THE ESSENTIALS OF THE LEGAL ENVIRONMENT OF BUSINESS

D1397799

John David Blackburn and Elliot Irwin Klayman

THE OHIO STATE UNIVERSITY

XanEdu
Change the course.

Printed in the United States of America

ISBN 13: 978-1-50669-592-1

Cover Image: © Pixabay/

530 Great Road
Acton, MA 01720
800-562-2147
www.xanedu.com

Professor Blackburn dedicates this book to his wife,
Vita Berezina-Blackburn
and their daughter,
Iris Mae Blackburn

Professor Klayman dedicates this book to his Aunt Annette Appel, who is the reason he and his wife currently enjoy sunny San Diego. Her zest for life and vigor serves as an inspiration and model for approaching each day with a positive attitude in spite of its challenges.

This book fills the need for quality teaching material for the legal environment of business course. It combines highly readable text with interesting cases and challenging review problems suitable for business students. The book responds to the accreditation standards of the American Assembly of Collegiate Schools of Business (AACSB), as well as those of the Association of Collegiate Business Schools and Programs (ACBSP).

The book surveys the essential fields of the legal environment of business with a goal of helping the student become an executive who is knowledgeable of the legal context in which the business organization operates. The book provides an introduction to American legal institutions, including the sources of law. It presents the basic concepts of public and private law related to business decisions, highlighting the information necessary to train students in good ethical decision-making.

The book consists of eight chapters, organized into four parts:

- *Part One: Law and Ethics in the Business Environment*, covers the interconnection of law and ethics, the nature of law and legal reasoning, and the American legal system.
- *Part Two: Civil Law Foundations of the Legal Environment of Business*, presents the law of property, the law of contractual transactions, and the law of injuries (tort law).
- *Part Three: The Legal and Ethical Environment of Business Organizations*, covers the subjects of agency, partnerships, corporations, and limited liability companies.
- *Part Four: The Legal and Ethical Environment of Business and its Employees*, focuses on equal employment opportunity law.

The thesis of this book is that business law and business ethics are interconnected. The book includes case studies within the Current Ethical/Legal Issues boxes, which invite students to determine whether the business practice is ethical. The court cases in the form of appellate court opinions that are included in the book show the intersection of law and business practice. At the conclusion of each chapter are review problems that challenge the student to identify legal and ethical issues, and to consider their resolution.

The goal of this book is for the student to develop a deeper understanding of the social-legal responsibilities of the business community. It is also a goal that the student will set a high standard of ethical decision-making. This book is the authors' contribution toward achieving these goals.

We have had considerable help in writing this book. Cory Barnes, an undergraduate student majoring in political science deserves special mention for his invaluable research assistance. Joyce Klayman, with her superb library science skills, used her online prowess to locate, and make suggestions for, case and link inclusion. A special thanks to our editors at Pearson, Anthony Howard and Jan Scipio; and to Ben Stephen, publisher's representative at Pearson, without whose services this edition could not have been so efficiently produced. None of these people is responsible for the views expressed or material used.

John David. Blackburn, J.D.
Elliot I. Klayman, J.D.
Fisher College of Business
The Ohio State University

B R I E F C O N T E N T S

vii

I LAW AND ETHICS IN THE BUSINESS ENVIRONMENT

1 LAW AND ETHICS

Chapter Outline

Learning Objectives

After learning this chapter the student should be able to:

- Explain the relationship between business ethics and law.
- Recite the fundamental ethical principles reflected in law.
- Describe how businesses address ethics via codes of ethics, compliance programs, by enlisting ethics officers, and by forming creative solutions to ethical problems.

Law consists of rules of human behavior and justice. These rules are often sanctioned by authority. They are often tied to consequences determined by someone empowered to effect them. Law reflects social values. Ethics are rationally justified views about what is right and wrong, moral and immoral, just and unjust. Chapter 1 discusses the relationship of law and ethics.

Law and Ethics Are Interconnected

Many people think of the businessperson as a selfish individual who maintains that it is a dog-eat-dog world where only the fit survive. They consider this view justified by the theory of evolution. This view is not justified by the natural world, human nature, or the world of business.[1]

What separates humans from other animals is that humans are rational creatures. They form communities based on cooperation to live sane lives in safety and security in peace and harmony, seeking fairness, equality, love and compassion. Law is one of the social institutions that human communities rely upon to achieve these goals.

Law is society's way of providing for the safety, security and happiness of its members. It does this by sanctioning rational rules of behavior, and by devising fair ways for resolving disputes. Law works most effectively and efficiently when it is supported by the moral opinion of the members of the community. In harmonious communities, the governmental, educational, religious, economic and social institutions support and are supported by the rule of law.

This book tries to show that business law and business ethics are interconnected.[2] Perceived unethical business behavior often spurs public outcry for increased regulation of business. What is considered ethical business conduct often finds expression as formal law. Contemporarily, law often affects the opinions of individuals and organizations about what conduct is right and wrong, ethical and unethical.

This is not to say that all governmental law is ethical. History supplies examples of unethical governmental laws. The pre-Civil War slave laws in the United States are an example. The slave labor law in Nazi Germany is another. Governments and government officials can commit crimes. People can distinguish governmental laws that promote peace and security among all members of a society from governmental laws that are clever legalisms and subterfuges for doing violence on some, peaceful members of society. You may find more recent exam-

---

[1] S.I. HAYAKAWA AND ALAN R. HAYAKAWA, LANGUAGE IN THOUGHT AND ACTION Ch. 1, "Language and Survival," (Harcourt Brace & Co. 5th Ed. 1990) ("Cooperation within a species (and sometimes with other species) is essential to the survival of most living creatures." at pp. 4–5.).

[2] *See,* Thomas W. Dunfee, *On the Synergistic, Interdependent Relationship of Business Ethics and Law,* 34 AM. BUS. L.J. 317 (1996).

ples of governmental laws that do not meet your standards for business conduct and law.

Throughout the book, as seen in this chapter, there are court cases showing the intersection of law and business practice. This book also includes case studies within the Current Ethical/Legal Issues boxes. They invite you to determine whether the business practice is ethical and legal. They also invite you to consider what you think should be expressed in the legal environment surrounding the activity. At the conclusion of each chapter there are review problems. These are business fact patterns. These business problems/cases invite you to identify legal and ethical issues and explain how you think they should be resolved.

You have the ability to understand and form rational opinions about the subject matter content of this book. All you have to do is draw upon the resources that are accessible to anyone. These include your ability to reason as an ordinary rational human being. Included also are your knowledge and experience about facts of the real and practical world. You also understand social life and can consider the most rational organization of it according to present needs.

The goal of this book is that you develop a deeper understanding of the social-legal responsibilities of the business community. It is also a goal that you will set

---

Current Ethical/Legal Issues

Joe, a business student at Go Beyond University, worked as a waiter at The Moldau, an upscale restaurant in town. Joe's performance appraisals were superb. Joe left his employment at The Moldau in good standing when he took an internship with Sorata Corporation.

When Joe returned from his internship, he reapplied for an opening as a waiter at The Moldau. While Joe was away, a new supervisor at The Moldau took over the supervisor's position. The new supervisor is gay and hires only waiters that the supervisor knows are gay. Joe is not gay, and consequently, did not get the job.

No law in the city or state where the Moldau is located forbids sexual orientation discrimination by employers. There is also no federal law in the United States forbidding sexual orientation discrimination by employers like the Moldau. (The Moldau does not fall under an executive order forbidding sexual orientation discrimination by companies with U.S. government contracts.)

Do you think the supervisor's action was ethical? Do you think it should be unlawful for an employer to discriminate on the basis of sexual orientation? Explain.

a high standard of business ethics. This book is part of the process of discovery and development of your personal values. Your personal values should guide you toward a happy and productive life as a member of the business/social community. The hope is this book will promote a sane and harmonious world full of freedom, justice, fairness and compassion.

Fundamental Ethical Principles Reflected in Law

Law and Ethics in Business Policies

The following link is to *The Kroger Company* ethics policy.

http://www.thekrogerco.com /docs/default-document -library/ethicspolicy

See page 15 for the company's treatment of sexual harassment, which is illegal, and other forms of harassment that are not illegal.

Law and ethics interconnect. What is considered ethical often finds expression in governmental law. Similarly, law may influence the values of individuals and organizations. Often, individuals and organizations look to the law for guidance in deciding what is right and wrong. For example, business people often refer to their fiduciary obligation when deciding what to do in their relations with others. When making company policy, business people often turn to the law for the principles to include in their policy documents. Examples of this include a company code of ethics, or a company's sexual harassment policy.

One result of this law/ethics interaction is that what is considered ethical business conduct often becomes formal law. Another result is the law often influences the values of individuals and companies, affecting the way business is practiced.

This section discusses some legal principles so fundamental that they are part of the everyday vocabulary of business. These legal principles serve as guideposts to business people to determine what is appropriate and ethical business behavior. When encountering situations where you are unsure what to do, the following principles may apply and provide guidance. The principles are:

1. Maintain fiduciary standards to act solely for the benefit of the person whose property or interests you are entrusted
2. Avoid the appearance of conflicts of interest
3. Respect confidential relationships
4. Exercise due care and diligence in the performance of your duties
5. Act in good faith and deal fairly with others

The principles listed above will be discussed at various places throughout this book. For example, the duty of due care is discussed in the chapters on torts and business associations, among others. These principles are well known in the business community and society at large. For example, accountants and psychologists are familiar with the principle of respecting confidential relations. But the following principles are not the only examples of legal principles that have influenced the ethics of the business community. Much of what is practiced by members of the business community is a reflection of what is provided by the law. For example, employment policies, such as sexual harassment policies, reflect the concepts developed in equal employment opportunity law. Much of what is required by law and is considered ethical business practice are two sides of the same coin.

Maintain Fiduciary Standards

The highest legal duty and standard for ethical business conduct is the fiduciary rule. A fiduciary is someone who occupies a position of power, trust and confidence regarding the property of another. Examples of fiduciaries include agents (such as real estate agents), business partners, and directors of corporations. The **fiduciary rule** requires the fiduciary to act solely in the interest of that other person's property and interests.

The following is an excerpt from *Meinhard v. Salmon*, a 1928 decision of New York's highest court. The case involves the duties owed by partners and those engaged in joint business ventures to one another. The excerpt is the most often quoted expression of the fiduciary rule:

For an edited version of the New York high court's opinion in *Meinhard v. Salmon* please see p. 208 in the Appendix of Chapter Extension Files.

> *Joint adventurers, like copartners, owe to one another, while the enterprise continues, the duty of the finest loyalty. Many forms of conduct permissible in a workaday world for those acting at arm's length, are forbidden to those bound by fiduciary ties. A trustee is held to something stricter than the morals of the marketplace. Not honesty alone, but the punctilio of an honor the most sensitive, is then the standard of behavior. As to this there has developed a tradition that is unbending and inveterate. Uncompromising rigidity has been the attitude of courts of equity when petitioned to undermine the rule of undivided loyalty by the "disintegrating erosion" of particular exceptions. Only thus has the level of the conduct for fiduciaries been kept at a level higher than that trodden by the crowd.*

Avoid the Appearance of a Conflict of Interest

A **conflict of interest** exists when your personal interest or duty conflicts with a professional interest or duty. One example is a real estate agent, representing a seller, having an ownership interest in a company wanting to buy the seller's property. Another example would be where a real estate agent represents both the seller and the buyer. In the first example, the agent has a personal interest that conflicts with the agent's duty to the seller. In the second example, the agent's duty to the buyer conflicts with the agent's duty to the seller.

Conflicts of interest create the impression that the person in the conflict situation cannot be fair and impartial. The rule against conflicts of interest is as old as the biblical expression that one "cannot serve two masters." The legal rule stems from the fiduciary rule. It also is rooted in the law of agency (covered in the chapter on business associations). There the rule is that an agent owes a duty of undivided loyalty to the principal (employer). The agent cannot allow his or her personal interests to conflict with that of the principal. The agent cannot deal with the principal as an adverse party.

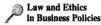
**Law and Ethics
in Business Policies**

The following link is to
The Coca-Cola Company's
ethics policy.

http://assets.coca-cola
company.com/45/59/f85d53a
84ec597f74c754003450c
/COBC_English.pdf

See pages 20–27 for the
conflict of interest policy.
Notice the first two
paragraphs on page 26.

Someone in a conflict of interest situation has two options: (1) disqualification or (2) disclosure and consent. Disqualification means the person having the conflict avoids the conflict by disqualifying him or herself from the opportunity presented.

In the first example, the real estate agent could disqualify him or herself by either resigning as the seller's agent or selling his or her ownership interest in the company that wants to buy the property. The other way the agent could resolve the conflict is to disclose the conflict to both the seller and the buyer and obtain their consent to continue with the transaction. If the second alternative is taken, a good practice would be to get an independent third party to provide an opinion on the fairness of the transaction. In our example, an independent real estate appraiser could provide an opinion as to the property's value.

Many companies have policies dealing with conflicts of interest. Often these policies are part of a company's code of ethics. (Codes of ethics are discussed later in this chapter.) These policies often require the employee to report a conflict on a company form, which often is available on the company website.

Respect Confidential Relations

When someone receives information "in confidence," or when they are said to be in a "confidential relation," or when they are held to "maintain confidentiality," they are expected to keep information secret. Certain relations and conditions give rise to a legal duty to maintain confidentiality. Examples of relations giving rise to a duty to protect confidentiality are attorney-client, accountant-client, and principal (employer) and agent (employee). An example of a condition creating a duty to maintain confidentiality is where an employee has access to a company trade secret, such as where a company keeps its customer lists or cost information a secret.

Federal law requires confidentiality in certain situations. Federal securities laws make it a crime for those possessing material, non-public information concerning a company to disclose such inside information. (This is explained more thoroughly in Chapter 7 on business organizations.) As a result of federal securities law, many companies have policies providing guidelines to employees, officers and directors for protecting the confidentiality of inside information.

Another federal law (the *Gramm-Leach-Bliley Act*, or *GLB*) requires all financial institutions to safeguard customer information. One purpose of the law is to reduce the risk of identity theft. Financial institutions are defined by the law to include not only banks, but also, among others, credit card companies, securities firms and insurance companies. As a result of this federal law, many companies have customer or client "confidentiality programs" designed to ensure that access to customer or client data is controlled at all times and that data breaches are identified and reported in a timely manner.

Other situations where business people expect information to be kept confidential include instances where one company seeks to buy another, where a company enters into a joint marketing venture with another company, and where employees work with critical company information. It is common in these situations for companies to enter into confidentiality agreements to protect company information.

In the situations described above, and in cases where you enter into a confidential relation or confidentiality agreement with your employer, you should respect that confidentiality. Failing to do so could cost you your job. In the case of violating the securities law, it could result in imprisonment.

Exercise Due Care and Diligence

A principle in the law that is based upon ethical obligation is the requirement to exercise **due care**. Basically, "due care" means that people and companies must be careful not to injure others. A breach of the duty of due care can lead to liability for negligence, which is explained in Chapter 6 in its discussion of tort law. The concept of due care also derives from the law of agency, discussed in Chapter 7 on business organizations, where an agent (employee) is required to exercise skill and care in performing the agent's obligations on behalf of the principal (employer).

The duty of due care requires action at times. For example, it may become necessary to exercise due care and remove a hazard from a store aisle, or to repair the brakes on a company vehicle. As well, the duty of due care may require inaction. An example of this would be a duty to refrain from driving heavy equipment across thick ice, or not working in a construction area without a hard hat.

Due care in business can find expression in the simple statement, "Be careful." It also finds expression as "due diligence" in other areas of law, such as corporate law and securities law (discussed in Chapter 7 on business organizations).

As can be seen from the discussion above, the concept of due care is one that finds expression in several areas of law, and it also is one that is familiar to business people. Your employer will expect you to be diligent, careful, in short, to be competent. Employees who do not exercise due care in performing their jobs do not bring that "added value" to their jobs that employers expect of their employees. Executives who do not perform due diligence functions may create liability for themselves and their employers. The last thing you want to be considered is a liability by your employer.

Act in Good Faith and Deal Fairly with Others

The obligation of **good faith** and fair dealing is fundamental in business. For example, a provision in the *Uniform Commercial Code, (UCC)* which is law in every state, provides: "Every contract or duty within this Act imposes an obligation of good faith in its performance or enforcement." Another section of the Code provides that " 'good faith' means honesty in fact in the conduct or transaction concerned."

Included in honesty in fact is telling the truth. The general principle is that it is good to tell the truth. Yet, most would agree that not every lie is wrong. Everyone is familiar with little white lies, such as telling a spouse that what they are wearing looks good. These untruths are exceptions to the general rule to tell the truth, because they are made out of a good faith motivation to not hurt the other person.

Lying under oath, or even on some documents not under oath, for example, tax returns, is punishable as the offense of perjury. Also, it is a crime to lie to an official of the federal government. Martha Stewart, the founder of *Martha Stewart Living Omnimedia*, was convicted of lying to federal prosecutors, and spent time in a federal penitentiary, even though she was found not guilty of insider trading (prohibited by federal securities law) in the same case.

While it is not against the law to lie to your boss, it might get you fired. It is not ordinarily against the law to lie on an employment application, but there may be consequences. If later the employer discovers the lie, the employer can terminate you for cause.

Withholding the truth by silence may also be considered lying. For example a half-truth regarding a material fact during contract negotiations is considered misrepresentation, making the agreement unenforceable.

Another component of good faith and fair dealing is disclosure. The law requires disclosure in many areas. Four examples are instructive:

**Law and Ethics
in Business Policies**

The following link is to
Merk's Code of Conduct,
entitled *Our Values and
Standards: The Basis of
Our Success (Edition III).*

http://www.merck.com/about
/code_of_conduct.pdf.

See pages 7–8 for the
discussion entitled "Honest
Communication."

1. Federal securities regulation, discussed in Chapter 7, requires full disclosure of the details of a stock offering so investors may be fully informed. It is also fraud under the federal securities laws to make a material misstatement or *omission* in connection with the sale of a security.

2. Most states require that the seller of a house fully disclose any hidden defects which are known to the seller. Additionally, almost every state now requires that the seller provide the buyer with a signed form answering various questions designed to inform the buyer of such hazards or defects as water leakage, the presence of radon gas, mold, and insect problems.

3. The federal Food and Drug Administration mandates labeling disclosure requirements designed to fully disclose to consumers the contents of food, including the calorie, sugar, protein, carbohydrate and fat content. More recently, there has been a push for uniform "green" packaging that would inform consumers that the animals used in producing the food were "antibiotic free," "grass fed," "cage free," "farm raised," "wild caught," or that the food is "fair traded," meaning that the farmers received a fair price. This is an example of ethics driving the law by promoting good faith through full disclosure.

4. The *Federal Trade Commission Used Car Rule* requires that car dealers disclose whether there is a warranty or no warranty; and, if there is a warranty, to make available the written terms. However, the rule only applies to those who sell at least five cars in the previous 12 month period. That means that the rule does not apply to the casual seller of cars.

The obligation of good faith and fair dealing generally arises in the setting of contractual dealings. The contract is essential to a functioning economic system. The law generally enforces contacts. People need to rely upon contractual promises. "A deal is a deal," "You promised," and "freedom of contract," are expressions of the ethical sentiment that promises are binding. While the law enforces contracts, the law does not enforce every promise. When contracts are deemed unconscionable or when they are against public policy, the law employs a form of balancing of the equities to nullify the promise of the party. This is a function of the fundamental obligation of good faith and fair dealing.

Ways Businesses Address Ethics

How seriously do business organizations and their executives take business ethics? There was a time when the words *business* and *ethics* were thought to be mutually exclusive terms. However, today an executive will not be considered a sophisticated executive if he or she maintains a cavalier attitude toward business ethics.

A prominent concern of many U.S. corporations is developing a corporate culture that encourages ethical behavior and discourages unethical behavior. Organizations have developed and enforced codes of ethics, instituted formal ethics training programs, maintained standing ethics committees, hired ethical consultants, and their top managers have actively addressed ethical problems confronting their organizations.

One motivation that companies have for developing corporate ethics codes and compliance programs is to receive favorable treatment under the *Federal Sentencing Guidelines* if their employees are convicted of a federal corporate crime. The *Sentencing Guidelines* make companies responsible when their employees are convicted of federal crimes. The *Sentencing Guidelines* also permit dramatic reductions in penalties for companies that have in place an effective compliance and ethics program to prevent and detect violations of the law. The absence of these programs may be used to increase the punishment a company may receive. In addition to the *Sentencing Guidelines*, the *Sarbanes-Oxley Act*, discussed in detail in Chapter 7, on business organizations, effectively requires a public company to have a **code of ethics** for financial officers and provide mechanisms for protecting whistleblowers who report financial misconduct of the company.

Whatever the motivation, many businesses and their executives take seriously the management of a company's values. Corporate ethics codes and **compliance programs** show that companies are dealing with ethics in a systematic way.

The combination of the *Federal Sentencing Guidelines* and the *Sarbanes-Oxley Act* has provided an incentive for companies to create ethics codes and compliance programs.

Ethics Codes

Securities and Exchange Commission (SEC) regulations set out the requirements of a code of ethics. According to the SEC, a code of ethics means written standards designed to deter wrongdoing and promote:

1. Honest and ethical conduct, including the ethical handling of actual or apparent conflicts of interest between personal and professional relationships.
2. Full, fair, accurate, timely and understandable disclosure in the periodic reports required to be filed by the company.
3. Compliance with governmental laws, rules and regulations.
4. Prompt internal reporting of violation of the code to appropriate persons identified in the code.
5. Accountability for adherence to the code.

Compliance Programs

The *Sentencing Guidelines* set out the seven requirements of an effective compliance and ethics program. They are:

1. The company must establish standards and procedures to prevent and detect criminal conduct.
2. The company's governing authority must be knowledgeable about the content and operation of the compliance and ethics program and exercise reasonable oversight to implement and ensure that it is effective. This means that high-level personnel are assigned overall responsibility for ethics and compliance programs. Specific individuals within the company are delegated day-to-day responsibility for the program and report periodically to high-level personnel on the effectiveness of the program.
3. The company must keep any individual the company knows or should know engaged in illegal acts from serving a high-level position.
4. The company must communicate periodically and in a practical manner its standards and procedures by conducting effective training programs and disseminating information to individual employees that is appropriate to their roles and responsibilities.
5. The company must monitor and audit its program to ensure that it is followed, evaluate periodically the effectiveness of the program, and provide mechanisms for employees to anonymously report violations without fear of retaliation.
6. The company must provide incentives to employees to act ethically and discipline employees who engage in criminal conduct.
7. The company must take reasonable steps to respond appropriately to criminal conduct and to prevent future misconduct.

**Law and Ethics
in Business Policies**

The following link is to the *Whirlpool Corporation's* Code of Ethics. *http://assets.whirlpoolcorp .com/wp-content/uploads /code_of_ethics.pdf*

See *"Support for Our Code of Ethics"* at page 12, and notice the connection with requirement number 5 of the *Sentencing Guidelines.*

Ethics Officers

Business ethicists, sometimes referred to as **ethics officers** or compliance officers, are another level of protection against unethical business practices. They are considered experts in assessing conflicts of interests that arise within the company and outside the company, instituting and monitoring compliance programs, and providing educational programs for the various levels of company executives and employees. Some companies employ the ethicist when the perceived need arises. However, the larger firms hire them in-house.

The *Ethics & Compliance Officer Association* is a professional association for those responsible for assuring ethical best practices (BEP). Its well-developed website at http://www.theecoa.org is instructional on the depth of that independent organization's offerings and is worth a visit. The *Federal Sentencing Guidelines*, discussed above, have further fueled the employment of ethicists, who often are the ones to testify as experts in corporate fraud cases. The *Sarbanes-Oxley Act* has added still more incentive for the employment of ethics officers.

Creative Global Ethics

In today's global economy, corporations and executives encounter ethical issues that arise when different cultural traditions are confronted. How should U.S. companies and their employees respond when doing business in countries where bribery of political officials is common, or in countries that permit discrimination against certain ethnic groups?

Some argue that cultural relativism, the concept that no culture has better ethics than any other, is the answer. Their position is captured by the old saying, "When in Rome, do as the Romans do." On the other hand, others reject the notion of relativism. They argue that U.S. companies are expected to stand by their values.

When encountering cross-cultural ethical conflict, companies and manager often seek creative solutions to ethical problems. For example, companies can negotiate with their international trading partners regarding concerns about unethical practices. Companies sometimes try to establish international standards through organizations like the *International Chamber of Commerce*. At times, American companies have asked the U.S. government to negotiate treaties to have American ethical standards (e.g., labor standards) of business adopted abroad.

Case

(*Fiduciary Obligation*)
DESIGN STRATEGIES, INC. v. MARC DAVIS, ET AL.
384 F.Supp.2d 649 (S.D.N.Y. 2005)

Design Strategies, Inc. ("Design") is in the business of providing trained personnel to companies needing technical support on specific projects requiring computer technology services. That aspect of the industry is known as "staffing." Design sued its former employee, Marc Davis ("Davis"), alleging that Davis, while still employed at Design, wrongfully diverted a lucrative business opportunity from Design to Info Technologies Web Solutions ("IT Web"), and subsequently benefitted from that diversion by accepting an offer of employment with IT Web. IT Web is a "web solutions" provider. Unlike staffing, web solutions work in the industry involves providing the services of trained personnel employed by the company on its premises and using the computers and other technical equipment supplied at the provider's laboratory on specific projects to design and develop websites for clients in accordance with given specifications. IT Web is a subsidiary of Info Technologies, Inc. ("Infotech"), a web staffing provider.

The court concluded that Design proved its claim against Davis for breach of fiduciary duties. What follows is the court's opinion, setting forth the court's reasons.

MARRERO, District Judge.

Davis's work entailed marketing Design's staffing services. He was compensated with a fixed annual salary plus commissions.

Davis left Design in February 2000 to accept a position with IT Web. At the time of his departure, Davis was earning an annual salary at Design of approximately $85,000.

Sometime during the summer of 1999 Davis became aware that Microsoft was involved with a partner, Brill Media, in a venture that would be soliciting companies for a contract worth approximately $10 million. The project, which came to be known as ("Contentville"), entailed establishing a high-profile website using Microsoft software to engage in electronic commerce in books and related products and thus compete with similar businesses operated by Amazon.com and Barnes and Noble.

The services to be provided by the company chosen to work on Contentville involved providing "web solutions" work.

Microsoft awarded the Contentville contract to IT Web in mid-December 1999. IT Web extended an offer of employment to Davis by letter dated December 14, 1999, which Davis accepted.

Davis promoted Design for what eventually became the Contentville contract from the time he learned about it until sometime in November 1999. In or before early November 1999, Davis ceased attempting to solicit the Contentville contract for Design and, instead, commenced trying

to promote IT Web for the contract. He took steps to inform IT Web and Infotech about a business opportunity with Microsoft and to encourage Microsoft to consider IT Web for Contentville.

Under New York law, an employee owes a duty of good faith and loyalty to his employer.

The New York Court of Appeals emphasized the broad nature of this duty in *Elco Shoe Mnfrs., Ins. v. Sisk*: "[N]o man can serve two masters with equal fidelity when rival interests come into existence. Agents are bound at all times to exercise the utmost good faith toward their principals. They must act in accordance with the highest and truest principles of morality."

An employee who is found to have breached his duty of loyalty is generally disentitled to recover his compensation, whether commissions or salary. Disloyal employees may be held liable for their compensation even if the principal suffered no provable damage as a result of the breach of fidelity.

The Court concludes that, even if strictly speaking Design and IT Web were not themselves competitors in the web solutions niche of the computer industry, they had sufficiently conflicting business interests at the relevant time to be deemed competitors in the present context. During the time when Davis attempted to procure Contentville for IT Web, that entity was a division of Infotech and its success directly contributed to Infotech's, which did squarely compete with Design in the staffing business.

Having determined that Davis violated his duty of loyalty to his employer, the Court must consider whether that violation warrants forfeiture of his relevant compensation, and, if so, to what extent.

Forfeiture is warranted because Davis acted "adversely to his employer." Davis's actions aimed at promoting the success of a company that was a division of a direct competitor of Design.

The court finds that the two pay periods from November 11 to December 9, 1999 encompass the time of Davis's disloyal acts. Thus, the Court determines that Davis must forfeit his salary for those two pay periods. For each of these pay periods, Davis received a salary of $3,269.00. The remainder of his compensation during these periods was comprised of commissions. Davis is not alleged to have acted disloyally in relation to any of the Design staffing sales on which he earned those commissions. Consequently, the Court finds that Davis must forfeit $6,538.00 to Design, plus any applicable interest.

Chapter Extension

For additional material relating to Chapter 1, see p. 208 in the Appendix of Chapter Extension Files.

Chapter Problems

1. Define the following terms:

   a. Law
   b. Ethics
   c. Fiduciary rule
   d. Conflict of interest
   e. Confidentiality
   f. Due care
   g. Good faith
   h. Code of ethics
   i. Compliance program
   j. Ethics officer

2. David is a research and development chemist employed by Acme Chemical Company. Acme has a range of chemical products marketed strictly in the northeastern region of the United States. David has developed a chemical that he knows will generate a high demand in the United States and, perhaps, worldwide. However, he feels Acme does not have a reputable enough name to market his discovery. David decided to approach a large, western-based chemical corporation. They are willing to hire him, provided they obtain the rights to produce and market the chemical. In return, David will be given a large block of the corporation's common stock and his salary will be tripled. David is considering the offer. He figures the most Acme will do is give him a bonus for his discovery. Should David accept the offer from the western corporation? Explain. If you were in his position, would you feel obligated to notify Acme of your discovery and not search for alternative companies to market it? Explain.

3. George works for Big Corporation as the manager of one of its departments. He supervises twenty employees. From time to time he has departmental meetings in which he orders food from a local caterer. When the staff works late at night, George often orders pizza for the staff. George's brother has started a restaurant in town. The restaurant sells take-out and makes deliveries. George wants to stop ordering from the caterer and start

ordering food from his brother's restaurant for those occasions when he orders food for the department staff. Should George do this? Explain.

4. Matthew Foote was employed by Dow Chemical Company. After learning of billing irregularities by its uniform provider, Cintas, Dow assigned Foote and his co-worker, Mike Hollies, the task of tracking and monitoring uniform charges. At a monthly meeting with Foote, Cintas invited them, as well as other Dow employees, to a Detroit Pistons basketball game. Dow's management approved the attendance at the game. However, Foote believed the attendance at the game presented a conflict of interest. At the time, Foote raised this concern with his supervisor, Dominic Zoeller.

Around the time that the Dow employees attended the Pistons game, Foote also began a consensual sexual relationship with a direct subordinate Libby Soler. Shortly after beginning the relationship, Foote took steps to remove Soler from his direct reporting line, swapping her for a different employee whose skills were similar. Foote discussed the proposal with Tara Kutchey of Dow's Human Resources Department, and he told Zoeller the details of the situation. Shortly after that, Foote received a letter advising him that his employment was terminated.

Dow's Code of Business Conduct contains an anti-retaliation policy. Foote believed his termination was in retaliation for his report of his concerns surrounding the Pistons basketball game. He maintained that nowhere in any of Dow's policies is a relationship between employees prohibited.

Dow asserted that the termination was due to loss of confidence in Foote as a result of his relationship with Soler and the manner in which he handled the situation. Dow pointed to language in its Code of Business Conduct that states: "Nothing in this document constitutes a contract of employment with any individual." It also pointed to the application for employment that Foote completed 19 years earlier, which concludes with the statement, "I understand that I have the right to terminate my employment with Dow at any time without notice and for any reason. I understand that Dow has the same right." Just below that provision is Foote's signature, agreeing that he had read and understood the contents of the application. The employment agreement that followed repeats that statement under the heading of "Employment at Will".

Foote sued Dow for wrongful termination of employment and breach of the employment contract. The court decided the case in favor of Dow. The court explained that Foote's employment arrangement with Dow was an at-will one; therefore, Dow could terminate him for either reason. (*Foote v. Dow Chemical and Zoeller*, 2010 Mich. App. LEXIS 112.).

Do you think Foote acted appropriately? Explain. Do you think Dow acted appropriately? Explain. Do you agree that the law should allow an employer to terminate an employee for any reason where the employer's code of conduct contains a disclaimer stating that the code is not a contract, that the employment relation is an employment-at-will, meaning that both the employer and the employee may terminate the employment relation without notice and for any reason? Explain.

5. Sandra Erwin submitted a prescription to Nichols Pharmacy for a drug that treats a sexually transmitted disease. A pharmacy technician who filled the prescription was aware that Sandra was dating the technician's ex-boyfriend. Concerned for his well-being, the technician informed her ex-boyfriend of Sandra's condition. Did the Nichols Pharmacy employee act appropriately toward Erwin? Explain.

6. Fisheries Incubation Service Health, Inc. (FISH) has been raising fresh water fish on their farms for many years. They cater to a health-minded set of consumers and sell their fish to health food stores across the country. They are government inspected by the local health commission and certified by that state agency as "Superior." FISH has been doing research for years and most recently found that their fish have a mercury and PCB level that makes it unsafe for women of childbearing age to eat more than two servings per month. There does exist a private "Seafood Safe" label that would warn women of this hazard; however, that label has not as yet been adopted by FISH. The law does not require it. You are a clerk in the research and development labs who records the data, and as a result are aware of the findings. You have signed a confidentiality agreement with the company whereby you agree not to reveal any information that you acquire from the job in the research laboratory. What should you do? Explain.

7. Skyhigh Construction Corporation specializes in multifloor office buildings predominately located in major cities throughout the United States. Skyhigh is a much respected firm in the high-rise construction industry. It has the reputation of completing all contracts on time and on budget. Frank Cook, a site supervisor for Skyhigh, comments:

    Skyhigh employs an average of 240 construction workers per site. For those who work up on the beams, this is a high health-risk occupation. There is a small but considerable number of serious and sometimes fatal accidents at every site before the job is completed. To meet deadlines, I sometimes must send the crew up when weather conditions are not favorable. My crew members are working in a potentially dangerous environment, but they are compensated with attractive wages. If one of them complains about going up every time it gets a little windy, I fire that person. When Skyhigh signs a contract, my job is to ensure completion of it on time!

    How do you feel about Skyhigh's policy as reflected in Frank Cook's comments?

8. You are a securities broker for Stock & Bond, a major Wall Street firm that is active in a wide variety of financial services. Your firm offers on-line trading. For $10.00 per trade a customer can buy or sell any stocks listed on the national exchanges. You know that one of the customers, Anthony, a family friend, has been committing "economic suicide" by trading recklessly, with

the passion of a gambling addict. From time to time Anthony consults with you on mortgage and other securities transactions, seeking your advice. You render full advice to him on these transactions and he pays the full fee. There is a company policy that prohibits you from rendering any advice on less than full service transactions. In fact, an in-house rule states: "Under no circumstances shall a broker render any opinion to a customer who inquires concerning on-line transactions." Anthony comes to you for advice on a full commission stock transaction, and, while engaging in conversation tells you what has been happening in his high risk on-line transactions. You are aware of his financial condition and are alarmed that Anthony is selling off much of his reliable blue-chip stock and real estate holdings in order to support his "on-line habit." You feel compelled to caution against his reckless trading. However, you know that it is against the company's policy to do so, and, if you are caught, you will be fired. What will you do? Explain.

9. Frank Senour is the president of Intercontinental Oil Company. Intercontinental maintains its corporate headquarters in the United States, but also has offices in several Southeast Asian and South American countries, where Intercontinental does much of its business. Intercontinental is looking for a manager of international marketing for its Southeast Asian and South American operations. The position requires that the manager travel to Intercontinental's several Southeast Asian and South American offices and interact with present and prospective customers of the company. Beth Reichman is qualified for the position, has been with the company 12 years, and has been the manager of Intercontinental's marketing operations in the United States for the last four years. She is the only applicant for the position. Frank is aware that according to the practices currently in force in several Southeast Asian and South American countries where Intercontinental does business, many of Intercontinental's customers would prefer to do business with men rather than women. As a result, Frank realizes that Beth will have great difficulty performing the job of international marketing manager. Nevertheless, Beth tells Frank that she can do the job, if given the chance. What should Frank do? Would he be justified in refusing to promote Beth? Explain.

10. Your company is considering selling its product in a foreign country. To do business in this country, your company needs a license from the government. It is accepted practice, and expected by the officials, that to get the license you must hire a certain local individual and pay him $250,000. If payment is not made to this individual, and your company decides to go through proper channels, your company can expect the granting of the license to be delayed by two years. Once the license is obtained, your company can expect to make at least $50 million a year from sales in that country. You are the vice president of marketing for your company. What will be your recommendation regarding making this payment to the foreign individual? Explain.

2 NATURE OF LAW AND LEGAL REASONING

Learning Objectives

After learning this chapter the student should be able to:

- Compare and contrast the following conceptions of law: ideal conceptions, positivist conceptions, historical conceptions, sociological conceptions, realist conceptions, economic conceptions, and critical conceptions.
- Describe how the legislature, the executive, the judiciary, and administrative agencies are sources of law.
- Describe the doctrine of stare decisis and why it is important to managers.
- Describe some of the rule-based rationales, precedent-based rationales, and policy rationales commonly used in legal reasoning, and recognize these rationales when they are used in court opinions.
- Compare and contrast formalistic and purposive methods of interpreting legislation.

This chapter considers the nature of law and legal reasoning. Not everyone would agree on how to define *law*. Therefore, we first examine the various definitions and conceptions of law that have developed over the years. Second, we discuss the sources of law. Finally, we conclude with an examination of legal reasoning, an analytical method distinctive to the legal system.

The Nature of Law: What Is Law?

The simple question, "What is law?" leads to a complex answer that reveals the many-faceted nature of the subject. Each person seems to have his or her own answer to this question. Some think law is a body of rules. Others see it as a means of restricting human conduct. Still others see it as an instrument for protecting basic freedoms. Similar to other basic concepts dealing with human behavior, law is susceptible to many definitions. A historian may regard law as a reflection of a society's mores at a particular time. A sociologist may regard it as a social institution.

When defining law, one can refer to several schools of jurisprudence. **Jurisprudence** is the study of legal philosophy. The following discussion outlines several major philosophical conceptions of law, namely:

- Ideal
- Positivist
- Historical
- Sociological
- Realist
- Critical
- Economic
- Feminist Jurisprudence

Ideal Conceptions: Natural Law

Natural law philosophers think law is ordained by nature. For them, law consists of a body of higher principles existing independently of human experience, and it exists as an ideal condition that is either inherent in human nature or derived from a divine source.

According to this conception of law, people cannot create natural law, but they can discover its principles through reasoned thinking. Knowledge of natural law is thus an informed intuition of what is fair and just. The principles of natural law, discoverable by reason, are universally valid. Thus, **natural law** is a body of principles of right and justice existing for all peoples irrespective of time and culture. It transcends human notions of what is right and just.

Positivist Conceptions

In word-association exercises, the word *law* often evokes the response *rules,* because most people think of law as a body of rules.

In jurisprudential terms, this is the positivist conception of law. The *positivist* school of jurisprudence regards law as any body of rules imposed by a sovereign or sovereign body. The term *positivist* stems from the root word *posit,* which means to place, put, or lay down something. A **positive law** is a law laid down by the duly constituted authority. A legal positivist might point to a speed-limit sign as an example of law.

Positivists distinguish between the law as it is and the law as it ought to be. They believe that an immoral command of a duly constituted authority is still law. In this regard, they differ from natural law theorists.

For example, in its early history, the United States enacted the Fugitive Slave Act, requiring the return of escaped slaves to their slaveholders. Positivists regarded the Fugitive Slave Act as law even though it was immoral. Natural law theorists did not regard it as law because it was immoral.

Historical Conceptions

Those who define law only as the current command of a sovereign may be criticized for ignoring the many rules that bound people in the past. Because law is often older than the state, some argue that the state is an incidental product of more mature legal systems rather than the distinguishing characteristic of all law.

The historical school of jurisprudence defines law as the embodiment of a society's customs. Historical jurisprudence asserts that custom is the chief manifestation of law, and that law evolves with social development. Custom may influence and become the basis of positive law. According to this conception, as customs and cultural values change, so does the direction of positive law. Laws patterned after custom are likely to meet with greater social acceptance.

Sociological Conceptions

Closely associated with the historical view is the sociological view of law. Sociologists define law in present human conduct. Thus, law is the sum of what the lawbooks permit and what human behavior provides. Under this view, for example, if you wanted to know what constitutes a business contract, you would look at business conduct to ascertain when people in business treat their agreements as binding, as well as when courts would declare such agreements to be contracts. Under this approach, formal law should reflect present human conduct; therefore, it might be necessary to bring about law reforms to have legal rules that reflect human experience.

The similarity between the historical and the sociological conceptions is obvious—both treat human conduct as the source of law. However, the historical conception embodies a long-range perspective, whereas the sociological view focuses on more immediate experience.

The sociological approach to law is not necessarily in conflict with the positivist approach. Positive law may reflect current human conduct. However, where human conduct is not in accord with a formal proposition of law, those adhering to the sociological conception would change the law to bring it into line with human conduct. Stretched to its limits, this logic would reduce formal law to its least influential level if people chose to ignore it.

Realist Conceptions

A conception of law closely allied to the sociological school is the realist conception. Realism looks beyond logic and reasoning and examines what actually occurs in the legal process. Both sociological and realist jurisprudence view life experiences as affecting the development of law. However, the realist conception focuses primarily on the social influences affecting the judicial decision-making process. It views law as the product of various social influences on official discretion. For example, if a speed-limit sign on a highway stated that the speed limit was 55 mph, but a police officer on patrol would not pull drivers over unless they drove over 65 mph, a legal realist would say that the law was 65 mph.

Critical Conceptions

A school of jurisprudence called *critical legal studies* is a type of legal realism. Its proponents contend that law is the product of political and sociological judgments made by judges. Critical legal theorists contend that judges make law in such a way as to preserve the existing political and economic order. Critical legal scholars claim that what appear to be legal reforms actually perpetuate the status quo by avoiding reconsideration of the basic assumptions behind the economic system.

Economic Conceptions

The law and economics school of jurisprudence affirms a link between law and economic activity. It contends that good law reflects good economics. It sees law as an instrument by which efficient economic outcomes are achieved. A concern for efficiency is an important, if not overriding, value for those who subscribe to this conception of law. Those belonging to the law and economics school turn to the study of economics in the belief that it can provide a stable basis for legal decisions.

Feminist Jurisprudence

There are three branches of feminist jurisprudence. Liberal feminists focus on traditional legal doctrines of individual rights, expose ways in which women have not been treated equally with men, and seek to correct the injustice.

Cultural feminists argue that the law's focus on individual rights reflects a male perspective. They contend that women, primarily due to their roles as bearers and caretakers of children, do not emphasize individualism to the same extent as traditional notions of law; rather, women emphasize a "culture of caring." Cultural feminists call for reevaluating the law in light of this culture of caring. For example, they call for a reevaluation of the traditional legal rule that a person has no duty to rescue a stranger even though he or she has the ability to do so.

Radical feminists view women's roles as caregivers as a source of their oppression. They view the law as a means of male dominance that perpetuates the oppression. For example, they consider the First Amendment's protection of pornography not as a guarantee of free speech, but as a protection of violence against women.

Sources of Law

It is often said that the legislative branch of the government makes the laws, the executive branch enforces them, and the judicial branch interprets them. Although this is a valid outline of the separation of powers among the three branches of government, it is not entirely accurate. In reality, each branch makes law. Additionally, administrative agencies, which collectively have come to be called the fourth branch of government, often have lawmaking authority. The following discussion focuses on the four primary sources of law, namely:

- The legislature
- The executive
- The judiciary
- Administrative agencies

The Legislature

One source of law is the legislature. A legislature is an organized body of persons having the authority to make laws for a political unit (e.g., Congress). It often exercises other functions, such as the control of government administration (e.g., Congress approves funding for federal agencies and oversees their regulatory efforts).

The Legislative Process

Laws created by a legislature are called *statutes, enactments, acts,* or *legislation.* Such law is sometimes called *written law.* The term **legislation** refers either to the process by which a statute is enacted or to the statute itself.

The procedure by which the U.S. Congress enacts a statute is typical of the legislative process. A federal statute begins as a bill introduced in either the House of Representatives or the Senate. Many bills are introduced by sponsors who realize that they have little or no chance of passage. These sponsors use such bills to satisfy constituent demands or to call public attention to particular issues.

After a bill is introduced, it is referred to the appropriate committee. Most bills die in committee from inaction. Those that receive serious consideration result in public hearings and, not infrequently, studies by the committee's staff. The committee then meets in executive session to "mark up" the bill, reviewing it line by line and rewriting it.

Finally, the committee sends the bill to the floor of the house of Congress in which it was introduced. It is accompanied by a committee report detailing the policy reasons for the bill and explaining the bill's intended effect on existing law. A minority report may also be included, if members of the committee disagree with the majority view. Following debate, the bill is voted on. If it receives support, it is sent to the other house of Congress for similar treatment.

When both houses pass similar but different bills, a conference committee consisting of members of both houses is established. This committee develops a compromise bill that satisfies both houses, and then submits it to each house for a vote.

Bills that pass both houses of Congress are forwarded to the president for signature. Pursuant to Article I, Section 7, of the U.S. Constitution, the president may sign the bill into law or return it to the house in which it originated (i.e., veto it). If the president takes no action within 10 days following the bill's transmittal, the Constitution states that the bill becomes law "unless the Congress by their Adjournment prevents its Return, in which case it shall not be a Law." Thus, if Congress adjourns after transmitting a bill to the president, the president may pocket-veto the bill by simply doing nothing.

State laws are enacted through similar procedures, specified in state constitutions.

The Business and Government Interface

The following link is to the official website for U.S. federal legislative information:

https://beta.congress.gov/

There you can find timely information about the status of bills introduced in Congress, among other matters.

The Executive

The executive branch of government also makes law. However, its lawmaking authority is limited by applicable constitutional provisions. For example, Article II of the U.S. Constitution provides that "the executive Power shall be vested in a President." The executive branch of the government consists of the president, the cabinet, and the agencies and bureaus operating under the president's authority. The president's exercise of official discretion is a source of law. In addition, the Constitution gives the president limited authority to make law in foreign and domestic affairs.

Presidential Authority over Foreign Affairs

The president's ability to make law regarding foreign affairs derives from the presidential power to make treaties, subject to the advice and consent of two thirds of the Senate. By virtue of the Supremacy Clause in Article VI of the U.S. Constitution, treaties confirmed by the Senate become part of the supreme law of the land, along with the Constitution and congressional enactments. All lawmakers of every state are bound by a treaty, notwithstanding any state law or state constitution to the contrary. The treaty controls, whether its ratification precedes or follows the enactment of state law.

The Business and Government Interface

The following link is to the official website for the White House:

http://www.whitehouse.gov/

There you can find timely information about the activities of the President of the United States and the operations of the executive branch of the federal government.

Treaties are an important source of law for international businesses. They often determine the type and quantity of goods that may be sold in foreign markets.

Presidential Authority over Domestic Affairs

The president's authority over domestic affairs is yet another source of law. Article II of the Constitution of the United States provides that the president "shall take Care that the Laws be faithfully executed." Executive lawmaking in domestic affairs is exemplified by the executive orders issued and implemented by presidents throughout U.S. history.

Presidential power to make law has been limited by the Supreme Court's interpretation of the Constitution. For example, during the Korean Conflict, President Harry Truman directed seizure of the nation's steel mills to prevent a threatened strike. The Supreme Court held the seizure unconstitutional for two reasons: first, the Court found no constitutional basis for the seizure; and second, the Congress had refused to confer such authority on the president.[1] The Court stated that the president's power to issue such an executive order must stem from an act of Congress or from the Constitution itself.

The Judiciary

Courts are also a source of law. When a court decides a dispute, it makes law. Through the application of general legal principles to actual controversies, these principles are refined and shaped into a more precise statement of law. A court's application of a statute to a particular case gives meaning to the statute.

Judge-made law is referred to as **common law**. Following the Norman Conquest of England, William the Conqueror sent his court officials throughout the realm to keep the king's peace. William's purpose was to bring the various parts of his newly conquered country under one law. These court officials resolved disputes by applying custom. Thus, there developed in England a body of judicial decisions that constituted the country's common law. As England had no Parliament or written constitution at that time, these decisions became the law of the country. Today, the term *common law* refers to those areas of law that have been developed principally by the courts.

Administrative Agencies

Administrative agencies have the power to affect the rights of private parties. Administrative agencies are housed in the executive branch of government but are created by the legislature. An administrative agency may have functions that are

---

[1] 72 S. Ct. 863 (1952).

traditionally executive, such as investigating, administering, and prosecuting. It may also have functions that are traditionally legislative or judicial, such as rule-making and adjudication.

Later chapters discuss lawmaking by administrative agencies in more detail. However, it is helpful to realize that administrative agencies may make law in much the same way that the legislative, executive, and judicial branches. For example, if Congress confers rulemaking authority on an agency, that agency's duly authorized rules and regulations have the same legal stature as if Congress itself had acted on the matters.

Interaction among the Various Sources of Law

Law and Ethics in Business Policies

Businesses understand the need to be aware of the laws that are being created, especially by administrative agencies. The following link is to the GE's policy document, *The Spirit and the Letter.*

http://www.gesustainability .com/wp-content/uploads /2014/05/English_Spirit -Letter-Booklet.pdf

See p 6, "Regulatory Excellence." Note especially *Responsibilities of All Employees,* and *Responsibilities of All Leaders.*

The various sources of law in the United States do not operate in a vacuum. The three branches of government frequently interact. This interaction provides a system of checks and balances in which the branches may aid or block each other. For example, as already noted, a congressional enactment needs presidential approval to become law, and a treaty negotiated by the executive branch needs Senate ratification.

People often think that the judiciary stands isolated from the other two branches and has the final word on any issue. Students often accept appellate court opinions in their casebooks as the final word on the law. In reality, a dynamic interaction occurs between the judiciary and the other branches of government. Congress, for example, can overrule a Supreme Court decision by legislation or constitutional amendment.

The judicial opinions presented in this book should be assessed carefully. You should question not only what the law is but also what it should be.

Legal Reasoning

The rest of this chapter looks at a method of thinking called *legal reasoning*. Legal reasoning cannot be precisely defined. Because it is a method of reasoning, the most that can be hoped for is a functional description of the process. Indeed, it is ironic but true that generations of law students have been taught to "think like a lawyer" without ever having been told explicitly just what is meant by that statement.

Although the method of reasoning that underlies legal reasoning is not unique to the legal system, we find the method most prominently displayed there. This is due in part to the methods and doctrines developed by courts to guide their decision making. Because courts explain their decisions in written opinions, we turn to court opinions for examples of legal reasoning.

Thus, to understand legal reasoning, we must first understand that judicial decision making uses prior cases to decide a present controversy. This method of decision making is referred to as the *rule of precedent*, or more frequently, the *doctrine of stare decisis.*

The Doctrine of Stare Decisis

The doctrine of **stare decisis** (Latin for "let the decision stand") is a policy that courts have developed as a general rule; thus, past judicial decisions are applied to decide present controversies. Consequently, a rule of law decided by the highest court of a jurisdiction subsequently binds all lower courts within that jurisdiction. It also generally binds later cases decided by that same court. Unless a court overrules itself, the decision is followed in all future cases presenting the same material facts and legal issues. Thus, a decision is a full-fledged precedent only for future "like" cases, that is, for future cases involving the same material facts.

The decision is not binding on courts in other jurisdictions. However, they may find its reasoning persuasive and follow it when considering similar cases in their jurisdictions. For example, although the Supreme Court of California is not bound by the decisions of the Supreme Court of Pennsylvania, it may adopt the Pennsylvania court's reasoning in a particular case.

Several bases underlie the doctrine of stare decisis. One is fairness. Inconsistent decisions of the same kinds of factual disputes seem unfair. Another basis for the doctrine is predictability. When a court decides a present case the way it decided a similar one before, parties are better able to anticipate and plan for the future.

Although a policy of applying prior cases to decide present controversies appears to look backward, it is important to recognize the way in which the method looks forward. A court's decision today will be tomorrow's precedent. A court, therefore, often carefully considers the future effects of a decision.

Obiter Dictum

Only the decision of a court is binding on future courts. What a court says and does that is necessary to its decision to settle the parties' dispute has precedential, or binding, effect. However, sometimes a court makes statements by way of explanation that are not really necessary to its decision. These remarks are referred to as **obiter dictum** or **dicta** (in the plural), which is Latin for "a remark by the way." Although these statements lack precedential value, they nevertheless indicate what the court is likely to do in the future. These statements may have some persuasive effect on a future decision of the court.

Some Common Rationales Used to Support Legal Reasoning

Although one of the justifications for the doctrine of stare decisis is that it advances the law's predictability, one quickly discovers decisions of appellate courts in which the judges are divided in their decisions. For example, it is not unusual for the nine justices on the Supreme Court of the United States to be divided five to four over the outcome of a case. If stare decisis works, why are there split votes?

The answer rests in the fact that those cases clearly controlled by precedent are usually either settled before trial or are disposed of routinely by the trial courts. The cases that go to the higher appellate courts involve issues where there are disagreements about the application of precedents or what constitutes sound legal policy.

Just as the parties may disagree about what the rule of law is or should be in a given case, so do judges often disagree. When the court announces its decision, the majority opinion states the court's rationale for reaching its result, and any dissenting judges may register their rationale for their disagreement in dissenting opinions. Although dissenting opinions have no precedential effect, a dissenting judge may register a dissent in the hope of persuading a future court to overrule the present decision. Thus, the majority and dissenting judges may each argue that the other has misread the cases or the rules established by them. This form of argument or rationale relies heavily on rules and precedent.

Judges may also disagree on the probable social effects of their decision. This type of argument or rationale relies heavily on policy. The following discussion describes three of the rationales found in legal opinions: rule based, precedent based, and policy based.[2]

Rule-Based Rationales

Rationales or arguments that are based on rules deal with the meaning to be given to the words in cases and statutes. (More is said about the interpretation of statutes later in this chapter). Typically, one side asserts that the language of a past case or statute established one rule, while the other side disagrees, asserting that the rule is something else altogether. The reasoning typically falls into one of two broad categories: **formalist reasoning** or **purposive reasoning**.

Formalist reasoning takes the words in a case or statute out of context and defines them without taking into account their purpose, much in the way you would define the words in a sentence by using a dictionary. For example, consider the question of whether the Constitution's First Amendment provision that "Congress shall make no law . . . abridging freedom of speech, or of the press" applies to commercial advertising. A formalist approach to this question might be to look up the definition of the terms *speech*, or *press*, and *advertising* in various dictionaries to ascertain what these words mean. Notice that different meanings can be provided depending on whether you use a current dictionary or one from 1791, the year the First Amendment went into effect.

Purposive reasoning, in contrast, attempts to define the meaning of words in a case or a statute by ascertaining the purpose underlying them. Notice that, as with formalist reasoning, different meanings can be derived, depending on how one might characterize the purpose of a given statement. In the example of commercial advertising and the First Amendment, one might assert that the purpose

---

[2] Much of this discussion was drawn from J. Boyle, *Anatomy of a Torts Class,* 34 Am. U. L. Rev. 1003 (1985).

of the First Amendment's free speech clause is to promote an open society with access to all forms of information. Hence, laws forbidding certain forms of advertising would be unconstitutional. On the other hand, one could also assert that the purpose of the constitutional protection of speech is to provide for open communication of political ideas, which is necessary for the functioning of a democratic society. Hence, laws restricting political speech would be unconstitutional, but laws regulating commercial advertising would be constitutional.

As noted earlier, rule-based rationales are found in court decisions where a court is called on to interpret language in its prior cases, as well as in court decisions involving the interpretation of statutes or regulations. In disagreements over the interpretation of language in cases, the formalist approach typically quotes the language of a prior case without elaborating on its context. In contrast, in the purposive approach, the court emphasizes the asserted purpose the court had in mind when it decided the earlier dispute. With regard to statutes, the formalist approach tends to focus on the literal language of the statute, while the purposive approach argues that the legislature or Congress had a certain purpose or intent in mind when it wrote the law. This discussion of formalist and purposive rule-based rationales should be reviewed when examining the material on legislative interpretation later in this chapter.

Precedent-Based Rationales

Rationales or arguments based on precedent deal with the basic question of whether an earlier decision applies to the present case, or if it is in some significant way different from the present controversy. If one side wishes to justify a decision on the basis of a past case, it argues that the earlier and current cases have essentially similar facts and issues and concludes that the earlier case controls the current case. The other side may be expected to argue that the cases have essentially different facts and issues, or are distinguishable. Much, therefore, depends on how the two sides characterize the facts and issues of the earlier decision and the current case. Thus, the side that treats the earlier case as similar may give it a broad reading, for example, by drawing analogies. The other side may argue that the earlier case is distinguishable by tying the rule of the earlier case so closely to its facts that it cannot be given a broader application.

A similar form of reasoning involves disagreement over the facts of the current case. The majority and dissent may differ in their descriptions of the facts of the case under consideration. For example, the majority may emphasize facts that the dissent ignores and, in that way, fit the case under consideration into the mold of prior case law. The dissent might emphasize factual characteristics of the earlier case that differ from those of the current case. Of course, the majority may be the side that distinguishes the earlier case, while the dissent may regard it as controlling.

Policy-Based Rationales

Some arguments or rationales in legal opinions involve disagreements over policy rather than precedents. These arguments tend to focus on who should be making policy rather than on the policy issues themselves. However, a careful reading of an opinion reveals the policy choices being made.

One common rationale deals with judicial administration. An opinion, for example, may assert that what is needed is a firm rule, that this rule can be easily administered by the legal system, and any other rule would "open the floodgates of litigation" and bring down the judicial system or otherwise bring about social ruin. In contrast, the competing opinion's view may reason that what is needed is a flexible rule, that the courts are capable of deciding the matter on a case-by-case basis, and the public confidence in the judicial system would erode if courts did not assume the responsibility of administering justice.

A similar policy argument deals with institutional competence. One opinion may reason that the rule should be developed by the courts because the judiciary is the only legal institution that combines the capability of determining complex factual issues and the capability of considering changing circumstances. However, the other opinion may assert that the issue involves public policy, which should be left to the legislature because it is the governmental body closest to public opinion and best suited for the task of considering the broader social implications.

Ethical Dilemmas/Issues

Howard Ross is a sales representative for the Page Printing Company. Page's employee handbook provides a progressive discipline procedure for employees. Under this procedure, if an employee violates the rules contained in the manual, he or she receives harsher penalties for each new violation. The company can discharge an employee after three violations of company rules.

The county prosecutor indicted Ross for rape. Ben Johnson, Ross's supervisor, suspended Ross from his duties pending the outcome of his criminal case. Johnson told Ross, "You will have your job back if there is a satisfactory outcome to your case."

The jury in Ross's trial could not reach a verdict, so the judge dismissed the indictment against Ross.

Ben Johnson went to see Donald Altai, Page's vice president of human resources, and asked what to do about Ross. Altai contacted Page's attorney, Anne Penn, who wrote an opinion letter.

Penn's letter concluded that under present state law, Page could fire Ross and disregard the employee manual and Johnson's statement. Her letter also mentioned that the law in this area was dynamic. Some states had recently declared employment manuals and supervisor's statements binding on the employers. Even under these views, it is unclear whether Page would have to honor the statements in the manual or those made by Johnson.

What are the ethical issues? What would you do?

Legislative Interpretation

Legal reasoning is not confined to the interpretation of case law; it is also used to interpret and apply legislation to legal disputes. Thus, the meaning of a statute is not fully known until the statute is interpreted by the courts.

In interpreting statutes, the courts begin by attempting to determine the legislature's intent, which may be expressed explicitly in the statute. However, the legislature may not have envisioned the particular controversy before a court, so legislative intent may be nonexistent. In such cases, the court attempts to determine how the legislature would have wanted the statute applied in the given case.

The most obvious indirect indication of the legislative intent is the statute's language. Where the language is clear, a court does not go beyond the plain meaning of its words to determine what a statute means. This is known as the **plain meaning rule**. A court will not apply a statute literally, however, where doing so produces an absurd result or renders the statute unworkable.

In examining the statutory context, a court considers the statute as a whole, not merely the particular clause at issue in the case. In this way, the court avoids considering a particular statutory clause out of context. Thus, courts do not divorce a single phrase or section of a statute from its other portions.

Where the context of the statutory language does not reveal legislative intent, courts frequently consider the statute's legislative history. This includes the social conditions that gave rise to the legislative response and any documents, such as committee reports, proceedings, and records of legislative debates. This approach aims at arriving at the purpose of the statute.

Case

(Legislative Interpretation)

ABRAMSKI V. UNITED STATES

No. 12-1493, United States Supreme Court, June 16, 2014

Bruce Abramski (Abramski) offered to purchase a handgun for his uncle. The form that federal regulations required Abramski to fill out asked whether he was the "actual transferee/buyer" of the gun, and clearly warned that a straw purchaser (namely, someone buying a gun on behalf of another) was not the actual buyer. Abramski falsely answered that he was the actual buyer. Abramski was convicted for knowingly making false statements "with respect to any fact material to the lawfulness of the sale" of a gun, 18 U.S.C. §922(a)(6), and for making a false statement "with respect to the information required ... to be kept" in the gun dealer's records, §924(a)(l)(A). The Fourth Circuit Court of Appeals affirmed the conviction. Abramski appealed to the U.S. Supreme Court. He argued that his false statement was not "material."

The Supreme Court affirmed the lower court decisions. What follows is the Supreme Court's majority opinion, delivered by Justice Kagan and joined by justices Kennedy, Ginsburg, Breyer, and Sotomayor. The Court's majority opinion is followed by the dissenting opinion, filed by Justice Scalia and joined by justices Roberts, Thomas, and Alito.

Justice Kagan

At its core, [Abramski's] argument relies on one true fact: Federal gun law regulates licensed dealers' transactions with "persons" or "transferees," without specifically referencing straw purchasers. Section 922(d), for example, bars a dealer from "sell[ing] or otherwise disposing] of" a firearm to any "person" who falls within a prohibited category—felons, drug addicts, the mentally ill, and so forth.

But that language merely raises, rather than answers, the critical question: In a straw purchase, who *is* the "person" or "transferee" whom federal gun law addresses? Is that "person" the middleman buying a firearm on someone else's behalf? Or is that "person" instead the individual really paying for the gun and meant to take possession of it upon completion of the purchase? In answering that inquiry, we must (as usual) interpret the relevant words not in a vacuum, but with reference to the statutory context, structure, history, and purpose. All those tools of divining meaning—not to mention common sense, which is a fortunate (though not inevitable) side-benefit of construing statutory terms fairly—demonstrate that §922, in regulating licensed dealers' gun sales, looks through the straw to the actual buyer.

The overarching reason is that Abramski's reading would undermine—indeed, for all important purposes, would virtually repeal—the gun law's core provisions. [T]he statute establishes an elaborate system to verify a would-be gun purchaser's identity and check on his background. It also requires that the information so gathered go into a dealer's permanent records. The twin goals of this comprehensive scheme are to keep guns out of the hands of criminals and others who should not have them, and to assist law enforcement authorities in investigating serious crimes. And no part of that scheme would work if the statute turned a blind eye to straw purchase—if, in other words, the law addressed not the substance of a transaction, but only empty formalities.

To sum up so far: All the prerequisites for buying a gun refer to a "person" or "transferee." Read Abramski's way ("the man at the counter"), those terms deny effect to the regulatory scheme, as criminals could always use straw purchasers to evade the law. Read the other way ("the man getting, and always meant to get, the firearm"), those terms give effect to the statutory provisions, allowing them to accomplish their manifest objects. That alone provides more than sufficient reason to understand "person" and "transferee" asreferring not to the fictitious but to the real buyer.

No piece of information is more important under federal firearms law than the identity of a gun's purchaser—the person who acquires a gun as a result of a transaction with a licensed dealer. Had Abramski admitted that he was not that purchaser, but merely a straw—that he was asking the dealer to verify the identity of, and run a background check on, the wrong individual—the sale here could not have gone forward. That makes Abramski's misrepresentation material under §922(a)(6). And because that statement pertained to information that a dealer must keep in its permanent records under the firearms law, Abramski's answer to also violated §924(a)(l)(A). Accordingly, we affirm the judgment of the Fourth Circuit.

Justice Scaliea, dissenting

Contrary to the majority's assertion that the statute "merely raises, rather than answers, the critical question" of whether Abramski or his uncle was the "person" to whom the dealer "[s]old" the gun, the statute speaks to that question directly. Giving the text its plain, ordinary meaning, Abramski, not his uncle, was that "person." That being so, the Government has identified no reason why the arrangement between Abramski and his uncle, both of whom were eligible to receive and possess firearms, was "material to the lawfulness of" the sale.

The majority's purpose-based arguments describe a statute Congress reasonably might have written, but not the statute it wrote.

The only thing which can justify [the majority's] leap is the false imperative to make the statute as effective as possible, rather than as effective as the language indicates Congress desired.

[P]erhaps Congress drew the line where it did because the Gun Control Act, like many contentious pieces of legislation, was a compromise among highly interested parties attempting to pull the provisions in different directions. Perhaps those whose votes were needed for passage of the statute *wanted* a lawful purchaser to be able to use an agent. A statute shaped by political tradeoffs in a controversial area may appear imperfect from some perspectives, but our ability to imagine ways of redesigning the statute to advance one of Congress' ends does not render it irrational. We must accept that Congress, balancing the conflicting demands of a divided citizenry, wrote the statute it wrote—a statute going so far and no further.

Chapter Extension

For additional material relating to Chapter 2, see p. 213 in the Appendix of Chapter Extension Files.

Chapter Problems

1. Define the following concepts and terms:
   a. Jurisprudence
   b. Natural law
   c. Positive law
   d. Legislation
   e. Common law
   f. Stare decisis
   g. Obiter dictum
   h. Formalist reasoning
   i. Purposive reasoning
   j. Plain meaning rule

2. What conception of law is embodied in the following statement from the Declaration of Independence?

   When in the Course of human events, it becomes necessary for one people to dissolve the political bonds which have connected them with another, and to assume among the powers of the earth, the separate and equal station to which the Laws of Nature and of Nature's God entitle them, a decent respect to the opinions of mankind requires that they should declare the causes which impel them to the separation. We hold these truths to be self-evident, that all men are created equal, that they are endowed by their Creator with certain unalienable Rights, that among these are Life, Liberty and the pursuit of happiness.

3. In 1973, the U.S. Supreme Court was called on to decide the constitutionality of a state statute making it a crime to obtain an abortion. In deciding that the statute was unconstitutional, the Court stated:

   We forthwith acknowledge our awareness of the sensitive and emotional nature of the abortion controversy, of the vigorous opposing views, even among physicians, and of the deep and seemingly absolute convictions that the subject inspires. One's philosophy, one's experiences, one's exposure to the raw edges of human existence, one's religious training, one's attitudes toward life and family and their values, and the moral standards one establishes and seeks to observe, are all likely to influence and to color one's thinking and conclusions about abortion. . . . Our task, of course, is to resolve the issue by constitutional measurement free of emotion and predilection.

   Which conception of law best describes the Court's statement? Do you think that the Court can resolve the issue "by constitutional measurement free of emotion and predilection?" Explain.

4. Martin Luther King, Jr., once wrote: "I think we all have moral obligations to obey just laws. On the other hand, I think we have moral obligations to disobey unjust laws because noncooperation with evil is just as much a moral obligation as cooperation with good." Lewis F. Powell (retired associate justice of the Supreme Court of the United States), when he was president of the American Bar Association, deplored the doctrine "that only just' laws need to be obeyed and that every man is free to determine for himself the question of 'justness.'" He added, "An ordered society cannot exist if every man determines which laws he will obey." Which conception of law was Justice Powell expressing? Which position was Dr. King espousing? Explain. With which position do you agree? Explain.

5. The federal Equal Pay Act (EPA) forbids sex-based wage discrimination. It states, "No employer . . . shall discriminate between employees on the basis of sex by paying wages to employees at a rate less than the rate he pays employees of the opposite sex for equal work on jobs the performance of which requires equal skill, effort, and responsibility, and which are performed under similar working conditions." Congress took the terms, "equal skill, effort and responsibility" and "similar working conditions" from the language of job evaluation system, developed in the field that was then called industrial relations/human resource management (IR/HRM). What conception of law is reflected in Congress's use of the language of IR/HRM when writing the EPA? Explain.

6. The Uniform Commercial Code (UCC) is a statute, enacted in part in all states, that provides rules regulating many types of commercial transactions. Section 1-102 of the UCC states the following: "(1) This Act shall be liberally construed and applied to promote its underlying purposes and policies. (2) Underlying purposes and policies of this Act are (a) to simplify,

clarify and modernize the law governing commercial transactions; (b) permit the continued expansion of commercial practices through custom, usage and agreement of the parties, and (c) to make uniform the law among the various jurisdictions." Which conception of law does Section 1-102 of the UCC reflect? Explain.

7. Explain the role of legal precedents in the development of the law.

8. The president of the United States concludes a commercial treaty with Russia. The treaty is subsequently ratified by the U.S. Senate. After ratification, a group of citizens files a lawsuit in a federal court attacking the treaty as unconstitutional. Will the citizens win? Explain.

9. The Federal Trade Commission, a federal agency, brings action against Conglomerate Car Company as a result of a complaint filed with the commission by Bigdome Car Company. After reviewing the complaint, the commission concludes that Conglomerate is guilty. The commission's opinion provides its reasons for reaching this conclusion. Is the commission's opinion law? Explain.

10. Arthur and Ava Strunk have two sons, Tommy, age 28, and Jerry, age 27. Tommy is married, employed, and a part-time college student. He suffers from a fatal kidney disease and is being kept alive by frequent dialysis treatment, a procedure that cannot be continued much longer. Jerry is incompetent and has been legally committed to a state institution for the mentally retarded. He has an IQ of approximately 35, which corresponds to a mental age of approximately six years. He is further handicapped by a speech defect that makes it difficult for him to communicate with people who are unacquainted with him. When it was determined that Tommy would need a kidney transplant to survive, doctors looked for a donor. Possible donors include cadavers as well as live persons. Because of compatibility of blood type and tissue, the only acceptable live donor is Jerry. The parents petitioned a court for authority to proceed with the operation. There are no statutes or prior case law to guide the court's determination. How should the court decide?

3   THE AMERICAN LEGAL SYSTEM

Chapter Outline

Learning Objectives

After learning this chapter the student should be able to:

- Recognize when a business should consult an attorney and how to select one.
- Determine whether particular communications are protected by the attorney-client privilege.
- Evaluate whether a firm not directly transacting business in a state is likely to be subject to suit in that state.
- Recognize the different stages of the litigation process and their importance to a firm facing possible litigation.
- Determine in particular settings the advantages and disadvantages of using alternatives to litigation for settling disputes.

Businesses come into contact with the legal system under a variety of circumstances. Disputes with suppliers or customers may result in lawsuits that bring the manager face to face with the legal system and its process. Contact with the judicial system creates a need for legal advice.

This chapter begins by explaining the attorney-client relationship. The next sections describe the judicial system. Finally, the chapter surveys alternatives to litigation (the traditional way to resolve disputes).

The Firm and Its Attorney

Businesses call on lawyers to assist them through the red tape of government regulation. In the past, a business usually did not contact lawyers until a problem arose—for example, when it was sued or when a distributor would not pay an outstanding debt. However, now more and more businesses are concerned with preventive law. By contacting lawyers early and following their legal advice, companies may avoid the consequences that accompany uninformed business practices. Business managers today have more of an ongoing relationship with lawyers than in the past; hence, they need to know more about lawyers.

Lawyers have a common base of education: law school. There, law students receive generalized training that enables them to adapt to a wide range of tasks. The average person thinks that lawyers know the law. It is more accurate to say that lawyers are versed in general legal principles and methods. They are trained to find the relevant law and to apply it to particular circumstances.

Corporate Legal Strategy

A long-standing tension has characterized the relationship between lawyers and business managers. Lawyers tend to be conservative in their advice and often dampen a business's desire to do creative things. Many business executives believe that attorneys should be consulted only to find out what cannot be done. Because they use attorneys only on an *ad hoc* basis, they do not know how to incorporate them into their business organization charts.

Some businesses, however, recognize the need to develop a comprehensive corporate legal strategy. This corporate strategy may appear in any of several forms. A *preventive* strategy employs attorneys to review new programs and documents with an eye to avoiding legal problems. An *enforcive* strategy uses legal activity to protect a company against patent infringement and other violations of its rights. A *creative* strategy employs legal counsel to help formulate corporate goals. An *active* strategy brings the manager and the attorney together to explore various ways of achieving those goals, through, for example, a merger with another corporation, legal loopholes, or lobbying for a change in the law. The preventive, enforcive, creative, and active corporate legal strategies may be used together, depending on the circumstances that confront the company.[1]

---

[1] This discussion of corporate legal strategy is derived from F. Sturdivant and C. Green, *Building a Strong Corporate Strategy*, College of Administrative Science, The Ohio State University, Working Paper Series 83–70 (October 1983).

The Lawyer's Roles

Lawyers play many roles in relation to the business firm. They counsel the firm's managers regarding transactions, compliance with regulations, and similar matters. They draft and review legal documents. Their primary goal as counsellors and drafters is to prevent legal problems from developing.

Lawyers also represent their clients as advocates. They negotiate to settle disputes with other parties on terms favorable to their clients. They represent their clients before courts, administrative agencies, and arbitrators. As advocates, their duty is to present the facts and argue the law in the light most favorable to the client. Counsel for opposing parties will do the same for their clients. Lawyers serve as partisan advocates in a legal system that is based on an adversarial model.

To perform their various roles, lawyers often must investigate relevant facts. Because of the need to investigate, communication between a firm and its attorney is very important.

Communicating with Lawyers

A person needing a lawyer's services should contact counsel early, before the problem intensifies. It is better to have a lawyer draft a contract than to call in a lawyer to solve a problem caused by a contract poorly drafted by the client.

The client should fully disclose the facts relevant to the question at hand. If an attorney's opinion is based on less than full information, the opinion is incomplete. A general understanding of the law affecting the business helps a client detail the material facts and avoid irrelevancies when communicating with a lawyer. Understanding the lawyer's role also facilitates communication.

The client should actively assist the lawyer's search for solutions. Also, the client should inform the lawyer of the company's goals so that the lawyer seeks solutions compatible with those goals. Finally, the client should expect high-quality service from counsel and should communicate that expectation. After all, the client is paying the bill.

The Attorney-Client Privilege

The law protects confidential communications between the attorney and client from disclosure to a third person. Without the client's permission, the attorney may not divulge communications made during the attorney-client contact. The client may, however, waive the privilege and authorize the attorney to make disclosure. The privilege applies only to confidential communications; it does not include statements made to an attorney in the presence of third parties other than the client's or attorney's agents or employees.

A corporation communicates with its lawyers through its employees. The courts have grappled with the question of which employees speak for the corporation so that their statements are protected by the privilege. Some states limit the privilege to statements from senior management who guide and integrate the firm's operations.

In federal court, however, the Supreme Court has refused to limit the privilege to the senior managers who control the firm.[2] The Court applies the privilege on a case-by-case basis, inquiring:

- Was the employee directed by his or her superiors to speak with counsel?
- Was the communication to enable the firm to get legal advice?
- Did the communication concern matters within the scope of the employee's job?
- Did the employee know the reason for the communication?
- Was the communication confidential?

The attorney-client privilege protects only the communication between the client and the attorney. The communication must be for the purpose of obtaining legal advice. The underlying information is not protected. A client cannot hide information just by telling it to the attorney.

The reason for the attorney-client privilege is to promote compliance with the law. The purpose of seeking legal advice is to avoid violating the law. A client who trusts the attorney not to reveal communications between them should be forthcoming with the facts needed by the attorney in forming a legal opinion.

Exceptions to the attorney-client privilege exist when there is an overriding public policy. For example, an exception allows an attorney to disclose communication where the client is trying to use the lawyer's services to commit a crime or fraud.

Work Product Doctrine

A doctrine akin to the attorney-client privilege is the work-product doctrine. Any materials that have been prepared in anticipation of a lawsuit fall under this doctrine, and are privileged. Neither the attorney nor the client can be compelled to disclose these materials. The doctrine covers not only materials that have been prepared by the client or the attorney, but also any materials prepared by, for example, consultants.

In some cases a party to a lawsuit may obtain these materials if there is a substantial need and there is no other way to obtain them without undue hardship. However, even in this case the court will still protect against disclosure of the mental impressions, conclusions, opinions or legal theories of an attorney or other representative of the party concerning the litigation.

Professional Conduct Rules for Attorneys

Every state has ethical rules of conduct governing lawyers' professional behavior. Lawyers have certain responsibilities to their clients, to the legal system, and to their own consciences. These responsibilities often result in ethical dilemmas.

---

[2] Upjohn Co. v. U.S., 449 U.S. 383 (1981).

The Business and Government Interface

The following link is to the ABA's *Model Rules of Professional Conduct* for attorneys:

http://www.americanbar.org
/groups/professional
_responsibility/publications
/model_rules_of_professional
_conduct.html

They have been adopted as law in most states. Clicking *Model Rules Table of Contents* takes you to the rules. Clicking *Rule 1.6, Confidentiality of Communications* gives you the full rule on this aspect of the lawyer-client relation. Clicking *Rule 1.5 Fees* takes you to a rule most potential clients find interesting.

To guide attorneys and bodies that regulate their conduct, the American Bar Association (ABA), a national organization of attorneys, has approved The Model Rules of Professional Conduct (usually known just as the Model Rules). Most states have adopted the Model Rules, with variations from state to state. Lawyers who violate the Rules of Professional Conduct may be disciplined or disbarred.

The Model Rules require the lawyer to provide competent representation to a client. According to the Model Rules, competent representation "requires the legal knowledge, skill, thoroughness and preparation reasonably necessary for the representation." The lawyer must act with reasonable diligence and promptness in representing a client. This must be accomplished while abiding by the client's decision regarding the objectives of the representation and while exercising candor to the tribunal hearing the case.

The Model Rules provide that lawyers may not represent clients whose interests conflict with those of other clients, unless each affected client gives informed consent, confirmed in writing. The Model Rules require lawyers to adopt reasonable procedures to determine whether there are any conflicts of interest.

Under the Model Rules, a lawyer must keep confidential all information relating to the representation, unless the client consents to its disclosure. This rule does not apply if a lawyer knows that a client intends to commit a crime that would result in death or substantial bodily harm. A client has the right to discharge a lawyer with or without cause.

The Court System

The judicial system in the United States, includes the federal system and the judicial systems of the 50 states. Separate federal court systems exist for the District of Columbia and U.S. territories such as Puerto Rico, the Virgin Islands, and Guam. This means there are more than 50 distinct judicial systems. It is not unusual for a firm to do business in a number of states and, hence, to be subject to the judicial processes in many jurisdictions. The business manager therefore needs a general understanding of the workings of federal and state judicial systems.

Jurisdiction

Jurisdiction is the power of a court to hear and decide a case. To exercise this power, a court generally must have jurisdiction over both the subject matter of, and the parties to, the dispute.

Jurisdiction over the subject matter is accomplished by selecting a court that has power to hear the type of case. State courts of general jurisdiction are usually empowered to hear any type of case. The federal courts, as discussed in the next section, have limited subject-matter jurisdiction.

Jurisdiction over the person may be accomplished by serving the defendant with notice of the suit within the state in which the court is located. The notice is called a *summons.*

The requirement that the process be served on the defendant in the state in which the court is located poses a severe limitation. Suppose a defendant who resides in Alaska strikes a pedestrian while driving a car in Florida. If the Alaskan resident returned home, the injured pedestrian might be forced to sue in Alaska. To combat this shortcoming, states enacted long-arm statutes. A **long-arm statute** is a means of gaining service over an out-of-state defendant. Most states have long-arm statutes that subject an out-of-state defendant to the jurisdiction where the defendant is doing business or has committed a civil wrong. Long-arm statutes must comply with the Constitution's requirement of due process. In *International Shoe Co. v. Washington,* the U.S. Supreme Court held that the U.S. Constitution requires a defendant, if not present within the state, to have certain minimum contacts with the state where the suit is filed.[3]

Venue

Jurisdiction must be distinguished from venue. *Venue* is concerned with the geographic locality within the jurisdiction where an action should be tried. Venue is specified by statute; it may require that the case be heard in the county where the defendant resides or where the property that is the subject of the action is located. When the location of a trial would result in an inconvenience and a hardship, the doctrine of **forum non conveniens** permits a defendant to transfer the case to another geographic location where venue is proper.

The Federal System

The federal judicial system derives from the U.S. Constitution. Article III provides that "the judicial Power of the United States shall be vested in one supreme court, and in such inferior courts as the Congress may from time to time ordain and establish." Pursuant to Article III, Congress has created 14 circuit courts of appeal and 94 district courts (see Figure 3–1).

District Courts
The basic federal trial court is the U.S. district court. There is at least one district in every state and territory. Many states are divided into more than one district, depending on size, population, and number of lawsuits filed. District courts also hear appeals from a few federal agencies, such as the Social Security Administration.

---

[3] 326 U.S. 310 (1945).

FIGURE 3–1   **Federal Court System**

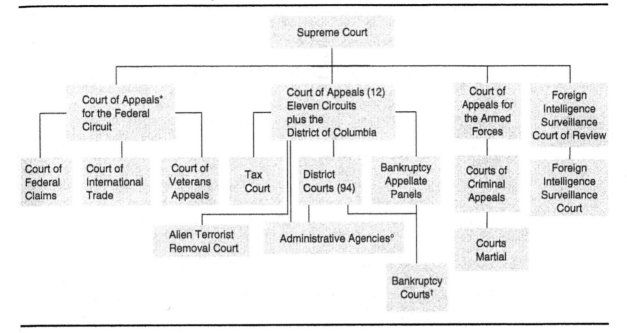

*Cases invoving patents, trademarks, copyrights, and contract claims against the United States are reviewed by the Court of Appeals for the Federal Circuit.

†Some appeals proceed to the Bankruptcy Appellate Panel; others go directly to the District Court.

°Most appeals are reviewed by the Court of Appeals; some are reviewed de novo in the District Court.

The Business and Government Interface

The following link is to United States Courts website:

http://www.uscourts.gov /Home.aspx

There you will find information, including videos, podcasts, statistics and other information about the federal courts.

The district court has subject matter jurisdiction only if a statute gives it jurisdiction. The two broadest statutes give district courts jurisdiction over cases involving a federal question and diversity of citizenship.

Federal question jurisdiction cases include any claim arising under a federal statute, a treaty, or the U.S. Constitution. Cases involving robbery of federal banks, federal antitrust violations, and interpretations of U.S. treaties with foreign nations are all properly heard by a federal district court because they present federal questions.

U.S. district courts also have **diversity jurisdiction** over cases between citizens of different states where the amount in contest exceeds $75,000. A corporation is considered a citizen of the states in which it is incorporated and in which it has its principal place of business. A partnership, even a limited partnership, is considered a citizen of every state in which a partner is a citizen. There must be complete diversity of citizenship; no plaintiff (the party who initiates the suit) may be a citizen of the same state in which any defendant (the party who is sued) is a citizen. If there are multiple plaintiffs, each must claim, in good faith, damages exceeding $75,000 (not counting interest or court costs).

For example, assume that four individual plaintiffs sue Chemical, Inc. because wastes it dumped into a waterway ultimately polluted the plaintiffs' property. Each seeks more than $75,000 in damages. Three of the plaintiffs are citizens of Ohio, and the fourth is a citizen of Michigan. Chemical, Inc. is incorporated in Delaware and has its principal place of business in Michigan. Here, diversity of citizenship is not present because a plaintiff and a defendant are citizens of Michigan. If the Michigan plaintiff were eliminated from the suit, then diversity jurisdiction would be present.

The federal district court sitting in a diversity case hears and resolves the case according to the law of the state in which it sits. This is known as the *Erie Doctrine,* named after a case in which this principle was first announced.[4] The court does, however, apply its own procedural rules, such as rules of evidence and rules of conduct regarding the administration of the trial.

Plaintiffs are not required to sue in federal district court, even though that court would have jurisdiction. In most cases, they may elect instead to file suit in a proper state court. The district court has concurrent jurisdiction, with the state courts, as opposed to exclusive jurisdiction. However, if plaintiffs sue in a state court, the defendant may have the case removed to the federal court as long as the case could have originally been brought in that court.

Court of Appeals

Appeals from the district courts are heard by the U.S. circuit courts of appeals. There are 11 numbered circuit courts of appeal, the District of Columbia circuit, plus the Courts of Appeals for the Federal Circuit and for the Armed Forces. They also hear appeals from the Tax Court and review most administrative agency actions. The Tax Court hears disputes involving tax deficiencies assessed against a taxpayer.

U.S. Supreme Court

Sitting atop the federal legal system is the U.S. Supreme Court. Review in the Supreme Court is not automatic. Parties seeking review must request that the Court hear the case by filing a petition for **certiorari**. The Court has absolute discretion to grant or deny certiorari, and it rarely gives a reason for a denial. Certiorari is granted if any four of the nine Supreme Court justices are in favor of it. Certiorari is likely to be granted when a constitutional issue of national importance is posed or when an issue has been decided in a conflicting manner by the circuit courts of appeals.

---

[4] Erie Railroad Co. v. Tompkins, 304 U.S. 64 (1938).

The State System

The Business and Government Interface

The following link is to the website of the Supreme Court of Ohio & The Ohio Judicial System:

http://www.supremecourt.ohio.gov/

This is provided as an example of a typical state court system.

State trial courts consist of courts of general and limited jurisdiction (see Figure 3–2). A court of general jurisdiction is one that can hear any type of case unless specifically prohibited by statute. Some cases, such as admiralty, bankruptcy, and patent infringement actions, may be brought only in federal court. Most state trial courts of general jurisdiction are organized at the county level. Their names vary from state to state. The most popular names are circuit court, court of common pleas, and superior court.

State trial courts of limited jurisdiction are those that can hear only specific types of cases. A probate court, for example, cannot hear a divorce case; a small claims court cannot try a felony case. Some courts are limited in that they can only hear disputes up to a maximum monetary ceiling.

Many states have an intermediate court of appeals, similar to the federal circuit court of appeals. Following a decision by the court of appeals, review may be sought in the state supreme court; similar to the U.S. Supreme Court, it reviews most cases by certiorari. In the smaller and less populous states, which lack intermediate courts of appeals, appeals from trial courts are taken directly to state supreme courts.

A state supreme court is the highest authority on the law of its state. The U.S. Supreme Court has no power to decide issues of state law. State supreme court decisions interpreting federal statutes, treaties, and the U.S. Constitution are, however, subject to U.S. Supreme Court review.

FIGURE 3–2   Typical State Court System

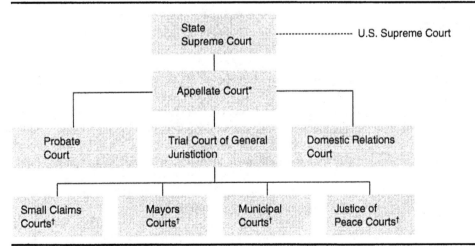

*Not present in the system in smaller, less populous states.

†In some cases, appeals are made directly to the Appellate Court.

The Civil Process

A dispute must involve a case or controversy before a court will decide it. Courts do not act when there is no real dispute.

Courts are best equipped to decide cases when the parties have a personal stake in the outcome. Under these circumstances, the parties have the incentive to expend their best efforts in prosecuting or defending a case. This is the adversary system. In this adversarial environment, courts are in the best position to examine the arguments, find the truth, and apply justice.

When an event triggers a dispute, the potential for a lawsuit exists. A lawsuit is a civil case. Table 3–1 contrasts civil and criminal cases. The civil process is the sequence of events from the beginning of the suit to the final appeal. It consists of four stages: the *pleading stage*, the *discovery stage*, *trial stage*, and *appellate stage* (see Figure 3–3).

The Pleading Stage

The *pleadings* are the documents that tell each party's claims or defenses against the other parties. See Table 3–2 for a summary of the pleadings.

Class Action Suits

Under certain circumstances, a person may bring a suit on behalf of a class of people who have been similarly injured. This is known as a **class action suit.** For example, assume that many members of the public have been injured as a result of illegally inflated utility prices. It may not be feasible for every injured person to sue the utility company individually, and not everyone may be aware of the illegal activity. The cost of maintaining the suit also may discourage people from suing, especially if the amount of potential recovery is too small to be worth the effort. The law in these cases may permit one or more persons to undertake a suit against the utility company on behalf of all the injured customers. By consolidating in one suit the claims of many, the class action suit avoids the potential for repetitious, inefficient litigation.

Class actions have involved thousands and even hundreds of thousands of people. The administration of a class suit is often very difficult because of the number of persons involved. The distribution of the proceeds of a settlement or judgment may be equally difficult. Not all members of the class may be identified or found. Additionally, the amount of distribution to each individual may be disputed. Some courts, aware of this problem, have ordered that damages be distributed to benefit the public. For example, in a case where a utility company charges illegally high rates, a court might order the company to reduce its rates to all consumers for a period of time.

In a class action lawsuit, one or more members of a class sue as representative parties on behalf of all members of the class. The court must determine

---
TABLE 3–1   Civil versus Criminal Cases

	Civil	*Criminal*
Who institutes the action?	Individual or business enterprise	Sovereign
Who has been wronged?	Individual or business enterprise	Society
What is the burden of proof?	Preponderance of the evidence*	Beyond a reasonable doubt†
What is the remedy?	Damages, injunction, or other private relief	Punishment (fine and/or imprisonment)

---

* By the greater weight of the evidence.

† To satisfy this burden the trier of the facts (judge or jury) must have an abiding conviction amounting to a certainty of the guilt of the accused. This is a greater burden of proof than "preponderance of the evidence."

FIGURE 3–3   The Civil Process

Complaint
Answer
Reply

Pleading
stage

Deposition
Written interrogatories
Requestfor production
    of documents
Request to inspect
    premises
Request for admissions
Request for physical
    examination
Request for mental
    examination

Discovery stage

Selection of jury
Opening statements
Cases in chief
Closing arguments
Instructions to jury
Verdict
Judgment

Trial stage

Review by
appellate
court

Appellate
stage

---

whether to certify the action as a class action. The requirements for certification as a class action include that questions of law or fact must be common to the class, and the claims of the representative parties must be typical of the claims or defenses of the class. When the court certifies a lawsuit as a class action, it defines the class, the claims or defenses, and appoints counsel to represent the class. The court directs that notice be given to all members of the class who can be reasonably identified. The notice states that absent class members may enter an appearance through an attorney, or request exclusion from the class action (which permits the absent member to bring an individual lawsuit). The notice also states that any class judgment is binding on all members of the class.

TABLE 3–2   **Pleadings**

Pleading	Who Files against Whom	Purpose
Complaint	Plaintiff against defendant	States the factual basis for the claim.
Answer	Defendant against plaintiff	Admits or denies the allegations of the complaint; may also raise affirmative defenses.
Counterclaim	Defendant against plaintiff	States basis for claim by defendant against plaintiff.
Reply	Plaintiff against defendant	Answers counterclaim.
Cross claim	Defendant against another defendant	States basis for claim.
Impleader	Defendant against a nonparty	Defendant adds another party to the lawsuit.
Intervention	Nonparty against a party	Another party seeks to join the lawsuit.
Interpleader	Plaintiff or Defendant against two parties	Forces the court to determine the rightful holder of monies.

Motions

During the pleading stage it is not unusual for a party to file a **motion to dismiss** or a **motion for judgment on the pleadings.**

A motion to dismiss may attack any number of deficiencies in a pleading. It may be used, for example, by a defendant questioning whether the court has jurisdiction over the defendant or over the subject matter. Or, it may allege that the matter should be dismissed because the Complaint fails to state facts that would constitute a reason for the Plaintiff to win the lawsuit. In effect this motion, says, "So what. Even if you prove what you said, the law does not recognize this as actionable." For example, in a jurisdiction where a surrogate mother contract is not recognized, a complaint seeking relief under such a contract should be dismissed for failure to state a cause of action.

A motion to dismiss will also be warranted when it is clear on the face of the Complaint that the statute of limitations has run. In a jurisdiction where the statute of limitations for a wrongful discharge of employment is four years, for example, a motion to dismiss should be granted if it is clear from the Complaint that it was not filed within that time period. Finally, there are consequences when the defendant fails to answer the Complaint in a timely manner, or the Plaintiff fails to Reply to the Counterclaim within the time specified by law. In such a case a motion for default judgment may result in the movant winning.

A motion for judgment on the pleadings may be filed by either party. It is similar to the motion to dismiss, however it alleges that on the basis of an examination of all the pleadings, the movant should prevail. For example, assume that the plaintiff alleges in its complaint that defendant owes it a sum of money. Defendant, in his Answer, pleads poverty, but does not deny the debt. Based on these pleadings a motion for judgment on the pleadings should be granted in Plaintiff's favor.

Remedies

Most people sue for money damages, but in some cases a plaintiff asks the court for an **injunction**—an order compelling the defendant to do something or to refrain from doing something. The plaintiff is not entitled to a permanent injunction until the end of the case. In a proper case, however, the plaintiff may obtain a preliminary injunction by demonstrating that: (1) the plaintiff is very likely to win on the merits of the case, (2) the plaintiff will suffer irreparable harm if the preliminary injunction is not issued, (3) the injunction will not be unjustly harsh on the defendant, and (4) the injunction is in the public interest.

The Discovery Stage

Discovery refers to the process where each party attempts to learn what the other party knows. Each party may direct written questions, known as *interrogatories,* to the other party, who must provide written answers under oath. Each party may also ask the other parties to produce and allow the requesting party to inspect documents or electronically stored information, or the premises. Each party may ask the other parties to admit or deny specific facts, or submit to a physical or mental examination. Parties may also take each other's deposition, a procedure whereby individuals are questioned under oath before a court reporter.

The discovery process contributes substantially to the costs of litigation. In an effort to control these costs, the Federal Rules of Civil Procedure impose on parties a duty to disclose to the other party, without being asked, the following:

- names, addresses and phone numbers of individuals with knowledge relevant to disputed facts alleged with particularity in the pleadings
- copies or descriptions of documents, electronically stored information, and tangible things relevant to disputed facts alleged with particularity in the pleadings
- computations of all monetary damage claims
- copies of liability insurance policies covering the dispute
- names and copies of reports by expert witnesses
- names of witnesses the party plans to call

The Federal Rules rely on automatic disclosure as the primary means of discovery.

Litigation holds. A litigation hold is where a company suspends its usual document retention and preservation policy and directs its employees to preserve documents and electronically stored information (ESI) in anticipation of future litigation. The duty to preserve documents and ESI arises when litigation is anticipated. The duty is often triggered by a "litigation hold letter" the company receives from a potential adversary's attorney. However, the duty also arises when management is aware of potential litigation from other sources, such as when supervisors are overheard talking about harassment of employees.

The company's management, or its attorney, will usually direct employees to retain documents and ESI, putting a hold on all evidence that may be relevant to future litigation. The hold can extend to employee cell phones, text messages, and home computers that access the company network. The purpose of the hold order is to preserve evidence and protect against spoliation of evidence.

Failure to preserve relevant evidence can result in court ordered "discovery sanctions." These include court orders that: prevent the disobedient party from introducing certain evidence, that dismiss the disobedient party's claims and defenses, or award a default judgment against the disobedient party. Discovery sanctions can also include an order that the disobedient party pay the opposing party's attorney fees.

Motions

During the discovery stage, it is common for parties to file a **motion for summary judgment**. This motion is not confined to an examination of the pleadings. It calls attention to the discovery materials, and may include additional sworn statements not part of the discovery. It is not unusual for both parties to file a motion for summary judgment and seek a favorable ruling based upon the sworn facts as applied to the law. Movants are required to file a memorandum that argues why the court should rule in its favor, based upon the uncontroverted facts, as applied to the law.

In a motion for summary judgment, the court is required to construe the facts in the light most favorable to the party against whom summary judgment is sought. Hence, if the question is whether the traffic light was red or green, and there is sworn testimony to both versions, then the court will overrule the motion since these facts are contested.

Pretrial Conference

The judge is interested in an efficient trial. Toward that end, the court will seek out ways to decrease the length of the trial. Parties will be asked to mark their exhibits beforehand and to provide the opponent a copy. Stipulations of evidence whereby the parties agree to the admission of certain documents, or to certain findings, is another way to streamline the trial. The number of witnesses should be realistic and duplication of testimony by different witnesses should ordinarily be avoided.

The court is also interested in the status of settlement negotiations, and will strongly encourage settlement. Of course, settlement will avoid the time and the risk of trial. Usually, the court will be proactive in moving the parties to agreement, and may even suggest or require ADR.

The Trial Stage

If the plaintiff is seeking monetary damages (known as *legal relief*), the parties are ordinarily entitled to a trial by jury. They may, however, waive this right and try the case to the court. If the plaintiff is seeking equitable relief, such as an injunction or other court order, the parties are not ordinarily entitled to a jury trial.

In most civil cases, the plaintiff has the burden of proving the case by a preponderance of the evidence. Preponderance of the evidence means by the greater weight of the evidence. To sustain that burden of proof, the plaintiff must convince the judge or jury that the facts are probably as the plaintiff alleges. If at the end of the case the trier of the facts is undecided, then the defendant wins.

After selection of the jury (if a jury trial is proper and not waived), counsel for the plaintiff makes an opening statement, explaining what he or she intends to prove. Defense counsel may make an opening statement immediately thereafter, or reserve opening statement until the close of plaintiff's case. Plaintiff then presents a case-in-chief by calling witnesses who testify and by presenting other evidence, such as business records, photographs, or other tangible objects, called *exhibits*. The defendant is given the opportunity to cross-examine the plaintiff's witnesses. The judge decides on the admissibility of the evidence, based on the law. The plaintiff rests after completing the case-in-chief.

The defendant then proceeds with an opening statement, if previously reserved, and presents his or her case-in-chief. When the defendant rests, the plaintiff may offer evidence to rebut the defendant's case-in-chief. The defense may follow with surrebutal.

When all of the evidence is in, the parties' lawyers deliver their closing arguments. If the case was tried without a jury, the judge makes findings of fact and conclusions of law. In jury trials, the judge instructs the jurors on the relevant law; they then deliberate and reach a verdict.

Motions

At the trial stage two motions are common: motion for directed verdict and motion for judgment notwithstanding the verdict. Both motions basically say the same thing, but come at different times during the trial.

The **motion for directed verdict** may sound like this in the voice of the attorney moving for it:

> Your Honor, based upon the evidence that has been presented, reasonable minds cannot differ. There is nothing to send to the jury because the evidence is clear, and as a matter of law, your Honor must find for my client.

The motion requesting that court direct a verdict in the movant's favor is customarily made by both parties at the end of the opponent's case-in-chief. Of course, if either party's motion is granted, that ends the case.

The **motion for judgment notwithstanding the verdict** is ordinarily made by the losing party after the return of an unfavorable verdict. It states in essence that the case should never have been sent to the jury because reasonable minds

---

Ethical Dilemmas/Issues

Burger Town, Inc. is a chain of hamburger stands with 20 establishments located in 15 towns in Kentucky. Big Time Burgers, Inc. is an international hamburger restaurant chain with over a thousand restaurants located throughout the United States, Canada, and Europe. Last week Burger Town started running full-page ads in newspapers stating: "Burger Town hamburgers and fries are healthier than Big Time's Burgers. An order consisting of a Burger Town hamburger and french fries contains less saturated fat than a Big Time hamburger and fries."

John Killbuck is the vice president of operations for Big Time Burgers, Inc. Killbuck's department includes the legal department. Teresa Vermilion, an attorney in the department, has informed Killbuck that Big Time could bring a lawsuit against Burger Town for false advertising. However, the success of the lawsuit would depend on the evidence presented in court.

Big Time cooks its hamburgers and fries in beef tallow. It is quite likely that a Big Time hamburger and fries contain more saturated fats than Burger Town's, if Burger Town cooks its hamburgers and fries in vegetable oil.

Killbuck knows that Burger Town is a small, regional chain and cannot withstand the expense of a lengthy lawsuit. However, Big Time's financial and legal resources could enable it to sue and tie up Burger Town in costly litigation for years. Killbuck is considering filing a lawsuit against Burger Town and immediately seeking to negotiate a quick settlement. Killbuck tells Vermilion, "Teresa, if I were in Burger Town's shoes, I would settle the case quickly even if it cost me several thousand dollars rather than face us in court with all the expense that would involve. Also, suing Burger Town would teach those small fries who's the boss of burgers."

What are the ethical issues? What would you do?

---

could not differ on the facts, and as applied to the law, the movant should win. In effect this gives the judge another opportunity to rule in favor of the movant, whose motion for directed verdict was previously overruled. It is rare that the court would upset the jury verdict and enter a judgment notwithstanding the verdict, but it does happen from time to time.

The Appellate Stage

Once the trial court makes a final judgment in the case, the losing party may not institute a new suit against the same parties involving the same issues. This would be barred by a doctrine called *res judicata* (the matter has been decided), which bars a second suit involving the same parties and the same issues.

However, the legal system provides an opportunity for a party to ask a higher court to review a case for error committed by the trial court judge. The basis for such a request might be that the judge's ruling on a motion was wrong, the judge improperly admitted or excluded evidence, or the judge's instruction to the jury misstated the law. The courts that review trial court decisions are called *appellate courts*. An appellate court does not hold a new trial, nor does it hear additional evidence; it merely reviews the record of the trial and listens to the arguments of the party (called the *appellant*) claiming some serious error in that trial. The appellate court also listens to the arguments of the opposing party (called the *appellee*), who may be claiming that no serious error occurred.

After reviewing the record of the trial and the arguments of the parties involved, the appellate court has several alternatives. It can: (1) affirm the verdict of the trial court, that is, accept it as is and change nothing; (2) reverse the verdict, that is, decide that the outcome of the trial was wrong and enter judgment for the appellant; (3) modify the legal remedy provided by the trial court; or (4) reverse and remand the case to the trial court for further proceedings.

Abuse of the System

In recent years, courts and legislatures have tried to curb parties from abusing the judicial system. Rule 11 of the Federal Rules of Civil Procedure is typical of these efforts. It requires that a party or lawyer sign every document filed in the lawsuit and attest that to the best of the signer's knowledge, after reasonable inquiry, the document is well grounded in fact and law and is not being filed for an improper purpose. If the other party believes the rule was violated, it must so advise the alleged violator. If the violator fails to withdraw the offending document, the lawyer and client may be liable for the other party's expenses, including reasonable attorney's fees. Additionally, many states by statute or common law permit parties who have been subjected to frivolous lawsuits to sue for attorney fees and costs, and other damages.

Alternative Dispute Resolution

Two problems plague our civil justice system: delay and expense. These problems result from the heavy volume of lawsuits and the formalities and technicalities of the discovery and motion practice. Consequently, parties and courts have developed a number of alternative dispute resolution (ADR) techniques for resolving legal disputes.

ADR Techniques

Most legal disputes never actually go to trial. Instead, they are settled. A variety of procedures have developed to assist the parties in settling disputes. If the parties are unable to settle, they can avoid court by agreeing to one of the many alternatives to litigation.

Mediation

Mediation involves an intermediary to assist the parties in resolving the conflict. The mediator has no power to force a solution; his or her job is to persuade the parties to come to agreement. A skillful mediator helps the parties understand their opponent's perspective; grasp the strengths of their opponent's case and the weaknesses of their own; and assess the benefits of settlement and the costs of continuing to fight. Often, the success of mediation turns on the mediator's ability and the parties' desire to settle.

Early Neutral Evaluation

Parties using early neutral evaluation submit written memos detailing their positions to a neutral evaluator. The evaluator issues a report on the strengths and weaknesses of each side's case. The parties use the report in an effort to settle their dispute.

Minitrials

The minitrial is a procedure structured to convert a legal dispute into a business problem. Lawyers argue their case to business executives of the disputing companies. These executives are usually high-level officers and have the power to settle the dispute. Time limitations are agreed on in advance. A neutral advisor (a judge or an expert in the topic of dispute) presides at the hearing and offers opinions and suggestions to the executives. After the case has been presented, the executives retire to deliberate. At this stage, the business executives settle the dispute, often by negotiation. The minitrial has been used successfully in several multi-million-dollar disputes.

Summary Jury Trial

In this procedure, each side is given a limited time to present its best case to a jury. Then each party meets with the jury to discuss the strengths and weakness of its case. This is followed by a settlement conference.

The Business and Government Interface

The following link is to website of the American Arbitration Association:

www.adr.org

Arbitration

Arbitration replaces the judge and jury with a private arbitrator, who holds a hearing and decides the dispute. Many associations, such as the American Arbitration Association, and the Better Business Bureau, provide arbitration services.

Disputants may voluntarily agree to use one or more ADR techniques, either on their own or at the suggestion of a court. Arbitration is the most extensively used voluntary ADR technique. Ad hoc arbitration occurs when the parties agree to submit a particular dispute to arbitration. Increasingly, however, parties are agreeing, before any disputes arise, that all disputes will be arbitrated. These blanket arbitration agreements are standard practice in some industries, such as construction, securities, and commodities.

In voluntary arbitration, the parties control the procedures, the timing, and even the identity of the arbitrator. Thus, arbitration provides greater flexibility than litigation and can solve the problems of delay, cost, and lack of expertise. For example, the parties can require that the arbitrator hear and decide the case by a specified date. If the arbitrator is unable to do so, they can select a different arbitrator. The parties can agree to limit or eliminate the formal discovery process. This can save a great deal of time and expense. Parties can also save money in appropriate cases by limiting or eliminating transcripts and briefs.

The parties can require that the arbitrator have expertise in the technical matters involved in the dispute. This can save the parties the time and money they would spend on educating a generalist judge and jury. It would also provide for a more informed decision.

In addition, the parties can also control whether the arbitration is public. They can agree to exclude the media and to keep the record confidential.

On the other hand, arbitrators do not have the same powers that judges have. Judges have the power to swear witnesses and issue subpoenas. Judges can hold witnesses who refuse to obey subpoenas in contempt and jail or fine them until they agree to comply.

More than three fifths of the states and the District of Columbia have adopted the Uniform Arbitration Act (UAA). The UAA gives arbitrators the power to swear witnesses and issue subpoenas. But an arbitrator has no contempt power. If a witness refuses to obey a subpoena, the parties must sue the witness in court. If the court orders the witness to obey and the witness persists in refusing, the court can then hold the witness in contempt.

An arbitrator's decision is called an *award*. The award may order a party to take action, such as paying money to the other party. However, an arbitrator has no power to enforce the award. As with subpoenas, a party must sue in court if the other party refuses to comply with the award.

Arbitrators have the power to award compensatory damages. There is considerable uncertainty, however, over whether an arbitrator has power to award punitive damages, attorney fees, or equitable relief. The trend in court decisions is to recognize broad arbitrator authority, but the law in this area is still developing.

Courts will not overturn arbitration awards for errors of law or fact. Arbitrators need not give reasons for their decisions. A court will only overturn an award if it displays a manifest disregard for the law.

Mandatory ADR

Many courts and administrative agencies are now requiring parties to use various ADR techniques. It is likely that these requirements will increase in the years to come. The Federal Civil Justice Reform Act requires every federal district court to adopt an expense and delay reduction plan. Many of these plans impose mediation or arbitration on certain types of cases.

When a court imposes arbitration on the parties, it usually does not bind them to the result. The losing party may reject the arbitration award and proceed to trial.

Typically, however, there is a disincentive for doing so. In some jurisdictions, the party must pay a fee for rejecting the award. In others, if the rejecting party loses at trial, it must pay the winner's costs and attorney fees for the trial. Due to overcrowded dockets it is very likely that the incidence of mandatory ADR imposed by the courts will continue to increase.

Case

(Arbitration)

AT&T MOBILITY LLC V. CONCEPTION
563 U.S. 321 (2011)

Vincent and Liza Concepcion entered into an agreement for cellular phone service with AT&T Mobility. The deal was advertised as including free phones, which they got from AT&T. The contract contained a clause requiring arbitration of all disputes between the parties in the parties' "individual capacity, and not as a plaintiff or class member in any purported class or representative proceeding." This clause prohibited the Conceptions from participating in class action lawsuits.

AT&T charged the Conceptions $30.22 sales tax for the phones. The Conceptions filed suit against AT&T in federal district court in California. They alleged that AT&T had engaged in false advertising and fraud by charging sales tax on phones it advertised as free. The suit was consolidated with a class action lawsuit. AT&T moved the court to compel arbitration under the terms of its contract with the Conceptions.

The district court denied AT&T's motion, relying on a California Supreme Court case, *Discover Bank v. Superior Court, (Discover Bank)*, which decided that under California law arbitration clauses that disallowed class-wide proceedings were unconscionable and therefore unenforceable. The federal court of appeals for the Ninth Circuit affirmed the district court decision.

The Supreme Court of the United States reversed the lower courts. The Supreme Court held that the Federal Arbitration Act (FAA) preempted state law, and the FAA required enforcement of the arbitration clause. What follows is the Supreme Court opinion.

Justice Scalia

Section 2 of the Federal Arbitration Act (FAA) makes agreements to arbitrate "valid, irrevocable, and enforceable, save upon such grounds as exist at law or in equity for the revocation of any contract."

We have described this provision as reflecting both a "liberal federal policy favoring arbitration," and the "fundamental principle that arbitration is a matter of contract."

The "principal purpose" of the FAA is to "ensur[e] that private arbitration agreements are enforced according to their terms." This purpose is readily apparent from the FAA's text. Section 2 makes arbitration agreements "valid, irrevocable, and enforceable" as written (subject, of course, to the savings clause); §3 requires courts to stay litigation of arbitral claims pending arbitration of those claims "in accordance with the terms of the agreement"; and §4 requires courts to compel arbitration "in accordance with the terms of the agreement" upon the motion of either party to the agreement (assuming that the "making of the arbitration agreement or the failure . . . to perform the same" is not at issue). In light of these provisions, we have held that parties may agree to limit the issues subject to arbitration, to arbitrate according to specific rules, and to limit *with whom* a party will arbitrate its disputes.

The point of affording parties discretion in designing arbitration processes is to allow for efficient, streamlined procedures tailored to the type of dispute. It can be specified, for example, that the decisionmaker be a specialist in the relevant field, or that proceedings be kept confidential to protect trade secrets. And the informality of arbitral proceedings is itself desirable, reducing the cost and increasing the speed of dispute resolution.

California's *Discover Bank* rule interferes with arbitration. Although the rule does not *require* classwide arbitration, it allows any party to a consumer contract to demand it.

[T]he switch from bilateral to class arbitration sacrifices the principal advantage of arbitration—its informality—and makes the process slower, more costly, and more likely to generate procedural morass than final judgment. In bilateral arbitration, parties forgo the procedural rigor and appellate review of the courts in order to realize the benefits of private dispute resolution: lower costs, greater efficiency and speed, and the ability to choose expert adjudicators to resolve specialized disputes. But before an arbitrator may decide the merits of a claim in classwide procedures, he must first decide, for example, whether the class itself may be certified, whether the named parties are sufficiently representative and typical, and how discovery for the class should be conducted. A cursory comparison of bilateral and class arbitration illustrates the difference. According to the American Arbitration Association (AAA), the average consumer arbitration between January and August 2007 resulted in a disposition on the merits in six months, four months if the arbitration was conducted by documents only. As of September 2009, the AAA had opened 283 class arbitrations. Of those, 121 remained active, and 162 had been settled, withdrawn, or dismissed. Not a single one, however, had resulted in a final award on the merits. For those cases that were no longer active, the median time from filing to settlement, withdrawal, or dismissal not judgment on the merits was 583 days, and the mean was 630 days.

Because it stands as an obstacle to the accomplishment and execution of the full purposes and objectives of Congress, California's *Discover Bank* rule is preempted by the FAA. The judgment of the Ninth Circuit is reversed, and the case is remanded for further proceedings consistent with this opinion.

Chapter Extension

For additional material relating to Chapter 3, see p. 225 in the Appendix of Chapter Extension Files.

Chapter Problems

    1. Define the following terms and concepts:
       a. Jurisdiction
       b. Long-arm statute
       c. Federal question jurisdiction

   d. Diversity of citizenship jurisdiction
   e. Certiorari
   f. Class action suit
   g. Discovery
   h. Injunction
   i. Mediation
   j. Arbitration

2. Plastic Corporation manufactures plastic containers sold to bottling companies. The bottling companies fill the containers with liquid and secure them with leakproof caps. John T. purchased from Ace Hardware a bottle of Prevention Plus, a sulfuric acid-based liquid drain unstopper. While carrying the bottle home, it leaked, causing severe burns to John T.'s body. The container was manufactured by Plastic Corporation and the Prevention Plus was bottled by Sure Bottle Company. John T. threatens to sue. Plastic Corporation seeks to hire an attorney. How should Plastic Corporation select an attorney? As a managerial executive in Plastic Corporation, what is your objective in this conflict? Assume that your lawyer informs you that John T. is willing to settle the case for $10,000. What other information do you need to determine whether to settle or not?

3. Al Ladin, attorney for Spray Lawn, Inc., suspected that two of Spray Lawn's lower-echelon employees were diverting the corporation's funds to their own use. Ladin confronted the employees with his suspicions, and they both confessed. At Ladin's insistence, the employees wrote a detailed account of their activities involving the diversion of company funds. Their employment was then terminated. Subsequently, the IRS conducted an audit of Spray Lawn, Inc. and issued a summons for the written statements in Ladin's possession. Must Ladin produce the statements? Explain. Could the IRS derive the information in any other way?

4. Your company is being sued by Tantalus Corporation for breaching a contract to build an air compressor which was to meet specifications contained in the contract. You claim that the air compressor meets the specifications. Tantalus claims that it does not. During discovery, Tantalus subpoenas all your documents and electronically stored information relating to the construction of the air compressor. You have a confidential hardcopy memo from one of your engineers that indicates that certain shortcuts were taken to reduce the cost of constructing the air compressor. Can you turn the memo over to your attorney and then successfully resist Tantalus's discovery request by claiming attorney-client privilege? Explain.

5. UHF, Inc., a citizen of the state of California, manufactured weather insulation. It sold the insulation to contractors who installed it in buildings throughout the United States. The insulation was found to be hazardous to health. Thousands of people suffered injury as a result of being exposed to it. Hundreds of thousands more have been exposed to the insulation, but have no symptoms at this time. What are the potential consequences to UHF, Inc.? Explain.

6. Helicopteros Nacionales de Colombia (Helicol) is a Colombian corporation that has its principal place of business in the city of Bogota. It provides helicopter transportation services for oil and construction companies in South America. Four U.S. citizens were killed when one of Helicol's helicopters crashed in Peru. The crash victims were working for Consorcio/WSH at the time of the crash. Consorcio/WSH was building a pipeline in Peru and needed helicopters to move personnel, materials, and equipment to and from the construction area.

   About two years before the accident, the chief executive officer of Helicol traveled to Houston, Texas, and conferred with representatives of Consorcio/WSH. They negotiated a contract later signed in Peru. It stated that controversies arising out of the contract would be decided by the Peruvian courts. It also provided that Consorcio/WSH would make payments to Helicol's bank account with Bank of America in New York. More than $5 million in payments received in these accounts were drawn on a Texas bank. Over an approximately seven-year period, Helicol purchased helicopters and spare parts for more than $4 million from Bell Helicopter Company in Fort Worth. Helicol sent pilots for training to Fort Worth. It also sent management and maintenance personnel to visit Bell Helicopter in Fort Worth. Are there sufficient contacts to confer personal jurisdiction over Helicol in Texas? Explain.

7. Asahi Metal Industry, a Japanese manufacturer of tire valve assemblies, sold them to Cheg Shin Rubber Co. in Taiwan. Cheng Shin used the assemblies in making tires, which it distributed worldwide. Asahi knew that its assemblies would be incorporated into tires sold in California and other states.

   Gary Zurcher sued Cheng Shin in the Superior Court in California for injuries he sustained allegedly caused by a defective motor cycle tire manufactured by Cheng Shin. Cheng Shin, through the use of the California long arm statute, sought to add Asahi to the lawsuit, alleging that the valve assembly was defective. Are the contacts with California sufficient for the California court to exercise jurisdiction over Asahi? Why or why not?

8. Professor Ephriam Cross is employed by New York University to teach French, Spanish, and Romance linguistics. He and his wife sailed from New York for France via Portugal, Morocco, Algeria, and Italy. On arriving in Marseilles, they split up. Mrs. Cross continued to tour, and Mr. Cross, though not pursuing a formal course of study, visited schools, courts of law, churches, book publishers, and restaurants; read magazines; listened to radio broadcasts; conversed with students and teachers; and attended political meetings. Cross and his wife returned to New York in time for Cross to resume his teaching schedule at NYU. Cross filed his income tax return and deducted the full cost of the trip he and his wife took to Europe.

   The IRS objected to the deduction and brought suit against Cross, demanding payment of the amount he allegedly underpaid. Cross contended that the deduction was pursuant to the Internal Revenue Code provision that allows deductions for all expenses incurred in carrying on a trade or business. Cross presented affidavits of other professors that indicated the desirability and necessity of foreign travel for a professor of foreign languages. He then moved for summary judgment. Cross contended that the summary judgment was appropriate under the circumstances. Do you agree? What is the criterion for granting a summary judgment? What if Cross listed separately the expenses incurred by his wife and himself and sought to deduct only his own expenses? Would additional information still be required? Explain.

9. Stanford University had a contract with Volt Information Sciences, Inc. to install electric conduit as part of a construction project. The contract contained a broad arbitration clause. Volt billed Stanford for extra work. When Stanford refused to pay, Volt demanded arbitration. Stanford filed a lawsuit against Volt and two companies that designed and managed the construction project. The suit accused Volt of fraud and alleged that the other two companies were responsible for the extra costs and should indemnify Stanford. Stanford's contracts with the other two companies did not have arbitration clauses. Should Stanford be forced to arbitrate the Volt claim? Why or why not?

10. XYZ Corporation is negotiating a contract with Computer Consultants, Inc. (CCI). Under the contract, CCI will provide customized computer programming, software support, and hardware consulting for five years. XYZ will pay an hourly fee. CCI has proposed that the contract require submitting all disputes to arbitration. Should XYZ agree to this? Explain.

II CIVIL LAW FOUNDATIONS OF THE LEGAL ENVIRONMENT OF BUSINESS

4   THE LAW OF PROPERTY

Learning Objectives

After learning this chapter the student should be able to:

- Define property.
- Categorize property as real or personal.
- Compare and contrast lost, stolen, and mislaid property.
- Identify the types of bailments.
- Identify a fixture by applying the appropriate tests.
- Compare and contrast patents, copyrights, and trademarks.
- Differentiate between those processes that are patentable and copyrightable from those that are not.

All around us we are surrounded by "things." From the smallest seed in the ground to the most distant star in the sky, these things occupy our existence. Things have certain properties. They are made up of molecular structures. However, property, in the legal sense, is concerned with relationships—the relationship between a thing and a person. This chapter deals with the law of property. It highlights the definition of property, and then focuses on personal property, real property, and intellectual property. The chapter concludes with an observation about property rights in other countries.

Definition of Property

Property can be thought of as a bundle of rights. This bundle of rights includes the right to possess, use, sell, donate, lease, improve, and destroy property. A distant star does not fit this definition; however, a house, a car, and a patent do.

Property may be real or personal. **Real property** is the land and anything that is permanently attached to land. In contrast, **personal property** is property that has no fixed site but is moveable. Personal property may be further divided into tangible and intangible property. Tangible personal property, such as clothing, frying pans, and doorknobs, may be touched. Intangible personal property has no physical being and, as such, may not be touched. It includes stocks, bonds, patent rights, and copyrights.

Personal Property

We are dependent upon personal property for our existence. The food we eat, the clothing we wear, and even the bed we sleep in are all personal property. Personal property may be acquired in a number of ways, and may be entrusted to another. The law regarding the acquisition and entrustment of personal property follows.

Acquiring Personal Property

The normal way of acquiring personal property is by purchase. The purchase may be by cash or by credit. However, some acquisitions do not involve an exchange of money. They occur as a matter of law, as, for example, when property is abandoned, lost, stolen, mislaid, or gifted.

Abandoned Property
Abandonment occurs when the owner voluntarily and intentionally surrenders property. When this occurs the property is unowned. The next person to appropriate the property owns it. By example, assume that someone places a stuffed animal and a sofa on the curb by the street with the intent of surrendering possesion and control. The first person to retrieve them owns this abandoned property.

Lost Property
Lost property is property that is involuntarily left somewhere. One who finds lost property has good title to the property against anyone in the world except the true owner. The finder, in fact, has an obligation to return the property to the known owner. Many states have statutes governing the disposition of lost property. Under these finder's statutes, the finder usually becomes the absolute owner of the property after the find is made public, a certain period of time elapses, and the owner fails to claim the property.

Stolen Property

Property that is stolen is ordinarily treated as lost property. The owner of the property has superior title to the world. A thief does not gain title to the property stolen. However, there is at least one instance where the Uniform Commercial Code (UCC) holds that one who acquires property from a thief becomes the absolute owner.

UCC § 2–403(2)

Any entrusting of possession of goods to a merchant who deals in goods of that kind gives him [or her] power to transfer all rights of the entruster to a buyer in ordinary course of business.

Assume that on Monday, Romeo and his girlfriend Juliet go to Badunov's Jewelry Store to size an engagement ring that was previously purchased by Romeo. Badunov tells them to come back in one week to pick up the ring. On Tuesday, Dick and Liz come into Badunov's in order that Dick may buy Liz a diamond to celebrate their engagement to be married. Badunov sells them Juliet's ring. It fits Liz's hand perfectly. Dick pays for the ring and takes it out of the store. Juliet and Liz, who have been friends since childhood, decide to go out for dinner Saturday night to celebrate their engagements. During dinner, Liz proudly displays her new engagement ring, and Juliet quickly discovers that Liz is wearing Juliet's ring. Between Juliet and Liz, who owns the ring?

Badunov is a thief, and, under common law, cannot convey good title to the ring. Normally, Juliet would be entitled to a return of her ring. However, under Uniform Commercial Code, section 2–403(2), which controls in cases involving the sale of goods, as here, Liz would be the owner of the ring. Naturally, Badunov would be subject to criminal liability, and civil liability to Juliet.

Note that this provision applies only to merchants—those who customarily deal in a particular type of good. The provision would not apply to the street vendor from whom one would buy a stolen watch. Consumers expect to obtain clear title to items they buy in a store. If a consumer could not have that expectation, retail sales could suffer greatly. The rights of the consumer have been balanced against the rights of the person entrusting goods to merchants. The balance is clearly in favor of the consumer knowing that he or she is getting good title when purchasing an item.

Mislaid Property

Mislaid property is property that is left somewhere and forgotten. The finder of mislaid property must surrender it to the owner of the premises where it is found. The reason for this requirement is that the owner of mislaid property will eventually remember where he or she left it and return to the premises. The owner of the premises then holds the property in trust for the true owner. Finding statutes, in some states, specify the rights and obligations of the true owner, the finder, and the owner of the premises.

Gifts

Property may also be acquired by gift. A gift occurs when one individual or entity gives something to another person or entity without any value given in return (consideration). Gifts come in a variety of forms. An *inter vivos*, or living gift, is made by a person when the donor is alive and has no expectation of imminent death. When three necessary elements occur, the gift is completed, and irrevocable. First, the donor (or gift giver) must intend to make a gift to a donee (gift receiver). Second, that gift must be delivered to the donee or the donee's agent. Delivery must be either physical, by turning over control of the item to the donee, or may be achieved by giving the donee some evidence of title. For example, a gift of an automobile may be completed by handing over an endorsed certificate of title and the keys, even if the automobile is located elsewhere at the time. Unless the element of delivery is present, there is no gift. Finally, the donee must accept the gift.

A gift *causa mortis* is a gift in contemplation of death in the near future. In this type of gift, intent, delivery, and acceptance are still necessary. However, even when these three elements are present, the gift may still be revocable by the donor. Consider the situation where Carlos is to have major surgery, and has been told that he has only a 30 percent chance of recovering. Carlos gives his watch to his close friend Bruce, telling Bruce he wants him to have the watch if the surgery is unsuccessful and Carlos dies. If Carlos recovers, he can invalidate the gift. He can also revoke the gift for any reason before he dies, and the gift is invalid if the donee (in this case, Bruce) dies before the donor.

A gift may be complete subject to a condition. Under the common law, for instance, an engagement ring is a gift to the bride-elect, conditional upon the marriage taking place. Consequently, if the marriage does not occur because of the actions of the bride-elect, no gift occurs and the man gets the ring back. Because of a spate of litigation, many states have now adopted specific statutes that alter the common law rule regarding the status of gifts made in anticipation of marriage.

Entrusting Personal Property

The law governing the entrustment of personal property is known as the *law of bailments*. A **bailment** occurs when one person (the bailor) transfers personal property to another (the bailee) with instructions to return it or otherwise dispose of it. For example, assume that Freda takes her car to a mechanic to have it repaired. Here, a bailment is formed. After the repair, the mechanic is obligated to return the car to Freda. Title to property does not pass by a bailment.

Types of Bailments

Most bailments are voluntary. However, an involuntary bailment may arise as, for example, when someone finds property that is lost. The finder becomes an involuntary bailee who holds the found property in trust for the owner. An involuntary bailee owes to the owner a slight duty of care, and is only liable for damages caused by intentional misconduct or gross negligence.

Another way of classifying bailments is by examining who benefits. Some bailments are solely for the benefit of the bailee. These bailments, sometimes referred to as *gratuitous bailments*, occur when, for example, one person lends a friend a car. Here, the bailee must return the car in the same condition and is liable for damages caused by even slight negligence. The duty here upon the bailee is to exercise extraordinary care. Other bailments are solely for the benefit of the bailor. These occur when a bailee takes possession of property without pay or benefit, but as an accommodation to the bailor, as, for example, when a friend agrees to temporarily store furniture. The bailee here will not be liable for damage to the property unless grossly negligent.

Finally, mutual benefit bailments are the most common. A mutual benefit bailment usually involves a contract for hire, for example, entrusting property to another for repair. Here, the bailor would benefit from having the item repaired, and the bailee would benefit by receiving compensation for the repair. The bailee will be liable for damages that result from a lack of ordinary care.

Rights and Duties

The rights and duties under a bailment may be part of a contract, express or implied. Any damages that occur as a result of a breach of the agreement may result in liability. However, bailees are often prone to include within the contract an exculpatory clause. An exculpatory clause limits or relieves liability for damages. Courts are apt to strike down such clauses when they are deemed to be against public policy—when there is an unequal bargaining position between the parties. For example, assume that Vera entrusts to Hank's Garage a car for the purpose of fixing the brakes. A clause within the contract states that Hank's is not liable for any damage to the car while in its possession. One of Hank's employees negligently rams the car into the gas pump island and damages the front end. Assume further that all the garages in the neighborhood have a similar exculpatory clause within their contracts. A court most likely would strike down the clause and hold Hank's Garage liable for the damage due to its employee's negligence.

Generally, in absence of specification, the bailee is entitled to reasonable compensation for the work done or for storage. The bailor is entitled to a return of the goods in substantially the same condition as when first received.

Special Bailments

Innkeepers, common carriers, and warehousers are deemed professional bailees, and, in addition to the ordinary rules of bailment, are subject to special rules. Innkeepers operate inns, hotels, motels, and lodges. At the common law, innkeepers were strictly liable for the loss or damage to personal property of their guests. This rule has been modified in many states that place a limit on liability, for example, $1,000.

A common carrier is in the business of transporting goods. Common carriers must serve the public on a nondiscriminatory basis and are strictly liable for damage or loss of goods. The common carrier is, in that sense, an insurer of the

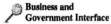
Business and Government Interface

These links, the first from the Bureau of Consumer Protection Business Center site and the second from a law firm site, contain information on the compliance standards for representing that a product is made in the USA, and the associated dangers.

http://www.business.ftc.gov /documents/bus03-complying -made-usa-standard; http://www.frostbrowntodd .com/resources-123.html

---

Ethical Dilemmas/Issues

Heart Felt is the President of Hi-Fly, Inc which owns a plant in the U.S. that produces high performance stunt kites. They come in various styles, shapes, colors and aerodynamic models. Their packaging says, "Made in the USA." In fact, the entire kite is assembled and package in a plant in Hope, Arizona. Of the 27 parts that comprise their Model 5X kite, 25 are manufactured in the Hope plant. Two small rings situated on the bridle of the kite can adjust the performance of the kite by moving the rings closer or farther from the nose. These rings are ordered from a U.S. supplier who purchases them from Taiwan. The total cost of the kite's parts is $89.00 and it sells for $199.00. The two rings cost $.14 each.

Every state that has a law concerning labeling of products "Made in USA," except California, requires only that the product be substantially made in the USA. California requires that all parts of any product that bears a "Made in the USA" representation must be made wholly in the U.S.

Hi-Fly's in-house attorney informs Felt about the California law. Consequently, Felt orders his production manager to come into compliance with the law. In the meantime he is hoping that the company will not be caught with the inventory already in the stores in California. He feels it is an unfair law to require 100% compliance. Yet, he is intent on complying, and says, "if we get caught in the meantime, then we will do the right thing and pay the fine."

What are the ethical issues? What are Felt's alternatives?

Understanding the private law sector

This Michigan State University link to an article highlights an inconsistency in the law of bailments when pets are delivered to their veterinarian for treatment.

https://www.animallaw.info /article/bailment-and -veterinary-malpractice -doctrinal-exclusivity-not

property. There are some exceptions: acts of God, of war, or of public authorities; the bailor's negligence; or the natural spoilage or deterioration of the goods. Additionally, by clear terms in a contract, common carriers may limit their liability.

A warehouse company stores property for others. It is usually subject to extensive state and local fire, health, and safety regulations. Like the common carrier, it may limit its liability.

Real Property

Real property is comprised of land and every thing that is attached to land. As such, it consists of air, surface, and subsurface rights. The old theory was that a landowner owned from his or her property straight up to the heavens and straight down to the center of the earth. With the advent of air transportation and modern methods of excavation, this theory was not very pragmatic and, hence, fell into disuse, in favor of the reasonable use theory. The property owner owns everything above and below the land that he or she may reasonably use. This is an attempt to balance the competing interests of different members of society.

This section considers the law of fixtures (which is a way of determining whether an article is personal or part of the real estate), the law of estates and of concurrent interests in an estate.

Fixtures

A **fixture** is personal property that has been affixed to the realty in such a manner as to become part of the realty. For example, a kitchen sinktop is personal property when it is carried into the kitchen to be installed. After installation, it is considered a fixture and it is part of the real estate.

Fixtures pass with real estate by deed whereas personal property does not. Fixtures are taxed as part of the real estate. It is also important to distinguish between fixtures and personal property for purposes of insurance claims. For example, assume that an insured house burns to the ground. If the carpeting is a fixture, it will be covered for real property insurance purposes; but, if it is personal property, then it would not. Additionally, there may be a difference in taxing of the property, depending upon whether it is deemed personal or real.

The controlling test of whether an item is a fixture is the intent of the attacher. The law has three tests to determine this intent—annexation, adaptation, and relation tests.

Annexation

When an item is attached to the real estate in such a manner that it would cause damage to sever it or leave it in an unfinished condition, then it is probably a fixture. Built-in medicine cabinets, wall-to-wall carpeting, light fixtures, antennas, and permanent fences are examples. Throw rugs, davenports, and stacked timber do not meet this definition, and are probably personal property.

Adaptation

When an item that is not physically attached nonetheless is specifically adapted to the real estate, it is deemed a fixture. Hence, rugs that are not tacked down but are custom cut would be considered a fixture under the adaptation test. Custom-made storm windows or an air conditioner specially modified to accommodate a window meet the adaptation test and hence are fixtures.

Relation

In cases where it is difficult to come to a conclusion based upon the annexation and adaptation test, the relation test may tip the balance. Under the relation test, the law prefers purchasers over sellers and tenants over landlords. For example, consider an air conditioning unit, installed by the owner, that has been occupying a window for several years. Assume further, the owner sells the house. In favoring the buyer the law presumes that the intent of the seller when affixing the unit was that it be part of the house. The air conditioner, hence, would pass to the buyer by the deed, as it would be considered a fixture. However, in the event that a tenant installed the same air conditioner in an apartment, the law would favor the interpretation that the tenant did not intend for the air conditioner to become a fixture. As such, the tenant would be entitled to remove and retain it after the

Decision-making in the legal environment

This link from a Chicago Tribune article contains practical information about the law of fixtures in relation to what is included in the sales price of a home and what is not.

http://articles.chicagotribune
.com/1996-11-09/news
/9611090182_1_dining
-room-chandelier-attached
-fixture

termination of the lease. As in most cases a written agreement clearly characterizing the item goes along way to avoid ambiguity.

Trade Fixtures

The law of fixtures relating to business use of property is different than it is for residences. Often, a business must make significant improvement to a property in order to be able to use that property effectively. A pizza parlor, for example, must install ovens, bolting them to the floor and venting them through the roof, creating a hole in the roof. A restaurant may install a walk-in cooler that attaches to the floor and/or walls. If the law of fixtures were to be applied in the same manner to both businesses and residences, businesses could be at a severe disadvantage in trying to do business, knowing that if they change location they lose all their business fixtures. Business fixtures are known as *trade fixtures*, and the business tenant is allowed to remove them prior to the expiration of the lease. The business tenant does have the obligation, however, to restore the property to its original condition once the personal property has been removed. For instance, the pizza parlor owner would have to repair the ceiling and roof once the pizza ovens were removed.

Estates and Interests

Estates are interests in real property. Some, like the fee simple absolute, fee tail, life estate, and leaseholds are possessory estates, while easements, profits and licenses are nonpossessory interests. Each is discussed.

Fee Simple Absolute
The **fee simple absolute** is the greatest quantum of interest that one may own in real property. The owner in fee simple may use the property as he or she sees fit, subject to local zoning laws, nuisance laws, and other laws of the municipality and state in which the property is located. One who owns a fee simple has the fullest interest in the bundle of rights, and, as such, has the power to sell, lease, improve, destroy, and pass the property to heirs. The fee owner may transfer less than the fee interest in the property to other entities without giving up the whole fee simple interest. For example, Tom purchases a parcel of property with a building on it. He gives the right to farm the land to his brother-in-law and he leases the building to Ichabod's Insurance Company for three years, but he still owns the fee. Most property today is owned in fee simple absolute.

Fee Tail
The fee tail passes the property from lineal generation to generation. It promotes family wealth, since the property is kept in the family. A transfer in fee tail is accomplished by transfer "to the grantee and the heirs of his or her body." This would continue the property to the lineal descendants. The property is not very marketable as a result. Hence, most states have abolished the fee tail or have afforded ways where it may be converted to a fee simple absolute.

Life Estate

A life estate is an interest in land. It is a right of use and enjoyment of land as measured by the life of that person or another person. At the death of the person whose life determines the length of the estate, the fee simple interest reverts to the grantor or to others, known as *remaindermen.* Holders of life estates may not do any act to damage or cause a decrease in the value of the land.

Leaseholds

A leasehold is an interest in land created by a contract called a *lease.* The tenant, or lessee, obtains the right to use the property for a specific purpose, usually for a specified period of time, in return for a periodic cash payment, known as *rent,* paid to the landlord, or lessor. A lease may apply to a residential unit or to commercial property. Lease provisions vary widely. For example, a residential lease may require the lessor to make all repairs and the lessee to pay a specified fee in dollars per month for rent. A commercial lease may provide that the tenant makes all repairs, and may further provide that the tenant pay a percentage of the real estate taxes on the leased property. In a commercial lease, other provisions may specify that the lessee must stay open for business a given number of hours each day, and that the lessee must pay a specified percentage of gross sales to the lessor.

Leases terminate at the expiration of the term. If no term is stated and rent is payable periodically, the lease is terminable upon giving one full period's notice. When the lease ends, possession of the property reverts to the owner.

Easements

An easement gives a right to use the land of another for a specified purpose, but not to possess the land. As an example, Paul may give Art an easement to drive across the back of Paul's paved parking lot so that Art may have access to another street. Easements may be bought or sold, or may be created at the time of transfer of the fee from one owner to another. Easements can also be implied by law. Assume, for example, that Ginger sells half of her land to Fred, and that Fred's portion of the land has no access to a street. The law will imply an easement allowing Fred the right to gain access to the street by driving over Ginger's property.

Profits and Licenses

A profit gives one a right to remove something from another's land, such as trees or oil. While a profit is an interest in the land, a license is not. A license is a right to enter land for a particular purpose. For example, a license may grant an individual a right to play 18 holes of golf on the owner's course or to watch a movie in a theater.

Co-Ownership of Property

Ownership of real property is often shared by two or more individuals or other entities such as partnerships, corporations, or trusts. There are various methods of holding concurrently. They include tenancy-in-common, joint tenancy and tenancy by the entireties, community property, condominiums, and cooperatives. Each is discussed.

Tenancy-in-Common

In a tenancy-in-common, each co-owner has an undivided fractional interest in the property. The potential interests need not be equal. Each tenant-in-common has a right to possess the property. One tenant-in-common may sell his or her share to another entity without affecting the existence of the tenancy-in-common.

Tenancies-in-common may also be used in time sharing agreements, where property is shared by a number of people, each having the right to use that property for a defined period each year. For example, 52 people may each have the right to use of an estate in Palm Beach, Florida, for one week each year. These people are tenants-in-common. They may sell their interests without disturbing the tenancy-in-common.

When a tenant-in-common dies, his or her share passes to heirs. If disputes arise as to the benefits from, or use of, the property among the co-tenants, a *partition* action may be undertaken in the courts. In such an action the court will either physically divide up the property among the co-tenants, or will order the sale of the property, with proceeds to be divided among the co-tenants according to their proportional share of ownership. If no particular type of relationship between co-tenants is specified in the deed, the law will ordinarily imply the existence of a tenancy-in-common.

Joint Tenancy and Tenancy by the Entireties

In a joint tenancy, upon the death of one joint tenant, his or her share passes to the other joint tenants. Each joint tenant owns an equal undivided share in the property. A joint tenancy will be terminated if one joint tenant conveys all or a part of his or her interest to another party, or if that interest is sold by a creditor to satisfy a debt. In either of those events, the remaining owners will then be tenants-in-common.

A form of joint tenancy, between husband and wife, called a *tenancy by the entireties*, is allowable in some states. This tenancy, like a joint tenancy, has a right of survivorship feature, so that when one spouse dies, the other immediately becomes sole owner of the property. Unlike the joint tenancy, however, neither party may sell his or her share without the consent of the other, nor may a creditor sever the tenancy to satisfy the debt of one of the spouses. Should the husband and wife sever the marriage relationship, the tenancy by the entireties ceases to exist. Because of a couple's ability to shield their real property from creditors through the tenancy by the entireties, many states have abolished this type of co-ownership.

Community Property

Some jurisdictions, including California, Texas, and a number of southern states, are community property states. Under this type of ownership, each spouse owns half of all property, real or personal, acquired by the efforts of either spouse during the marriage. Property owned by a spouse prior to marriage, or acquired with the proceeds of separate property owned by that spouse, remains the individual property of that spouse.

Condominiums

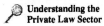

Understanding the Private Law Sector

This link to a Washington Post article examines the differences between condos and cooperatives.

http://www.washingtonpost
.com/realestate/condos-vs
-co-ops-whats-the-difference
/2013/04/25/f673e29c-a5e6
-11e2-b029-8fb7e977ef71
_story.html

In a condominium, individuals own units of a larger parcel in fee simple, and are tenants-in-common with other owners in the parcel as to common areas such as elevators, swimming pools, and land. The individual owners also share the costs of maintaining the common areas. Since owners own their units in fee simple, they have the right to mortgage their property interests or the right to transfer title to their units.

The developer of the condominium records a Declaration of Condominium, which describes the land on which the condominium is to be developed, and includes rules for how the condominium is to operate. For example, the bylaws may provide that all owners must be at least 55 years of age, and that no individual under 18 years of age is allowed to live in the condominium more than a specified number of days each year. Once a certain number of units are sold, the unit owners form their own condominium association which governs the affairs of the condominium.

Co-Operative

A co-operative, or co-op, is usually established for an apartment or office building. The building in question is owned by one entity, such as a corporation. Individuals purchase shares in the corporation, which allows them the right to lease units in the co-operative. The bylaws of the corporation establish the rights and duties of tenants, and control the rights these shareholder-tenants have to sublease their unit or transfer their share in the corporation to others. A share in the co-operative is not an ownership interest in land; consequently, the shareholders cannot obtain a mortgage loan to finance the purchase of their units.

Intellectual Property

Business and Government Interface

From the World Intellectual Property Organization (WIPO) this link imparts a summary of what you need to know about intellectual property rights.

http://www.wipo.int/about
-ip/en/

Intellectual property deals with rights of individuals and businesses in applied ideas. For example, an author's idea may be translated into, and published as, a novel. The law of intellectual property does not protect the physical book itself. Stealing the book does not violate the author's intellectual property rights. Use of the plot and characters of the novel in a movie, however, does constitute misappropriation of the author's intellectual property.

Intellectual property is a form of intangible personal property. It includes several rather distinct areas of the law. Patents, copyrights, and trademarks are traditional areas of intellectual property rights. Each is discussed on the next page.

Patents

U.S. Constitution, Art. I § 8

Congress shall have the power: "To promote the Progress of Science and useful Arts, by securing for limited Times to Authors and Inventors the exclusive Right to their respective Writings and Discoveries."

Patents are authorized by the U.S. Constitution. A patent is a limited monopoly to make, use, and sell an invention, granted by the government. To encourage innovation and technology, the government generally grants an inventor a 20-year monopoly on an invention, provided an application is filed, making public disclosure of the details of the invention.

Patentable Subject Matter

Patents are obtainable on an invention that is novel and useful, and that falls under one or more classes listed in the federal statute. Specifically, the statute authorizes patents for any processes, machines, manufacture, composition of matter, or improvement on one of these classes. In addition, specific statutory provisions authorize patents on designs, asexually reproduced plants and even genetically engineered bacteria.

Procedure to Obtain a Patent

The process for obtaining a patent can be long and expensive. An inventor must prepare and file an application in the United States Patent Office. To comply with the Constitutional mandate, the application must fully describe the invention. The description must have sufficient detail such that upon expiration of the inventor's limited monopoly the invention may be reproduced by others.

The Patent Office examines the application to be sure that it is new and useful, and that it falls within one of the statutory classes. Not every development by an inventor rises to the level of an "invention." The Patent Office over the years has developed the objective test of **non-obviousness**. The question posed is, would the development described in the application have been obvious to the ordinarily skilled worker in the art at the time the "invention" was made? If it would have been obvious, the development is not patentable. Only those developments that represent a real step forward rise to the level of invention.

The Patent Office is an administrative agency under the Department of Commerce. An applicant dissatisfied with any decision by the patent examiner is entitled to an appeal within the agency to the Patent Office Board of Appeals, and, if dissatisfied with the decision of the board, may appeal to the Court of Appeals for the Federal Circuit, a special appellate level federal court that has jurisdiction in all patent matters.

Patent Owner's Rights

The patent statutes give the owner of a patent the exclusive right to make, use, and sell the invention. The application for a patent must be filed by the individual who made the invention. However, the inventor may assign (transfer ownership) all or any part of the patent rights to another individual or entity. Employees of a company, who work in technical areas, generally sign, at the time of employment, an agreement surrendering to their employer all rights to any inventions made during the course of their employment.

A license involves the transfer of rights under a patent, without transferring ownership. The owner of a patent may license one company to manufacture the patented product, while retaining the right to sell the product. Or, in the reverse, the inventor may manufacture the product and license someone else to sell the product.

Licenses may be either exclusive or nonexclusive. Under an exclusive license, only a single person or entity has the exclusive right; not even the inventor or patent owner retains a right to manufacture. A nonexclusive license, on the other hand, gives the patent holder the right to invest other entities with similar rights under the patent.

The owner of a patent may enforce patent rights through a suit for patent infringement filed in the federal courts. If successful, the patent owner is entitled to statutory damages, which include actual damages (at least in the amount of a reasonable royalty), which may be trebled, and attorney fees, as well as an injunction ordering the infringing party to stop the infringing activity.

Copyrights

A **copyright**, like a patent, is a limited monopoly that finds its origin in Article I, Section 8 of the U.S. Constitution. While the Constitution speaks in terms of writings and authors, copyright protection today covers a very broad span of business and the creative arts. Copyright law is governed exclusively by a federal statute.

The statute lists specific classes of copyrightable works, for example, literary works; musical works; dramatic works; choreographic works; pictorial, graphic, and sculptural works; motion pictures and other audiovisual works; sound recordings; and architectural works. At the same time, the statute expressly excludes copyright protection for any idea, procedure, system, method of operation, concept, principle, or discovery.

Procedure to Obtain a Copyright
The procedure for obtaining a copyright is very different from the procedure involved in patenting an invention. Copyright protection is obtained by publication of the work with the statutory notice, which is the word *copyright*, its abbreviation *copr.*, or the international copyright symbol ©, followed by the year of first publication, and the name of the owner of the copyright. The copyright is perfected by filing an application to register the copyright, along with copies of the work, in the copyright office in Washington, D.C.

Copyright Owner's Rights
The statute provides that the copyright owner has the exclusive right to do and to authorize reproduction of the copyrighted work, distribution of copies or phonorecords of the work to the public, and public performance or display of the work. The major limitation upon the exclusive rights is the doctrine of fair use,

which permits use of the copyrighted work for purposes such as criticism, news reporting, teaching, or research.

Licensing of copyrights is very much like assignment and licensing of patents. Like patents, the various rights granted by the statute may be divided up in licensing arrangements.

The copyright statute provides one major exception to the general rules of licensing. Specifically, if the owner of a music copyright permits a recording to be made and distributed, then anyone is free to make their own recording, provided the copier pays the royalty provided by statute. These are known as the *compulsory licensing provisions* of the copyright law.

The statutory remedies for copyright infringement include actual damages to the copyright holder, punitive damages, profits of the infringer, temporary and permanent injunctive relief, and impoundment and disposition (usually destruction) of the infringing articles.

Trademarks

While patents and copyrights have their origin in the U.S. Constitution, and are both the exclusive domain of federal statutory law, **trademarks** originate in the common law, and involve both federal and state law. Federal involvement with trademarks is limited to cases affecting "interstate commerce."

The federal law of trademarks is codified in the Lanham Act, which defines a trademark as ". . . any word, name, symbol, or device or any combination thereof adopted and used by a manufacturer or merchant to identify his goods and distinguish them from those manufactured or sold by others." For example, look at the following list of trademarks: Old Spice®, Kool Aid®, Tylenol®, Kleenex®, Q-Tips®, and Listerine®. These are immediately recognizable (see Table 4–1).

These trademarks are identifiable, and carry with them some concept of quality and performance. Even if people do not know the specific manufacturer, they buy the brand because of its known reputation for quality. Thus, the trademark is the basis for the purchase decision.

At the state level, trademark laws vary rather widely. Many states have adopted broad protection for trademarks, while other states offer more limited protection. Obviously, state protection is operative only within the bounds of a given state,

TABLE 4–1	**Trademarks**	
Trademark	*Product*	*Owner*
Old Spice®	Deodorant	Shulton
Kool Aid®	Powdered drink mix	General Foods
Tylenol®	Pain medication	McNeil PPC
Kleenex®	Facial tissues	Kimberly-Clark
Q-Tips®	Cotton-tipped swabs	Chesebrough
Listerine®	Mouthwash	Warner Lambert

and hence all but local companies opt for federal trademark protection. The balance of our discussion of trademarks will be limited to the Lanham Act and the federal law of trademarks.

Classification of Trademarks
Trademarks may be categorized in several ways. They may be classified by form (word marks, symbol or design marks, or composite marks), by use (use on a product, use on a service, or use as a certification), or by relative strength. It is this last classification that is most important to the businessperson in understanding the nature and scope of trademark protection.

A *generic* mark is one employing the common descriptive name for a product. For example, the term *carbonated* is the generic term for a beverage having carbonation. This is the weakest of marks. No one is permitted exclusive rights in a generic term.

A *descriptive* mark is one that merely describes the product or qualities of the product to which it is applied. For example, a bakery might employ the trademark "Oven-Fresh" on its goods. Because the term *oven-fresh* is simply descriptive of the qualities of baked goods, it would be unfair to permit any one merchant to develop exclusive rights in the mark. Thus, anyone in the bakery business is free to use this descriptive term. A merchant can use such a phrase as a trademark, but will be unable to develop any exclusive rights in the mark.

A *suggestive* mark is one that may suggest the product or the qualities of the product to which it is applied, but yet is not merely descriptive of that product. If a term requires imagination, thought, or perception to reach a conclusion as to the nature of the goods, it is "suggestive." For example, the Second Circuit Court of Appeals held that "Roach Motel" was a suggestive mark when used on an insect trap. Hence, suggestive marks are stronger than descriptive ones.

A trademark is considered *arbitrary* if it is a new word, or if it is a common word that has no relation whatsoever to the product to which it is applied. For example, the well-known trademark Kodak® is arbitrary. It is a combination of five letters that has no independent meaning at all. A more subtle example would be Ivory®. You can look in any dictionary and find a number of standard definitions for the word *ivory*. However, as applied to soap, the mark is considered "arbitrary." In the trademark sense, arbitrary trademarks are the strongest.

The federal statute that is controlling provides that a mark that is not arbitrary may be registered only if it can be shown that ". . . the mark has become distinctive of applicant's goods in commerce." Such a showing is called **secondary meaning**. In reality, it means that through widespread, continuous, and exclusive use, a particular mark has developed a new or secondary meaning in which it serves to identify the specific goods of a particular merchant.

Federal Registration and Remedies
Under the common law, trademark rights were acquired by adopting a mark and applying it to goods sold in the trade. As originally codified in the Lanham Act, use of the mark in commerce was required before an application could be filed to register the mark.

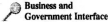
Business and Government Interface

This United States Patent and Trademark Office link helps the student understand the trademark protection process.

http://www.uspto.gov /trademarks/process/index.jsp

Business and Government Interface

This link, an excerpt from a U.S. Department of State publication, contains a concise guide to international property rights treaties and protection.

http://iipdigital.usembassy .gov/st/english/publication /2008/04/20080429214132 myleen5.741519e-02 .html#axzz3AQRfLzFz

The Lanham Act provides for registration of trademarks in the United States Patent Office. An application for registration is filed, and examined by the Patent Office to be sure that all statutory conditions are met. Specifically, the Patent Office ensures that generic marks are not registered, and that nonarbitrary marks are registered only if an appropriate showing of secondary meaning is provided.

When the examiner is satisfied with the application, the mark is published for opposition. An official publication of the United States Patent Office lists all marks that have been passed by the trademark examiners, and anyone who may be damaged by registration of the mark is entitled to file an opposition. This is a contested administrative proceeding, adjudicated by the Patent Office. The amendments to the Lanham Act in 1988 provided for the first time an opportunity to register a mark based upon "intent to use." This provision had been widely sought by major corporations who wished to establish their trademark position prior to actually putting a product on the market with a new trademark.

Registration provides many major advantages to the trademark owner. First of all, it provides constructive notice throughout the entire country of the trademark user's claim to rights in the mark. In other words, if a small firm starts operations in the Pacific Northwest, registration will give the firm nationwide protection for its mark. Second, after six years of continuous use following registration, the mark becomes "incontestable." This incontestability gives the trademark owner significant procedural advantages to enforce rights in the mark. And finally, the statutory remedies become available in enforcement.

Under the Lanham Act, the trademark owner may bring an action for infringement seeking the statutory remedies of treble damages, attorney fees, and destruction of infringing labels. The fundamental issue in a trademark infringement action is likelihood of confusion. Where the marks are the same, and the goods on which they are used are the same, the issue is clear. However, when either the marks or the goods are different, the issue becomes much more difficult, and takes into account the strength of the mark, the similarity of the marks, the similarity of the goods upon which the marks are used, the similarity of the channels of distribution, and evidence, if any, of actual confusion. For example, Coca-Cola was able to stop a competitor from using the mark "LaCoq" on soft drinks. Even though the marks look different, they sound very similar, and Coke® is a very strong mark. The owner of the mark Johnny Walker® for whiskey was able to stop use of the identical mark on shoes. Again, the court found the mark to be very strong and accorded protection, even though the goods were very dissimilar.

International Property Rights

With the increase of multinational companies—those doing business in more than one country—there is a concomitant concern about protecting intellectual property. Patents, copyrights, and trademarks are afforded great protection in this country; however, not every country's laws are as protective. Some countries do have adequate protection. The United States does have patent, trademark, and copyright treaties with a number of nations. Some are nondiscrimination treaties. Others provide for limited protection, while others provide for protection upon registration. Still others give automatic protection without registration. Companies need to be wary of those nations that have a reputation for pirating intellectual works and either not deal in those nations when their property rights are at risk or take special precautions to protect those rights. Currently, serious problems exist with countries that are lax on enforcement of intellectual property laws. The United States has the power to impose trade restrictions on those nations.

Case

(*Patentable Subject Matter*)
IN RE: ROSLIN INSTITUTE (EDINBURGH)
United States Court of Appeals (Federal Circuit, 2014)
2013–1407

Keith Henry Stockman Campbell and Ian Wilmut successfully produced the first mammal ever cloned from an adult somatic cell: Dolly the Sheep. A clone is an identical genetic copy of a cell, cell part, or organism. The cloning method Campbell and Wilmut used to create Dolly constituted a breakthrough in scientific discovery. Known as somatic cell nuclear transfer, this process involves removing the nucleus of a somatic cell and implanting that nucleus into an enucleated (i.e., without a nucleus) oocyte. A somatic cell is any body cell other than gametes (egg or sperm). An oocyte is a female gametocyte (an egg cell prior to maturation), and a nucleus is the organelle that holds a cell's genetic material (its DNA).

Once the nucleus of a somatic, donor cell is removed, that nucleus is fused with an oocyte, which develops into an embryo. The embryo can then be implanted into a surrogate mammal, where it develops into a baby animal. The resulting cloned animal is an exact genetic replica of the adult mammal from which the somatic cell nucleus was taken.

Campbell and Wilmut obtained a patent on the somatic method of cloning mammals, which it assigned to Roslin Institute of Edinburgh, Scotland. The examiner issued a nonfinal rejection of Campbell's and Wilmut's patent claims because she found that they were directed to nonstatutory subject matter under 35 U.S.C. § 101. The Patent Board affirmed the examiner's rejection of Campbell's and Wilmut's claims. It concluded that the claimed subject matter was ineligible for patent protection under § 101 because it constituted a natural phenomenon that did not possess "markedly different characteristics than any found in nature."

Roslin Institute appealed the decision of the Patent Board. The Federal Circuit Court of Appeals affirmed the Board decision.

Circuit Judge Dyk

An inventor may obtain a patent for "any new and useful process, machine, manufacture, or composition of matter, or any new and useful improvement thereof." An invention that falls within one of these categories of patentable subject matter may still be ineligible for patent protection if it meets one of three exceptions. Laws of nature, natural phenomena, and abstract ideas are not eligible for patent protection.

■　　　■　　　■

. . . [N]aturally occurring organisms are not patentable.

■　　　■　　　■

Accordingly, discoveries that possess "markedly different characteristics from any found in nature," . . . are eligible for patent protection. In contrast, any existing organism or newly discovered plant found in the wild is not patentable.

More recently, in *Myriad*, the Court held that claims on two naturally occurring, isolated genes (BRCA1 and BRCA2), which can be examined to determine whether a person may develop breast cancer, were invalid under § 101. The Supreme Court concluded that the BRCA genes themselves were unpatentable products of nature.

While Roslin does not dispute that the donor sheep whose genetic material was used to create Dolly could not be patented, Roslin contends that copies (clones) are eligible for protection because they are "the product of human ingenuity" and "not nature's handiwork, but [their] own." Roslin argues that such copies are either compositions of matter or manufactures within the scope of § 101. However, Dolly herself is an exact genetic replica of another sheep and does not possess "markedly different characteristics from any [farm animals] found in nature. Dolly's genetic identity to her donor parent renders her unpatentable.

In *Myriad*, the Court concluded that "isolated," naturally occurring DNA strands are not eligible for patent protection. Here, as in *Myriad*, Roslin "did not create or alter any of the genetic infor-

mation" of its claimed clones, "[n]or did [Roslin] create or alter the genetic structure of [the] DNA" used to make its clones. Instead, Roslin's chief innovation was the preservation of the donor DNA such that the clone is an exact copy of the mammal from which the somatic cell was taken. Such a copy is not eligible for patent protection.

Related areas of Supreme Court patent case law reinforce this conclusion. For example, Supreme Court decisions regarding the preemptive force of federal patent law confirm that individuals are free to copy any unpatentable article, such as a live farm animal, so long as they do not infringe a patented method of copying. . . In *Sears*, the question was whether the defendant, Sears Roebuck & Co., could be held liable under state law for copying a lamp design whose patent protection had expired. . . . The Court . . . clarified that "[a]n unpatentable article, like an article on which the patent has expired, is in the public domain and may be made and sold by whoever chooses to do so." Roslin's claimed clones are exact genetic copies of patent ineligible subject matter. Accordingly, they are not eligible for patent protection.

However, Roslin argues that its claimed clones are patent eligible because they are distinguishable from the donor mammals used to create them. First, Roslin contends that "environmental factors" lead to phenotypic differences that distinguish its clones from their donor mammals. A phenotype refers to all the observable characteristics of an organism, such as shape, size, color, and behavior, that result from the interaction of the organism's genotype with its environment. A mammal's phenotype can change constantly throughout the life of that organism not only due to environmental changes, but also the physiological and morphological changes associated with aging.

Roslin argues that environmental factors lead to phenotypic differences between its clones and their donor mammals that render their claimed subject matter patentable. . . . Indeed, the word "cloned" in the pending claims connotes genetic identity, and the claims say nothing about a phenotypic difference between the claimed subject matter and the donor mammals. Moreover, Roslin acknowledges that any phenotypic differences came about or were produced "quite independently of any effort of the patentee." Contrary to Roslin's arguments, these phenotypic differences do not confer eligibility on their claimed subject matter. Any phenotypic differences between Roslin's donor mammals and its claimed clones are the result of "environmental factors."

Second, Roslin urges that its clones are distinguishable from their original donor mammals because of differences in mitochondrial DNA, which originates from the donor oocyte rather than the donor nucleus. . . . Mitochondria possess their own DNA, which is distinct from the DNA housed in the cell's nucleus. In the cloning process, the clone inherits its mitochondrial DNA from its donor oocyte, instead of its donor somatic cell. Therefore, Dolly's mitochondrial DNA came from the oocyte used to create her, not her donor mammary cell. Roslin argues that this difference in mitochondrial DNA renders its product claims patent eligible.

. . . Roslin's patent application does not identify how differences in mitochondrial DNA influence or could influence the characteristics of cloned mammals. As the Board found below,

> [a]s for the influence of the oocyte into which the donor nucleus is transferred, the . . . Specification teaches that "[a]nimals produced by transfer of nuclei from a source of genetically identical cells share the same nucleus, but are not strictly identi-

cal as they are derived from different oocytes. The significance of this different origin is not clear, but may affect commercial traits." The Specification cautions further that "[i]t remains . . . to consider whether it is possible or necessary in specific situations to consider the selection of oocytes." Thus . . . the Specification does not disclose any systematic differences in the clones that arise from the capture of the recipient oocyte.

There is nothing in the claims, or even in the specification, that suggests that the clones are distinct in any relevant way from the donor animals of which they are copies. The clones are defined in terms of the identity of their nuclear DNA to that of the donor mammals. To be clear, having the same nuclear DNA as the donor mammal may not necessarily result in patent ineligibility in every case. Here, however, the claims do not describe clones that have markedly different characteristics from the donor animals of which they are copies.

Finally, Roslin argues that its clones are patent eligible because they are time-delayed versions of their donor mammals, and therefore different from their original mammals. But this distinction cannot confer patentability. As the Board noted, "[t]he difficulty with the time-delayed characteristic is that it is true of any copy of an original." Thus, we affirm the Board's finding that Roslin's clones are unpatentable subject matter under § 101.

AFFIRMED.

Chapter Extension

For additional material relating to Chapter 4, see p. 236 in the Appendix of Chapter Extension Files.

Chapter Problems

    1. Define the following terms and concepts:
       a. Real property
       b. Personal property
       c. Bailment

   d. Fixtures

   e. Fee simple absolute

   f. Patent

   g. Non-obviousness

   h. Copyright

   i. Trademark

   j. Secondary meaning

2. Karen Ray worked as a receptionist at Flower Hospital. One evening she noticed a soft-shell eyeglass case on the top of the information desk. It contained rings, earrings, and other jewelry. What should Ray do? Why?

3. Johnson played a round of golf at the Firestone Country Club. Prior to teeing off at the first hole, he took off his Rolex watch and placed it in the front compartment of the golf cart he had obtained from the club. At the end of the game one of the players drove the cart to the pro shop and dropped it off. About 20 minutes later, Johnson realized that he was not wearing his watch and remembered that he had left it in the cart. The watch was never found. What should Johnson do, and why?

4. The Premonstatensian Fathers (Fathers) owned a one-story building that was insured. The Fathers leased out the building to a tenant that used it as a supermarket. A major fire damaged the building. The insurer refused to pay for the damage to five Hussman walk-in coolers situated in the building, contending that they were personal property installed by the tenant. The construction of the coolers was as follows:

   a. The exterior walls of the cooler, in four instances, constituted the interior wall of another room.

   b. In the two meat coolers, a meat-hanging-and-tracking system was built into the coolers. These tracks were used to move large cuts of meat from the cooler area into the meat preparation areas, and were suspended from the steel girders of the building structure by means of large steel bolts. These bolts penetrated through the roof of the cooler supporting wooden beams, which, in turn, supported the tracking system. The tracking in the coolers was a part of a system of tracking throughout the rear portion of the supermarket.

   c. The coolers were attached to hardwood planks that were, in turn, attached to the concrete floor of the supermarket. The attachment of the planks to the floor was accomplished through the use of a ramsetting gun. The planks were laid on the floor, and the bolts were driven through them into the concrete floor, where they then exploded, firmly fixing the coolers into place. There was a material placed on the planks that served as both an adhesive and an insulation.

   d. The floor of the coolers was specially sloped during the construction of the building so that the slope would carry drainage into a specially constructed drain in the concrete. In addition, four of the coolers were coated with a protective coating to seal the floors. In the freezer, a special concrete buildup was constructed in the nature of a trough, the purpose of which was to carry away moisture as frozen chickens melted.

e. A refrigeration unit was built into each cooler. The unit was suspended from the ceiling of the cooler, and tubing was run through the wall of the cooler to compressors located elsewhere in the store.

f. Electric lights and power receptacles were built into each cooler and were connected by electrical wiring through the walls and the ceiling of ·the cooler to the store's electrical power supply.

g. The walls of the cooler were interlocked and set into the splines, and the hardwood planks ramset into the concrete floor, in tongue-and-groove fashion.

Are the Fathers entitled to be compensated for the damage to the coolers? Explain.

5. John, Mary, and James owned real estate in fee simple absolute as "joint tenants with the right of survivorship." John died, leaving Candy and Rollins as heirs. Then Mary sold her interest to Van. Who has what, and why?

6. John Moore was diagnosed with hairy-cell leukemia. Dr. David Golde, a physician attending Moore at the University of California-Los Angeles (UCLA) Medical Center, removed Moore's spleen to slow down the progress of the disease. Dr. Golde was aware of the scientific and commercial value of blood components from Mr. Moore as a result of his specific disease. In follow-up sessions, Dr. Golde withdrew blood and bodily fluids from which he was able to grow a culture to produce lymphokines on a continuous basis (cell line). Lymphokines are proteins that regulate the immune system, and they have particular therapeutic value. Dr. Golde and UCLA obtained a patent on the cell line.

Genetics Institute has made Dr. Golde and UCLA an attractive financial offer for the exclusive access to the materials and research performed on the cell line and products derived from it. They are contemplating the offer.

What are the ethical issues? What should the result be?

7. Universal (respondent) owned the copyrights on a variety of television programs that were broadcast over the public airwaves, and brought suit against Sony (petitioner) for copyright infringement. Sony manufactured and sold the Betamax home video tape recorders, called at the time *VTRs*.

Universal argued that customers who had purchased the VTRs had used them to unlawfully record copyrighted programs, and that Sony, because of its marketing of the device, was liable for copyright infringement. Both parties conducted surveys that showed that the primary use of the machine for most owners was "time-shifting"—the practice of recording a program to view it once at a later time, and thereafter erasing it. Both surveys also showed, however, that a substantial number of interviewees had accumulated libraries of tapes. Has Sony infringed? Is the practice fair use? Explain.

8. Kinko photocopied excerpts of several copyrighted books, without permission and without payment, compiled them into course "packets," and sold them to college students. The owner of one of the copyrights sued for copyright infringement. Kinko defended by asserting that its copying was a "fair use" of the copyrighted material for educational purposes. Argue the case for the copyright owner. Who do you think should prevail, and why?

9. Rolls Royce, a British company that has a worldwide reputation as a producer of luxury automobiles and jet engines, obtained a U.S. registration of the words "Rolls Royce" as a trademark for its products. Alexander Knock-off formed a small company and began producing a low-cost reproduction of a roll-top desk that he called "The Rolls Royce." What action, if any, would you recommend that Rolls Royce take? Explain.

10. Owings-Corning Fiberglass Corp (OCF) filed an application to register the color "pink" as a trademark for the company's fibrous glass residential insulation. It uses the color in advertising, employing the "Pink Panther" in a cartoon-type animation in connection with the rolling out of pink insulation.

    Do you think that OCF will be able to obtain a trademark registration for the color pink? Explain.

5   THE LAW OF CONTRACTUAL RELATIONS

Chapter Outline

Learning Objectives

After learning this chapter the student should be able to:

- Determine whether a promise is legally enforceable.
- Determine whether particular promises require writings to be enforced and the legal significance of reducing a contract to writing.
- Evaluate whether particular promises are not enforceable because of a party's status or conduct or because of its substantive provisions.
- Evaluate the effects of unforeseen changes in circumstances on a party's duty to perform under a contract.
- Assess the remedies a court is likely to award for a breach of contract.

Most people associate the word *contract* with formal written documents, such as a contract to purchase real estate, a contract in a complex business transaction, or a professional athlete's employment agreement. The legal term *contract* is far broader than that, however; a contract is a promise that the law will enforce. The definition suggests that the law does not enforce every promise.

Most contracts consist of exchanges of two or more promises. In the typical case, the *promisee,* that is, the party to whom one of the promises was made, is attempting to enforce that promise against the *promisor,* the party who made it. At its core ethical and economic considerations drive the law's policy of enforcement of certain types of agreements. This chapter explores the factors that determine whether the law will enforce particular promises.

Sources of Contract Law

The basic law of contracts is common law, that is, it is judge-made law. However, the National Commission on Uniform State Laws believed that some common-law rules did not serve the commercial community as well as they could, and tried to write new rules that more closely reflected how most people conducted business. These new rules were codified in the Uniform Commercial Code (UCC). The UCC consists of nine articles, governing such commercial transactions as security interests in property, checks, drafts and other commercial paper. The UCC has been enacted as a statute in 50 states and the District of Columbia. (Louisiana has enacted part of the UCC, but not Article II.)

Article I of the UCC contains general provisions. Article II governs contracts for the sale of goods. A *good,* as the term is used in the UCC, is a tangible commodity capable of being moved from place to place. Pens, books, desks, appliances, cars, factory equipment, and office supplies are examples of goods. Real estate, services, stocks, bonds and other securities, and intangible property—such as patents and copyrights—are not goods.

When a contract involves the sale of goods, the UCC applies. The UCC's influence on the law of contracts has not been limited to contracts for the sale of goods; at times, courts considering contracts outside the UCC view the UCC changes positively and adopt them into common law.

Intent to Contract—The Objective Theory of Contracts

Every day, people make promises they do not intend to carry legal consequences. Many of these are social obligations, such as a promise to meet for lunch or to study together; and family obligations, such as a promise to visit parents next month. Companies often sign nonbinding letters of intent, expressing their expectations that after negotiations, agreements will be reached, but providing that neither party will be obligated until an agreement is reached. Additionally, some promises are simply just made in jest. If the parties do not intend to be legally bound, their promises are not legally enforceable.

Intent to contract does not refer to a party's subjective state of mind. Contractual intent is determined objectively by examining the parties' observable behavior—their words and conduct. The relevant legal inquiry thus becomes whether a reasonable person in the position of the promisee would conclude that the promisor intended to be legally bound.

For example, assume that Smith, a farmer, and Jones, the owner of a retail store, are enjoying a beer at their favorite tavern and discussing the low prices farmers are receiving for their crops. Jones says to Smith, "If you're fed up with farming, I'll buy your farm from you for $200,000." Smith thinks that Jones is joking and decides to play along. In a serious tone of voice he says, "You have a deal." Jones replies that he will need time to obtain financing. Smith still thinks the discussion is a joke, but discusses details of the transaction with Jones for a half hour and writes all the details on a piece of paper that Smith and Jones sign.

Subjectively, Smith did not intend to sell the farm to Jones, rather thinking that the matter was a joke. Nevertheless, a reasonable person in Jones's position would conclude that Smith intended to sell. Therefore, Smith would be legally bound to sell the farm to Jones.[1]

The Bargain Theory of Contracts

The law of contracts is the backbone of business. It enables parties to transact business with the knowledge that if one party fails to live up to the agreement the other party can seek redress from the courts. It is a primary guarantor of transactional integrity.

There are many reasons why parties would keep their promises even if the courts did not enforce them. For example, if a business developed a reputation for not abiding by its agreements, others would be very reluctant to do business with it.

The basic type of promise that a court enforces is one that is part of a bargained-for exchange. The elements of a bargained-for exchange are offer, acceptance, and consideration.

Offer

An **offer** is made by the *offeror* and gives the *offeree* the power to bind the offeror by accepting the offer. The objective theory is used to determine whether an offer has been made. The test is whether a reasonable person in the position of the offeree would interpret the offer as signifying the offeror's intent to be bound.

Offers must be distinguished from invitations to negotiate. Parties frequently send out announcements that they are seeking to do business and invite others to deal. These announcements may be contained in circulars, price quotes, catalogs, and advertisements. They are frequently indefinite concerning quantity and other terms. Most important, they usually do not identify the offeree.

There are some exceptions to the rule that an advertisement does not constitute an offer. The first are the reward cases. For example, Kelley promises a reward of $100.00 to the person who locates Duchess, her chihuahua dog. This promise is an effective offer, and is enforceable should someone accept the offer by locating and returning Duchess to Kelley.

---

[1] Lucy v. Zehmer, 196 Va. 493; 84 S.E. 2d 516 (1954).

An offer is not effective unless it is communicated to the offeree. For example, assume that John offers a $500 reward for the return of an antique watch he lost. Sarah, unaware of the offer, finds the watch and turns it over to the police, who return it to John. Sarah learns of the offer two days later. Sarah is not entitled to the reward because her acceptance, that is, her return of the watch, occurred before the offer was communicated to her.

Termination of an Offer

Offers do not last forever but expire at a time depending on the circumstances. An offer may specify its expiration date. If it does not do so, the offer terminates after passage of a reasonable time. Death of the offeror also terminates an offer.

Also, a rejection by the offeree terminates the offer. A counteroffer is both a rejection and a new offer. It terminates the original offer.

The most common method of terminating an offer is by **revocation.** A direct revocation occurs when the offeror advises the offeree that the offer is revoked. An indirect revocation occurs when the offeree receives truthful information from a reliable source that is inconsistent with the offer remaining open. For example, Susan offered to sell her house to James. The next day James learned from Carol that Susan had just sold her the same house. A sale to Carol is inconsistent with a possible sale to James. If the statement from Carol is truthful, the offer to James has been indirectly revoked.

Irrevocable Offers

If an offeror states that the offer will remain open until next Tuesday, the offeror usually can revoke prior to that time. Next Tuesday simply fixes the offer's expiration date in the event there are no intervening circumstances that cause termination of the offer. Even if the offeror promised not to revoke, the offeror could still revoke it unless the offeree gave money or other value for the promise. If the offeree gives value, such as the payment of money, the offer would be part of an option contract and would be irrevocable.

Under the UCC, a merchant's firm offer is irrevocable. A merchant is a party who regularly deals in, or otherwise has expertise in, the goods involved in the transaction. A firm offer must be in writing and must be limited to a reasonable period of time, not to exceed 90 days.

Acceptance

An **acceptance** consists of words or actions by which an offeree signifies his or her intention to be bound by the offer. Acceptance binds the offeree and the offeror. Acceptance must occur before the offer is terminated.

An offer may only be accepted by the offeree. For example, assume that Ace Widget Co. writes Deuce Gizmo Co., offering to sell Deuce 100 widgets for $200. The president of King Gizmo Co., while visiting the president of Deuce, sees the offer on the desk. The King president writes to Ace, "We hereby accept your offer of 100 widgets for $200." There is no contract between King and Ace. Because King was not the offeree, King cannot accept the Ace offer. King's letter is merely an offer to Ace, which Ace is free to accept if it wishes to do so.

An acceptance must signify the offeree's clear intent to be bound. Ambiguous actions or statements, such as "sounds like a good deal," are not acceptances. An offeror cannot declare that an ambiguous action will be treated as an acceptance. For example, assume Jack says to Jill, "I offer to sell you my car for $1,500. You may accept by taking the business law final exam next week." If Jill takes the final exam she will not have accepted Jack's offer because her action is ambiguous. She may be taking the final because she wishes to accept the offer, or she may be taking the final because it is required for the course.

Usually, silence by the offeree is ambiguous and cannot serve as an acceptance. Silence in the context of a prior course of dealings or silence plus acceptance of the benefits of the offer is not ambiguous and can serve as an acceptance.

The Mirror Image Rule and UCC 2–207

At common law, the acceptance must mirror the offer. If it adds new terms or changes any terms, it is not an acceptance but a counteroffer.

In commercial transactions, buyers and sellers frequently use printed forms with terms that do not agree, sometimes referred to as "the battle of the forms." Under the mirror image rule, each form exchanged is a counteroffer, even though it may be intended as an acceptance. The terms of the last form sent by either party govern the transaction when that counteroffer is accepted by the other party's shipment or acceptance of the goods.

Section 2–207 of the UCC changes this common-law rule. It provides that a document intended to be an acceptance is an acceptance even though it has terms different from or in addition to those in the offer. The acceptance creates a contract on the offeror's terms. The new terms found in the acceptance are proposals to add to the contract. Unless both parties are merchants, the new terms only become part of the contract when both parties expressly agree to them.

If both parties are merchants, the new terms automatically become part of the contract unless one of three conditions is met: (1) the offer expressly limited acceptance to the terms of the offer; (2) the offeror notifies the offeree of its objection to the new terms; or (3) the new terms materially change the contract.

For example, assume that Buyer sent Seller an offer to purchase 100 widgets for $200 on Buyer's printed order blank. The terms on the order blank included statements that full warranties apply and that the goods were to be delivered by Speedy Delivery Service. Seller responds with a printed acknowledgement form, promising to ship the widgets on the requested date. Seller's form specifies delivery via Quick Delivery Service and limits the warranty to replacement of defective widgets. Seller ships the widgets, Buyer accepts them, and two weeks later a defective widget causes $5,000 damage to Buyer's equipment. To determine the contents of the contract under the common law and the UCC, see Table 5–1.

Acceptance by Promise or Performance

Most offers contemplate contracts in which promises are exchanged for promises. For example, Owner offers to pay Roofer $1,500 for reroofing Owner's house. If Roofer accepts, the contract consists of Owner's promise to pay the money and Roofer's promise to do the work. This is called a *bilateral contract*. Roofer may accept by promising to do the job or by actually starting. If Roofer begins performance, Roofer is impliedly promising to do the entire job.

Sometimes the offeror is not interested in the offeree's promise, but is only concerned with full performance. For example, if a company offers a reward for the return of some lost documents, it is not bargaining for someone to promise to search for the documents; the company is only interested in the documents. The offeree can accept only by producing the documents. This is called a *unilateral*

TABLE 5–1   The Mirror Image Rule and UCC 2–207

	Common Law	UCC (At least 1 party is not a merchant)	UCC (Both parties are merchants)
Buyer's order	Offer	Offer	Offer
Seller's acknowledgment	Counteroffer because of the delivery and warranty terms	Acceptance; changes in delivery company and limitation on warranty are proposals to change the contract	
Buyer accepts the goods	Acceptance of Seller's counteroffer	Irrelevant	Irrelevant
Change in name of delivery company	Part of contract as Buyer accepted Seller's counteroffer	Not part of contract as Buyer did not agree to it	Part of contract because Buyer did not specify in its offer that acceptance must be limited to the offer's terms, Buyer did not object to it, and it does not materially change the contract
Limitation on warranty	Part of contract as Buyer accepted Seller's counteroffer	Not part of contract as Buyer did not agree to it	Not part of contract as it materially changes the terms of the contract

contract. Because the offeree makes no promise, the offeree is not obligated to perform; but if the offeree performs, the offeror is bound to perform.

After the offeree commences performance, but prior to completion of performance, the offeror might try to revoke the offer. Because only complete performance would bind the offeror, the offeree needs protection against revocation midway through performance. The law affords that protection; when the offeree begins to perform, the offeror cannot revoke for a reasonable time in order to give the offeree a chance to complete the performance.

Effective Date of Acceptance—The Mailbox Rule

The offeror is the master of the offer and can set any conditions on the acceptance. The offeror can expressly limit the means of communicating acceptance, for example, by specifying overnight delivery, and can expressly provide that acceptance will be effective only on receipt.

If the offeror does not restrict the method of acceptance, the offeree may use any reasonable means to accept. If the offeror does not specify otherwise, acceptance is effective on dispatch by the offeree. This principle is frequently called the **mailbox rule**, as a mailed acceptance is effective on its deposit in the mailbox. The rule protects the offeree from unknown revocations. Because revocation is effective on receipt, an offeree who has not received a revocation can dispatch an acceptance knowing that a contract has been formed.

Consideration

Consideration refers to the requirement that a promise be part of a bargained-for exchange in order for it to be enforceable. Offer and acceptance are the bargaining process. Consideration consists of two elements: (1) a legal detriment by the promisee that (2) is bargained for by the promisor. A legal detriment exists where the promisee does or promises to do something he or she was not previously obligated to do, or refrains from or promises not to do something he or she had a legal right to do. The detriment is bargained for if it is given in exchange for the promise. See Table 5–2 for an illustration of how consideration is present in a contract between Roofer and Owner to roof Owner's house for $2,500.

Past consideration is not bargained for and, therefore, cannot provide the consideration for a present promise. For example, assume that Employer says to Worker, "In consideration of your many years of service to this company, I promise to pay you a pension of $2,000 per month when you retire." Worker's past services were not given in exchange for the promise of a pension. Therefore, there is no consideration for the promise.

The Preexisting Duty Rule

A promise to perform or the performance of a preexisting legal duty is not a detriment and, therefore, is not consideration. For example, if Professor says to Student,

TABLE 5-2	**Consideration**		
Promise	*Consideration*	*Detriment*	*Bargained for*
Owner's promise to pay $2,500	Roofer's promise to roof the house	Roofer was under no prior obligation to do the job	Roofer's promise induced Owner's promise
Roofer's promise to roof the house	Owner's promise to pay $2,500	Owner was under no prior obligation to pay Roofer	Owner's promise induced Roofer's promise

"I promise to pay you $50 if you don't cheat on the final exam," the promise is unenforceable because Student is already under a legal duty not to cheat.

The preexisting duty rule has made modifications of existing contracts unenforceable. For example, assume that Owner and Builder contract for the construction of a swimming pool at a price of $5,000, with payment due on completion. After Builder starts work, Builder finds that due to unanticipated soil conditions the pool will cost $7,000 to build. Owner promises to pay Builder an extra $2,000 and Builder completes the job. Under the preexisting duty rule, Owner's promise of an additional $2,000 is unenforceable because the only consideration given by Builder was completion of the pool, something Builder was obligated to do by the original contract. However, if Builder also promised that Owner could pay for the pool 30 days after completion, Builder has given new consideration—30 days' credit—which would satisfy that element of the contract.

Recently, a trend away from strict application of the preexisting duty rule has emerged. The *Restatement (Second) of Contracts* provides that for executory contracts, that is, those not fully performed on either side, a good faith modification in response to unanticipated conditions is enforceable without consideration.

Courts in a growing number of states are adopting this approach. UCC Section 2-209 provides that any good faith modification of a contract for the sale of goods is enforceable without consideration.

🔍 **Understanding the private law sector**

This link, from the U.S. Small Business Administration site, succinctly explains the nature of a legally binding contract.

http://www.sba.gov/blogs /contract-law-how-create -legally-binding-contract

Mutuality of Obligation

When the consideration for a promise is another promise, the parties must be under mutual duties to perform. If one party's promise is illusory, such as a promise to perform "if I feel like it," mutuality is lacking and the other party's promise is unenforceable. This problem can arise where one party retains discretion over whether, and to what extent, he or she will perform. Courts frequently infer duties to use reasonable efforts to perform or to exercise the discretion in good faith to avoid interpreting such promises as illusory.

Statute of Frauds

Generally, oral contracts are enforceable, although their existence may be difficult to prove. Certain types of contracts, however, are not enforceable unless they are evidenced by a writing. The **Statute of Frauds** requires written evidence for promises:

- Made in consideration of marriage.
- For sales of goods priced $500 or more.
- For transfers of real property other than a lease of less than one year's duration.
- That cannot, by their terms, be performed within one year.
- To answer for the debt of another.

The first three promises are self-explanatory. Promises that by their terms cannot be performed within one year refer only to those promises that expressly call for more than a year's commitment. If the promise can be performed within one year, it does not fall within the Statute of Frauds even if a longer duration is contemplated. For example, if Worker promises Company to work for the next two years, the contract must be evidenced by a writing because it cannot be performed within one year. But if Worker promises Company to work until retirement, the Statute of Frauds does not apply because Worker can retire at any time. A writing is not required, even if Worker is 25 years old and intends to work for 40 more years.

Promises to answer for the debt of another come within the Statute of Frauds only if they are made to the creditor. A promise made to the debtor does not require a writing. Even where the promise is made to the creditor, a writing is not required if the promisor is also the debtor. For example, if Jill telephones the Ace Department Store and says, "Jack is coming over. Sell him a new suit and send me the bill," no writing is required. Jack never becomes indebted to Ace. When Jack makes a purchase, Jill becomes a debtor; thus, she has promised to pay her own debt rather than Jack's.

A promise to answer for the debt of another does not require a writing if the main purpose of the promise is to benefit the promisor. For example, assume that Big Bank holds a mortgage on David Debtor's home. Bank promises an insurance company that if Debtor fails to pay the premium for fire insurance, Bank will pay. Bank's main purpose is to protect its interest in the property, as the mortgage would be of little value if the property was destroyed by fire and was not insured.

Compliance with the Statute of Frauds

The Statute of Frauds does not require that the contract be in writing; it requires only that there be a written evidence of the contract signed by the party to be charged with enforcement of the contract. For example, a typical laundry ticket could be sufficient to satisfy the Statute of Frauds' requirement of a signed writing in a lawsuit against the laundry. Courts can also integrate several documents to arrive at the written evidence needed to satisfy the Statute of Frauds. Letters between parties or internal company memos may combine to show the existence of a contract.

The requirement of a signature is satisfied by any mark that is intended to authenticate a document. For example, a company's name on stationary letterhead would satisfy the signature requirement. A federal statute known as E-Sign was enacted to encourage the use of electronic signatures, such as those used in online transactions, in interstate commerce. E-Sign states that a contract may not be denied legal effect, validity, or enforceability solely because an electronic signature or electronic record was used in its formation.

In goods transactions between merchants, UCC 2–201 permits a written confirmation of a contract to satisfy the requirement of a signed writing if the party who receives the confirmation has reason to know its contents and does not send written notice of objection to the sender of the confirmation within ten days after the confirmation is received. This allows the sender to enforce the contract against the recipient of the confirmation even though the recipient's signature is not on any writing. For example, if a merchant telephoned an order to a supplier for goods priced over $500, and the supplier sent an invoice to the buyer, who sees it and does not object to it within 10 days, the supplier can enforce the purchase agreement against the buyer even though the buyer did not sign anything. The written confirmation without written notice of objection substitutes for a signed writing in these circumstances.

Even where no writing exists at all, courts may enforce an oral contract where the parties have performed part of their obligation, and the performance is referable to the contract. That is, if the performance can be explained only on the basis of the existence of a contract, the performance serves as a substitute for a signed writing.

Decision-making in the legal environment

This link instructs on what to look for in a business contract.

http://smallbusiness.findlaw.com/business-contracts-forms/how-to-write-a-business-contract.html

Alternatives to the Bargain Theory of Contracts

Alternatives to the bargain theory of contracts exist for courts to provide remedies in cases not meeting classical contract law's requirement of a bargained-for exchange. These alternative theories stem from an area of law known as the *law of equity*. Courts have drawn upon equity law to apply doctrines to do equity in a given case. The three alternative theories are: promissory estoppel, the doctrine of moral obligation, and the doctrine of quasi contract.

Promissory Estoppel

Under the doctrine of **promissory estoppel**, courts have enforced promises that lacked consideration and oral promises that would otherwise be unenforceable under the Statute of Frauds. Under the doctrine, a party is "estopped" to deny the existence of a promise. Three conditions must be met for the doctrine of promissory estoppel to apply:

1. There must be a *promise* from a promisor to a promisee.
2. There must be *reliance* by the promisee upon the promise.
3. The reliance must be to the promisee's *substantial economic detriment.*

The promise must be one that a reasonable promisor should foresee would induce reliance. The promisee's reliance must be reasonable. The requirement of substantial economic detriment means that an injustice can be avoided only by enforcing the promise.

Promissory estoppel has been traditionally used as a defense. For example, if a landlord told a tenant that the landlord would not enforce a provision in the lease that says that interest would be charged on late rental payments, the tenant could raise promissory estoppel as a defense to a claim by the landlord for interest in addition to the unpaid rent. The trend is for courts to permit promissory estoppel to be used as an affirmative claim to enforce promises that are not contracts under contact law because they lack the requirements of a contract (such as consideration).

Moral Obligation

Generally, a moral obligation to keep a promise is not sufficient to make the promise legally enforceable. However, if a promise becomes unenforceable by operation of law, a subsequent promise to keep the original promise is enforceable without new consideration. For example, assume John owes Mary $500, but because the statute of limitations period for bringing suit has expired, John's debt is uncollectible. If John promises to pay the $500 anyway, the promise is enforced without new consideration.

Quasi Contract

If a doctor finds a pedestrian unconscious on the street and treats the pedestrian, no contract has arisen between the two. An unconscious pedestrian cannot accept the doctor's offer.

However, where a party confers a benefit on another party with a reasonable expectation of payment, and the recipient of the benefit would be unjustly enriched if not required to pay for it, a court implies a contract as a matter of law. Under such a *quasi contract,* a doctor is able to recover the reasonable value of the services provided.

Policing the Bargain

Courts generally do not get involved in reviewing the fairness of particular contracts. If an agreement has been reached, a court cannot protect a party from a bad deal. In certain cases, however, courts refuse to enforce a promise because of a party's status. Courts protect particularly vulnerable parties deemed to lack the capacity to contract. In other cases, courts may rescind or reform a contract if a party's conduct produces a defect in the bargaining process. Finally, courts may refuse to enforce all or part of a contract if its substantive provisions are illegal or unconscionable.

Capacity

People so mentally infirm that they cannot understand the nature and consequences of their actions lack the capacity to contract. People who have not yet attained the age of majority—usually 18 but in some states 21—also lack contractual capacity. The overwhelming majority of capacity problems arise in contracts made by minors.

Minors have the right to disaffirm their contracts at any time prior to reaching the age of majority. On reaching the age of majority, a party may choose to disaffirm or ratify the contract. Ratification may be implied from the party's conduct or from the party's failure to disaffirm within a reasonable time after reaching the age of majority. An adult has no power to disaffirm. An adult is bound by a contract with a minor unless the minor disaffirms.

If a minor disaffirms, the law in most states only requires the minor to return to the adult any remaining consideration. It does not require the minor to make restitution. For example, assume that Minor buys a car on credit from Dealer. After making only one payment and with an outstanding balance of $8,000, Minor is involved in an accident that totally destroys the car. In most states, if Minor disaffirms, Minor need only return the remaining wreck to Dealer and need not make restitution for the damage or the value of the use of the car.

Minors are responsible for their contracts for necessities, such as food, clothing, shelter, and medical care. A minor who disaffirms such a contract is liable in quasi contract for the reasonable value of the benefit received.

Defects in the Bargaining Process

Defects in the bargaining process may result in a court rescinding, or occasionally reforming, an agreement. A party's consent may have been obtained through misrepresentation or under duress or may be the result of a mistake.

Misrepresentation
Where a misrepresentation of a material fact is made and a party justifiably relies on the misrepresentation, the deceived party may rescind the transaction and receive restitution for any benefits conferred on the deceptive party. Misrepresentations need not be fraudulent (i.e., intentional), or even negligent, as long as they are material. A misrepresentation is material if it would likely influence the conduct of a reasonable person.

Only misrepresentations of fact are actionable. Misrepresentations of opinion are not actionable unless the deceived party is relying on the deceiver's expertise. Statements that an item is the "best buy" or a "superb value" usually are dismissed as nonactionable opinion. Similarly, predictions of future events are usually considered to be nonactionable opinion.

In certain circumstances, nondisclosure may amount to actionable misrepresentation. Deliberate concealment is actionable, as is deceptive partial disclosure. There is a duty to disclose latent defects and to correct misconceptions caused by the nondisclosing party. A duty to disclose also arises if the parties are in a fiduciary or other special relationship.

Nondisclosure or misrepresentation is actionable only if justifiably relied on. Reliance is not justified if the deceived party knows the representation is false or could discover it through a reasonable investigation.

Duress

Duress occurs when one party's wrongful act overcomes the free will of another party. If a party's agreement is obtained with threats of physical harm, the contract is void because of duress. The law considers the contract to have never been made. Duress can also result from economic pressure. Economic duress that results from a wrongful act renders a contract voidable. The victim of the duress may rescind the contract.

For example, assume that Repairer had a contract to repair a machine for Mechanic. Because the machine was indispensable to Mechanic's business, Repairer agreed to pick up the machine at the close of business on Friday and have it ready for Mechanic to pick up Monday morning. When Mechanic arrived on Monday, Repairer said that the machine was ready but would not be returned to Mechanic unless Mechanic promised to pay a debt that Mechanic's brother owed to Repairer and had refused to pay. Mechanic desperately needed the machine, so she promised to pay her brother's debt. Mechanic may rescind her promise because of duress.

Mistake

The parties may allocate the risk of mistake in their contract. The allocation may be expressed, or it may be implied from what a reasonable person would expect under the circumstances. For example, assume that Jack finds a gemstone and sells it to Jill for $50. Neither party knows what type of gem it is, but both assume that, although it is pretty, it is not very valuable. Under these circumstances, it is reasonable to imply that Jill is assuming the risk that the gem is worthless and Jack is assuming the risk that it is valuable. If the gem turns out to be a diamond worth $5,000, the mistake is not grounds for Jack to rescind the contract.

If the parties have not allocated the risk, a mutual mistake in a basic assumption allows either party to rescind the contract. If only one party is mistaken, rescission is allowed under some circumstances. Many courts allow rescission if the nonmistaken party knew or should have known of the other party's mistake. More liberal courts allow rescission if enforcement would be oppressive to the mistaken party and rescission would not impose a hardship on the nonmistaken party.

Sometimes the parties reach an oral agreement but make a mistake in reducing it to writing. In such a case, a court reforms the writing to conform to the original agreement.

Law and Ethics in Business Policies

This link supplements the discussion on unconscionable contracts.

http://www.legalmatch.com /law-library/article/what-is -an-unconscionable-contract .html

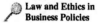

Unconscionability

UCC Section 2–302 authorizes a court to deny or limit enforcement of a contract or part of a contract that it finds to be unconscionable. Unconscionability is determined as of the time the contract is made. Unconscionability exists where one party did not have a meaningful choice and where the terms are so one-sided as to be oppressive. Absence of meaningful choice has been found where there was a large disparity in bargaining power, the terms were hidden in fine print, or the term were presented on a take-it-or-leave-it basis.

Courts have analogized to the UCC and applied the concept of unconscionability to contracts that did not involve sales of goods. Unconscionability is most commonly found in consumer transactions.

Ethical Dilemmas/Issues

You are the president of a large real estate rental company. Your standard residential lease has a clause that provides, "Tenant agrees that landlord shall not be liable for any personal injuries or property damage sustained by tenant on landlord's property or resulting from landlord's negligence." A recent decision from your state's supreme court held that a similar clause in another landlord's lease was unconscionable. The court refused to enforce the clause.

Several of your resident managers have advised you not to drop the clause from your leases. They reason that although a court would not enforce the clause, the tenants do not know that. In their experience, the clause deters tenants from pressing claims for minor injuries. As one resident manager explained, "If you take the clause out, every time someone slips and skins a knee, we'll see a claim." Your liability insurance company agrees and will raise your premiums if you do not retain the clause.

What are the ethical issues in this problem? What would you do? Explain.

Illegality

A contract is illegal if its formation or performance is tortious, forbidden by statute, or contrary to public policy. For example, contracts to bribe public officials, to embezzle money, to gamble in a state that prohibits gambling, and to sell cocaine are illegal.

The concept of public policy is difficult to define with precision but it enables courts to deny enforcement to contracts which they believe injure the public interest. One such contract that has received considerable judicial attention is the covenant not to compete.

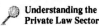

**Understanding the
Private Law Sector**

This link supplements the
discussion on non-compete
agreements.

http://www.nolo.com/legal
-encyclopedia/noncompete
-agreements-how-create
-agreement-29784.html

Covenants not to compete arise out of basically two situations: the sale of a business and an employment contract. In the sale of a business the buyer may push to include a provision within the sales contract that would prevent the seller from turning around, opening up a new business and competing against the new buyer's business. Likewise, an employer who trains an employee and imparts skills and knowledge of the business would be concerned about the employee, upon leaving the employ, using those skills and knowledge to compete against the former employer. This protection against that threat could be covered in an employee signing a covenant not to compete in such event.

Covenants not to compete come with a presumption that they are illegal because preventing someone from employment appears to be an unreasonable restraint of trade. Hence, courts scrutinize covenant not to compete provisions to determine if they are, in fact, reasonable, and thus enforceable.

First, in order to be enforceable a covenant not to compete must be reasonable as to the duration of the restriction. Restrictions that are five or ten years in duration are more suspect than those that are one or three years in duration. The final determination on reasonableness as to time turns on the length of time necessary to protect the business establishment against a new competitive threat by a former employee or the seller of a business.

Second, the restriction should be reasonable as to geographics. The territorial restriction should be no greater than the radius within which the business competes. To restrict an employee of a local hardware store from securing another such job any place within the United States is unreasonably broad and hence not enforceable.

Third, the covenant not to compete should be reasonable as to the scope of the restriction. The restriction should be confined to the relevant type of business or employment. Hence, it is unreasonable to restrict a seller of a grocery business to refrain from work in a plumbing business regardless of how short a period of time or how narrow the geographic restriction. The plumbing business is just too far afield from the grocery business.

If an agreement is illegal, usually a court will not enforce the agreement. There are several exceptions to this general rule. Courts enforce a contract that contravenes a statute if enforcement would be consistent with the purpose of the statute. For example, if a party does business without a required license and the license statute's purpose is a "tax" to raise money rather than protect customers and clients, courts would enforce the unlicensed party's contracts. If the license is required for protection, courts would enforce the contracts on request of the customers or clients but not on the request of the unlicensed party.

Courts considering illegal contracts often inquire into whether the illegality involves *moral turpitude,* that is, serious misconduct. If the illegality does not involve moral turpitude and the parties are not *in pari delicto,* that is, not equally blameworthy, courts allow the more innocent party to recover in quasi contract for benefits conferred on the other party. If the illegality does not involve moral turpitude, a party who renounces the bargain and prevents the illegal act from taking place may recover in quasi contract.

Contract Interpretation

Frequently, contract disputes do not involve the existence or enforceability of a contract. Rather, they focus on what the contract's provisions mean. In interpreting contracts, courts inquire into how a reasonable person in the position of the parties would interpret the agreement. Often, courts look to the past practices of the industry. In written documents, ambiguities often are resolved against the drafter because that is the party responsible for the ambiguity.

The Parol Evidence Rule

Decision-making in the legal environment

This link discusses the pros and cons of written employment contracts.

http://www.nolo.com/legal
-encyclopedia/written
-employment-contracts-pros
-cons-30193.html

The **parol evidence rule** provides that if a contract is reduced to writing and the parties intend the writing to be the final and complete evidence of the agreement, prior or contemporaneous representations or agreements (i.e., parol evidence) may not be used to vary or contradict the writing. Parties often specify that their writings are intended to be the final expressions of their agreements to the exclusion of all prior representations. Such clauses are called *integration, merger,* or *zipper clauses.* Nonetheless parol evidence may establish reasons for rescinding the contract, such as fraud, duress, mistake, or lack of capacity. Parol evidence may also be used to explain the meaning of ambiguous terms contained in the writing. Finally, parol evidence may be used to establish modifications agreed to after the original written contract.

Performance and Breach

A breach of contract occurs if a party has a duty to perform and fails to do so. A party may not have a duty to perform if conditions precedent to that duty have not been fulfilled. A party's duty to perform may be discharged by unforeseen subsequent events.

Conditions

The two types of conditions contained in contracts are express and constructive. **Express conditions** are those established by the parties themselves. For example, if George buys a $100,000 life insurance policy naming Sally as beneficiary, the insurance company has promised to pay Sally $100,000 if George dies. George's death is an express condition precedent to the insurance company's duty to pay Sally.

Constructive conditions are implied as a matter of law from the order of performance contemplated by the parties. If one party is to perform first, that party's performance is a constructive condition precedent to the other party's duty to perform. If both parties are to perform at the same time, each party's performance is a constructive condition concurrent to the other party's duty to perform.

Constructive conditions need only be substantially fulfilled for a party's duty to perform to arise. For example, assume that Owner contracts with Builder to build a house according to stated specifications, with Owner to pay for the house on completion. Although the specifications call for using a certain brand of pipe for the plumbing, Builder uses a different brand that is identical in quality to the pipe specified.

Builder's completion of the house as specified is a constructive condition precedent to Owner's duty to pay. The condition has not been literally fulfilled because of the deviation from the specified brand of pipe. However, because the construction condition precedent of completing the house has been substantially fulfilled, Owner must pay.

Excuses for Nonperformance

The parties in their contract may expressly or impliedly allocate the risk of unforeseen changes in circumstances. Often, they fail to do so. Generally, if unforeseen events render performance impossible, the duty to perform is discharged. For example, if the subject matter of the contract is destroyed, the duty to perform is discharged. Similarly, supervening illegality discharges the duty to perform. Death of an individual who was to personally render services also discharges the duty to perform.

UCC Section 2–615 extends the doctrine of impossibility to cases of unforeseen impracticability. Courts in a few states have added this liberalization to their general law of contracts, but the majority of states have confined it to the sale of goods.

A related doctrine is the rule of frustration of purpose. It was first recognized in a 1903 English case.[2] The defendant agreed to pay the plaintiff £75 to use the plaintiff's apartment for two days to view the coronation of King Edward VII. The coronation was unexpectedly canceled due to the King's illness. Performance of the contract remained possible, but the purpose of the contract had been frustrated. Accordingly, the duty to perform was discharged.

Breach by Anticipatory Repudiation

Most breaches of contract occur at the time for performance. Sometimes, a party may declare prior to the time for performance that he or she has no intention of ever performing. In such a case, the other party may treat the anticipatory repudiation as a current breach of contract and sue immediately for relief. For example, assume that Seller agrees to sell Buyer 100 widgets a month for six months. After two months, Seller tells Buyer that it will not sell any more widgets. Although

---

[2] Krell v. Henry, 2 K.B. 740 (1903).

the time for performance of the next four months' supply of widgets has not yet arisen, Buyer may treat Seller's repudiation as an immediate breach.

Remedies

The basic remedy for breach of contract is an award of money damages. The basic measure of damages is lost expectation. Expectation damages are calculated to place the victim of the breach in the position he or she would have been in had the contract been performed. The two alternative measures of damages are reliance and restitution. Reliance damages are calculated to place the victim of the breach in the position he or she would have been in had the contract never been made. Restitution damages are designed to place the breaching party in the position he or she would have been in had the contract never been made.

To illustrate the differences among the three measures of damage, assume that Builder agreed to subdivide a lot and build two apartment buildings and Owner agreed to pay Builder $1 million. Builder completed the first building at a cost of $350,000. The building had a market value of $600,000. Before Builder started work on the second building, Owner repudiated the contract. It would cost Builder $300,000 to build the second building.

If the contract had been fully performed, Builder would have made a profit of $350,000. It will take $700,000 (the lost profit plus the $350,000 spent on the first building) to put Builder in the same position as if the contract had been fully performed. Thus, Builder's expectation damages are $700,000.

Builder spent $350,000 that it would not have spent if there had been no contract. It will take $350,000 to put Builder in the same position as if no contract had been made. Thus, Builder's reliance damages are $350,000.

Owner received a building worth $600,000 that Owner would not have had if there had been no contract. To place Owner in the same position as if no contract had been made, Owner must pay Builder $600,000. Thus, Builder's restitution damages are $600,000.

There are several limitations on the amount of damages. First, damages must be calculable with reasonable certainty. Uncertainty is frequently a problem when the damages requested include lost profits. A new business with no track record to use as a basis for calculating lost profits may be unable to recover them because they are too uncertain.

Second, damages must be reasonably foreseeable. This principle was established in an 1854 English case.[3] The plaintiffs mill was shut down because of a broken shaft. The defendant agreed to ship the shaft to a company that would make a new one. The defendant breached the contract by excessively delaying the ship-

---

[3] Hadley v. Baxendale, 156 Eng. Rep. 145 (1854).

ment, thereby prolonging the period that the mill was closed. The plaintiff sought to recover the profit lost during the excessive closing, but the court denied recovery because the defendant had no way of knowing that the mill was shut down.

Third, the victim of the breach must make reasonable efforts to mitigate damages. For example, if a supplier breaches a contract to supply widgets to a manufacturer, the manufacturer must make a reasonable effort to obtain an alternate source of supply.

Sometimes the parties may specify the amount of damages in the contract. Such provisions are called **liquidated damages**. They are enforceable if they are intended as remedies rather than penalties, if actual damages would be difficult to calculate, and if they represent reasonable estimates of the damage done.

Sometimes a party wants a court to order the breaching party to actually perform the contract rather than pay damages. Orders of **specific performance** are available if money damages would not provide an adequate remedy. However, an award of specific performance is subject to the court's equitable discretion. A court would not order specific performance if the order would be difficult to enforce or overly harsh on one of the parties. The party requesting specific performance must have acted promptly in asserting his or her rights and must be free of wrongdoing or bad faith.

Case

(Covenant not to Compete)

H&R BLOCK EASTERN ENTERPRISES, INC., V. VICKI D. MORRIS
606 F.3d 1285 (Ct Appeals, 11th Cir. 2010)

Block prepares taxes and related services for individuals and companies nationwide. It employed Morris as a seasonal tax preparer in its College Park, Georgia 2000–2005 tax seasons. In 2004 Morris and Block entered into an agreement that included a non-competition covenant. The pertinent section contains a non-competition covenant that restricts Morris for a period of two years after the termination of the Agreement, resignation or termination as an employee from providing tax services to any of Block's clients with whom Morris had serviced, within Morris' district of employment or within a twenty-five (25) mile radius of the office to which Morris was assigned.

Block declined to re-hire Morris for the 2006 tax season. Morris started Dreams Tax Service. She prepared 47 returns for former Block clients whom she had serviced while at Block. Block sued seeking injunctive relief and damages.

The District Court found in favor of Morris reasoning that the covenant not to compete was unenforceable because it prevented Morris from accepting unsolicited business from former clients. Morris appealed.

PER CURIAM

A restrictive covenant in an employment contract . . . is considered to be in partial restraint of trade and will be enforced only if it (1) is reasonable, (2) is supported by consideration, (3) is reasonably necessary to protect the restraining party's interest, and (4) does not unduly prejudice the interests of the public. . Georgia courts apply strict scrutiny to restrictive covenants in employment contracts, and the reasonableness of the restraint is a question of law for determination by the court, "which considers the nature and extent of the trade or business, the situation of the parties, and all other circumstances." . . . "A three-element test of duration, territorial coverage, and scope of activity has evolved as a helpful tool in examining the reasonableness of the particular factual setting to which it is applied."

■   ■   ■

The Non-Competition Covenant

The district court determined the non-competition covenant was unenforceable because it prevented Morris from accepting unsolicited business from her former Block clients. In reaching this decision, the district court applied rulings involving non-solicitation covenants rather than non-competition covenants.

On appeal, Block argues the district court erroneously concluded the non-competition covenant was invalid. Block contends the non-competition covenant is enforceable when evaluated under the proper standard and considering the interplay of provisions in the Agreement. In response, Morris argues the provision is unreasonable in geographic scope because it has two geographic restrictions — a district restriction and a 25-mile radius restriction. Morris also asserts the non-competition covenant contravenes public policy by limiting the number of businesses providing tax preparation and filing services.

A non-competition covenant, "which is de-signed primarily to protect the employer's 'investment of time and money in developing the employee's skills.' prohibits the employee from performing competitive activities in a certain geographic area for a limited time." A non-competition covenant "may preclude the employee from accepting related business (whether solicited or not) from any clients (whether previously contacted by him or not) if the employee is officed in, or is to perform the restricted activities in, the forbidden territory." A restrictive covenant subject to strict scrutiny may apply to the territory in which the employee served. A non-competition covenant must also "contain a territorial limitation sufficient to 'give the employee notice of what constitutes a violation of the restrictive covenant [by] specify[ing] with particularity the territory in which the employee[s' conduct] is restricted.' "To determine whether a non-competition covenant satisfies this requirement, "a court must examine the 'interplay between the scope of the prohibited behavior and the territorial restriction.' "For example, "[a] broad territorial limitation may be reasonable if the scope of the prohibited behavior is sufficiently narrow.".

Applying the three-element test of duration, territorial coverage, and scope, we conclude the Agreement's non-competition covenant is reasonable, considering the nature and extent of the business, the situation of the parties, and other relevant circumstances. With respect to duration, the two-year duration of the . . . clause is within the time frame permitted by law. . . .

With regard to territorial coverage, the non-competition covenant was geographically limited to (1) Morris's district of employment and (2) a 25-mile radius from the Block office where Morris worked. . . . The restricted geographic area was illustrated by a map accompanying the Agreement, and was thus identified and disclosed to Morris at the time she signed the contract. Although Morris contends the geographic restrictions are unreasonable, the district court found "Block . . . presented evidence showing that Morris serviced clients from communities in the extreme outer-edges of the twenty-five mile territor[y]." Moreover, the geographic restrictions are reasonable considering the "interplay" between the territorial restriction and the scope of prohibited behavior– the covenant applies only to clients served by Morris, and only covers territory in which she actually worked. Accordingly, in these circumstances, the non-competition covenant's territorial limitation is reasonable.

Finally, the scope of prohibited activities is sufficiently narrow. A non-competition covenant "must balance an employee's right to earn a living without unreasonable restrictions, and an employer's right to protection from the former employee's possible unfair appropriation of contacts developed while working for the employer." Here, the non-competition covenant prohibited Morris from preparing tax returns or providing any other service Morris "provided or offered as an employee of the Company" to any of the Company's Clients. The Agreement limited Company Clients to those persons or entities "with whom [Morris] had contact" by providing services as an

employee of the Company. This covenant does not prohibit Morris from preparing taxes or providing a related service to the general public, or Block clients generally. Morris is only prohibited from serving those clients she serviced while employed at Block during the 2005 tax season. The covenant appropriately balances Morris's right to earn a living with Block's right to protect its customer relationships and Block's investment in developing Morris's skills.

The non-competition covenant is limited to a specific geographic area, the types of activities performed by Morris at Block, the customers serviced by Morris at Block, and a two-year duration. After considering the nature of the tax preparation business, the situation of the parties, and after applying the three-element analysis, we conclude this non-competition covenant is reasonable under Georgia law.

■　■　■

REVERSED on the issue of the Covenant Not to Compete.

Chapter Extension

For additional material relating to Chapter 5, see p. 249 in the Appendix of Chapter Extension Files.

Chapter Problems

1. Define the following terms:
   a. Offer
   b. Acceptance
   c. Mailbox rule
   d. Consideration
   e. Statute of Frauds
   f. Promissory estoppel
   g. Parol evidence rule
   h. Express and constructive conditions
   i. Liquidated damages
   j. Specific performance

2. Sally Black sent an unsolicited recipe for fruit flavors to be used in making ice cream to General Foods Corporation, along with a letter asking General Foods to compensate her if the company should decide to use it. A vice president of General Foods replied with a letter thanking her for her suggestion, but added, "We shall be happy to examine your suggestion but only with understanding that our use of it and your compensation, if any, rest entirely at our discretion." Ms. Black did not reply to the letter. Six months later General Foods introduced a new product that followed Ms. Black's suggestion exactly. Is Ms. Black entitled to compensation? Explain.

3. First Colonial Bank ran an advertisement in a local newspaper which invited investors to "Deposit $14,000 for 3 1/2 years and receive an RCA 20″ color t.v. and $20,136.12 upon maturity. Rate shown is 8 3/4 percent. T.V. carries manufacturer's warranty; deposits are fully insured to $100,000 by FDIC. Substantial penalty for early withdrawal."

   The advertisement contained an error. To get $20,136.12, an investment of $14,000.00 earning 8 3/4 percent had to remain on deposit for four years. Pamphlets on display in the bank's lobby advised this.

   Sally Saver responded to the advertisement and deposited $14,000. She did not see the display. First Colonial gave her the advertised t.v. and a certificate of deposit (CD) redeemable in 3 1/2 years with interest at a rate of 8 3/4 percent. No one advised her of the mistake in the ad. Three and one-half years later, Sally liquidated the CD. She received $18,823.93, representing three and one-half years' interest at 8 3/4 percent. Is the bank liable for the remaining $1,312.19? Explain.

4. Architectural Glass & Metal Co. (AGM), an Indiana company, telephoned Falconer Glass Industries, a New York company, and ordered a special type of glass manufactured by Falconer for use in a construction project in Indianapolis. Over the phone, the parties agreed on quantity, price, delivery, and payment terms. Falconer then mailed to AGM a form confirming the order. The form contained many preprinted terms, including one limiting Falconer's liability for defects in the product to replacement of the defective product or refund of the purchase price, and one requiring that any lawsuits arising out of the order be brought in New York. The product proved to be defective and the defects caused AGM $19,000 in damages. Is Falconer liable? If so, may AGM sue Falconer in Indiana, or must it sue in New York? Explain.

5. William Story made a promise to his nephew, William Story, 2d, that if he would refrain from drinking liquor, using tobacco, swearing, and playing cards or billiards for money until he became 21 years old, then he, William Story, would at that time pay William Story 2d, $5,000. William Story 2d fully performed his part of the agreement. William Story 2d had not been paid when William Story died. The executor of the estate of William Story would not allow the claim of William Story 2d for $5,000. Is William Story 2d's claim for the $5,000 enforceable? Explain.

6. Crabtree entered negotiations with Elizabeth Arden Sales Corp. concerning his employment as a sales manager. Ms. Arden, the corporation president, orally offered Crabtree a two-year contract starting at $40,000 per year, increasing to $45,000 after six months and $50,000 after one year, with an expense allowance of $5,000 per year. Crabtree replied, "Sounds interesting." Ms. Arden then had her secretary write a memo on a telephone order blank that happened to be at hand as follows:

EMPLOYMENT AGREEMENT WITH CRABTREE	
Begin	$40,000
6 months	45,000
6 months	50,000
$5,000 per year expense money (2 years to make good)	

Two days later Crabtree telephoned his acceptance. On his first day at work, a payroll card was made up and signed by the company's general manager. It classified Crabtree as a sales manager and further stated:

First six months of employment	$40,000 per annum
Next six months of employment	$45,000 per annum
After one year of employment	$50,000 per annum

Crabtree received the first scheduled $5,000 pay raise but did not receive the second. When he inquired about it, Ms. Arden fired him. If Crabtree sues, will the contract be enforceable? Why or why not?

7. You own and operate a department store. For many years, you have rented space to Acme Furriers, Inc., to operate a fur concession in your store. Although Acme was a separate company, the appearance given the general public was that it was a department within your store. Unknown to you, Acme contracted with Fur Storage, Inc. (FSI) to provide cleaning and storage services to it. Acme accepted furs from customers in the spring and, for a fee, agreed to clean and store them until the late fall. Acme, in turn, paid FSI to clean and store the furs.

   Acme went bankrupt and closed. Acme's customers came to you to retrieve their furs. You approached Acme's president, who told you about FSI. You then asked FSI for the furs. FSI told you that Acme owed $1,500 for cleaning and storage of the furs. You offered to pay the $1,500, but FSI stated that Acme also owed it $4,500 for other services not involving your store. FSI demanded that you pay the entire $6,000 before it would release the furs. The customers are demanding their furs. The weather is getting colder by the day. What should you do? Explain.

8. Owner contracted with Red Roof Co. (RRC) for a new roof to be constructed on Owner's house for $3,000. The contract specified the type of shingles to be used and the color—asphalt gray. RRC completed the job, but ran out of asphalt gray shingles. It used three other colors—two other shades of gray and a dark blue. As a result, the roof is perfectly sound but Owner thinks it looks terrible. Must Owner pay RRC? Why or why not?

9. Gravel Contractors, Inc. (GCI) was the low bidder for a road construction contract and was awarded the contract by the state of Alaska. GCI's bid was so low because it owned a gravel pit near the site and intended to use gravel from that pit. After GCIs contract was announced, residents living near the gravel pit objected to GCIs hauling gravel from it. The local zoning board ruled that GCIs proposed use of the pit violated local zoning laws. GCI now has to purchase and haul gravel from a site 25 miles away and will incur an additional $20,000 in costs. Instead of making a $10,000 profit on the job, GCI will lose $10,000. Must GCI perform under the contract? Explain.

10. Al's Restaurant leased a storefront from Jane's Realty for three years. The lease provided that Al would pay a monthly rent of $2,000, maintain the premises in good repair, arrange for trash collection, and hold the restaurant open for business at least five days per week. The lease further provided that for any breach, Al's would be liable for $4,000 liquidated damages. Is this provision enforceable? Explain.

6 THE LAW OF INJURIES (TORT LAW)

Learning Objectives

After learning this chapter the student should be able to:

- Distinguish a tort from a breach of contract and a crime.
- Classify various torts under the appropriate headings: intentional, negligent, or strict liability.
- Recite the elements of a variety of torts, and apply them to factual situations involving business operations.

A **tort** is a civil wrong other than a breach of contract. The law recognizes the right of a victim of a tort to recover compensation in the form of money damages from the wrongdoer (tortfeasor).

    A tort is not a crime, although many torts may also lead to criminal proceedings. In a tort action the victim sues to recover compensation from the tortfeasor

TABLE 6–1	**Classification of Torts**	
Intentional Torts	*Negligence*	*Strict Liability*
Intentional wrongdoing	Unreasonable conduct	Vicious animals Defective products Abnormally dangerous activities

for the injury that occurred. In contrast, in a criminal case the government brings charges seeking punishment (usually a fine or imprisonment) against the wrong-doer.

A breach of contract is not a tort. Contract duties arise by agreement of the parties. Tort duties, however, arise by operation of law and exist whether or not a person agrees to them. Tort law reflects society's determination of which injuries should be compensated, which interests protected, and which conduct deterred. In this way the law establishes standards for actions and behavior of people and companies.

Tort law is important to business. Businesses harmed by the wrongful conduct of others may sue to recover damages. When businesses or their agents cause damage to others—whether they are customers, competitors, or strangers—liability may result. Insurance against possible damage awards is a necessary cost of doing business.

When an employee of a business commits a tort, the liability of the business is determined under the principle of vicarious liability or *respondeat superior* (let the master answer). Under this principle a business is liable for the torts of an employee who is acting within the scope of his or her employment. For example, if a pizza delivery driver causes an automobile accident while delivering a pizza, the driver's employer would be responsible for the damages inflicted on the other motorist.

The various types of torts can be divided into three categories: intentional torts, negligence, and strict liability torts (see Table 6–1).

Intentional Torts

Intentional torts are voluntary acts that invade a protected interest. In each of these torts, the tortfeasor intends to do the act that causes injury. The tortfeasor is liable for all reasonably foreseeable harm resulting from that intentional act.

Punitive Damages

Because a high degree of culpability attaches to intentional torts, the victim is entitled to **punitive damages**. These are damages intended to punish the offender, and further compensate the victim for wounded sensibilities. They are damages awarded above and beyond the compensatory damages. Compensatory damages included those for medical expenses, loss of wages, disability and pain and suffering. The amount of punitive damages to be awarded is normally within the province of the jury. Over the years large punitive damage awards have grabbed public attention. In the O.J. Simpson civil case the jury awarded punitives amounting to $25,000,000. The McDonalds' coffee cup spill case was first reported with a punitive damage award of $4 million. However, The United States Supreme Court made it clear in *BMC vs. Gore* that excessive punitive damage awards would be a denial of Due Process.

The following torts, although not exhaustive, are categorized as intentional torts. They include intentional torts against person, property, or both (see Table 6–2).

Battery and Assault

Battery is an unprivileged, unwanted touching of another. Any unwelcome contact, from a slap on the back to a punch in the face, constitutes a battery. Some possess a privilege to commit battery; for example, soldiers in war, and executioners lawfully charged by the sovereign with carrying out the death penalty.

To be liable for a battery, the tortfeasor must intend to touch the other person, an article of clothing that person is wearing, or something the victim is carrying. A flick of another's hat or grabbing at an umbrella the victim is carrying constitutes a battery, although the injury here would ordinarily be slight.

Assault is causing another person to be apprehensive about a battery. Threatening to strike someone or advancing toward another with intent to sexually violate that person is deemed an assault, while the actual touching is the battery.

Intentional Infliction of Emotional Distress

The tort of intentional infliction of emotional distress provides a remedy for conduct intended to unjustifiably upset the victim. Simple insults and indignities do not give

TABLE 6–2	Classification of Intentional Torts
Against a Person	**Against Property**
Battery	Disparagement
Assault	Palming off
Intentional infliction of emotional distress	Interference with contract
False imprisonment	Trespass
Defamation: libel and slander	Nuisance
Deceit	
Invasion of privacy	**Against Property and Person**
	Wrongful discharge

rise to this tort. For the tort to occur, conduct must be outrageous; the perpetrator must intend to cause emotional distress. To recover damages for intentional infliction of emotional distress the plaintiff must actually suffer severe mental distress.

False Imprisonment

False imprisonment is interference with a victim's freedom of movement. A restraint that prevents a person from going where he or she pleases is considered false imprisonment, even if the restraint is accomplished nonviolently. It can take place on an open street or in a store. It is not necessary to actually harm the victim; the tort protects the victim's interest in freedom of movement. The victim of false imprisonment must be consciously aware of the restriction. Hence, an unconscious person or one who is sleeping may not be falsely imprisoned when in those states.

False imprisonment may arise when a merchant detains a suspected shoplifter. However, the law recognizes that merchants have a special interest in protecting themselves against theft. If a merchant reasonably believes that a person has taken goods without paying for them, the merchant is privileged to restrain the person for a reasonable period of time and in a reasonable manner. Restraint beyond what is reasonable to investigate the merchant's suspicions and summon the police, if necessary, destroys the privilege and leaves the merchant vulnerable to a successful lawsuit.

Defamation: Libel and Slander

The tort of defamation protects a person's interest in his or her reputation and good name. Libel is written defamation, while slander is oral defamation. A person who attacks another's reputation or causes another to be held up to hatred, contempt, or ridicule, or to be avoided or shunned, may be liable for the tort of defamation. The tort of defamation requires proof that:

- The tortfeasor made a defamatory statement.
- The defamatory statement identifies the victim to a reasonable reader or listener.
- The tortfeasor communicated the defamatory statement was communicated to a third party.
- The victim's reputation was damaged.

Because the First Amendment of the U.S. Constitution protects the right of free speech, defamation is more difficult to prove when the target of the statement is a public figure. In such cases, the public figure must prove that the tortfeasor knew the statement was false or made the statement in reckless disregard of the truth. In contrast, when the target of the statement is a private person, liability may exist where the tortfeasor negligently publishes a defamatory statement.

Another limitation on recovery for defamation in most states is the requirement that a victim of slander establish actual damage to his or her reputation. However, some statements that are clearly defamatory are presumed to cause damage. These statements are referred to as *slander per se*. The following statements fall under this category:

- A statement adversely reflecting on a person's business, trade, or profession.
- A statement that a person is afflicted with a communicable disease, usually a sexually transmitted one.
- A statement that a person has committed a crime that is morally reprehensible.
- A statement imputing sexual misconduct to a person.

Slanderous statements falling outside the per se category require proof that the statements caused actual damage to reputation, such as loss of business or a contract. Many states afford a presumption of damages for libel.

In some situations, an individual is privileged to make an otherwise defamatory statement. This occurs when the communication serves an important public interest. For example, a former or current employer is privileged to tell a prospective employer about a job applicant's qualifications. However, the privilege can be lost if the statement is made in bad faith. To avoid the danger of running the risk of committing the tort, defamation, many employers simply adopt a policy of providing only a neutral recommendation that states the date of hire, the position(s) held and the date of discharge.

Truth is an absolute defense to the tort of defamation. The burden, however, is on the defendant to prove that the defamatory statements were in fact true.

Deceit

Deceit is a knowing and intentional misrepresentation of a material fact. To recover damages, the following elements must be established:

- A knowingly false representation of a material fact.
- An intent to induce the listener to rely on the representation.
- Justifiable reliance on the representation by the listener.
- Damages to the duped party resulting from such reliance.

Clearly, the range of what can be considered fraud or misrepresentation is great; as the morals of the marketplace change, so does the definition of deceit. For example, in the distant past, negotiations between buyers and sellers were characterized by the notion of *caveat emptor*, or "let the buyer beware." This attitude gave way to an obligation on the part of a seller to inform a buyer of hidden defects. This is particularly true when vendors deal with consumers. This expansion of vendors' obligation of fuller disclosure is an example of law intersecting with high moral values. In commercial transactions between parties on relatively equal bargaining levels, for example, a manufacturer and supplier, the obligation to disclose is not as strict. These parties can generally be expected to investigate and protect their own interests.

Invasion of Privacy

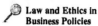

Law and Ethics in Business Policies

This Privacy Rights Clearinghouse link delves into the issues of workplace privacy and employee monitoring.

https://www.privacyrights .org/workplace-privacy-and -employee-monitoring

Most people assume that they have a right to privacy, but very few can describe the dimensions of this right. Tort law recognizes four distinct causes of action for interfering with privacy rights: (1) intrusion, (2) public disclosure of private facts, (3) false light in the public eye, and (4) appropriation.

Intrusion into Seclusion

The more traditional notion of what the right of privacy protects is represented by an intrusion. Tortious intrusions include unauthorized physical entry into another's premises or peering into someone's home or other private premises, eavesdropping, repeated or unwanted telephone calls, or unauthorized prying or access into someone's bank account or other personal affairs. Liability may occur if the nature of the intrusion is such that it would be objectionable or offensive to a reasonable person.

Public Disclosure of Private Facts

Another type of invasion of privacy, public disclosure of private facts, involves disclosing to the public the intimate facts of one's life. Information revealed to the public must not have been publicly known, and the disclosure must be offensive to a person of ordinary sensibility. Private facts that the courts have protected include the public disclosure of an unpaid debt, medical pictures of one's anatomy, and details of one's sexual relations.

False Light

The third form of interference with privacy involves placing someone in a false light in the public eye. A person has the right to be free from having false information publicly disseminated. Although similar to defamation, it is broader and includes acts that would be objectionable to a reasonable person even though they are not necessarily defamatory. Examples of the tort are publicizing that a person is dead when he is in fact not, or that a person heroically rescued people from a burning building when this is untrue.

Appropriation

Tort law prohibits the appropriation or use of the plaintiff's name or likeness for financial benefit without consent. This was the earliest form of privacy protection recognized by the courts. The most common example is the use of the name or picture of a celebrity for business purposes without the celebrity's consent. However, private, unknown people are also protected.

Disparagement

False statements that injure a person's interest in property, as opposed to one's reputation, amount to disparagement. Assume that a patron accuses a butcher of selling spoiled meat. Because this statement tends to injure the butcher's reputation, it would be defamatory. Assume, however, that the patron falsely informs potential customers that the butcher went out of business. This does not directly injure the butcher's reputation; however, it injures the business by keeping potential buyers away from the butcher's business. This statement may constitute disparagement.

Disparagement is harder to prove than defamation. Plaintiffs must prove that the statements were false and malicious and that they resulted in monetary loss by, for example, causing certain customers to avoid dealing with the business.

Palming Off

When an advertiser represents its goods in a way that deceives the average buyer into believing them to be the goods of a competitor, the advertiser is liable to that competitor for palming off. The misrepresentation may involve imitating the trademark, labels, containers, appearance of business, or any other distinctive characteristic of the competitor. Assume a local company that sells cheap wrist watches stamps the name Rolex (a watch of high quality) on the face of its watches and advertises them as such. This would amount to unlawful palming off—a practice that would injure Rolex in two ways. First, it would take away customers who would purchase the watches thinking that they were made by Rolex. Second, it would injure Rolex's image by associating the inferior watch with its name. Here, Rolex could obtain both an injunction restraining the company from misrepresenting its goods and damages for loss of business.

Palming off is not the only type of false advertising that injures competitors. Most often, false advertisements misrepresent the quality, price, or nature of the advertised goods. Some states, and a federal statute, give competitors an action against competitors who falsely advertise in this manner. These false advertisements harm competitors by taking customers away from them.

Interference with Contract

The intentional and wrongful interference with a contract is a tort. The origin of this tort can be traced to *Lumley v. Guy*, an English case decided in 1853.[1] In that case, an opera singer was obligated, pursuant to a contract, to sing at a theater. A competitor of the theater, aware of the contractual relationship, nevertheless persuaded the singer to break her contract. Liability was imposed against the competitor for interference with contract.

Tortious interference of contractual rights is not confined to existing contracts; it extends to potential contracts as well. Hence, it is a tort to prevent a person from obtaining employment, or to impede a business from contracting with customers, or to dissuade a publisher from contracting with an author.

---

[1] 118 Eng. Reprint 749.

Trespass

The tort of trespass is really two torts: trespass to personal property (movables, such as merchandise), and trespass to real property (land).

A trespass to personal property is committed by interfering with someone's right to possess his or her personal property by, for example, taking merchandise for a short time, or harming the goods. The tortfeasor is liable for damages if the victim can prove:

- Interference with the owner's right of possession.
- Intent by the tortfeasor to do the act that constituted the interference.
- Interference caused damage to the owner's personal property.

When the interference with personal property is so great that it deprives the owner of its value, courts find that the tortfeasor converted the property and order the tortfeasor to pay the fair market value of the property to the owner. This constitutes another related tort, known as *conversion*. Common acts constituting conversion are the destruction of property, theft, receipt of stolen goods, and wrongful transfer or retention of property. The owner has the option of demanding the property back or receiving the fair market value at the time of conversion.

Trespass to real property is an unlawful interference with another's land. This tort action protects a landholder's interest in the exclusive possession of his or her properties. A person who physically intrudes on another's property commits a trespass. However, the intruder need not physically set foot on the property to be liable; he or she may be held liable for setting events in motion that cause the intrusion. For example, someone on his or her land who sets a fire to a neighbor's land commits a trespass to real property. A trespass may be committed by a single act or by a continuing presence on another's land.

Nuisance

A nuisance is a substantial and unreasonable interference with the use and enjoyment of an interest in land. A cause of action for nuisance thus protects landholders' interests in the use and enjoyment of their properties. In environmental litigation, nuisance includes interferences in the form of smoke, odor, noise, and vibration.

Trespass and nuisance are distinguishable. A trespass is an invasion of the right to exclusive possession of land, as by entry on it. A nuisance is an interference with the interest in the private use and enjoyment of land and does not require direct interference with possession. For example, the flooding of another's land constitutes a trespass because it interferes with the landholder's interest in possession. In contrast, a noxious odor spewing from a nearby factory smokestack might constitute a nuisance to the neighboring owners' use and enjoyment of their properties. Some courts do not differentiate between such subtleties; the label is not as important as the wrongful action and injury.

When determining whether a nuisance exists, the courts balance various factors—a practice referred to as *balancing the equities*. All landholders' rights to use and enjoy their properties are necessarily subject to the rights of other land-holders to do the same. Consequently, the courts weigh the utility of the conduct of one landholder against the gravity of the harm caused to another. Generally, if the harm outweighs utility, the courts deem the conduct a nuisance. Other relevant considerations are the existence of practical means to avoid causing the harm and the location of the properties.

Wrongful Discharge

Employment relationships are based on contracts. Employees agree to perform services for their employers, who agree to compensate their employees. Most employees are hired for an indefinite period of time. Frequently nothing is said about when, how, or under what circumstances the contract may be terminated.

The traditional rule is that an employment contract of indefinite duration is terminable at the will of either party. If nothing is said about the length of employment, the employee is free to quit, and the employer is free to fire the employee at any time, for any reason, or for no reason at all.

This traditional employment-at-will doctrine has eroded over the years. Courts in most states still agree that an employer has the power to discharge an at-will employee for any reason. However, most states have decided that when an employer fires an employee in a manner that contravenes public policy, how-ever, the employee may recover for the tort of abusive or wrongful discharge. These courts disagree over what constitutes public policy. However, most of the courts that recognize the tort of wrongful discharge require that the public pol-icy be expressed by a constitutional provision or a statute. For example, in one case it was deemed a wrongful discharge for an employer to fire an employee when the employee refused to pump water out of the deck of a boat into the water-way because there was a statute that prohibited such pumping.[2] Some courts allow the public policy to be expressed in a state's common law. Recognition of wrong-ful discharge based upon employer actions that are contrary to public policy is an example of society's concept of morality influencing the law.

Defenses to Intentional Torts

Consent and privilege are two common defenses in intentional tort cases. A defen-dant can avoid liability by proving either that the plaintiff consented to the defen-dant's conduct or that the defendant was privileged to do what would otherwise be an intentional tort.

Whether a plaintiff has consented to the defendant's conduct is determined by the plaintiff's behavior under the circumstances, not by the plaintiff's actual feel-ings. Consent may be expressed. For example, it is common for hospitals to require patients to sign a consent form before undergoing medical procedures. Consent may also be implied by conduct, as, for example, where an employee engages

---

[2] Sabine Pilot Services v. Hauck, 687 S.W. 2d 734 (Tex. 1985).

voluntarily in an employer's drug testing program. Courts inquire into the reasonableness of the consent, and will declare consent ineffective if it violates law or public policy.

Conduct that would otherwise be an intentional tort may nevertheless be privileged. For example, someone acting in self-defense can avoid liability for what would otherwise be a battery. When creating privileges, courts are deciding that the importance of certain conduct outweighs the risks of harm. A privilege is lost if the defendant acts in bad faith.

Negligence

Often damage is caused by unintentional or careless conduct. Under certain circumstances, the injured party can recover damages for the tort of **negligence**. Negligence is unintentional conduct that falls below the standard of care that is necessary to protect others against exposure to an unreasonable risk of a foreseeable injury.

Elements of Negligence

Negligence is conduct that is unreasonable under the circumstances. A plaintiff must prove the following elements to recover against a defendant for the tort of negligence:

- The existence of a duty to exercise the degree of care that a reasonable and prudent person would exercise under similar circumstances.
- A breach of that duty by a failure to adhere to the standard of reasonable conduct.
- The unreasonable conduct was the actual and proximate cause of the plaintiff's injury.
- Actual injury to the plaintiff.

Duty

Before liability for negligence is imposed, a court must first determine that the defendant was under a duty to protect the plaintiff from the injury that occurred. For example, assume a passenger in the front seat of a van is injured when the van collides with a telephone pole. Could the passenger successfully sue the manufacturer of the van for negligence, claiming that the manufacturer had a duty to design the vehicle so that in collisions under 40 mph the passenger would not come into contact with the interior compartment of the van? Should the manufacturer be under a duty to design a crashworthy vehicle? In determining the existence of a duty, a court would weigh the nature and foreseeability of the risk of harm (here, the risk of collisions) against the social utility of the defendant's conduct (here, the social utility of a van) and the costs of taking precautions (here, the cost of redesigning the van).

In the example involving the van, a federal appellate court considered the foreseeability of automobile collisions, but found that it was outweighed by the burden of imposing precautions on the manufacturer, a burden that would require redesigning a van to the extent that it would no longer be useful for its intended purpose as a cargo carrier. The court also noted that imposing such a duty on the manufacturer would drastically increase the price of vans. In the court's opinion, this would have the effect of depriving society of a reasonably priced light-cargo carrier.[3] Thus, when determining the existence of a duty, courts balance as a matter of policy the social value of the parties' interests.

Breach of Duty

In the absence of a statute, the question of whether the defendant breached the duty of care is one that the jury determines (or the judge, if sitting without a jury). A standard of conduct, known as the *reasonable person standard*, is applied. Whether the defendant has breached a duty of care is determined by comparing the defendant's conduct to that of a reasonable and prudent person under the same or similar circumstances. When the defendant is a person with special training, such as a doctor, lawyer, or accountant, the standard takes into consideration the defendant's training. Thus, an accountant is held to the standard of a reasonably informed accountant; a certified public accountant would be held to the standard of a reasonably informed certified public accountant.

Actual and Proximate Cause

The plaintiff must also prove that the defendant's conduct was the actual and proximate cause of the injury. Determination of the existence of actual and proximate cause is a matter for the jury to decide (or the judge, if sitting without a jury).

Actual cause refers to the direct causal connection between the defendant's conduct and the plaintiff's injury. The simplest way to determine whether an injury resulted from the defendant's conduct is to ascertain whether the plaintiff would have been injured *but for* the defendant's action. For example, a landlord's negligent failure to provide a fire escape could cause the death of someone who is thereby prevented from fleeing a fire. However, the absence of a fire escape would not cause the death of someone who suffocated in bed during the fire. When there are several causes of an injury or damage, each defendant whose conduct contributed to the injury can be held responsible for the damage if his or her conduct was a substantial factor causing the injury.

In addition to being the actual cause of the plaintiff's injury, the defendant's conduct must also be the **proximate cause**. A defendant is liable only for those injuries that are proximate, as opposed to injuries that are remote. Proximate cause, thus, has to do with the likelihood (foreseeability) of the injury. If the plaintiff's injury could not be reasonably foreseen by the defendant at the time of the defendant's act or omission, the defendant's conduct will not be considered the proxi-

---

[3] Dreisonstok v. Volkswagen of America, 489 F. 2d 1066 (4th Cir. 1974).

mate cause of the injury. The element of proximate cause requires the plaintiff's injury to be the natural, probable, and foreseeable result of the defendant's conduct.

Injury

Generally, injury includes damage to property or person. A plaintiff who sustains physical injury is entitled to recover for damage, including medical expenses, loss of wages, and even pain and suffering. It may also include injury for loss of consortium, that is the loss of services, society and sex. The establishment of damages for physical or mental injury usually requires the testimony of medical experts. The defendant often has its own medical experts to rebut the plaintiff's medical experts. This "battle of the experts" generally requires the trier of the fact to determine whose expert opinion to believe.

Procedural Doctrines

Two procedural doctrines help plaintiffs prove their case of negligence. The first one, the doctrine of *negligence per se*, employs a statute to establish negligence; the second, the doctrine of *res ipsa loquitur*, employs reason to establish a presumption of negligence.

Negligence Per Se

Negligence may arise as a result of a violation of a statute or regulation. When enacting statutes or regulations, legislatures and agencies sometimes weigh the risk of harm resulting from certain conduct and the conduct's social utility. In many states the violation of such a statute or regulation in certain circumstances is considered **negligence per se**, which means that the violation, by itself, is considered unreasonable. For violation of a statute or regulation to qualify as negligence per se (1) the injured person must be within the class of persons the statute or regulation was designed to protect, and (2) the injury must be of a type that the statute or regulation was designed to prevent. Assume, for example, that a statute prohibits the mislabeling of any drug. From his local pharmacy Jack Plaintiff purchases a drug labeled aspirin; in reality it is a poisonous substance. If Plaintiff becomes ill or dies as a result of ingesting the mislabeled drug, the manufacturer would be negligent per se. Plaintiff is a consumer, a person within the class the statute was designed to protect, and the statute is designed to prevent the very type of injury that occurred.

However, assume that a local health ordinance requires a restaurant to have smooth flooring for drainage and cleaning. One Star Restaurant violates the statute by having corrugated flooring. Jill Patron trips and injures herself when her high heel lodges within a riveted portion of the floor. Here, the violation of the statute would not constitute negligence per se. The statute is for sanitation purposes and is not designed to protect patrons against the injury that befell Jill.

Res Ipsa Loquitur

In some accidents it is not easy for the plaintiff to discover which act or omission led to the injury suffered; the plaintiff can find no direct evidence of negligence.

For example, if a pedestrian is suddenly and unexpectedly struck by a falling brick while passing a construction site, the plaintiff may have difficulty knowing how or why the brick fell. To help deserving plaintiffs, courts have developed a rule of evidence referred to as **res ipsa loquitur** (the thing speaks for itself). Application of the doctrine of res ispa loquitur creates a presumption of negligence. The rule is applicable when the accident would not ordinarily occur without negligence. In addition, other causes—including conduct by the plaintiff—must be sufficiently eliminated by the evidence. As well, the instrumentality causing the injury must be within the defendant's control. Because of this rule, many plaintiffs are able to establish their cases without direct evidence of negligence.

Defenses to Negligence

Even when the plaintiff can successfully prove the elements constituting negligence, defenses may be raised to defeat recovery. Contributory negligence, comparative negligence and assumption of the risk are the more common defenses.

Contributory Negligence

In a few states the plaintiff's contribution to the injury, however slight, will bar plaintiff's recovery. Like negligence, the contributory negligence must be proximate, a contributing cause of the injury. In a few other states, for the bar to occur, the contribution must be substantial. The doctrine of contributory negligence has given way in the vast majority of the states to the doctrine of comparative negligence.

Comparative Negligence

Almost all states have adopted **comparative negligence** as a defense. Under this principle, recovery is reduced by the percentage that the plaintiff's negligence contributed to his or her injury. Assume, for example, that the defendant negligently designed a refuse bin so that it was unstable. The plaintiff purchased the bin and negligently placed it on an irregular and inclined surface. The plaintiff was injured when the bin overturned in a windstorm. If the jury determines that the plaintiff's damages are $40,000, that the defendant was 75 percent at fault, and that the plaintiff was 25 percent at fault, plaintiff's recovery would be reduced by 25 percent to $30,000. In many states the plaintiff would be barred from any recovery if his or her percentage of contribution was greater than or equal to the defendant's percentage of contribution.

Assumption of the Risk

Assumption of the risk prevents a plaintiff from recovering against a negligent defendant, because the plaintiff is held to have assumed the risk of his or her injury. Assumption of the risk consists of a voluntary exposure to a known risk. It differs from comparative or contributory negligence in that contributory or comparative negligence is based on carelessness, whereas assumption of the risk is based on voluntariness—willful exposure to a known risk. A plaintiff who continues to drive an automobile with full knowledge that it has defective brakes is deemed to have assumed the risk of injury that is likely to result. If the plaintiff does not know about the defective brakes but really should, then he or she is guilty of comparative or contributory negligence. Some states have collapsed the doctrine of assumption of the risk into the doctrine of comparative negligence on the basis that one who voluntarily assumes an unreasonable risk is, infact, negligent.

Strict Liability

By emphasizing the factors of intent and reasonable conduct, the areas of intentional torts and negligence use a fault standard to determine liability. The third area of tort law, **strict liability**, does not emphasize fault. Liability is strictly imposed in certain situations even if the actor does not intend to do the act or exercises all reasonable care.

The areas in which strict liability apply are where injuries (1) are caused by a defective product that is unreasonably dangerous because of its defect, (2) result from the keeping of dangerous or vicious animals, or (3) result from abnormally dangerous activities, such as blasting operations.

Abnormally Dangerous Activities

🔍 **Understanding the Private Law Sector**

This link expands on, "What is an Ultrahazardous Activity?"

http://www.legalmatch.com /law-library/article /ultrahazardous-activity -liability.html

Individuals or companies engaged in hazardous activities, such as oil drilling, are strictly liable for any injuries arising from those activities. It does not matter that the offender did not intend to cause injury or was exercising all reasonable care; nor does it matter that the victim may have failed to take reasonable precautions for his or her own protection. Fault does not matter; liability is strictly imposed. It is based upon economics and a policy of risk-spending over society for hazardous activities.

The theory of strict liability serves to reimburse victims harmed by abnormally dangerous activities carried on voluntarily. It treats the risk of injury as a cost of engaging in the activity. Under strict liability, those engaged in abnormally dangerous activities must pay for the damage they cause. Under negligence, the victim would not be compensated if reasonable care were undertaken in the performance of such dangerous activity. Negligence theory provides no recovery to the victims of dangerous yet reasonable activity; strict liability does.

Abnormally dangerous activities involve a serious risk of harm to people, land, or property. The risk is usually one that cannot be eliminated even if the actor exercises great care. Businesses engaged in abnormally dangerous activities bear responsibility for the injuries they cause despite any precautions taken to prevent them.

Activities are usually abnormally dangerous when they are out of place in their locality. Blasting operations and storage of large quantities of explosives or flammable gases are abnormally dangerous when conducted in cities. Such activities pose serious threats to human life and the integrity of property.

Ethical Dilemmas/Issues

Understanding the Private Law Sector

This link discusses insuring against tort liability.

http://tort.laws.com/liability-insurance

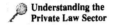

Early one December morning, methyl isocyanate (a lethal gas) leaked from a fertilizer production plant in Bhopal, India. The plant was owned by Union Carbide of India, a subsidiary of Union Carbide, a U.S.-based corporation. The leakage resulted in the worst industrial disaster in history—more than 3,500 people were killed and more than 200,000 people were injured. Union Carbide had insurance of $200 million to cover such a disaster. Because the disaster occured in India, for practical and legal reasons, the survivors and decedents' representatives are forced to sue in India.

India does not provide for jury trials. Its discovery rules are more restrictive than those in the United States. Judgments are generally significantly less than they are in the United States, and the court system is much slower.

Union Carbide had a similar plant with the same design in West Virginia. What are the ethical issues? What should Union Carbide do?

Case

(*Wrongful Discharge*)
DUKOWITZ v. HANNON SECURITY SERVICES

Supreme Court of Minnesota
841 N.W. 2d 147 (2014)

Hannon Security Services (Hannon) hired Jane Dukowitz as a security officer on the night shift. She was then transferred to a temporary day shift position. In early December her supervisor told her that the position would not be open past the end of the month. Dukowitz then informed the supervisor that she would have to apply for unemployment benefits, which she did. Hannon terminated Dukowitz, even though the day-time position became open two days after she applied for the benefits.

Dukowitz sued Hannon for wrongful discharge alleging that Hannon violated the public policy when it terminated her employment in retaliation for her seeking unemployment benefits. The trial court found in favor of Hannon and the court of appeals affirmed. The Supreme Court of Minnesota affirmed the court of appeal decision. There was a strong dissenting opinion.

Justice Stras

The . . . question presented in this case is whether the public-policy exception to the employment-at-will rule applies to a termination resulting from an employee's application for unemployment benefits. . . .

■ ■ ■

In Minnesota, the employer-employee relationship is generally at-will, which means that an employer may discharge an employee for "any reason or no reason" and that an employee is "under no obligation to remain on the job." In *Phipps*, we recognized a narrow public-policy exception to the employment-at-will rule. . . . We . . . limited the cause of action in *Phipps* to discharges resulting from an employee's good-faith refusal to violate the law.

■ ■ ■

Dukowitz interprets *Phipps* more broadly, arguing that the case implicitly recognized an exception to the employment-at-will rule for any violation of a clear mandate of the state's public policy. Dukowitz's interpretation, however, is inconsistent with the reasoning of *Phipps*. In that case, we did not reach "the policy question of whether or not Minnesota should join the three-fifths of the states that now recognize, to some extent, a cause of action for wrongful discharge."

Nelson, the other case relied upon by Dukowitz, was similarly limited in scope. In *Nelson*, we considered the effect of Minnesota's Whistleblower Act . . . on the cause of action we had recognized in *Phipps*. Although we acknowledged some possible overlap between the two, we held that the common-law cause of action that we had recognized in *Phipps* survived the enactment of the Whistleblower Act.

■ ■ ■

Phipps and Nelson, therefore, recognize a common-law cause of action for wrongful discharge only in those circumstances in which a termination is the result of an employee's refusal to do an act that the employee, in good faith, believes to be illegal. Neither case recognizes a broader cause of action that arises every time an employee's termination results from an employer's violation of a clear mandate of public policy. . . .

In light of the limited scope of *Phipps and Nelson*, Dukowitz's claim survives only if we recognize a new cause of action for wrongful discharge for terminations resulting from an employee's application for unemployment benefits. We decline to do so for two reasons. First, as we observed in *Nelson*, this court "has generally been reluctant to undertake the task of determining public policy since this role is usually better performed by the legislature." Although phrased broadly, the statement in *Nelson* reflects our general reluctance to expand a purely legislative statement of public policy by recognizing a new cause of action without any indication that the Legislature intends for us to do so. . . .

Moreover, neither Dukowitz nor the dissent can delineate the contours of the tort that they urge us to adopt, which presumably would make an employer liable whenever a court can identify a clear statement of public policy that the employer has violated by discharging an employee. . . .

Indeed, given the difficulties of defining a clear statement of public policy, it is not surprising that even those states that have adopted a public-policy exception to at-will employment have disagreed on the parameters of the cause of action. . . . The variation and lack of precision in the articulation of the exception reflect legitimate disagreement about how to identify and weigh the many interests at stake in employer-employee relationships. . . .

Second, we decline to expand the public-policy exception to the employment-at-will rule when the Legislature has already delineated the consequences for an employer that interferes with an employee' application for unemployment benefits. . . .

. . . [T]he Legislature has not created a civil action for retaliation in Minnesota's unemployment-insurance statutes. In contrast, the Legislature has explicitly furnished a civil remedy for retaliation in a variety of analogous situations, including when an employer discharges an employee for seeking workers' compensation benefits or for reporting an employer's violation of state or federal law. Recognition of a new common-law cause of action under these circumstances runs the risk of upsetting the careful balance adopted by the Legislature in the heavily regulated area of unemployment insurance.

Accordingly, we decline Dukowitz's invitation to expand the scope of the public-policy exception to the employment-at-will rule to reach a termination resulting from an employee's application for unemployment benefits.

■   ■   ■

Affirmed.
Justice Wright, dissenting.

■   ■   ■

. . . In my view, an employee who alleges that she was discharged from employment because she filed an application for unemployment benefits has a common-law cause of action for wrongful discharge under the public-policy exception to the employment-at-will rule. For that reason, I respectfully dissent.

■   ■   ■

The majority first expresses a "general reluctance" to recognize a new cause of action unless "the Legislature intends for us to do so." Indeed, the Legislature plays a significant—even the most significant—role in formulating the public policy of the state. But the Legislature's role is not exclusive. As a common-law court, we have "the power to recognize and abolish common law doctrines."

We have explained that the common law "is not composed of firmly fixed rules" and "[a]s society changes over time, the common law must also evolve." . . . When applied here, the majority's view—that any extension of public policy is better left to the Legislature—presents an overly narrow view of the common law and abdicates this court's responsibility for developing it.

The majority points to variation in the parameters of the public-policy exception across jurisdictions as evidence of the judiciary's inability to delineate the contours of the exception. . . .

Variation in the exception across jurisdictions indicates very little because each state is free to determine for itself which employment practices, such as retaliatory discharges, violate the public policy of that state. More importantly, the prospect that it might be difficult in some hypothetical future case for us to decide the limits of the public-policy exception does not require us to deny Dukowitz a remedy here. . . .

The second reason offered by the majority is even less compelling. The majority contends that the public-policy exception is inappropriate because "the Legislature has already provided other remedies to vindicate the public policy of the state." . . . In my view, the mere existence of another remedy is not sufficient to crowd out this common-law wrongful-discharge claim. Indeed, [in Nelson] we have specifically held that the existence of a statutory remedy does not preclude common-law wrongful-discharge claims. . . .

. . . Generally, when developing our common law, we look to the common law of other states. Here, the overwhelming majority of jurisdictions recognize the public-policy exception to the employment-at-will rule. I discern no compelling reason to reach a decision that is inconsistent with the prevailing practice of other common-law states.

With the foregoing principles in mind, I now turn to the question that the majority avoids— whether an employer's retaliation against an employee who files for unemployment benefits violates a clear mandate of public policy.

Under Minnesota law, an individual is considered unemployed, and therefore potentially eligible for unemployment benefits, if "(1) in any week that the applicant performs less than 32 hours of service in employment . . . and (2) any earnings with respect to that week are less than the applicant's weekly unemployment benefit amount." Thus, because an employee may qualify for unemployment benefits while still working a limited number of hours, it is possible for an employer to retaliate against an employee who applies for unemployment benefits by terminating the employee altogether. In this case, it is undisputed that Dukowitz was eligible for unemployment benefits at the time of her termination. . . .

■   ■   ■

. . . [W]e have recognized that the extension of unemployment benefits to those who are eligible is "the declared public policy of our state. . . ." To ensure that benefits are available to under—and unemployed workers, the Legislature has forbidden employers from obstructing or impeding an application for unemployment benefits. Indeed, that the Legislature has deemed such conduct criminal underscores the strong public policy at stake and allays any concerns about the judiciary's ability to discern "what employers" decisions contravene a clear mandate of public policy." A common-law wrongful-discharge claim arising from a discharge in retaliation for seeking unemployment benefits would advance that public policy by fostering additional deterrence. . . .

. . . Permitting employers to discharge employees who seek unemployment benefits deters eligible, economically vulnerable individuals— including part-time workers, seasonal workers, or workers who have their hours reduced—from seeking unemployment benefits to which they are statutorily entitled. Moreover, permitting such terminations exacerbates the very problem that unemployment insurance is designed to remedy—economic insecurity.

■   ■   ■

Because I conclude for the foregoing reasons that Dukowitz has a cognizable cause of action for wrongful discharge under the public-policy exception to the employment-at-will rule, I respectfully dissent.

Chapter Extension

For additional material relating to Chapter 6, see p. 263 in the Appendix of Chapter Extension Files.

Chapter Problems

1. Define the following terms:
   a. Tort
   b. Punitive damages
   c. Palming off
   d. Wrongful Discharge
   e. Negligence
   f. Proximate cause
   g. Negligence per se

> *h.* Res ipsa loquitor
> *i.* Comparative negligence
> *j.* Strict liability

2. Luella Davis was indebted to Public Finance Corporation. She informed Public Finance that she was no longer employed, was on public aid, and was unable to make payments on the indebtedness. Over an eight-month period, in attempts to collect the debt, employees of Public Finance called Mrs. Davis several times a week, sometimes more than once a day, and frequented her home weekly. On one occasion an agent of Public Finance telephoned Mrs. Davis at the hospital where she was visiting her sick daughter. On another occasion an employee of Public Finance persuaded Mrs. Davis to write a check on the promise that the check would not be cashed. The employee then informed an acquaintance of Mrs. Davis that she was writing bad checks. On still another occasion a Public Finance employee went to Mrs. Davis's home and took an inventory of her household furnishings, refusing to leave until Mrs. Davis's son entered the room. Public Finance was aware that Mrs. Davis suffered from hypertension and a nervous condition. Both of these ailments were aggravated as a result of Public Finance's conduct. Does Davis have any recourse against Public Finance? Explain.

3. Paul Luedtke and his brother Clarence were employed on Nabors Alaska Drilling, Inc.'s (Nabors) oil rigs. Paul supervised an oil rig crew. Nabors required him to undergo urinalysis as part of a physical exam conducted while off duty. He tested positive for use of marijuana. Consequently, he was suspended and told that he would have to pass two additional tests at monthly intervals to be reinstated. He refused and was fired. Clarence Luedtke, Paul's brother, was fired when he refused to submit to the drug testing. Do Paul and Clarence Luedtke have any recourse against Nabors? Explain.

4. Continental Telephone Company of Vermont (Contel) ran a series of advertisements in Vermont Newspapers featuring certain of its employees. Cynthia Staruski, a sales and service representative at Contel's office in Springfield, Vermont, was featured in one such ad. The ad included a photograph of Mrs. Staruski smiling broadly. In large letters beside her photograph were the words "Hi, I'm Cindy Staruski." Accompanying this was text, attributed with quotation marks to Staruski, describing her job responsibilities and saying that "it has been exciting and reassuring to know that Continental continues to expand its equipment and services to meet its obligations to serve you." Upset by Contel's publication of her name and likeness in this manner, Staruski sued in tort for invasion of privacy. What should be the result and why?

5. Geary was employed as a salesperson for U.S. Steel Corporation. He discovered that one of U.S. Steel's products was defective. He complained to his supervisor, who told him to mind his own business. He then contacted the vice president in charge of marketing for the product, who investigated. The investigation led to the removal of the product from the market and a

reprimand to Geary's supervisor. The supervisor fired Geary "for making me look bad." What cause of action, if any, does Geary have? Explain. What policy should U.S. Steel adopt to handle situations of this nature?

6. Hidell Corporation has offices in an isolated area with an unusually high crime rate. On several occasions, employees have been victims of robbery and other violent attacks. In December, Paul Peters was robbed and severely beaten in an unlit employee parking lot when getting in his car to go to an executive meeting scheduled for 7 P.M. The attacker, an unemployed drifter, was found. What causes of action would Paul Peters have and against whom? Explain. What if anything can Hiddell do to reduce potential liability for such episodes?

7. Hearn ran a classified advertisement in *Soldier of Fortune* magazine (SOF) that read "EX-MARINE—67–69 'NAM VET, EX-DI, weapons specialist—jungle warfare, pilot, M.E., high risk assignments, U.S. or overseas (404) 991–2684." After seeing the ad, Black called Hearn and proposed that Hearn kill Black's wife. Hearn did so. Black's mother-in-law and daughter sued SOF on the theory that SOF negligently published Hearn's classified ad. Analyze the suit under each of the elements of the tort of negligence. What is the result?

8. Hank Gathers played basketball in Los Angeles for Loyola Marymount University, which had an NCAA Division I basketball team. Gathers had a serious heart disorder and was under medication to normalize his heart rhythm. His doctor and coach knew of his medical condition. Nonetheless, Gathers insisted on playing. Because of Gathers's condition, the coach had a special medical device to revive him in the event he fell unconscious. On one occasion, Gathers passed out at the foul line during a game and was revived. During his final game, Gathers fell unconscious after a slam dunk. Efforts to revive him were of no avail and he died. Who is legally responsible for Gathers's death, if anyone? Explain. What should a college do under such circumstances?

9. Kathy Anderson sued Service Merchandise and Sylvania Lighting Services Corporation under the doctrine of res ipsa loquitur for injuries she suffered when an overhead light fixture fell and struck her as she stood in the checkout line of a Service Merchandise store. Service Merchandise has a maintenance contract with Sylvania, which had previously performed maintenance work on the lighting system. Notwithstanding this contract, Service Merchandise employees had occasionally changed light fixtures when they burned out.

The trial court granted summary judgment for Service Merchandise and Sylvania. The trial judge ruled that the lighting system was not under the exclusive control of each defendant and therefore the doctrine of res ipsa loquitur did not apply. No other information indicated any specific negligence by Service Merchandise or Sylvania. For that reason, the trial court dismissed Anderson's action. Anderson appealed. What should be the result?

10. On December 3, 1971, a dam burst at a phosphate mine operated by Cities Service Company in Polk County, Florida. Approximately 1 billion gallons of phosphate slime retained in a settling pond escaped into Whidden Creek. The slime reached the Peace River, killing countless fish and inflicting other damage. What recourse do affected property owners have against Cities Service? Explain.

III THE LEGAL AND ETHICAL ENVIRONMENT OF BUSINESS ORGANIZATIONS

7   THE LAW OF BUSINESS ORGANIZATIONS

Chapter Outline

Learning Objectives

After learning this chapter the student should be able to:

- Compare and contrast the relationships among principals, agents, and third parties.
- Identify the advantages and disadvantages of the major types of business organizations.
- Compare and contrast the partnership and the corporation in the areas of creation, operation, and termination.
- Compare the dissolution and winding-up process for partnerships and the dissolution process for corporations.
- Define the corporate structure and the interrelationship of the corporation's directors, officers, and shareholders.

Businesses are organized under a variety of legal structures. The dilemma faced by a new business is what organizational structure to embrace. The three most common organizational forms are the sole proprietorship, the partnership, and the corporation, although there are variants of these forms. Types of business organizations are compared in Table 7–1.

The sole proprietorship is the simplest form of business organization. It involves one person who owns and operates a business. Although this structure is discussed briefly, the chapter's main focus is on more complex business organizations—the partnership and the corporation. Both of these business forms are examined in terms of creation, operation, and termination.

These organizations—the partnership and the corporation—engage in a variety of activities to carry on business. To do this, they involve agents who act on behalf of the enterprises. Hence, before the discussion of partnerships and corporations begins, it is necessary to examine the law of agency.

Agency

An agent acts on behalf of another. The party for whom an agent acts is the **principal**. Every business organization, whether it be a sole proprietorship, partnership, or corporation, employs agents. Agents ordinarily have authority to bind their principals, and may enter into contracts on behalf of their principals. As well, principals are liable to third parties for some tortious acts committed by agents within the scope of their agency. The agent is liable to the principal for entering into unauthorized contracts and for the agent's torts.

TABLE 7–1   Business Organizations Compared

Organization	Ownership	Management Control	Liability Exposure	Duration	Tax-Paying Entity
Sole proprietorship	Self	Self	Unlimited	Limited	Yes
Joint venture	Venturers	Venturers	Unlimited	Limited	No
Partnership	Partners	Partners	Unlimited	Limited	No
Limited partnership	Limited partners	General partners	Limited for limited partners	Limited	No
Corporation	Shareholders	Board of directors	Limited	Perpetual	Yes
Subchapter S corporation	Shareholders	Board of directors	Limited	Year to year	No
Limited liability company	Partners	Partners	Limited	Perpetual	No

Creation of Agency Relationship

Agency relationships usually arise by mutual consent. For example, a national tire manufacturer may contract with a distributor of wholesale tires to be its exclusive agent within a local geographical area. This creates an agency relationship by contractual agreement.

Not every agency, however, is created so formally. All that is really necessary is assent to an agency relationship. Assume, for example, that Fred asks a neighbor to buy some baseball cards the next time he is at the baseball card store. The neighbor consents. No contract results because the agreement lacks consideration. Nonetheless, the neighbor is Fred's agent by consent.

An agent's authority is derived from the principal. That authority may be express, implied, apparent, or result from a ratification.

Express Authority

Many agencies are created by express direction. For example, a power of attorney is a written instrument that authorizes another to act as one's agent (see Form 7-1).

Many agency agreements are created orally, and they are just as effective as written agency agreements. One of the more common agencies created orally is the employer-employee relationship. Here, the employee acts as an agent of the employer.

FORM 7-1   **Power of Attorney**

I, Henry Hansome, of sound mind, and over the age of eighteen years, do hereby invest in my attorney in fact, Elma Nichol, the following powers:

1. To deposit and withdraw funds from my savings and checking accounts and to sign all checks, deposit slips, and any other instruments necessary to perform such.
2. To sell securities that I presently own and deposit the proceeds from such into my savings account, and to sign all instruments to accomplish such.
3. To manage my real estate; pay taxes, insurance, and mortgage payments; and sign all instruments to accomplish such.
4. To make all medical decisions on my behalf and in my stead, should I become incompetent to do so, including a decision that no extraordinary medical procedures be used to prolong my life when there is no reasonable prognosis for recovery from a comatose or vegetative state.

_____   _____
Witness signatures   Henry Hansome
_____
Witness signatures

On February 12, 2015, Henry Hansome appeared before me and acknowledged his signature.

_____
Notary Public

Implied Authority

Agency relationships may arise by implication. Usually agency authority by implication arises as a natural addition to express authority. For example, assume that an agent is hired to manage a swimming pool. This express authorization gives rise to the agent's implied authority to do all things reasonable and necessary to perform the managerial tasks. The agent could enter into contracts for the supply of chemicals to purify the water, repair the filtration system, and replace unsafe diving boards. This implied authority is derived from the express authorization.

Apparent Authority

In certain cases, a principal is estopped (prevented) from denying that he or she authorized an agent's act. This occurs when the principal clothes an agent with **apparent authority**, thereby giving third parties the impression that the agent is empowered to act.

Assume for example that HVAC Corporation employs service repair persons to repair air conditioning and heating units and to install new ones. Frank Delitch had been having trouble with his air conditioning unit for several winters. He called Delitch to repair his unit. Henry Gable, a long time service repairman for the company was dispatched. His truck was emboldened with the name of the company and writing that said "HVAC, All Brands, Best Prices in Town." Gable's uniform also reflected the same writing. Gable discovered that Frank's unit was not repairable. He wrote up a contract to sell him a new unit. Although Gable did not have the actual authority to negotiate the price of a new air conditioning unit, he in fact, negotiated a price that was actually below his employer's cost. Frank signed the contract. Gable signed on behalf of HVAC. Since HVAC Corp had clothed Gable in the appearance of authority by the lettering on the truck and on Gable's service uniform, HVAC must honor the below cost price.

Ratification

A principal may ratify, or approve, unauthorized action taken by an agent. When ratification occurs, the principal is fully responsible for the agent's action. For ratification to be effective, the principal must have full knowledge of the transaction; the fact of the existence of a principal must have been disclosed to the third party at the time of the unauthorized act.

Assume, for example, that Doakes's auto breaks down and she leaves it at Main Standard gas station, where she is known by the owner. The owner of the gas station mistakenly, without authorization, acts as agent for Doakes and contracts to sell Doakes's auto for $400 to an interested customer. When Doakes learns of the mistake she is at first upset, but thereafter accepts payment. The acceptance of payment is an act ratifying the transaction. Her ratification creates an enforceable contract.

Principal and Agent Relationship

Once an agency relationship exists, the law imposes certain duties and obligations on the parties to that relationship. The agent has certain responsibilities to the principal, and the principal, in turn, owes certain duties to the agent.

Duties of Agent to Principal

Agents are characterized as fiduciaries. A fiduciary holds a position of trust and is held to the highest standard in the law. As fiduciaries, such persons owe to their principals the duties of obedience, care, loyalty, and accounting. An agent who breaches any of these duties is liable for damages to the principal and forfeits any compensation.

Obedience. An agent owes a duty to obey the principal's instructions. For example, an agent may not bid higher on an item at an auction than the principal's instructions dictate. Or, if the principal instructs the agent not to purchase a particular brand of goods, the agent must comply.

Blind obedience, however, is not required. The agent is under no obligation to act contrary to law. Additionally, where a change of circumstances occurs that would jeopardize the principal's interest, the agent may deviate from the principal's instruction. For example, an agent is not required to comply with a principal's direction to store bales of hay at a particular location when a fire has rendered that location unsafe.

Care. The agent must exercise proper skill and care in carrying out agency responsibilities. Anything less than reasonable care subjects the agent to liability for negligence. As is explained later in the chapter, the principal may also be liable to third parties for injury negligently caused by the agent.

Loyalty. The agent owes a duty of loyalty to the principal. The agent may not act against the principal's interest, or in any way engage in self-dealing. A real estate agent may not, for example, secretly purchase the very property he or she is selling for a principal. Moreover, the agent may not represent both parties to a transaction—the buyer and seller—without fully disclosing this representation to each party. Neither may agents take advantage of a business opportunity without sharing that advantage with the principal.

Accounting. Agents owe a duty to the principal to account for all monies generated by the agency. This should be done by accounting statements at agreed-on intervals.

Agents must not commingle their personal funds with those of their principals. Professionals, such as lawyers, accountants, brokers, and others, seriously jeopardize their licenses if they do. Separate trust accounts must be maintained.

Duties of Principal to Agent

The principal owes certain duties to the agent. They include the duty to comply with the contract and to reimburse the agent for expenses and losses incurred as a result of the agency.

Contract Compliance. A principal has the power to breach a contract, but does not have the right to do so. Any breach results in liability to the agent. Assume, for example, that Tri-State Company lists its property for sale with XYZ Realty under an exclusive listing. This means that Tri-State agrees to authorize only its agent to sell the property and collect a commission. Tri-State would breach the exclusive agency contract by selling the property through another agent. If this occurred, XYZ Realty would still be entitled to the commission.

Reimbursement. The agent is entitled to reimbursement (or indemnification) for all expenses incurred as a result of duties performed within the scope of agency authority. Hence, a pilot hired to fly corporate passengers from New York to Atlanta would be entitled to reimbursement for fuel for the trip.

The agent is also entitled to indemnification for any losses incurred while operating within the scope of the agency. For example, assume that an agent is hired to dump a company's wastes at a particular site. The agent is then fined by the city for dumping without a license. The company is required to compensate the agent for the amount of the fine.

Principal and Third-Party Relationship

An agent acts on behalf of a principal. The principal is normally responsible for the acts of his or her agent. Acts engaged in by agents may involve (1) contracts, (2) torts, and (3) crimes. This section examines the principal's legal liability for each of these agency acts.

Contracts

Normally, a principal is liable for contracts entered into by his or her agent. This is true as long as the agent has authority—express, implied, or apparent—to enter into the contract. If, however, the third party is on notice or should reasonably know that the agent lacks authority, the principal would not be bound.

Assume that Dax, on behalf of his employer, Pixie Fish Market, enters into a contract with Fisher whereby Fisher is to sell, and Pixie is to buy, all the salmon Fisher catches. Pixie and Fisher are bound by contract. Assume, however, that before Dax entered into the contract Pixie informed Fisher that Dax was no longer authorized to enter into contracts for Pixie. Any contract after this notification would not bind Pixie.

Torts

The principal is normally liable for the tortious negligent acts committed by the agent within the scope of the agency. In the employer-employee context, this doctrine is known as *respondeat superior* (let the master respond).

Questions often arise as to whether the employee was operating within the scope of employment when the tort was committed. Assume that Hank, a truck driver, is to make a delivery for his employer. Instead of making the delivery, Hank deviates from the course, drives to a bar, and crashes the truck into the bar's plate glass window. Hank's employer would not be liable for the damages because it occurred outside of the scope of his employment, while Hank was on a frolic of his own.

Principals are not ordinarily liable for the acts of independent contractors. An **independent contractor**, a type of agent, must be distinguished from an employee. The employer possesses control over the physical conduct of the employee, and may dictate the means and method by which the employee accomplishes the employer's work. This is not the case with an independent contractor. Here, the principal may not dictate the means and methods of performance, but only the result. For example, assume that Frank hires Louise, a taxicab driver, to take him downtown. Louise is an independent contractor because Frank does not have the authority to control the specifics of the travel, such as the speed and route. Ordinarily, Frank could only dictate the destination. Consequently, Frank, the passenger-principal, would not be liable to a pedestrian whom Louise negligently injured.

Crimes

Generally, the principal is not liable for the crimes of an agent. Of course, a principal who directs the agent to perform an illegal act, or who is aware that the agent is acting criminally but does not act to stop crime, is criminally liable. And if the agent's act is committed in the scope of an illegal business, the principal is liable.

Some states impose criminal liability on business owners for violating certain laws designed to protect the health and safety of the public. For example, in those states a grocery store owner may be held criminally liable should an employee sell adulterated meat, even without the owner's knowledge.

Agent and Third-Party Relationship

The general rule is that an agent is not a party to a contract entered into with a third party on behalf of a principal. This general rule holds true, however, only if the specific identity of the principal is disclosed to the third party. If the principal is only partially disclosed, the agent also becomes a party to the contract. A partially disclosed agency occurs when the fact that the agent is acting for a principal is disclosed, but the identity of the principal is not (see Table 7–2).

TABLE 7–2   **Liability of Principals and Agents for Contracts**

	Disclosed	*Partially Disclosed*	*Undisclosed*
Agent liability		X	X
Principal liability	X	X	X

Liability of Principals and Agents for Contracts

Agents who enter into written contracts must clearly designate their authority to avoid liability. The designation, "H. B. Corporation, by J. Adams, agent," for example, is sufficient to inform the third party that J. Adams is acting only as an agent for an identified principal.

Agents are liable to third parties for their torts. Under the doctrine of respondeat superior, the principal is liable for the negligent torts of the agent committed within the scope of the agency. Hence, both the agent and the principal may be liable to a third party for the agent's wrongs. Their liability is termed *joint and several.* This means that the third party may collect an entire judgment against either the principal or the agent, or a share of the judgment against each.

Termination of the Agency Relationship

A principal-agency relationship may terminate in any number of ways. For example, it may terminate under the terms of the agency contract. Clauses stating, "This agency shall terminate in two years," or "This agency shall end when the sale of the building is complete," specify the moment of termination. Even absent a specific provision for termination in the contract, the parties may always terminate the agency relationship by mutual consent.

At times, a change in circumstances can cause an agency to end. Changes in circumstances resulting in termination of the agency include death of the principal or agent, impossibility of performance, and destruction of the subject matter of the agency.

The agency relationship may also terminate on the unilateral action of either party. Either party has the power to terminate the relationship, even if he or she does not have the right. Simply stated, the law does not force a party to continue in a personal service relationship against his or her will. Unilateral termination, however, may constitute a breach of contract, in which case the nonbreaching party may have an action for damages.

The principal has a duty to notify third parties of the termination of the agency relationship. Actual notice must be given to those who have extended credit or contracted with the principal through the agent. Absent such notice, the agent may still possess apparent authority and continue to bind the principal. Constructive notice of the termination should be given to all other third parties. Constructive notice may be accomplished by publishing the fact of termination in a newspaper that is designed to reach third parties with whom the agent has had contact. Notice is not required when the termination is due to death, insanity, or bankruptcy, as these are already on the public record.

Sole Proprietorship

A sole proprietorship is owned by a single person. This organization is normally a small business, such as the corner grocery.

The principal advantage of the sole proprietorship is that the owner has exclusive control over its operations. The proprietor may make managerial decisions without accounting to board members, partners, or stockholders. Sole proprietors may hire employees to act as agents for the proprietorship. This relationship is governed by the law of agency just discussed.

This form of business also has disadvantages. First, the owner is exposed to unlimited liability. That means the owner is personally liable for all debts of the business. These debts may be incurred as a result of a contract obligation or tort liability. Second, the sole proprietorship is normally not in the best position to raise large sums of money. This is true because its ability to repay loans is limited by the assets of the individual proprietor.

Partnership

The partnership form of organization involves two or more persons and, as such, is more complex than the sole proprietorship. In all states but Louisiana, partnership law is governed by the Uniform Partnership Act (UPA).[1] Partnership law employs the principles of agency law previously discussed.

Definition of Partnership

Decision-making in the legal environment

This U.S. Small Business Administration link provides help so you may think through the process for forming a partnership.

http://www.sba.gov/blogs/six
-elements-every-partnership
-agreement-needs

The UPA defines a partnership as "an association of two or more persons to carry on as co-owners a business for profit." To determine whether a partnership exists, each of the elements of the definition must carefully be examined.

An association implies voluntariness. Two or more persons may associate to form a partnership. Thus, a partnership is consensual and ordinarily formed by a contract.

The partnership is treated as a distinct entity for some purposes and as an aggregate of persons for others. For example, under the UPA the partnership may own, buy, and sell property in its own name. The partnership files a federal income tax return for information purposes. Each partner is an agent of the partnership. These characteristics make the partnership look like a distinct entity.

On the other hand, the partnership does not pay income taxes; rather, the individual partners pay taxes on respective portions of what the partnership earns. Also, a partnership dissolves on the death or departure of a partner. These characteristics make the partnership appear to be composed of an aggregate of persons.

The UPA requires that a partnership consist of "two or more persons." *Person* is defined broadly to include individuals, partnerships, corporations, and other associations.

A fundamental element of a partnership is that the persons must "carry on as co-owners." Evidence of co-ownership of the business includes sharing profits and

---

[1] The UPA was originally proposed and adopted in 1914 by the National Conference of Commissioners on Uniform State Law.

jointly owning property, contributing capital, and jointly participating in managerial decision making.

Finally, the UPA specifies that the business must be for profit. This would exclude ventures formed for religious, charitable, or fraternal purposes.

Formation of Partnership

Under most circumstances, the creation of a partnership does not require a formal written agreement. Partnerships may be formed informally, by handshake, or may arise by implication, as when, for example, the parties share profits and co-manage the business.

Nonetheless, it is desirable to have an agreement in writing, referred to as *articles of partnership*. The existence of such an agreement often helps to avoid conflict by clarifying the rights and responsibilities of the parties. The normal partnership writing covers the matters found in Table 7–3.

In the absence of an agreement, the UPA controls. For example, the UPA states that absent an agreement, partners shall share profits and losses equally.

Rights of Partners

The partnership agreement should be consulted to determine the rights of partners as to each other. In the absence of an agreement covering the specific issue in question, the UPA governs. Rights concerning partnership property, profit sharing, and management participation are discussed next.

Partnership Property

Each partner has a right to possess partnership property in furtherance of the partnership business. The partners have an equal right to use or possess the property for this purpose. Hence, each partners' right in partnership property is indivisible: each has a full right to the whole.

TABLE 7–3   Matters Covered in a Typical Partnership Agreement

---

Names of the partners
Name of the partnership
Location of the partnership
Purposes of the partnership
Duration of the partnership
Allocation of profits and losses among partners
Capital contributions by partners
Partners' rights and responsibilities
Dissolution procedures
Buyout provisions for death or withdrawal

Ordinarily, the initial contributions made by the partners, referred to as *capital contributions,* constitute partnership property. Any additional property acquired by the partnership is also deemed partnership property. Of course, the intent of the parties controls whether an item is owned by a partner personally or by the partnership. Offering some help in this area, the UPA states: "Unless the contrary intention appears, property acquired with partnership funds is partnership property."

Profit Sharing

The UPA provides that the partners share profits and losses equally. This may be altered by agreement. For example, partners may agree to share profits in proportion to their capital contributions. Assume that X contributed $20,000, Y contributed $30,000, and Z contributed $50,000. Under such an agreement, X would receive 20 percent ($20,000/$100,000) of the profits; Y would receive 30 percent ($30,000/$100,000); and Z would receive 50 percent ($50,000/$100,000). The parties similarly could designate the same or a different ratio for loss sharing. Failure to do so would result in the same ratio of loss distribution as that specified for the profit sharing.

Partners are not entitled to salaries, absent an agreement to the contrary. This is true even if one partner does the bulk of the work, or even all of the work. A partner is, however, entitled to reasonable compensation for services rendered for winding up the partnership affairs (as discussed later in this chapter).

Management Participation

Each partner has an equal right to participate in the management of the partnership. As with profit sharing, this may be altered by agreement.

On ordinary decisions, the vote of the majority controls unless the partnership agreement specifies otherwise. Any decision on extraordinary matters, however, requires unanimous consent. Extraordinary matters include a change of the partnership purpose, admission of a new partner, or a decision to relocate the business.

Additional rights enjoyed by partners include reimbursement, inspection, accounting, and assignment. Partners are entitled to *reimbursement* for payments made in connection with the ordinary conduct of the business. This includes, for example, the purchase of office supplies or the payment of taxes on partnership property. Partners are also entitled to be indemnified for personal liability resulting from conducting the partnership business.

Every partner has the right to *inspect* and copy any part of the partnership books. The books contain financial information, minutes of meetings, and other information germane to the conduct of the business.

The UPA grants a partner the right to an accounting. An accounting is a detailed statement of the financial affairs and condition of the business. Partners may desire and demand an accounting when, for example, they have been wrongfully excluded from the partnership business.

Finally, any partner has the right to assign (sell or give away) his or her monetary interest in the partnership. This may be accomplished without the other partners' consent. However, the assignee (the one to whom the property is assigned) does not become a partner unless all partners consent. Hence, the assignee does not obtain any nonfinancial rights in the partnership, such as, for example, the right to management participation. The assignee is entitled only to the respective share of the profits and any other financial rights.

Obligations of Partners

Each partner stands in a fiduciary relationship to each other partner. (This relationship was discussed in the section on agency.) The partner, as fiduciary, owes certain obligations to the partnership, among which is the duty of loyalty. This duty exists between partners. This duty existed within the common law and was expressed well in the words of Justice Benjamin Cardozo in *Meinhard v. Salmon*:

> Joint adventurers . . . owe to one another, while the enterprise continues the duty of the finest loyalty. Many forms of conduct permissible in a workaday world for those acting at arm's length are forbidden to those bound by fiduciary ties. A trustee is held to something stricter than the morals of the marketplace. Not honesty alone, but the punctilio of an honor the most sensitive, is then the standard of behavior. As to this there has developed a tradition that is unbending and inveterate. Uncompromising rigidity has been the attitude of courts of equity when petitioned to undermine the rule of undivided loyalty by the disintegrating erosion of particular exceptions. Only thus has the level of the conduct for fiduciaries been kept at a level higher than that trodden by the crowd. It will not consciously be lowered by any judgment of this court.

The fiduciary duty of loyalty means that one partner may not exclude other partners from the benefits of the partnership property. For example, one partner may not rent out partnership property without sharing the information and the rental income with all partners. Moreover, when partnership opportunities arise, a partner must afford all partners the right to participate. This is true even when the opportunity derives from the partnership business. For example, assume that the partnership is in a relationship with a condominium agency from which it purchases condo units in hotels. When a "deal" is offered by that condo agency to one of the partners, that partner owes a duty of loyalty to the other partners. The partner may not appropriate a partnership opportunity that has arisen through business relations of the partnership. Only after offering the opportunity to the partners, and the partners decline, may the partner "go it alone." The partner must make full disclosure to the other partners of the details of the proposed transaction and not present it in a way so as to discourage other partners. The rule here is the duty of highest loyalty and good faith.

The UPA adopts this "high road" of fiduciary duties. Although the UPA does not expressly adopt the partnership duty of loyalty, the duty has nonetheless been deeply rooted in case law since Justice Cardozo's pronouncement in *Meinhard v. Salmon*. This foundational concept came under attack with the Revised Uniform Partnership Act (RUPA), which declares that "[a] partner does not violate a duty or obligation under the [Act] or under the partnership agreement merely because the partner's conduct furthers the partner's own interest." The RUPA has been adopted by most states and the District of Columbia. The RUPA further states that a partnership agreement may not "eliminate the duty of loyalty . . . but . . . may identify specific types or categories of activities that do not violate the duty of loyalty, if not manifestly unreasonable." The battle lines between "freedom to contract" and fiduciary notions of loyalty are drawn. The battle continues to rage between the state legislatures who have adopted the RUPA and the courts that generally disdain the overthrow of the fiduciary duty of loyalty. It remains to be seen if Justice Cardozo's words were prophetic when he declared that the fiduciary duty of loyalty "will not consciously be lowered by any judgment" of a court.

Relationship to Third Parties

A partnership creates a principal-agent relationship. The partnership is the principal. Partners are agents of the partnership. As such, the previously discussed agency principles are applicable.

Partners are jointly liable on the contracts of the partnership. Joint liability requires that all partners be sued on the contract obligation. The individual partners, however, would not be held liable unless all the partnership assets were first used up to satisfy the indebtedness.

Unlike contractual liability, partners are jointly and severally liable for torts. That means that all partners need not be sued at once. For example, one partner may be sued for the whole amount. Additionally, the release of one partner does not release other partners from liability. As well, partnership assets do not have to be used up first to satisfy the judgment; the partners are personally liable. Any partner, however, who is required to pay on the judgment and who did not personally commit the tort, may recover against the partner(s) who committed the tort.

In some cases, partner and partnership liability to third parties may arise by estoppel, or **apparent partnership**. This may occur under two circumstances. First, a person (apparent partner) may represent that he or she is a partner when in fact this is not true, and the partnership has no knowledge of the representation. If a third party, in reliance on this representation, extends credit to the partnership, the apparent partner would be liable for any injury the third party sustains.

Second, a partner may have knowledge that a nonpartner is misrepresenting himself or herself as a partner. Any partner with such knowledge who consents to the misrepresentation is liable to third parties who sustain injury as a result of reliance on the representation.

Termination of Partnership

Termination of a partnership is a legal process that involves two stages: dissolution and winding up.

Dissolution

The UPA defines dissolution as a "change in the relation of the partners caused by any partner ceasing to be associated in the carrying on . . . of the business." Some dissolutions are merely technical. They occur, for example, when a partner dies or retires. These events result in a dissolution because there is a change in the relation of the partners. However, in most of these cases, the surviving partners wish to continue the business; the dissolution is only a bookkeeping entry whereby a new partnership is formed. In the absence of agreement, the UPA provides that a retiring partner or the estate of a deceased partner is entitled to the value of his or her share in the partnership plus interest or, in lieu of interest, profits.

The partnership agreement may designate a date for termination, or the partners may at any time mutually agree to dissolve the partnership. In either case, dissolution occurs and the liquidation process begins.

A partner may seek to dissolve the partnership by obtaining a court decree. A court issues the decree if a partner is judicially declared to be insane or is otherwise incapable of performing the partnership duties; a partner is guilty of impairing the ability of the business to continue; or where it is impractical to continue the business, as when the partners are constantly unable to cooperate and make decisions.

When a partnership dissolves for any reason other than death of a partner, illegality or bankruptcy, notice must be given to third parties. Specific notice must be given to those creditors with whom the business has dealt. Constructive notice, by publication in a newspaper distributed in the area of the business, must be given to all other third parties. Failure to give proper notice may result in liability for unauthorized contracts and debts.

Winding Up

The winding-up process involves the liquidation of assets and distribution of its proceeds. The UPA establishes the rules for distribution of assets in the following order: (1) to creditors other than partners; (2) to partners who are creditors; (3) to partners to repay capital contributions; and (4) to partners for profits. In the event of insufficient partnership assets to pay creditors, the partners must contribute the amount necessary to satisfy the liabilities.

Difficulties may arise when assets are insufficient to satisfy partnership debts and when the partners are indebted to personal creditors. The general rule is that partnership creditors have first priority on partnership property and personal creditors have first priority on partners' property.

Limited Partnership

The basic disadvantage of the general partnership is that it subjects all partners to unlimited personal liability. However, all state except Louisiana have adopted legislation affording an alternative to the general partnership limiting the liability of some partners. This alternative is called **limited partnership** and is governed in these states by the Uniform Limited Partnership Act (ULPA).[2] Under this uniform act, the partnership consists of general and limited partners. General partners manage and control the partnership and they are liable without limit. Limited partners enjoy limited liability, as long as they do not participate in the management or control of the partnership and as long as they comply with state law.

Limited partnerships may be formed only by compliance with the state statute. This requires the filing of a certificate of limited partnership with a state agency, often the secretary of state. The certificate contains the name of the partnership, its purpose, and its location; the names of partners; and other information.

Limited partnerships are usually formed for investment purposes. The limited partners are the investors. The partnership may be formed for the purpose of, for example, erecting an outlet mall or drilling for oil. As members of a partnership, the partners enjoy tax advantages.

The limited partnership involves passive investors who are like shareholders in a corporation. Consequently, this form of business ownership, like the corporate form, creates securities questions.

Corporations

The corporate form of business has existed in some form as far back as the days of the Code of Hammurabi (about 1750 B.C.). Its early usage, however, was restricted to the government and the church. Later, the sovereign, through special legislation, chartered private corporations to perform trade. In the United States, corporations were introduced in the 18th century and since then have been growing in numbers and popularity. Today, corporations are a dominant institution in our economy, accounting for about 90 percent of the gross national income.

---

[2] Since its adoption by the National Conference of Commissioners on Uniform Laws in 1976 ULPA has undergone amendment in 1985 and 2001.

Characteristics of Corporations

Corporations are distinct from sole proprietorships and general partnerships in several respects (see Table 7–1). First, a corporation is a separate legal entity for all purposes. It is an artificial being created by legislation. As such, a corporation can purchase, hold, and sell property in its own name. It enters into contracts in its own name. It can be sued and can sue in its own name. It is a tax-paying entity.

Second, a corporation is not mortal; theoretically, it has a perpetual existence. A partnership certainly terminates at the death of the last partner. A corporation, in contrast, is not dependent on the life of particular individuals for existence. Corporations continue until dissolved, merged, or otherwise terminated.

A third distinct characteristic of the corporation is that the owners of the corporation, called *shareholders,* enjoy limited liability. This is a prime feature of the

---

Ethical Dilemmas/Issues

As a successful tire salesperson for Swift Wholesale Tire, Inc., Louis Rosenmund called on Warren Hubbard, manager of the King Tire Store. On one visit, Rosenmund told Hubbard that the owner of the Tough Tire Store in Westerville wanted to sell his store due to a lack of business. Hubbard replied: "Louis, with your sales ability and my business judgment, we could turn that business around. I'll put up the money to buy the business, if you will manage the daily operations. You can take a monthly salary of $3,500, and the rest of the profits will be ploughed back into the business. We can split the profits later. Since we'll have to act quickly, I'll go ahead and buy the property. The incorporation papers will be filed as soon as possible after the purchase."

Rosenmund quit his $40,000-per-year position with Swift and started working at the Tough Tire Store. Hubbard purchased the store and named himself owner on the title. Rosenmund had business cards and newspaper advertising printed that included both his name and Hubbard's under the name of the business. Three months later, the Tough Tire Store was a success.

Whenever Hubbard visited the store, Rosenmund asked about the corporation papers. Hubbard's response was vague. Finally, Hubbard told Rosenmund to meet him at the office of Richard Stone, an attorney, who opined that Rosenmund was an employee and that Hubbard had no additional obligation to him.

When Rosenmund arrived, Stone introduced himself as Hubbard's attorney. He told Rosenmund that his services as an employee of Tough Tire were no longer required.

What are the ethical issues? What should Rosenmund have done to protect himself legally.

corporation that makes it attractive to investors. Unlike general partners, a shareholder can lose only what he or she invests. Creditors cannot, under ordinary circumstances, reach the personal assets of the shareholder to satisfy debt. In this respect, shareholders resemble limited partners.

A fourth important characteristic of the corporation is the ease of transferring ownership interests. Sale of a partnership normally involves a detailed process of valuation and an interruption of the affairs of the partnership. A corporation's ownership, represented by shares of stock, may be bought and sold freely without business interruption.

A fifth characteristic of the corporate form is the separation of ownership from management. Shareholders always own the corporation but often do not manage it. This separation in functions between investment and management makes corporations subject to the securities laws.

Sixth, and perhaps an undesirable aspect of the corporation, is that it pays taxes on its earnings. Then, when it distributes dividends to its stockholders, they pay taxes on those earnings. This results in double taxation, which has led many small corporations to elect the form of subchapter S status.

A subchapter S corporation is a creation of the tax laws. It is treated as a partnership for purposes of taxation. Hence, only the shareholders are taxed on earnings, not the corporation. This type of election is available only to corporations that have 100 or fewer shareholders, and all shareholders must elect the subchapter S status. To qualify for favorable subchapter S treatment, a corporation must strictly adhere to IRS filing guidelines.

Finally, the corporate form requires compliance with an array of formalized procedures. Incorporation can be very costly as a result. Also, government more closely supervises corporations than partnerships or sole proprietorships. Each state has detailed statutes covering the regulation of corporations.[3]

Business and Government Interface

These links help determine what state to incorporate your business.

http://www.sba.gov/blogs /which-best-state -incorporate-your-brick-and -mortar-or-online-business; https://www.incorporate.com /choosing_a_state.html

Creation of Corporations

The formation of a corporation is controlled by state statutory law. Normally, promoters come together to form a corporation. They handle the plans for financing the corporation and draw up the corporate charter, referred to in many states as the *certificate,* or *articles, of incorporation* (see Form 7–2).

Promoters involve themselves in the sale of stock subscriptions and in contracting for loans, goods, and supplies. The promoters are normally personally liable for these contracts because the corporation is not in existence during this state of formation. After the corporation forms, however, it may adopt the promoters' actions and agree to indemnify them.

The next step is to file the articles of incorporation with the designated state office, usually with the secretary of state. This is accomplished by incorporators

---

[3] About one-half the states have adopted the Model Business Corporation Act (MBCA) as approved by the National Conference of Commissioners on Uniform State Law (NCCUSL) and the House of Delegates of the American Bar Association (ABA), or a revision of that act, in whole or in part.

who may be the same persons as the promoters. Articles of incorporation normally include the name of the corporation, principal place of business of the corporation, purpose of the corporation, powers of the corporation, names of incorporators, amount and types of authorized stock, and designation of an agent of the corporation who is to receive all official papers.

After the state receives the filing and issues a charter, the first shareholders' meeting occurs. At that meeting stockholders participate in three events: They (1) receive stock certificates, (2) elect a board of directors of the corporation, and

---

FORM 7–2   **Certificate of Incorporation**

The undersigned, desiring to form a corporation for profit, do hereby certify:

First.   The name of the corporation shall be TransAir Mobile, Inc.

Second.   The principal place of business will be in City, State.

Third.   The purposes for which said corporation is formed are

1. Manufacturing air mobiles for use as public transportation within cities.
2. Marketing the concept of air mobiles as a more efficient form of public transportation.
3. Lobbying cities, counties, and other governmental agencies in attempts to influence them to adopt air mobiles as a major form of city transportation.
4. Doing all things necessary and lawful to accomplish these purposes.

Fourth.   The following persons shall serve as interim directors until the first meeting called to elect a board of directors:

Dr. Angela Moore

Dr. Angela Moore

Laura Williams

Laura Williams

Nelson Odis

Nelson Odis

Fifth.   The corporation shall be authorized to issue 1 million shares of no par value common stock.

In witness whereof, we, the incorporators, subscribe our names this 5th day of January, 2015.

Ruth Anne Hills

Ruth Anne Hills

Constance Rivers

Constance Rivers

Howard Randal

Howard Randal

(3) adopt a set of bylaws to govern the operation of the corporation. The next meeting is that of the newly elected board of directors. The board elects officers and covers any other matters necessary to begin business.

After all of the procedures for formation of the corporation have been completed, a *de jure* corporation exists. Neither the state nor other parties may challenge its existence. At times, although the incorporators make a good-faith attempt to comply with the statute, they fail. In these cases, a court may find that a *de facto* corporation exists, that is, even though there has not been full compliance, nonetheless it is treated as a corporation. This may occur if, for example, the incorporators failed to pay the filing fee.

To exist, a *de facto* corporation must act as a corporation. A *de facto* corporation may not be challenged by any parties except the state. Shareholders in a *de facto* corporation enjoy limited liability.

When an organization substantially deviates from the statutory mandated procedure, it is neither a *de jure* nor a *de facto* corporation. Many states require the filing of articles of incorporation before a corporation comes into being. Even here, however, it is still possible for a court to treat a business which has not filed its articles as a corporation under estoppel principles. For example, a business that holds itself out as a corporation and incurs debts as a corporation but is not a corporation is not allowed to deny its corporate existence for purposes of avoiding repayment of the debt.

Sometimes a corporation is used for the exclusive purpose of hiding the assets of shareholders, and thereby shielding them from personal liability. Often, these organizations do not act like corporations but are only such in name. They are merely the alter ego of the shareholders. For example, in one case, the owners of a taxicab company incorporated the operation of each taxicab. They did not have board of directors' meetings, keep any minutes of the "corporations," or even keep separate financial books for each "corporation." The scheme was a sham to protect the assets of the taxicab company from creditors. In such cases, creditors are able to **pierce the corporate veil** and hold shareholders personally liable for the business's debt.

Types of Corporations

Corporations may be classified in a number of ways (see Table 7–4). Some corporations are domestic. A corporation is considered domestic within the state in which it is incorporated. It is considered foreign when transacting business in any other state. Transacting business does not include merely maintaining bank accounts, holding directors' or shareholders' meetings, or borrowing money. Each state regulates foreign corporations doing business within the state. States usually require that the corporation register in the state and obtain a certificate of authority from the secretary of state. Failure to do so may result in criminal penalties and limitations on the corporation's right to enforce its contracts.

Public corporations are established by the government. For example, a local municipality may incorporate. The U.S. Postal Service is an example of a federal public corporation.

Quasi-public corporations are public service companies, such as public utilities. Although they are private, the high degree of government regulation and protection makes them public in nature. An example would be a public utilities corporation, e.g., a gas and electric company that services the public.

Private corporations are those established for private interests and include the bulk of existing corporations. Private corporations may further be divided between nonprofit and profit. Nonprofit corporations are formed for charitable or religious purposes. Profit corporations are usually formed to carry out business for profit.

Private corporations for profit may be further subdivided into closely held corporations and publicly held corporations. A corporation owned by one or a few shareholders (who normally have family or other close ties and also manage the business) is termed a *closely held corporation*. These corporations do not publicly offer their stock. Ninety percent of all private-profit corporations fall in this category. The *publicly held corporation,* in contrast, has a number of unrelated shareholders who are passive investors; they do not actively manage the company. The shares of stock are traded freely on stock exchanges.

Some corporations, however, do not fall in either group. They are too small to be publicly held and yet they are larger than closely held corporations.

The professional corporation has been legalized by every state. Until the 1960s, lawyers, doctors, accountants, and other professionals could not incorporate. They could not take advantage of certain corporate tax breaks and pension benefits. Professional corporation statutes now allow them to do so; however, these professionals are still personally liable for their wrongful acts.

TABLE 7–4   **Types of Corporations**

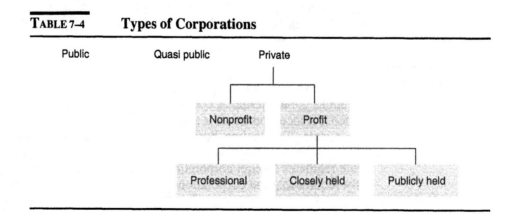

Corporate Management

Shareholders elect a board of directors to manage the corporation. The board, in turn, delegates the day-to-day operations to officers. The directors and the officers comprise the management of the corporation.

Directors

The articles of incorporation normally list the initial board of directors that serves until the first shareholders' meeting. At that meeting, shareholders elect a new board or, as often is the case, reelect the same board.

State statutes, the articles of incorporation, and bylaws may establish eligibility requirements for board membership. For example, the corporation's bylaws may require that a board member own stock in the company or be a resident of the state of incorporation. In the absence of such restrictions, anyone is eligible to be elected to the board of directors.

Ordinarily, board members serve one-year terms. This, however, is also governed by the bylaws. Although boards normally consist of at least three members, some states permit as few as one board member.

Directors must meet regularly. Some boards meet only once a year, others monthly, and still others more frequently. A quorum of board members must be present to hold a meeting. The number necessary for the quorum—normally a majority—is designated in the bylaws. Bylaw provisions may permit the board to make decisions by telephone or by writings through the mail.

The board of directors establishes the policy of the company and is responsible for guiding the company in a manner consistent with that policy. Other decisions made by the board include declaring dividends, proposing amendments to articles of incorporation and bylaws, proposing candidates for the board, and removing officers.

Commonly, some boards delegate some of their powers to executive committees. Executive committees may be composed of board members, officers, and others. They normally relieve the boards of detail work by studying alternatives and making suggestions. For example, the board may decide to implement a pension/profit-sharing plan and ask the executive committee to research alternatives and come up with a proposal.

Directors stand in a fiduciary relationship to the corporation. They must act with loyalty and due care in their actions and decision making. They may not act in their own self-interest; in all business relationships with the corporation they must make full and fair disclosure. Where a conflict of interest arises, a director may not vote on the issue that is the subject of conflict.

Board members are protected in their decision making by the **business judgment rule**. The business judgment rule, when applicable, affords board members great latitude in their decision making. This rule is designed to encourage board members to freely make difficult decisions, free from the fear of liability, even should those decisions, in hindsight, turn out to be harmful to the corporation. In effect, courts recognize their limitations in reviewing business decisions and

Decision-making in the legal environment

Business and government interface: These links explain various board governance and management styles.

http://garberconsulting.com /governance%20models%20 what%27s%20right.htm; http://papers.ssrn.com/sol3 /papers.cfm?abstract_id =1323124 defer to the company directors who are presumed to act in the best interests of the company. For the business judgment rule to be applicable, the board must have made an informed and rational decision, free from conflicts of interests.

Officers

Officers of the corporation are appointed by the board of directors pursuant to the bylaws. They are responsible for implementing the policies of the board and for the oversight of the day-to-day operations of the business. Officers include a president, vice president, secretary, and treasurer. Large corporations may have a number of vice presidents, including such specialized officers as vice president–marketing, comptroller, and financial secretary.

   Officers are agents of the corporation, and, as such, may bind the corporation. Like directors, officers owe fiduciary duties to the corporation.

Shareholders

🔍 **Decision-making in the legal environment**

This article from an International Journal of Leadership Studies link explains the leadership role of the Board chairperson through a team approach.

https://www.regent.edu/acad/global/publications/ijls/new/vol3iss1/gabrielsson/GabrielssonHuseMinichill_IJLS_V3Is1.pdf

The publicly held corporation is usually financed by issuing securities to investors, known as *shareholders*. Of the various classifications of shareholders, the most common distinction is between common stockholders and preferred stockholders. A primary difference between the two is that, ordinarily, preferred stockholders are entitled to receive their dividends before common stockholders and, on dissolution, preferred stockholders are entitled to distributions of assets before common stockholders.

Voting

Some stockholders have voting rights. Other stockholders may lack those rights or only be entitled to vote on extraordinary matters.

   At the annual shareholders' meeting, the voting members elect directors and vote on other matters of corporate concern. There are two principal methods for voting for directors: straight and cumulative.

   Under the straight method, each shareholder is entitled to one vote per share per director's position. Each vacant director's position is voted on at a time. The second method, cumulative, affords each shareholder one vote times the number of shares owned times the number of directors' vacancies to be filled. The election for all board members takes place at one time. For example, assume five vacant board positions must be filled. Harriet owns 1,000 shares of stock. She has 5,000 votes (1 x 1,000 x 5). She may vote the entire 5,000 shares for one candidate, or she may split her votes in any combination among several candidates. Cumulative voting gives minority shareholders the chance to elect some members(s) to the board.

Dividends

Dividends are portions of corporate earnings distributed to shareholders. They are declared by the board of directors. A board maintains almost absolute discretion to declare or not declare dividends. It may not, however, declare dividends if the corporation is insolvent, or if the declaration would push the corporation into insolvency. In contrast, it may not refuse to declare dividends in bad faith—for example, to squeeze out minority shareholders.

Dividends may be in the form of cash or stock. Cash dividends are the most common type of dividend. They increase the wealth of the stockholder and are taxable to the receiver. Stock dividends may be declared by the board of directors. For example, a 10 percent increase in stock may be declared and distributed. In such a case, a shareholder who owns 100 shares would receive 10 additional shares. This does not change shareholders' percentages of ownership of the company; although a stockholder's net worth may be increased, there is no immediate taxable gain.

The stock split is sometimes confused with a stock dividend. In a stock split, the existing shares are divided, for example, two for one. A shareholder receives two shares for every one he or she owns. Again, this does not give the shareholder any additional interest or even theoretically increase net worth. If the stock is selling for $100 a share, in a two-for-one split the value of a share is theoretically reduced in half to $50 a share (although in reality the market value is usually a little higher). The prime reason for issuing a stock split is to make the stock more affordable to more people, thereby stimulating a flow of capital into the corporation.

Preemption

Shareholders may be granted **preemptive rights** by the articles of incorporation. Preemptive rights ensure that existing shareholders may maintain their proportionate interest in the company. They require the corporation to offer new shares to existing shareholders before offering them to the public. Assume that Phil owns 100,000 shares in a corporation that has 1 million shares outstanding. Phil owns 10 percent of the company. Now assume that the company desires to raise more capital and does so by issuing 1 million new shares. If Phil does not have a first right to buy a proportional number of shares, his interest in the company could be diluted to 5 percent. If, however, Phil has preemptive rights, he would be entitled to purchase 100,000 shares and thus preserve his percentage of the relative ownership interest (10 percent). Of course, preemptive rights do not help Phil if he cannot afford to purchase the shares.

Inspection

Stockholders have the right to inspect the books and records of the corporation; this includes the shareholders list, the minutes of meetings, and financial records. The one qualification on this right is that the shareholder must show a proper purpose. The purpose must be related to the status of a shareholder. It would not be a proper purpose if the shareholders list is to be used to buttress the mailing list for one shareholder's personal business. It would be proper, however, if the shareholder's purpose is to gain control of the company by soliciting proxies.

Suits

Shareholders may sue the corporation individually or on behalf of the corporation. A shareholder who has been injured by wrongful corporate acts may sue the corporation. These acts may include a refusal to permit inspection of the shareholders list and illegal inside trading.

Derivative actions to recover monies on behalf of the corporation may be filed by individual shareholders when the board of directors refuses to act. Assume one of the directors has illegally absconded with company monies. Should the majority of the board refuse to sue to recover, any shareholder would have the right to sue on behalf of the corporation. Any recovery would directly inure to the benefit of the corporation.

Dissolution

Decision-making in the legal environment

This Internal Revenue Service link provides a practical checklist for closing a business.

http://www.irs.gov/Businesses /Small-Businesses-&-Self -Employed/Closing-a -Business-Checklist

In theory, a corporation can live forever, although it can and does expire under various circumstances. The termination of corporate existence is referred to as *dissolution*. Dissolution may occur voluntarily or involuntarily.

Voluntary dissolution occurs when the corporation files a certificate of dissolution with the secretary of state. This normally requires both board of directors' and shareholders' approval. The main reason for voluntary dissolution is unprofitability of the company. Some profitable corporations, however, voluntarily dissolve to fend off hostile takeovers.

Involuntary corporate dissolutions are accomplished by administrative or judicial process. A corporation's failure to comply with certain administrative requirements, such as filing of forms, payment of taxes, and maintaining a statutory agent, may result in an action by the state attorney general to dissolve the corporation. Additionally, shareholders may file suit seeking dissolution of the corporation under circumstances where, for example, there is gross mismanagement or unfair treatment of shareholders.

On dissolution, the board of directors, or in some cases a court-appointed trustee, must wind up the affairs of the corporation. This entails liquidating the corporate assets and distributing the proceeds, first to creditors, and then to the shareholders.

Limited Liability Company

Business and government interface

This U.S. Small Business Administration link answers the question, "How and Why Choose an LLC?" as a form of business organization.

http://www.sba.gov/content /limited-liability-company-llc

The newest type of organization on the business scene is the **limited liability company (LLC)**. All states have adopted the LLC form of business organization, with variations. The LLC is a hybrid of the partnership and the subchapter S corporation, selecting the best characteristics of each. Like the subchapter S corporation, its owners enjoy limited liability, without, however, the restriction of number of owners and the necessity of electing the status annually. Like the partnership, the LLC avoids double taxation, and unlike the limited partnership there is no restriction on control and management of the business.

There are, however, some practical limitations. First, some states place restrictions on the transfer of interests, requiring unanimous agreement for the transferee to have management input. Additionally, jurisdictions that do not have LLC statutes may not recognize the limited liability aspects of an LLC transacting business in that jurisdiction.

Case

(*Business Judgment Rule*)
FEDERAL DEPOSIT INSURANCE CORPORATION V. LOUDERMILK
Supreme Court of Georgia.
2014

The Federal Deposit Insurance Corporation (FDIC) sued nine former officers and directors of the bank, alleging that they were negligent with respect to the making of loans, which led the bank, to sustain nearly $22 million in losses. The defendants moved to dismiss the lawsuit, arguing that the business judgment rule relieves officers and directors of any liability for ordinary negligence. The FDIC responded that such a business judgment rule is not part of the common law in Georgia, and even if it were, it does not apply to bank officers and directors, insofar as the statutory law in Georgia explicitly requires bank officers and directors to exercise ordinary diligence and care. The United States District Court for the Northern District of Georgia certified the following question to the Supreme Court of Georgia:

Does the business judgment rule in Georgia preclude as a matter of law a claim for ordinary negligence against the officers and directors of a bank in a lawsuit brought by the FDIC as receiver for the bank?

Justice Blackwell.

. . .The business judgment rule is a fixture in American law, and it is a settled part of the common law in many of our sister states. But defining the rule is "no easy task," insofar as the particulars of the rule may vary a bit from one jurisdiction to another. Nevertheless, we find a classic statement of the rule in [a New York case]:

> Mistakes in the exercise of honest business judgment do not subject the directors to liability for negligence in the discharge of their fiduciary duties. . . . The directors are entrusted with the management of the affairs of the [corporation]. If in the course of management they arrive at a decision for which there is a reasonable basis, and they act in good faith, as the result of their independent judgment, and uninfluenced by any consideration other than what they honestly believe to be for the best interests of the [corporation], it is not the function of the court to say that it would have acted dif-

ferently and to charge the directors for any loss or expenditures incurred.

■   ■   ■

The question is frequently asked, how does the operation of the so-called business judgment rule tie in with the concept of negligence? There is no conflict between the two. When courts say that they will not interfere in matters of business judgment, it is presupposed that judgment—reasonable diligence—has in fact been exercised. A d[i]rector cannot close his eyes to what is going on about him in the conduct of the business of the corporation and have it said that he is exercising business judgment. Courts have properly decided to give directors a wide latitude in the management of the affairs of a corporation provided always that judgment, and that means an honest, unbiased judgment, is reasonabl[y] exercised by them.

■ ■ ■

As the rule pertains to the liability of officers and directors for money damages, it distinguishes between the merits of their business decisions, on the one hand, and the basis of those decisions, on the other. If an officer or director has honestly exercised "judgment" with respect to a business matter—that is, if her decision was made in a deliberative way, was reasonably informed by due diligence, and was made in good faith—the wisdom of the judgment cannot ordinarily be questioned in court. . . . So understood, the rule reflects the principle that managing the affairs of a corporation is a matter committed by law to the discretion of the directors, the reality that the making of profits involves the taking of some risks, and the recognition that businesspeople generally are more competent than judges to exercise business judgment.

Although this Court never has spoken of the "business judgment rule" in so many words, we find an implicit acknowledgment of the rule in a number of our decisions. At common law, corporate officers and directors in Georgia owed a duty to exercise ordinary care. The same was true of bank officers and directors. But in several cases in which business decisions by officers and directors were alleged to be negligent, this Court distinguished between . . . cases in which a business decision was assailed for [the] way in which it was made . . . and those in which the merit alone of the decision was disputed.

■ ■ ■

Although our decisions at common law speak in terms of a general duty on the part of officers and directors to exercise ordinary diligence and care, they do so mostly with respect to the way in which business decisions are made, not the wisdom of the decisions. The cases suggest that, if the only dispute is about the wisdom of a business judgment—an "exercise of discretion—the law at least would require something more than a mere want of ordinary care to establish liability .... But whether a business decision was, in fact, an exercise of "judgment"—whether it was a product of deliberation, reasonably informed by due diligence, and made in good faith—is open to judicial scrutiny. . . . In this sense, our decisions at common law about the liability of officers and directors for money damages implicitly acknowledge the business judgment rule.

■ ■ ■

From our precedents, we conclude that the business judgment rule is a settled part of our common law in Georgia, and it generally precludes claims against officers and directors for their business decisions that sound in ordinary negligence, except to the extent that those decisions are shown to have been made without deliberation, without the requisite diligence to ascertain and assess the facts and circumstances upon which the decisions are based, or in bad faith. Put another way, the business judgment rule at common law forecloses claims against officers and directors that sound in ordinary negligence when the alleged negligence concerns only the wisdom of their judgment, but it does not absolutely foreclose such claims to the extent that a business decision did not involve "judgment" because it was made in a way that did not comport with the duty to exercise good faith and ordinary care. We note as well that the business judgment rule applies equally at common law to corporate officers and directors generally and to bank officers and directors. Having concluded that such a business judgment rule is a part of our common law, we must consider whether the General Assembly has modified or abrogated the business judgment rule by statute. . . .

■ ■ ■

Our examination of the statutory law starts with OCGA § 7-1-490 (a), which concerns the care with which bank officers and directors are to perform their duties:

> Directors and officers of a bank or trust company shall discharge the duties of their respective positions in good faith and with that diligence, care, and skill which ordinarily prudent men would exercise under similar circumstances in like positions. In discharging his duties, a director or officer, when acting in good faith, shall be entitled to rely upon information, opinions, reports, or statements, including financial statements and other financial data, in each case prepared or presented by:
>
> (1) One or more officers or employees of the bank or trust company whom the director or officer reasonably believes to be reliable and competent in the matters presented;
>
> (2) Counsel, public accountants, or other persons as to matters which the director or officer reasonably believes to be within such person's professional or expert competence; or
>
> (3) A committee of the board upon which the director or officer does not serve, duly designated in accordance with a provision of the articles of incorporation or the bylaws, as to matters within that committee's designated authority, which committee the director or officer reasonably believes to merit confidence. . . .

■   ■   ■

In the light of this statutory history, we conclude that OCGA § 7-1-490 (a) is perfectly consistent with the business judgment rule acknowledged at common law in the decisions of this Court. To be sure, subsection (a) provides that an officer or director who acts "in good faith and with that diligence, care, and skill which ordinarily pru-

dent men would exercise under similar circumstances in like positions" "shall have no liability by reason of being or having been a director or officer of the bank or trust company." And no doubt, these provisions imply strongly that, if an officer or director *fails* to act in good faith or with such ordinary care, he is subject to liability. But taken in its legal context, the statutory reference to ordinary "diligence, care, and skill" is most reasonably understood to refer to the care required with respect to the process by which a decision is made, most notably the diligence due to ascertain the relevant facts. So understood, the implication of liability means only that an officer or director who acts in bad faith or fails to exercise such ordinary care with respect to the process for making a decision is liable.

■   ■   ■

We conclude that the business judgment rule acknowledged at common law in the decisions of this Court is consistent with, and has not been superseded by, OCGA § 7-1-490 (a).

■   ■   ■

Both at common law and by statute, the standard of ordinary care for bank officers and directors is less demanding than the standard of "ordinary diligence" with which most ordinary negligence claims are concerned. As this Court explained . . .

> [A bank director] is not bound to exercise the same degree of care which a prudent man would exercise in his own business. This is too high a standard. To expect a director under such circumstances to give the affairs of the bank the same care that he takes of his own business is unreasonable, and few responsible men would be willing to serve upon such terms. In the case of a city bank doing a large business, he would be obliged to abandon his own affairs entirely. A business man generally understands the details of his own

business, but a bank director cannot grasp the details of a large bank without devoting all his time to it, to the utter neglect of his own affairs. A director is expected to attend the meetings of the board with reasonable regularity, and to exercise a general supervision and control.

The same limitation appears in the statutory law concerning bank officers and directors, which does not demand the "care which is exercised by ordinary prudent persons under the same or similar circumstances," but instead requires only the "diligence, care, and skill which ordinarily prudent men would exercise under similar circumstances *in like positions.*"...

■   ■   ■

Finally, the business judgment rule makes clear that, when a business decision is alleged to have been made negligently, the wisdom of the decision is ordinarily insulated from judicial review,

and as for the process by which the decision was made, the officers and directors are presumed to have acted in good faith and to have exercised ordinary care. Although this presumption may be rebutted, the plaintiff bears the burden of putting forward proof sufficient to rebut it. All together, the limited standard of care, the conclusive presumptions as to reasonable reliance, and the rebuttable presumptions of good faith and ordinary care offer meaningful protection, we think, to officers and directors who serve in good faith and with due care. The business judgment rule does not insulate "mere dummies or figureheads" from liability, of course, but it never was meant to do so. . . .

As described above, the business judgment rule precludes some, but not all claims, against bank officers and directors that sound in ordinary negligence. With that qualification, we answer the certified question in the negative.

Chapter Extension

For additional material relating to Chapter 7, see p. 279 in the Appendix of Chapter Extension Files.

Chapter Problems

1. Define the following concepts and terms:
   a. Principal
   b. Apparent authority
   c. Independent contractors
   d. Apparent partnership
   e. Limited partnership
   f. Pierce the corporate veil
   g. Private corporations
   h. Business judgment rule
   i. Preemptive rights
   j. Limited liability company (LLC)

2. Wheeler spoke with Stewart, an agent of Stewart Insurance, an independent insurance agency, about obtaining insurance for his mobile home. Wheeler

filled out an application for insurance on a Puritan Insurance Company form and made partial payment. Stewart informed Wheeler, "As quick as I write this receipt out and accept your money, you will be covered by Puritan." Stewart failed to send Wheeler's application to Puritan and to obtain insurance protection for Wheeler.

Stewart did not have any express authorization from Puritan to bind the company. Puritan considered each application on arrival. Fire destroyed Wheeler's mobile home. Stewart informed Wheeler that the loss was not covered by Puritan. Do you agree? Explain. Would Wheeler have any other alternatives to recovery? Explain.

3. Loehr's is a used car dealer. One of its salespeople misrepresented the mileage of a used car in a sale to a customer. Under agency principles, is Loehr's liable for the damages due to the misrepresentation? What additional information, if any, do you need to answer the question? Explain. What can the owners of car dealerships do to minimize the risk of such misrepresentation occurring?

4. Lancaster was a mechanic in the locomotive shop at Norfolk and Western Railway Co. Lachrone, a hot-tempered foreman, lost his temper and approached Lancaster with a broom in a menacing manner. Lancaster developed a severe mental disorder as a result. Is Norfolk and Western Railway Co. liable for Lancaster's injury under agency principles? Explain.

5. Harris and Zajac worked together in a salvage operation business. They bought wrecked cars and rebuilt them or sold them for salvage. Zajac had a controlling voice in the management of the business. There was no written partnership agreement; neither did the business file a partnership tax return. Harris used his own money to buy cars, as did Zajac. The parties split the profits on the sales from time to time. Zajac withheld federal withholding and social security taxes on Harris's share of the profit. Is this a partnership? Why or why not?

6. Able, Baker, and Carter formed ABC Partnership. Able contributed $5,000, Baker $10,000, and Carter $15,000. During the term of the partnership, Baker loaned ABC $5,000 and Able loaned ABC $6,000. The partnership is winding up its affairs after a voluntary dissolution. It owes creditors $100,000. Assume ABC has assets in the amount of $150,000 to distribute. How will Able, Baker, and Carter divide the profits or losses? What if ABC had $132,000 to distribute?

7. Dr. Bennet signed articles of incorporation for Aero-Fabb Co. Because these articles were not in accord with the state statutes, the secretary of state did not issue a certificate of incorporation. Timberline leased equipment to Aero-Fabb Co. Aero-Fabb refused to pay. May Timberline enforce payment against Aero-Fabb? Explain.

8. Gries Sports Enterprises, Inc. (GSE) and Gries own 43 percent of the outstanding stock of the Cleveland Browns Football Co., Inc. (Browns), a Delaware corporation. Gries is a director and officer of the Browns. Modell owns 53 percent of the stock in the Browns and is a director, president, and chief executive officer of the Browns. Other board members include Modell's wife; Bailey, general counsel of the Browns; Berick, outside legal counsel; Wallack, a full-time employee; and Cole.

   Modell formed Cleveland Stadium Corporation (CSC). CSC leased the Cleveland Municipal Stadium from the city and subleased it to the Browns. Modell owned 80 percent of the stock in CSC. Berick, Bailey, Cole, Wallack, and Gries also owned stock in CSC.

   Modell had an outstanding personal indebtedness of $4 million. In an effort to retire that debt, he set about to sell CSC to the Browns for $6 million. Since he owned 80 percent of the shares in CSC, that would net him sufficient funds to pay off his $4 million debt. A brokerage and investment firm rendered an opinion that CSC would be worth from $6.2 million to $6.9 million if acquired by the Browns.

   At the Browns meeting of the directors, Gries objected to the acquisition. By a four-to-one vote the board approved the acquisition. The Modells abstained.

   Gries and GSE filed suit seeking to set aside the transaction, contending that the transaction was "intrinsically unfair." The Browns defended by contending that the board's decision was protected by the business judgment rule. What additional information would you want to present to support the Browns' contention?

9. Mesa Petroleum owned 13 percent of Unocal's stock. It attempted to gain control of Unocal's stock by a cash offer for outstanding shares. It offered to purchase 64 million shares for $54 per share. It then intended to eliminate the remaining shares by exchanging Mesa stock for Unocal stock. Unocal's board is unanimously against accepting and recommending to its shareholders Mesa's offer. Assuming that Mesa's offer is fair and that the offering price is above the market price, what are some alternatives for the board to consider?

10. Home Owners Warranty Corp. (HOW) administers a homeowner's program for the benefit of member-builders. Two shareholders demand to inspect the books, records, and membership lists of HOW and its subsidiaries. Under which circumstances, and for what purpose, would HOW shareholders be entitled to such inspection?

IV   THE LEGAL AND ETHICAL ENVIRONMENT OF BUSINESS AND ITS EMPLOYEES

8   EQUAL EMPLOYMENT OPPORTUNITY

Chapter Outline

Learning Objectives

After learning this chapter the student should be able to:

- Recognize employment decisions having a high risk of disparate treatment liability.
- Determine the likelihood that an employment practice would result in disparate impact liability.
- Apply the bona fide seniority system, bona fide occupational qualification, and bona fide employee benefit plan exceptions to different problems.
- Evaluate the likelihood that an affirmative action plan is lawful.
- Determine when harassment amounts to illegal discrimination.
- Determine when to accommodate an employee's religious practices or physical or mental disability.

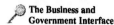

The Business and Government Interface

The following link is to the website for the Equal Employment Opportunity Commission, the federal agency that administers the EEO laws discussed in this chapter:

http://www.eeoc.gov/

Notice that the website contains links for employees & applicants as well as for the employers. Clicking the link "About EEOC" gets you to the laws and regulations, statistics, and publications, among other topics.

During the Reconstruction period, Congress passed several civil rights acts to protect the newly freed slaves. These acts were soon ignored, as segregation and discrimination became widespread within America's social institutions. Although many Americans worked against segregation in the late 19th and early 20th centuries, it was not until the 1950s that the civil rights movement began to gain momentum. The movement achieved its most significant legislative victory with the passage of the Civil Rights Act of 1964, a comprehensive assault on discriminatory practices in America. Title VII of the Civil Rights Act prohibits discrimination in employment on the basis of race, color, religion, national origin, or sex. It is the broadest federal statute regulating employment practices. Today, it is one of several major sources of federal equal employment regulation.

These regulations weave a tangled legal web that can snare today's employers. They establish the following categories of illegal discrimination: race, sex, sexual orientation and gender identity, religion, national origin, age, veteran status, genetic information, and disability. Each of these categories is known as a *protected class*. The federal equal employment opportunity laws contain different provisions concerning coverage of protected classes, defenses, and enforcement. They are summarized in Table 8–1.

The Concept of Discrimination

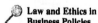

Law and Ethics in Business Policies

The following link is to the Exelon Corporation Code of Business Conduct:

http://www.exeloncorp.com /assets/people-culture/docs /bro_codeofconduct.pdf

See, "Fair Treatment, Diversity and Inclusion" at page 12. In what ways does the policy reflect federal regulatory law? In what ways does it go beyond federal regulation?

Regardless of which protected class or statute is involved, the concept of discrimination is basically the same. Discrimination in any employment decision is illegal. This includes hiring, firing, promotion, job assignments, training programs, compensation, and similar decisions. The law does not require an employer to hire, promote, or retain anyone; it simply prohibits an employer from using membership in a protected class as a basis for an employment decision. The two types of illegal discrimination are:

* Disparate treatment of a member of a protected class.
* Disparate impact of an employment practice on a protected class.

The disparate treatment and disparate impact approaches were first developed by the courts in cases interpreting Title VII. They have also been applied in cases involving other federal equal employment opportunity laws.

Disparate Treatment

Disparate treatment results when an employer, union, or employment agency treats one employee less favorably than another because of race, sex, religion, national origin, age, or disability. Thus, disparate treatment is intentional discrimination. In a disparate treatment case, the focus is on the defendant's motive.

TABLE 8–1   **Federal EEO Laws**

Law	Coverage	Protected Class(es)	Defenses	Enforcement
Title VII, 1964 Civil Rights Act	Employers with at least 15 employees; unions; employment agencies	Race, sex, religion, national origin	Seniority systems, ability tests, bona fide occupational qualifications (except race)	EEOC or private lawsuit after using EEOC remedies
Equal Pay Act	Similar to FLSA coverage	Sex (equal pay for equal work)	Seniority system, factors other than sex, quantity or quality of output	EEOC or private lawsuit
Age Discrimination in Employment Act	Employers with at least 20 employees; unions; employment agencies	Age (40 or older)	Seniority system, bona fide occupational qualification, reasonable factors other than age, employee benefit plan	EEOC or private lawsuit after using EEOC remedies
Americans with Disabilities Act	Employers with 15 or more employees	Disability, including a duty to accommodate	Undue hardship	Same as Title VII
§§503, 504, Rehabilitation Act of 1973	Federal contractors and recipients of federal financial assistance	Handicap, including a duty to accommodate		Private lawsuit, debarment from federal contracts
1866 Civil Rights Act Executive Orders	Employers; unions Federal contractors	Race, national origin Affirmative action re race, color, national origin, sex, sexual orientation, gender identity		Private lawsuit Debarment from federal contracts
Genetic Information Nondiscrimination Act	Employers with at least 15 employees; unions; employment agencies	Genetic Information	Inadvertent acquisitions and those through: wellness program, Family and Medical Leave Act certification, commercially or publically available sources, biological monitoring for workplace toxic substance exposure, limited law enforcement purposes	EEOC or private lawsuit after using EEOC remedies

A plaintiff may prove disparate treatment with direct evidence of discriminatory motive. For example, an employer may have sent a rejection letter to a female applicant stating, "You are certainly well qualified, but this is a man's job.

Usually, direct evidence of discriminatory motive is not available. Motive, therefore, must be inferred from a defendant's conduct in view of the surrounding circumstances. A plaintiff may raise an inference of discrimination by showing that he or she (1) belonged to a protected class, (2) applied and was qualified for a job for which the employer was seeking applicants, and (3) was rejected, after which the position remained open and the employer continued seeking applicants with similar qualifications. A plaintiff who accomplishes this is said to have established a prima facie case of disparate treatment, or intentional discrimination. This approach may be adapted to establish a prima facie case of disparate treatment with regard to matters other than initial hire.

When a prima facie case of disparate treatment has been established, the defendant must provide a legitimate, nondiscriminatory explanation for the employment decision. The defendant is not required to prove that it did not discriminate, nor must it prove the factual validity of its explanation. However, a demonstration that an employment practice is required by business necessity may not be used as a defense against a claim of intentional discrimination.

Once the defendant provides an explanation, the plaintiff must prove that the explanation is really a pretext for discrimination. To do so, the plaintiff may attempt to show that the defendant's rationale lacks credibility, that the rationale was not uniformly applied, or that statistics indicate a general practice of discrimination by the defendant. The ultimate issue is a factual one: is the defendant's apparently valid reason really a cover-up for intentional discrimination?

Strong circumstantial evidence of intentional discrimination is provided by a statistical comparison between the percentage of minorities in the employer's workforce and the percentage of minorities in the relevant labor market. Employers are not required to hire a specified percentage of minorities, but the minority composition of the employer's workforce may suggest that the employer has discriminated.

For example, assume that an employer has 1,000 qualified applicants for 100 openings, and that 500 applicants are black and 500 are white. If the employer hires randomly, one would expect 50 blacks and 50 whites to be hired. Fifty is said to be the "expected value." If the employer hires 47 blacks, it is still very likely that the selection is random and that the deviation from the expected value occurred by chance rather than by design. If only 10 blacks were hired, one may suspect discrimination. If no blacks are hired, it is almost certain that the employer discriminated. One cannot be absolutely certain, because it is possible to randomly select 100 whites. Nevertheless, the greater the deviation from the expected value, the less likely it is that the result occurred by chance.

If the frequency of all possible random outcomes is plotted on a graph, the result is a bell curve, as illustrated in Figure 8–1. A statistical measure, known as **standard deviation**, is derived from the bell curve. It measures the probability that a given result occurred by chance. On the curve below, point A is the expected value. Points B and C are equal distances away from point A. We expect to find 68 percent of all results between points B and C; and 34 percent between A and C. Points D and E are equidistant from points B and C, respectively. Between points D and E, we expect to find 96 percent of all results. The distance between each point and its closest neighboring point is one standard deviation. Thus, when the minority or sexual composition of an employer's workforce is two to three standard deviations less than the expected value, we are 96 percent to 98.8 per-

FIGURE 8–1   Bell Curve

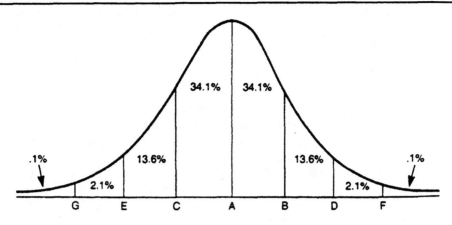

cent sure that the hiring did not occur randomly. Under these circumstances, a court infers that the employer has committed intentional discrimination.

An employer faced with statistical proof of intentional discrimination may attempt to rebut the inference in several ways. The employer may argue that the statistical comparison is not valid because the plaintiff failed to select the appropriate relevant labor market. The appropriate relevant labor market depends on the skill required for the job. If the job requires little specialized skill, general population figures would provide an appropriate basis of comparison. If the job is highly specialized, the relevant labor market must be restricted to those who are qualified. For example, the workforce of an employer charged with discrimination in hiring messengers may be compared to the general population, whereas the workforce of an employer charged with discriminating in hiring certified public accountants must be compared to CPAs generally.

The employer's location may also influence the composition of the relevant labor market. Commuting patterns in a given metropolitan area may be significant in determining the relevant market of an employer located in the central city or in a suburb.

Besides attacking the validity of the statistical comparison, the defendant may also attack its probative value. For example, the employer might show that its workforce has experienced little turnover and little expansion since the effective date of Title VII. The employer might also offer nondiscriminatory explanations for statistical disparities.

In some cases, the evidence may show that both discriminatory and legitimate reasons contributed to the defendant's actions. These cases are called **mixed motive cases**. The defendant may claim that it would have taken the same action even if the plaintiff had not been a member of a protected class. As long as the plaintiff proves that membership in a protected class was a motivating factor in the decision, the defendant is liable, even though other factors also motivated the practice. The defendant may avoid the remedies of damages, reinstatement, hiring, promotion, and back pay, however, by proving that it would have reached the same decision without considering the plaintiff's protected class status. The available remedies would be only declarative relief, certain types of injunctive relief, attorney fees and costs.

Disparate treatment can take many forms. For example, an employer that segregates its workforce for fringe benefits purposes engages in illegal disparate treatment. Thus, an employer may not offer male employees lower life insurance benefits or higher pension benefits than similarly situated female employees even though women, as a group, live longer than men.

Another type of disparate treatment occurs when an employer uses a double standard for members of a protected class. This conduct is illegal, even if the employer does not otherwise discriminate. For example, an employer whose workforce is predominantly female acts illegally if it refuses to hire women with preschool children but hires men with preschool children. Such a policy is often called *sex plus discrimination*.

Disparate Impact

Employers often impose requirements for particular jobs. For example, employers might require security guards to be at least six feet tall. On its face this requirement does not appear to disqualify any job applicant because of sex or national origin. However, if scrutinized, it may prove to disqualify a larger percentage of women, Latinos, and Asians than nonminority males. Because, on average, they are shorter than white males, these groups may be systematically excluded from consideration for the security guard jobs. The employment discrimination laws do not prohibit the use of such facially neutral criteria. When the criteria systematically exclude members of a protected class from job opportunities, the employer must justify their use or it will be liable for **disparate impact**.

In a disparate impact case, the plaintiff must prove that the challenged practice disqualifies a protected class at a significantly greater rate than the majority class. The defendant may avoid liability by proving that the practice is job related and consistent with business necessity. The defendant may still be liable if the plaintiff can prove that there was a less discriminatory practice available to meet the defendant's needs.

Exceptions

The federal laws contain a variety of exceptions to their prohibitions against discrimination. The three most common exceptions are:

- Bona fide occupational qualifications.
- Professionally developed ability tests.
- Bona fide seniority systems.

The Bona Fide Occupational Qualification

The **bona fide occupational qualification** (BFOQ) is a statutory exception to employment practices that might otherwise violate Title VII or the Age Discrimination in Employment Act. This exception allows an employer to discriminate in its hiring where religion, national origin, sex, or age is a bona fide occupational qualification reasonably necessary to the normal operation of the business. The exception does not apply to racial discrimination. To establish a BFOQ, the employer must show that employees of a given sex, religion, national origin, or age are a business necessity because any other groups would undermine the essence of the business operation. This may be done by showing that certain qualifications possessed by persons of a given sex, religion, national origin, or age are essential to the employer's business and that it is impracticable to find members of the excluded class who possess these qualifications.

The BFOQ is interpreted narrowly, and the employer bears a heavy burden of proof. The employer must prove that the discrimination is necessary, not merely convenient.

Professionally Developed Ability Tests

Title VII permits the use of any professionally developed ability test, provided that the test is not designed or used to discriminate. The EEOC has issued guidelines detailing the **validation** processes it approves for establishing the job relatedness of any selection procedure that has an adverse impact on a protected group. Under the guidelines, a test is considered discriminatory if it results in a selection rate for one race, sex, religion, or national origin that is less than four fifths of the selection rate for another. The burden then shifts to the user of the test to validate the test by one of three methods: criterion validity, content validity, or construct validity.

Criterion validity establishes a statistical relationship between performance on the test and an objective indicator of job performance. Criterion validity is established by a study comparing test scores to the specified measure of performance. For example, if a study showed that a statistically significant correlation existed between GMAT scores and grades in an MBA program, the GMAT exam would be criterion valid.

Content validity establishes that the test representatively samples a function of the job. A word processing test for a word processor is content valid.

Construct validity establishes that the test indicates a psychological trait required for the job. A test indicating leadership ability is construct valid for a police commander.

Seniority Systems

Title VII, the ADEA, and the Equal Pay Act permit employers to apply different standards of employment pursuant to **bona fide seniority systems** that are not the result of an intention to discriminate. In *Teamsters v. United States,* the Supreme Court held that a seniority system can be bona fide even though it perpetuates the effects of pre-act discrimination.[1] The Court further held that a seniority system is bona fide where it applies equally to all employees regardless of membership in a protected class, was not established or maintained for the purpose of discriminating, and operates rationally in accord with practices in the industry.

Special Topics in Equal Employment Opportunity

In addition to the basic types of discrimination, employers face special problems when dealing with affirmative action and workplace harassment. Employers also must handle issues that are peculiar to sex, sexual orientation and gender identity, religion, national origin, age, disability, and genetic information discrimination.

Affirmative Action

Law and Ethics in Business Policies

The following link is to GE's Code of Conduct:

http://www.ge.com/files _citizenship/pdf/TheSpirit &TheLetter.pdf

Pages 39–41 discuss equal employment opportunity. Notice at page 41 the company explicitly addressess affirmative action.

Affirmative action issues arise in two settings. First, employers might voluntarily adopt affirmative action plans that give preference to minority employees. Second, after finding that an employer has discriminated against minorities, a court might require the employer to take affirmative action. In either case, whites or males may argue that the voluntary plan or the court order illegally discriminates against them.

Employers adopt voluntary affirmative action plans for a variety of reasons. One reason an employer might do so is to be eligible for contracts with the federal government. Executive Order 11246, administered by the Office of Federal Contract Compliance Programs (OFCCP), requires that government contractors take affirmative action to ensure that their employees are hired and promoted on a nondiscriminatory basis.

All federal contractors and subcontractors who do more than $10,000 in business with the federal government in one year must, according to the Executive Order, not discriminate in employment on the basis of race, color religion, sex, sexual orientation, gender identity, or national origin. In addition, the Executive Order requires federal government contractors to take affirmative action to ensure that equal opportunity is provided in employment.

The federal government program requires that an acceptable affirmative action plan with realistic goals and timetables be prepared by each contractor or subcontractor. The employer must first perform a utilization analysis, including evaluation of the size of the minority and female population and labor force in the area, the requisite skills among minorities and women in the area, and the available training programs and facilities. Having completed this analysis, the employer

---

[1] 431 U.S. 324 (1977).

must identify the deficiencies in its workforce, and must then establish attainable goals for correcting and eliminating those deficiencies, along with timetables and methods for achieving the goals. An employer is not in violation of its plan if it fails to meet its goals provided that the employer has made good-faith efforts to do so. This is the principal difference between goals and quotas: if a contractor is required by law to meet the goals, they become quotas.

Harassment

Law and Ethics in Business Policies

The following link is to the Kroger Co. Policy on Business Ethics:

http://www.thekrogerco.com /docs/default-document -library/ethicspolicy

See pages 15–16 for Kroger's policy on harassment, which includes bulleted examples of both sexual harassment and other forms of harassment.

Harassment does not per se violate Title VII. Harassment that is discriminatory can violate Title VII. For example, an employee who is required to have sexual relations with a supervisor to secure, maintain, or advance in employment is subjected to conditions that are not imposed on employees of the opposite sex. An employee who is promoted as a reward for having sexual relations with a supervisor is given an opportunity that employees of the opposite sex do not have.

Sexual harassment is unwelcome sexual conduct that is a term or condition of employment. There are two types of sexual harassment: (1) quid pro quo harassment and (2) hostile environment harassment. Quid pro quo harassment is where job benefits are exchanged for sexual favors. ("Date me or lose your job.") Hostile environment harassment is where unwelcome sexual conduct creates an intimidating, hostile, or offensive environment.

Employer Liability.   An employer's liability for harassment (called *respondeat superior liability* or *vicarious liability*) depends on the status of the harasser. If the harasser is a co-worker, the employer is liable only if it was negligent in controlling the working conditions. This same negligence standard applies to nonemployee harassers, like customers or independent contractors, that the employer has control over (such as when they are on the employer's premises).

However, if the harasser is a supervisor, the employer is strictly, or automatically, liable if the harassment results in a tangible negative employment action, such as a lack of a raise or promotion, or termination of employment. But, if no negative action is taken, the employer may avoid liability by establishing as an affirmative defense that (1) the employer exercised reasonable care to try to prevent and correct any harassing behavior, and (2) that the employee unreasonably failed to take advantage of the preventive or corrective opportunities provided by the employer.

In *Vance v. Ball State University*[2] the U.S. Supreme Court held that an employee is a "supervisor for purposes of vicarious liability only if he or she is empowered by the employer to take tangible employment actions against the victim, like the power to hire, fire, demote, promote, transfer, or discipline.

---

[2] 133 S. Ct. 2434 (2013).

Sex

Sexual discrimination in employment is not a new phenomenon. The concepts of men's work and women's work have been ingrained in society since civilization began. Today, sex roles in our society are changing, yet the notion of gender-based jobs remains a threat to the freedom to work, regardless of sex.

Ethical Dilemmas/Issues

Frieda Rosenmund is a financial analyst for Stevedore Pants Company. Her supervisor is Gus Goyert. As the company's controller, Goyert hires the secretaries in the controller's office. Applications for secretarial positions are screened by Goyert. Selected applicants are then interviewed by Goyert and all the other employees in the controller's office. After conferring with the other employees, Goyert decides whom to hire.

Several applications have been sent to Goyert for an open secretarial position. Among the applicants is a male. Goyert looks over the man's application in Rosenmund's presence and announces with an air of finality, "Don't interview this one. I'm not going to hire any man as my secretary. He's probably gay, and I don't want any AIDS epidemic at Stevedore Pants."

What are the ethical issues? What would you do?

The Business and Government Interface

The following link is to the EEOC's *Enforcement Guidance on Pregnancy Discrimination and Related Issues:*

http://www.eeoc.gov/laws/guidance/pregnancy_guidance.cfm

It includes several examples to help guide understanding of how EEO law applies to pregnant workers.

Pregnancy

Only women can become pregnant, but not all women choose to do so. Title VII, as amended by the Pregnancy Discrimination Act of 1978 (PDA), equates discrimination on the basis of pregnancy, childbirth, or related medical conditions with sex discrimination.

An employer must treat pregnancy in the same manner as any other medical condition. It may not exclude pregnancy coverage from the medical insurance it provides for employees' spouses. To do so discriminates against male employees. The PDA, however, does not prohibit an employer from providing special pregnancy benefits, such as special maternity leave, that it does not provide to employees generally.

Compensation

Sex discrimination in compensation violates Title VII. It may also violate the Equal Pay Act of 1963 (EPA).

The EPA prohibits differences in pay between the sexes for employees who are performing work that requires "equal skill, effort, and responsibility" and is "performed under similar working conditions." If even one worker is paid at a higher rate than members of the opposite sex who are doing equal work, a violation of the act may be found.

The term *equal* does not require that the work of men and women employees be identical, but only that it be substantially equal, to justify equal pay. Thus, small differences in job description do not make jobs so unequal as to justify a higher pay scale for one sex.

In writing the EPA, Congress referred to equality of "skill," "effort," and "responsibility" exercised "under similar working conditions" because these are criteria by which industry evaluates jobs for classification purposes. For example, in *Corning Glass v. Brennan,* the Supreme Court considered whether the differences between the day and night shifts were sufficient to justify paying male night-shift employees more than female day-shift employees.[3] The Court rejected the employer's argument that different shifts constituted different working conditions, noting that in the glass industry working conditions did not usually refer to the time of day during which work was performed.

Several exceptions to the equal work-equal pay standard are:

- Bona fide seniority and merit systems.
- Earnings based on quantity or quality of output.
- Factors other than sex.

Pay differentials based on seniority or on performance evaluations are justified, provided that the policy is uniformly applied. Systems in which employees are paid according to an individual production piece rate are immunized from liability by the quantity or quality of output exception.

Exceptions for factors other than sex immunize other legitimate bases for wage disparities. For example, although a shift differential results in unequal pay for equal work under similar conditions, the inequity may be justified because it arises from a factor other than sex.

An EPA violation does not exist where a wage disparity arises out of a bona fide management training program that rotates employees of one sex through all departments, thereby requiring them to work temporarily with members of the opposite sex who receive a lower rate than the trainees. However, courts scrutinize training programs that involve employees of only one sex to determine whether they are, in fact, bona fide exceptions. If the programs are informal, do not regularly result in promotion to the position being trained for, and appear to be geared more to the employer's needs than to actual training, they are not likely to survive scrutiny.

Title VII has been interpreted to implicitly incorporate the EPA's affirmative defenses in compensation discrimination cases. However, intentional sexual discrimination in pay violates Title VII even though the employees do not perform equal work. Thus, an employer who pays truck drivers more than secretaries because the truck drivers are male and the secretaries are female does not violate the EPA but may violate Title VII.

---

[3] 417 U.S. 188 (1974).

Sexual Orientation and Gender Identity

The legal status of employment discrimination on the basis of sexual orientation and gender identity is in a state of flux. The answer to the question, "Can an employer discriminate on the basis of sexual orientation and gender identity?" is, "It depends."

At the federal level, there is no federal statute forbidding sexual orientation and gender identity discrimination in employment. Title VII does not explicitly forbid it. The EEOC's enforcement policy is that discrimination against a transgender individual is discrimination on the basis of sex.

Since 1994, a bill has been reintroduced in every Congress that would forbid employment discrimination based on sexual orientation and gender identity. The bill is entitled the Employment Nondiscrimination Act (ENDA), but it has yet to be enacted by Congress.

In 2014, President Barak Obama signed an executive order forbidding federal contactors from discriminating on the basis of sexual orientation and gender identity. The executive order applies to one part of the economy, those businesses that do business with the federal government.

At the state level, the answer to the question of whether employment discrimination on the basis of sexual orientation and gender identity is unlawful is similarly complicated. Some states forbid both discrimination on the basis of sexual orientation and gender identity (an individual's appearance, mannerisms, characteristics), some forbid sexual orientation discrimination in employment only; and some, like federal law, do not have legislation forbidding either type of discrimination, but have governor-signed executive orders. A majority of states have no law banning this form of discrimination. The legal landscape is in a state of change.

Religion

The term *religion* encompasses such traditional religions as Judaism, Catholicism, Protestantism, and Islam, but is far broader. It includes all moral or ethical beliefs that are sincerely held with the strength of traditional religious views. Atheism and agnosticism are considered religions for Title VII purposes.

The Duty to Accommodate Religion

Title VII requires an employer to make reasonable accommodations to employees' religious beliefs and practices unless accommodation would work an undue hardship on the business. The most frequent charges of religious discrimination dealt with by the courts and the EEOC involve not raw prejudice, but instances in which an employer's work rule, innocent in intent, conflicts with an employee's religious belief. Such conditions trigger the employer's duty to accommodate the employee's religious beliefs.

An employer need not accommodate an employee's religious beliefs if to do so would impose more than a *de minimis* cost. For example, an employer need not give an employee the day off for his or her religious Sabbath if this would require the employer to pay another employee at an overtime rate to fill in.

An employer fulfills its duty under Title VII when it offers a reasonable accommodation to the employee. The employer is not obligated to agree to the accommodation requested by the employee even if it would cost the employer nothing.

National Origin

Title VII forbids employment discrimination based on national origin against applicants or employees. National origin refers to the country from which an individual or the individual's ancestors came. It also includes persons with characteristics generally identified with particular national groups. Unlawful national origin discrimination includes discrimination directed at individuals because they are married or associated with persons or groups of a national origin.

Title VII prohibits treating people differently because of national origin. This includes harassment on the basis of national origin. Name calling would be an example of national origin harassment.

English-only language rules tend to have a disparate impact on national origin. The EEOC guidelines state that when an employer requires English to be spoken at all times, the agency will presume that such a rule violates Title VII and will closely scrutinize it.

Selection procedures that have an adverse impact on the basis of national origin and are not job-related and required by business necessity violate Title VII. For example, height or weight requirements tend to have an adverse impact based on national origin.

The Immigration Reform and Control Act (IRCA) prohibits employers from hiring illegal aliens. The IRCA also requires employers to verify the residence or citizenship status of every employee. However, the IRCA makes it illegal for an employer to discriminate in employment against someone who is not an illegal alien on the basis of that individual's citizenship or immigration status.

Age

The Age Discrimination in Employment Act covers employers with 20 or more employees, employment agencies, and unions with 25 or more members or who operate hiring halls. The ADEA prohibits age discrimination against persons age 40 or older.

The ADEA contains BFOQ and bona fide seniority system exceptions. It also excepts employment decisions based on reasonable factors other than age and discharges for cause. These two exceptions are essentially denials of, rather than justifications for, age discrimination. They have been interpreted as codifying the employer's burden of rebutting a prima facie case of disparate treatment with legitimate, nondiscriminatory reasons for its actions.

The ADEA excepts **bona fide employee benefit plans** that are not subterfuges to avoid the act. This exception applies only where employers reduce benefits to older workers to offset the increased costs of those benefits as employees age. For example, employers may reduce life insurance benefits based on age. Often it may be difficult to distinguish between age and other characteristics correlated with age.

Employers should be particularly sensitive to ADEA liability when terminating older employees. More than 90 percent of the cases brought under the ADEA have involved terminations. This is particularly true during economic recessions, when many companies lay off or terminate large numbers of workers.

Disability

The Americans with Disabilities Act (ADA) prohibits discrimination against a qualified individual on the basis of disability. An employer may not treat a qualified individual with a disability unfavorably because of the individual's disability.

A disability under the ADA means, with respect to an individual-

- a physical or mental impairment that substantially limits one or more major life activities of such individual,
- a record of such an impairment, or
- being regarded as having such impairment.

Major life activities include, among others, caring for oneself, performing manual tasks, seeing, hearing, sleeping, walking, standing, lifting, bending, speaking, breathing, learning, reading, concentrating, thinking, communicating and working. A major life activity also includes the operation of a major bodily function, such as functions of the immune system, digestive, bowel, bladder, brain, respiratory, circulatory, endocrine, and reproductive systems.

The ADA states that, mitigating factors, such as medication, prosthetics, hearing aids, etc. shall not be considered in determining whether someone has a disability. For example, an employer cannot conclude that just because someone wears a hearing aid they are not disabled. However, the statute excludes ordinary eyeglasses and contact lenses from the mitigating factors that must be ignored. (So, if you are wearing ordinary eyeglasses or contact lenses to read this, you cannot claim that your poor eyesight is a disability.)

An impairment that is episodic (for example seizures) or in remission (such as cancer) is a disability if it would substantially limit a major activity when active.

For someone to be regarded as having an impairment that substantially limits a major life activity, they do not have to show that the employer perceived them that way. All the individual has to prove is that he or she was subjected to an action prohibited by the ADA (for example, rejected for a job or a promotion) based on an impairment that is not minor or transitory.

The ADA states that this definition of disability shall be construed in favor of broad coverage of individuals to the maximum extent permitted by the statute.

Employers are required to provide reasonable accommodation to an applicant or an employee with a disability, unless doing so would cause an undue hardship to the employer, which under the ADA means imposing significant difficulty or expense. According to the EEOC, "a reasonable accommodation is any change in the work environment (or in the way things are usually done) to help a person with a disability apply for a job, perform the duties of a job, or enjoy the benefits

Law and Ethics in Business Politics

The following link is to GE's Code of Conduct:

http://www.ge.com/files _citizenship/pdf/TheSpirit &TheLetter.pdf

Notice the Q&A that starts on page 39 and is answered on page 40.

and privileges of employment." Examples of reasonable accommodation include modifying facilities, equipment, examinations, or other job requirements or working conditions. The duty to accommodate may involve providing readers or interpreters, or restructuring jobs. Individuals who are covered only under the "regarded as" part of the definition of disability are not entitled to reasonable accommodation. (They do not really need it.)

The ADA forbids using qualification standards, employments tests, or other selection criteria that tend to screen out individuals with disabilities, unless the practice is job related and consistent with business necessity.

The ADA prohibits employers from asking medical questions or requiring a medical exam before a job offer is made. The employer cannot ask an applicant if he or she has a disability or the extent of the disability. The EEOC tells employers that they "may ask job applicants whether they can perform the job and how they would perform the job, with or without a reasonable accommodation."

Employers may condition a job offer on passing a medical exam if it is job related and consistent with business necessity. This is allowed only if it is required of all employees regardless of disability.

Genetic Information

The Genetic Information Nondiscrimination Act (GINA) prohibits employers from discriminating on the basis of genetic information. GINA restricts the collection and disclosure of genetic information. The law's reach extends to applicants, employees, and their family members.

Genetic information means information about an individual's genetic tests, the tests of his or her family members, and the manifestation of a disease or disorder in the person's family members. However, under GINA, information about a person's sex or age is not considered genetic information.

According to the EEOC, which enforces GINA, "An employer may never use genetic information to make an employment decision because genetic information is not relevant to an individual's current ability to work."

There are six narrow exceptions to GINA's prohibitions. They are when genetic information is acquired:

1. Inadvertently
2. As part of a voluntary wellness program
3. As part of certifying leave under the Family and Medical Leave Act
4. Through commercially or publicly available documents (for example, newspapers and websites), so long as the employer was not intentionally searching for genetic information
5. As part of legally required biological monitoring of the workplace for toxic substance exposure, and the program is voluntary
6. From DNA testing for the law enforcement purpose of identifying human remains and the genetic information is used only for quality control to detect sample contamination.

Enforcement of Equal Employment Opportunity Laws

Table 8–2 summarizes the enforcement scheme of the major civil rights laws.

Title VII, the ADA, and the ADEA have similar enforcement provisions. All require victims to file charges of violations with the EEOC and their state employment discrimination agencies if they exist. The EEOC is allowed time to investigate the charges and to try informally to resolve the dispute. The EEOC or the individual victims can sue to correct the violations.

Title VII, the ADA, and the ADEA differ in their timing of the enforcement process. Under Title VII, and the ADA, the charge must be filed with the EEOC within 180 days following the discriminatory act if it arises in a state that does not have an antidiscrimination agency. If the state has an antidiscrimination agency, the charge must be filed first with the state agency. The charge may be filed with the EEOC after the state agency has had it for 60 days or has terminated proceedings, whichever occurs first. The charge must be filed within 300 days following the discriminatory act.

Individuals cannot file Title VII or ADA lawsuits until the EEOC notifies them of their right to sue. This EEOC notice is called a **right-to-sue letter**. If the EEOC's investigation of the charge discloses no reasonable cause to believe a Title VII violation occurred, the EEOC dismisses the charge and issues a right-to-sue letter. The EEOC's dismissal does not prohibit the charging party from suing.

If the EEOC finds reasonable cause, it issues a determination letter. The EEOC attempts to conciliate the dispute. If conciliation efforts fail, it issues a right-to-sue letter. In all cases, suit must be filed within 90 days after receipt of the right-to-sue letter.

Under the ADEA, the charging party can file charges with the state antidiscrimination agency and the EEOC in any order. The charging party is not required to file with the state first. The 180- and 300-day time limits for filing with the EEOC apply to the ADEA. The charging party need not receive a right-to-sue letter to file suit. He or she can sue anytime after the EEOC has had the charge for 60 days. ADEA lawsuits must be filed within 90 days following a right-to-sue letter.

TABLE 8–2   EEO Enforcement

Law	Who Enforces	Jury Trial	Punitive Damages
ADA, Title VII	EEOC and private plaintiffs	Yes	Yes, for actual malice or reckless disregard for victim's rights; maximum recovery $50,000–$200,000, depending on size of employer
ADEA, EPA	EEOC and private plaintiffs	Yes	Double damages for willful violations
1866 Civil Rights Act	Private plaintiffs	Yes	Yes, with no monetary limits
E.O. 11246	Federal agencies	No	No

Case

(Harassment)

MANDEL V. M & Q PACKAGING CORP.

706 F.3d 157 (3rd Cir. 2013)

Shannon J. Mandel (Mandel) sued M & Q Packaging Corp. (M & Q) alleging sexual harassment in violation of Title VII of the Civil Rights Act, and other claims not relevant here. The district court ordered summary judgment in favor of M & Q. Mandel appealed to the United States Court of Appeals for the Third Circuit, which reversed the district court's order regarding Mandel's sexual harassment claim. What follows is the Court of Appeals opinion.

ROTH, Circuit Judge:

On October 25, 1996, Shannon J. Mandel was hired as an Inside Sales and Customer Relations Coordinator by M & Q Packaging Corporation (M & Q), which manufactures and sells packaging film. Mandel claimed that, throughout her employment from October 25, 1996, to May 23, 2007, she was sexually harassed and discriminated against by male managers, supervisors, and owners in alleged incidents such as being referred to as "woman," "darling," "the woman," "fluffy," "missy," "hon," and "toots"; having her body, clothing, and physical appearance commented on; being told that she was "foolish not to use [her] assets"; being told by Systems Manager David Benetz, when she asked for directions to a meeting at corporate headquarters, that " [f]or you ... the meeting will start at my house tonight and we will conclude our part of it tomorrow morning"; being told by Quality Manager Harold Brenneman that he fantasized about her while he was having sex with his wife; being told in a review by Managing Director (and later President & COO) Michael Schmal that she was "too female" and "too emotional"; being solicited for dates by Vice President of Sales Curt Rubenstein even after she told him she was not interested; being told to clean the bathroom and make coffee when male employees were not asked to perform such tasks; and being paid less

and given less vacation time than a male manager.

On April 6, 2007, during a meeting regarding sample orders, Bachert became angry, repeatedly called Mandel a "bitch," and screamed "shut the fuck up." Bachert had previously referred to Mandel as a "bitch," both in and out of her presence. As a result of the meeting, Mandel resigned on May 23, 2007, by submitting a letter with two weeks' notice to Schmal.

In her resignation letter, Mandel did not complain of harassment or discrimination, apparently because she was concerned she would be denied her vacation time. She did, however, refer to the Employee Handbook. The Employee Handbook included an Equal Employment Opportunity Policy, which informed employees that they should contact the personnel manager-in this case, Conway- if they felt they were being discriminated against. The Employee Handbook also included an Open Door policy, which directed employees to discuss any issues first with their supervisor and then with the personnel manager. Mandel testified in her deposition that she understood the policies in the Employee Handbook but felt uncomfortable going to Conway or Schmal with her complaints. Conway testified in his deposition that other than giving each employee a copy of the Employee Handbook, there was no training regarding discrimination or sexual harassment.

Although Mandel complained to Schmidt about being told to make coffee, she did not complain to her supervisors about other alleged incidents of harassment or discrimination. Mandel occasionally used profanity and sent emails containing sexual humor. Mandel also called Bachert "gay" on a few occasions, apparently as a joke in reference to jealous husbands who claimed Bachert made advances to their wives. Mandel was never disciplined during her employment with M & Q.

Title VII prohibits sexual harassment that is "sufficiently severe or pervasive to alter the conditions of [the plaintiff's] employment and create an abusive working environment." *Meritor Sav. Bank, FSB v. Vinson*, 477 U.S. 57, (1986). To succeed on a hostile work environment claim, the plaintiff must establish that 1) the employee suffered intentional discrimination because of his/her sex, 2) the discrimination was severe or pervasive, 3) the discrimination detrimentally affected the plaintiff, 4) the discrimination would detrimentally affect a reasonable person in like circumstances, and 5) the existence of *respondeat superior* liability. The first four elements establish a hostile work environment, and the fifth element determines employer liability.

We note that the parties do not dispute the District Court's finding that Mandel satisfied the first element because she had presented "sufficient evidence from which a reasonable jury could infer that the alleged harassment was based on her sex."

ii. " Severe or Pervasive"

To determine whether an environment is hostile, a court must consider the totality of the circumstances, including "the frequency of the discriminatory conduct; its severity; whether it is physically threatening or humiliating, or a mere offensive utterance; and whether it unreasonably interferes with an employee's work performance." *Harris v. Forklift Sys., Inc.*, 510 U.S. 17 (1993). The District Court summarized the alleged incidents and concluded that "none of the alleged incidents is sufficiently severe to establish a hostile work environment." The District Court's reason-

ing suggests that it improperly parsed out each event and viewed them separately, rather than as a whole. On remand, the District Court must consider the totality of the circumstances, rather than parse out the individual incidents, to determine whether the acts that collectively form the continuing violation are severe or pervasive.

iii. " Detrimentally Affected"

We agree with the District Court that an objectively reasonable person in Mandel's place might be offended by the alleged incidents. We are troubled, however, by the District Court's conclusion that Mandel failed to show that she was detrimentally affected by the alleged incidents:

> Here, Mandel only complained about one of the alleged incidents (Bachert's name calling), and she complained to a friend at work and not a supervisor. Further, she has presented no evidence that she had any psychological distress or that her ability to perform her job was impaired. Finally, the record contains evidence that Mandel actively participated in creating a work environment in which vulgarity and sexual innuendo were commonplace. Mandel's use of explicit language and her e-mails involving ongoing sexual jokes demonstrate a casual ease with this type of workplace behavior. The use of sexual humor does not on its own demonstrate that Mandel is incapable of being offended by degrading comments, but when combined with a lack of evidence of any subjective distress, a reasonable jury could not find that Mandel has proven that the harassment had a detrimental effect on her.

Although Mandel engaged in certain unprofessional conduct, the comments and conduct to which she was subject were often worse and apparently uninvited. Mandel complained about being told to make coffee, and although she did not complain to her supervisors about the other alleged incidents, there is some evidence that she complained to other employees. She also resigned shortly after Bachert called her a "bitch" during a meeting and alleged in her sworn EEOC Charge and questionnaires that she was detrimentally affected. A jury could reasonably conclude that Mandel did not invite these comments or conduct and that, despite her own conduct, was offended by them. Because the inherently subjective question of whether particular conduct was unwelcome presents difficult problems of proof and turns on credibility determinations, the District Court erred in granting summary judgment.

iv. *Respondeat Superior* Liability

The basis of an employer's liability for a hostile work environment claim depends on whether the harasser is the victim's supervisor or coworker. Because the District Court concluded that Mandel failed to establish a hostile work environment, it did not reach the question of employer liability. There is an inadequate record before us on appeal from which to determine whether *respondeat superior* liability exists. Because we reverse and remand for further proceedings on the hostile work environment claim, we leave the issue to the District Court to determine on remand.

Chapter Extension

For additional material relating to Chapter 8, see p. 285 in the Appendix of Chapter Extension Files.

Chapter Problems

1. Define the following terms:
   a. Disparate treatment
   b. Disparate impact
   c. Mixed motive cases
   d. Standard deviation
   e. Bona fide occupational qualification
   f. Validation
   g. Bona fide seniority system
   h. Hostile work environment
   i. Bona fide employee benefit plan
   j. Right-to-sue letter

2. Rysy, Inc. is a janitorial company in Chicago. It advertised in a Spanish-language newspaper that it was looking to hire 15 men and 15 women. Applicants were to apply at the company's office in Chicago. Jean saw the ad and told her friend Natalie about it. Both Jean and Natalie are African-American.

   When Jean went to Rysy's office, there was another applicant who was Hispanic filling out an application. When the Hispanic woman turned in her application, she was asked to stay for an interview. The receptionist would not give Jean an application and told her that she needed a birth certificate to apply. Jean went home and came back with her birth certificate. She was then told that the company did not have any more applications. When Jean gave Rysy her resume, the receptionist told her that Rysy would call her if it was interested in her. The next day, Natalie went to Rysy's office, and had a similar experience. The receptionist took her application and told her that someone would call her if Rysy was interested in her. While she was there, she saw four Hispanic women and one Hispanic man filled out applications. All five of the other applicants were asked to stay for an interview. Rysy did not call either Jean or Natalie for an interview afterward.

According to Rysy's human resources manager, Rysy's president told the HR manager that Rysy was a Polish company, and that she needed to recruit more Europeans and not African-Americans. The HR manager also said that when the HR manager recruited from an African-American community, she was reprimanded by the president. According to the HR manager, the president of Rysy told the HR manager that she was hiring too many N-word and then fired the HR manager shortly after that.

Do the above facts provide a reasonable basis for believing that Title VII has been violated? Why or why not? Explain fully.

3. An insurance company has found that black people are more likely to buy insurance if approached by a black agent, while white people are more receptive to a white agent. The company plans to assign its black agents to offices in predominantly black neighborhoods and its white agents to offices in predominantly white neighborhoods. Is the practice legal? Why or why not?

4. The All African-American Co. (AAA), a real estate firm, hires only African-Americans, because its owner is African-American and the owner wants to promote the economic opportunities of African-Americans. Is AAA's practice legal? Explain fully.

5. The Vita Company has a job opening for a financial analyst. It advertises its position as requiring that the applicant possess an accounting undergraduate degree. Three applicants apply. Bob Bender, an African-American male, possesses an undergraduate business degree from a large state university, with an accounting major. Wilma Wood, a white female, possesses an undergraduate degree from a small private college, with three years of job experience. Joe Goodbar, a white male, possesses an MBA from an Ivy League college and an undergraduate accounting degree from a state university.

All three candidates are interviewed by members of the management team at Vita Company. Each member of the management team fills out an evaluation form. One management team member responds that "Wilma is cute but dumb." Another states that Bob "won't be able to get into the right clubs." All of the team members agree that Joe is preferable because his MBA provides flexibility for future promotions and work assignments beyond the financial analyst job. Who should be hired? Why?

6. An employer's hiring policy requires that all of its employees have a college degree, even for jobs such as receptionist and file clerk, which as recently as seven years ago were filled by employees who did not have a college education. If the employer's policy would result in a significantly

disproportionate exclusion of racial minorities, will adopting the requirement violate any equal employment opportunity laws? Explain fully.

7. Zugspitze Parking, Inc. manages parking facilities nationwide. It uses an Internet website to accept applications for all its job vacancies. If an applicant answers "yes" to the question, "Have you ever been convicted of a crime?" the system terminates the process with a screen telling the applicant that the application cannot be processed at that time. Is this selection practice legal? Explain fully.

8. A real estate management company manages an office building and employs a receptionist in the building lobby. The company requires the receptionist to wear a uniform that is a low-cut, tight-fitting body suit. The top of the receptionist's breasts are visible. Her legs and thighs are covered only by black fishnet stockings. Every day various people entering the building have whistled and stared at her and made cat calls, and a few have pinched her or put their arms around her. Does Title VII require the company to change the uniform? Explain.

9. Zulphia, who is from Jordan and a Muslim, wears a hijab, a headscarf that covers the head and neck but leaves the face clear. She applied for a job as a retail sales clerk at Great Gable Hardware. Gus Gable is concerned that if Zulphia wears the hijab, the store's customers, employees, and suppliers will be unnerved. What should Gus Gable do? Explain fully.

10. Ernest Employer provides medical insurance to its employees, who share in paying the premium. The employer also maintains a wellness program for employees, providing them with health care coaching, nutritional counseling, fitness activities, etc. Employer sends the employees an email notifying them that if they go to the wellness program's website and complete a questionnaire entitled *Personal Health & Well-Being Assessment (PHA)*, they will earn a $360 premium credit and have a choice of several medical plans. If they have a spouse/same-sex domestic partner on the medical plan, the employee will earn an additional $120 premium credit. If they do not complete the *PHA*, they will be able to enroll in only one of the medical plans, which carries the highest premium. The *PHA* asks for the employee to provide information about the employee's medical history as well as the medical history of his or her family members. For example, a question asks if the employee or anyone in the employee's immediate family (parents, brother, sisters) have experienced such medical conditions as hypertension (high blood pressure). Is Ernest Employer in violation of GINA? Explain.

Abusive discharge A tort, recognized in some states, committed when an employer discharges an employee in violation of a clear expression of public policy.

Acceleration clause A provision in a credit agreement that allows the creditor to demand full payment of the debt if the debtor does not make timely payments or otherwise fails to comply with the terms of the agreement.

Acceptance The offeree's assent to the terms of an offer to enter into a contract.

Act of state doctrine Principle preventing judicial examination of certain acts of a foreign government.

Action A suit brought in a court.

Actionable A term used to show that acts provide a basis or legal reason for a lawsuit.

Adequate protection Usually an amount of money paid by the trustee in bankruptcy to a secured creditor to compensate for depreciation or other loss to property in which the secured creditor has a security interest.

Adjudication The determination of a controversy and pronouncement of a judgment or decree in a case.

Administrative agency An agency of the government charged with administering particular legislation.

Administrative law judge An officer who presides at the initial hearing on matters litigated before an administrative agency. He or she is independent of the agency staff.

Administrative Procedure Act A statute establishing the procedural rules governing how federal agencies operate.

Affectation doctrine A doctrine, developed by the Supreme Court in interpreting the Commerce Clause of the Constitution of the United States, whereby Congress has the power to regulate any activity that has an appreciable effect on interstate commerce.

Affidavit A written declaration or statement of facts, sworn before a person who has the authority to administer such an oath.

Affirm To agree with. An appellate court affirms a lower court decision when it declares the decision valid.

Affirmative action The aggressive search to hire qualified minorities or those underrepresented in the workplace. An obligation undertaken by federal contractors to make special efforts to hire women and minorities. It is also a remedy which a court may decree under Title VII of the Civil Rights Act of 1964 and which the National Labor Relations Board is authorized to make under the National Labor Relations Act to effectuate the policies of those statutes.

Affirmative defense An assertion that, if true, relieves a defendant of liability or limits a plaintiff's recovery.

Agent One who acts for a principal.

Allegation In a pleading, a declaration or statement by a party to a suit.

Allege To make a statement of fact, an assertion, or a charge.

Amicus curiae Latin, "Friend of the court." An individual or corporation that, because of strong interest in a case, petitions the court for permission to file a brief.

Answer   A pleading of the defendant which responds to a complaint by either admitting or denying the allegations contained in the complaint.

Antitakeover statutes   Statutes that benefit incumbent management of a corporation in the event of a corporate takeover attempt.

Apparent authority   A doctrine whereby an agent binds a principal to a third party because the principal invests the agent with the appearance of authority, even though actual authority is absent.

Appeal   The process by which a party asks a higher court to review alleged errors made by a lower court or an agency.

Appellant   The party that takes an appeal from one court to another.

Appellate court   A court having jurisdiction of appeal and review.

Appellee   The party in a case who responds to an appeal.

Appraisal rights   Rights of minority shareholders to have their interests appraised and sold to the corporation at the appraised value.

Arbitrary and capricious standard of review   The standard of judicial review of agency action whereby a court sets aside agency action if the agency failed to consider relevant evidence or made a clear error in judgment.

Arbitration   A process wherein a dispute is submitted to a mutually acceptable person or board, each party to the dispute having agreed beforehand to comply with the decision.

Arguendo   For the sake of the purposes of argument. A statement or observation made as a matter of argument or hypothetical illustration.

Arraignment   A proceeding wherein the accused is formally informed of the charge(s) and is asked to plead guilty, not guilty, or nolo contendere.

Articles of Confederation   The name of the document embodying the compact made among the 13 original states of the Union, before the adoption of the present Constitution.

Assault   The intentional tort of causing another person to be apprehensive of a battery.

Assumption of the risk   An affirmative defense raised by the defendant that defeats the plaintiff's recovery because the plaintiff knowingly and voluntarily exposed himself or herself to the danger that caused the injury.

Attachment   The act or process of taking, apprehending, or seizing persons or property by virtue of a judicial process for the purpose of securing satisfaction of a judgment.

Attempt   In criminal law, an effort to accomplish a crime, amounting to more than mere preparation or planning for it, which, if not prevented, would have resulted in the full consummation of the attempted act, but which, in fact, does not bring to pass the party's ultimate design. In civil matters, an attempt ordinarily means an intent combined with an act falling short of the thing intended.

At-will employee   An employee who may be discharged by the employer for any reason without liability.

Authorization cards   Cards signed by employees in favor of a particular union as their collective bargaining representative.

Aver   To set out, assert, or allege in a formal complaint before a court of law.

Bailment   A delivery of goods by one person (bailor) to another (bailee) in trust for the accomplishment of a specific purpose involving the goods (e.g., repair) on an express or implied contract to carry out such trust and subsequently return the goods to the bailor.

Bailor   One who entrusts goods to another under a bailment.

Bait and switch   A method of selling in which a seller advertises at a low price a product that the seller does not intend to sell (the bait) and then disparages that product to the prospective buyer and directs the buyer to a higher-priced product (the switch) which the seller intended to sell all along.

Banc   French, "The full court." A court sits *en banc* when all the judges making up the court hear the case in contradistinction to having the case decided by one judge or a portion of the judges of the court.

Bargaining order   An order of the National Labor Relations Board directing an employer to bargain with a union. A bargaining order is made to remedy employer conduct during a board conducted election to decide whether the employees want a union to be their representative. The employer's conduct must be so serious an interference with employees' free choice as to render a new election incapable of being conducted.

Bargaining unit The group of employees sharing a community of interest and making up a unit for purposes of union representation and collective bargaining. Barred Obstruction; subject to a hindrance that prevents legal redress or recovery.

Battery The intentional tort of performing an unwanted touching.

Beneficiary One for whose benefit a trust is created.

Best efforts underwriting A type of underwriting whereby an underwriter agrees to use its best efforts to sell securities of an issuer to brokers in return for a commission on the sales that it makes. Under this type of distribution the underwriter is not obligated to sell any designated quantity of securities.

Bill The draft of an act of the legislature before it becomes law.

Bill of information A formal accusation of the commission of a crime made by a prosecutor in place of a grand jury indictment.

Bill of lading A document issued by a person engaged in the business of shipping goods. It serves as a receipt of goods received, a memorandum of the sales contract between seller and shipper, and a document of title evidencing ownership of the goods described in the bill of lading.

Blue sky laws State statutes regulating the sale of securities.

Bona fide Latin, "In good faith." Honestly, sincerely.

Bona fide occupational qualification A statutory exception to employment practices that might otherwise violate equal employment laws; it allows an employer to discriminate in its hiring where religion, national origin, sex, or age is reasonably necessary to the normal operation of a business.

Bona fide seniority system A seniority system which applies equally to all employees regardless of membership in a protected class, was not established or maintained for the purpose of discriminating, and operates rationally in accord with the practice in the industry.

Bond (security) A certificate issued by a governmental body or a corporation to represent a debt owed to the bondholder as well as a promise to pay interest.

Boycott A conspiracy or confederation to prevent anyone from carrying on business, or to injure anyone's business, by preventing potential customers from doing business with him or her.

Breach of contract Failure, without legal excuse, to perform any promise which forms the whole or part of a contract.

Bribe Anything given in value with the corrupt intent to induce or influence a public official in the performance of his or her duties.

Broker An agent who bargains, carries on negotiations, and makes contracts on behalf of his or her employer for compensation; also, a dealer in securities issued by others.

Brokerage The compensation of a broker, including wages and commission.

Bubble concept The treatment of all pollution-emitting devices collectively within an area, thus permitting increased pollution from sources as long as there is an equivalent decrease in pollution from other sources under the bubble.

Burden of proof The necessity or duty of affirmatively proving the fact or facts in dispute on an issue raised between the parties to a suit in court.

Business judgment rule A rule that affords board members of a corporation wide latitude in decisionmaking.

Canons of ethics Standards for the professional conduct expected of a lawyer, comprising the Code of Professional Responsibility. Initially adopted by the American Bar Association, it has been enacted into law in most states.

Capitalist model of justice A model based on the theory of economic justice that any distribution of things of value which results from unfettered economic competition is just.

Case law The law as developed or laid down in decided cases, as opposed to statutes.

Case of first impression A case which has no precedent on which the court may rely.

Cause of action The facts which evidence a civil wrong, thereby giving rise to a right to judicial relief.

Cease and desist order An order by an agency or a court directing someone to stop doing something.

Certiorari   A means of obtaining appellate review by petition; a writ issued by an appellate court to an inferior court commanding the record to be certified to the appellate court for judicial review.

Charging party   A person who files a complaint with a government agency alleging that there has been a violation of law. In labor law, the person who files an unfair labor practice charge with the National Labor Relations Board is called a charging party. Also, a person who files a charge with the Equal Employment Opportunity Commission, alleging that someone has violated one of the federal employment laws prohibiting employment discrimination, is called the charging party.

Checks and balances   A system of government whose branches provide checks and balances against each other.

Choice-of-forum provision   A provision in a contract specifying a jurisdiction's court to which the parties agree to submit any disputes that may arise under the contract.

Choice-of-law provision   A clause in a contract specifying the body of law the parties to the contract agree will govern their contract.

Churning   Abuse of a customer's confidence by a broker who initiates excessive transactions for the customer for personal gain.

Circumstantial evidence   Evidence of an indirect nature; evidence from which the existence of a fact is inferred.

Civil law   That body of law concerned with civil or private rights. Contrast *Criminal law*.

Claim   A cause of action.

Class action   An action brought by one or more persons as representatives of a large group of similarly situated persons.

Close corporation   A corporation with a small number of shareholders who are family members or otherwise related.

Closed-end credit   Refers to specific amount of credit for a definite time with loans repaid in installments.

Codetermination   A process of management in which employers and employees share in the decision making.

Collateral   Property pledged as security for the satisfaction of a debt.

Collective entity doctrine   A doctrine of constitutional law holding that the Fifth Amendment's privilege against self-incrimination is a personal right and does not apply to corporations or other collective entities.

Collusion   An agreement between two or more persons to commit a wrongful act.

Commerce   The exchange of goods, products, or property of any kind.

Commercial speech   A term used in constitutional law to refer to economic speech, such as advertising.

Commodity   A movable article of commerce, especially merchandise.

Common carrier   One that transports persons or property for compensation, providing such services to the general public.

Common law   The principles and rules which derive solely from custom or from the judgments and decisions of courts. It is judge-made law.

Comparative negligence   The doctrine under which a plaintiff's negligence as a factor in his or her own injury is assigned a percentage value, and his or her recovery from the defendant is reduced proportionately. Contrast with *Contributory negligence*.

Compensable   Capable of being compensated.

Compensable damages   Damages which compensate the victim for a loss; damages that put the victim in the position he or she was in before the injury occurred.

Compensable injury   Within workers' compensation statutes, compensation to an employee for injury arising out of and in the course of employment.

Compensatory damages   Damages compensating an injured party for the injury sustained, and nothing more; such compensation as will simply make good or replace the loss caused by a wrong or injury.

Competitive injury   An injury to competition or to a competitor.

Complaint   The first pleading by the plaintiff in a civil case. Its purpose is to give the defendant the information on which the plaintiff relies to support its demand. In a complaint, the plaintiff sets out a cause of action, consisting of a formal allegation or charge presented to the appropriate court.

Composition plan   A plan whereby a debtor pays a pro rata share to each creditor in satisfaction of debt.

Concerted action Action that has been planned, arranged, adjusted, agreed on, or settled between parties acting together pursuant to some design or scheme.

Conciliation The proceeding in which litigants are brought together by a third party.

Concur To agree.

Concurring opinion A printed opinion in which a judge agrees with the decision of the majority of the court for a different reason. With reference to appellate court opinions, a concurring opinion is one written by a judge who may agree with the majority opinion's conclusion, but for different reasons, and therefore writes a separate opinion.

Confederation A league or compact for mutual support, particularly of nations or states. Such was the colonial government during the American Revolution.

Confirmed letter of credit A letter of credit sent to a bank near the seller's place of business, indicating another bank representing the buyer will pay on presentation of required documents.

Conglomerate merger A merger among firms that operate in separate or distinct markets.

Conscious parallelism When a competitor copies the actions of a market leader absent contract, combination, or conspiracy.

Consent decree A decree entered by consent of the parties. It is not a judicial sentence, but is an agreement of the parties made under the sanction of the court.

Consent order An agreement by the defendant to cease activities which the government asserts are illegal. Also known as consent decree.

Consequential damages Damage or injury that is not a direct, immediate, or predictable result of a party's act, but is nevertheless shown to be a consequence of it.

Consideration Something given in exchange for a promise which makes the promise legally enforceable. Consideration consists of doing or promising to do that which the giver was not previously obligated to do or refraining from doing or promising to refrain from doing that which the giver had a legal right to do.

Consignee One to whom goods are consigned for sale or safekeeping.

Consignment Property delivered by a consignor to an agent for sale where title is held by the consignor until the property is sold.

Consignor One who delivers goods to another on consignment.

Conspiracy A combination or confederation between two or more persons formed for the purpose of committing, by their joint efforts, some unlawful or criminal act.

Construction defect In a product liability action, a defect which results from the negligent manufacture of a particular item rather than from a defect in its design.

Constructive conditions Conditions that the law implies into a contract based on the order of performance under the contract.

Consumer credit Credit that is extended primarily for personal, family, or household purposes.

Consumer Product Safety Commission A federal administrative agency which supervises and regulates consumer products.

Consumer product safety standard Performance or labeling standard, voluntarily assumed by product manufacturers, or imposed by the CPSC on product manufacturers.

Contempt A willful disregard or disobedience of a public authority.

Contempt of court An act which disturbs or obstructs a court or is intended to detract from its authority or dignity.

Continuing trespass A type of trespass that occurs over an extended period of time.

Contract An agreement that a court enforces.

Contributory negligence Conduct by the plaintiff which is a contributing factor in his or her injury, thus barring any recovery against the defendant. Contrast *Comparative negligence.*

Conversion An unauthorized assumption and exercise of ownership over goods belonging to another, to the alteration of their condition or the exclusion of the owner's rights.

Conviction The result of a criminal trial which ends in a judgment that the prisoner is guilty as charged.

Copyright A limited monopoly granted by the federal government to protect literary type works.

Corporate opportunity An opportunity that arises because of a corporation's business or situation; a doctrine which prevents corporate officials from personally appropriating an opportunity which belongs to the corporation.

Corporation A business organization which is a legal entity formed in compliance with statutory law whose owners enjoy limited liability.

Corrective advertising A remedy of the Federal Trade Commission by which one found guilty of violating the Federal Trade Commission Act with regard to unlawful advertising is ordered to correct the lasting impression of the advertising on the public by engaging in advertising that repudiates the earlier advertising.

Cost justification defense The justification of price discrimination under the Robinson-Patman Act based on the difference in cost.

Counterclaim A claim presented by a defendant which, if successful, defeats or reduces the plaintiff's recovery.

Countervailing duties A tax imposed by an importing country on goods to counter-act a subsidy given by the exporting country to the manufacture of the goods.

Court judgment The official decision of a court determining the respective rights and claims of the parties in a lawsuit.

Credit bureau An establishment that makes a business of collecting information relating to the credit, character, responsibility, and reputation of individuals and businesses for the purpose of furnishing the information to subscribers.

Creditor A person to whom a debt is owed.

Criminal law That body of law, commonly codified into penal codes, which declares what conduct is criminal and provides punishment for such conduct to protect society from harm. Contrast Civil law.

Criminal penalty Punishment attached to the conviction of a crime.

Cross claim A claim made in the course of an action by a defendant against a codefendant or by a plaintiff against a coplaintiff.

Cross elasticity of demand An economic measure of the relationship between price changes and demand changes for a particular good.

Cross-examination The examination of a witness at a trial or hearing, or on taking a deposition, by the party opposed to the one that produced said witness, on his or her evidence given in chief, to test its truth, to further develop it, or for other purposes.

Data acts from which to draw a conclusion. De facto In fact; in deed; actually.

De jure corporation A lawfully recognized corporation.

De minimis Something small or trifling.

De novo Latin, "To begin anew." Usually refers to the necessity of a new hearing on the same facts and law previously litigated.

Debt security Bonds, notes, debentures, and any other corporate securities which represent a debt owed to the holder.

Debtor One who owes money.

Deceit A fraudulent misrepresentation used by one person to deceive or trick another, who is ignorant of the facts, to the damage of the latter.

Decertify In labor law, to decertify a union is to take away its status as the exclusive bargaining agent of the employees of an employer. Decertification occurs usually after an election is conducted by the National Labor Relations Board to determine whether the employees wish to continue to have a particular union act as their exclusive bargaining agent.

Declaratory judgment A judgment which simply declares the rights of the parties or expresses the opinion of the court on a question of law without ordering anything to be done.

Defamation The disparagement of one's reputation; the offense of injuring a person's character, fame, or reputation by oral or written publication.

Default Failure; omission to perform a legal or contractual duty; the failure of a party to appear in court after being properly served with process.

Defendant The party against which an action is brought in a civil case; the accused in a criminal case.

Defense An assertion offered by a defendant which, if successful, relieves him or her of liability, reduces the plaintiff's recovery, or defeats a criminal charge.

Defined benefit plan A retirement plan that provides specific retirement benefits based on age and length of employment.

Defined contribution plan A pension plan whose benefits are based on the amount in the retirement account.

Demand The amount of a particular good that consumers buy in a given period of time.

Deposition Pretrial testimony of a witness taken orally and under oath before an officer of the court (but not in open court), subject to cross-examination and reduced to writing.

Design defect In the law of product liability, a defect in a product resulting from its design, so that every one produced is similarly defective. Contrast with *Construction defect.*

Dicta Plural of *dictum.* Opinions of a judge that do not embody the resolution or determination of the court.

Dictum The word is generally used as an abbreviated form of obiter dictum (a remark by the way). An observation or remark made by a judge in pronouncing an opinion in a case, concerning some rule, principle, or application of law, or the solution of a question suggested by the case, but not necessarily involved in the case or essential to its determination.

Disclosure The act of disclosing. In several areas of government regulation of business, it refers to the act of revealing required information to consumers, investors, and employees.

Discovery Devices that may be used by one party to obtain information about the case from the other party in preparation for trial.

Disparagement An untrue or misleading statement about a competitor's business or goods made to influence, or tending to influence, the public not to buy from the competitor.

Disparate impact The imposition of a rule of employment which disproportionately affects a protected class.

Disparate treatment The treatment of one employee or prospective employee less favorably than another because of race, sex, religion, national origin, age, or handicap.

Disposable earnings The portion of a person's income that he or she is free to spend or invest as he or she sees fit after payment of taxes and other obligations.

Dissenting opinion An opinion wherein a judge disagrees with the result reached by the majority of the court. Contrast Concurring opinion.

Distress sale A "going out of business" sale in which the seller receives less for the goods than would be received under normal conditions.

Distributive justice Theories of justice dictating the morally proper way to distribute things of value in society.

Diversity jurisdiction The jurisdiction of the federal courts to hear cases in which the parties are citizens of different states or one of the parties is an alien and the amount in controversy exceeds $50,000.

Diversity of citizenship A phrase used with reference to the jurisdiction of the federal courts, which, under Article III, Section 2, of the Constitution of the United States, extends to cases between citizens of different states. See diversity jurisdiction.

Dividend The share allotted to each of several persons entitled to participate in a division of profits or property. Dividends are what a shareholder earns from the stock owned in a corporation.

Draft A written order by the first party, called the drawer, instructing a second party, called the drawee (such as a bank), to pay a third party, called the payee. Due diligence defense A defense to a securities violation which requires a defendant to prove that he or she exercised ordinary prudence, but nonetheless was unaware of a material misrepresentation contained in the registration statement.

Effluent limitation The amount of pollutants legally dischargeable from a particular source.

Electronic Funds Transfer Act A federal statute that requires financial institutions to disclose the terms of electronic funds transfer services, establishes a procedure for error resolution, and specifies penalties for violations.

Eminent domain The power of a sovereign to take private property for public use, necessitating just compensation.

Emission limitation A specific rule that operators of pollutant sources must follow to reduce emissions.

Emissions offset policy A policy under the Clean Air Act whereby increased emissions are permitted by the applicant at a source in a nonattainment area as long as sufficient reductions in emission occur in the same area.

Employment-at-will doctrine The legal doctrine that holds that whenever an employment relationship is of an indefinite duration, either party—the employer or the employee—may terminate the relationship at will, for good cause or bad, in good faith or with malice.

Enabling legislation   A term applied to any statute that enables agencies, corporations, or persons to do something they could not do before. Such statutes confer a lawful power in an agency to act on a given matter.

Enactment   The process by which a bill becomes a statute.

Enterprise coverage   A type of coverage of the federal Fair Labor Standards Act whereby that act covers all the employees of a firm that engages in commerce.

Entrepreneur   Someone who organizes, manages, or assumes the risk of a business.

Environmental impact statement   A statement that details the environmental impact of proposed administrative action. The statement must be prepared by an agency whenever it plans or engages in major federal actions significantly affecting the quality of human environment.

Equal Credit Opportunity   Act A federal statute that prohibits discrimination in credit extension on the basis of sex, race, religion, national origin, age, and other protected statuses.

Equitable relief   Injunction, specific performance, restraining orders, and the like, as opposed to money damages.

Equity security   A share in a corporation, usually referred to as stock.

Escrow   A writing, deed, stock, or property delivered to a third person, to be held by that person until the fulfillment of a condition and then delivered to its owner.

Ethicist   One versed in the study of how moral decisions are justified.

Ethics   The study of how moral decisions are justified.

Ex parte   On the application of one party only. A judicial proceeding is ex pane when it is taken or granted at the request of, or for the benefit of, one party only, and without notice to, or contestation by, any person adversely interested.

Exclusive dealing agreements   Contracts on which the buyer is obligated to purchase all of its requirements of a given commodity from the seller.

Executive agencies   Federal agencies that are under the direct control of the president. Appointments to executive agencies do not need Senate approval.

Executive order   An order by the chief executive of a government affecting the administration of the executive branch of government.

Exhaustion   A doctrine requiring that a party utilize remedies provided within an agency before seeking review by a court.

Exonerate   To exculpate; to remove a responsibility or duty.

Experience rating provision   A rating of an employer, based on historical unemployment data, which determines the employer's state unemployment compensation tax contribution.

Export trading company   A company that acts as an intermediary in the marketing of goods overseas.

Express conditions   Conditions inserted in a contract by the parties that must be fulfilled before a party has a duty to perform or that when fulfilled relieve a party of a duty to perform.

Express warranty   A warranty which the seller creates by making a representation or a promise relating to goods or by showing the buyer a sample or model of them, regardless of whether such words as guaranty or warranty are used.

Expropriation   An act by which a foreign government takes over ownership of an American company or American property located in the foreign government.

Expunge   To destroy; to strike out wholly. "Expungement of the record" refers to the process whereby a record of a criminal conviction is sealed or destroyed after a designated period of time.

Extension plan   A plan whereby a debtor extends the time for payments to creditors past the due date.

Fair Credit Reporting Act   A federal statute that regulates consumer reporting agencies.

Fair use   A doctrine under copyright law which permits reasonable use of copyrighted works for limited purposes, such as criticism, news, reporting, teaching and research.

False imprisonment   The intentional tort of interfering with another person's freedom of movement.

Federal question jurisdiction The jurisdiction of the federal courts to hear cases arising under the U.S. Constitution, acts of Congress, or treaties.

Federal Register A federal publication providing notice of federal rulemaking by federal agencies.

Federalism The relationship between the states and the federal government whereby responsibility and autonomy is divided between them.

Fellow servant doctrine A common-law doctrine, now abrogated by all workers' compensation acts, that an employee injured by the negligent act of a fellow employee cannot recover damages from his or her employer.

Fiduciary A person having a duty, created by his or her undertaking, to act primarily for another's benefit.

Fiduciary duty The duty which arises whenever one person is in a special relationship of trust to another, such as the duty an attorney owes to a client.

Firm commitment underwriting A type of underwriting of securities whereby the underwriter is obligated to purchase a designated number of shares of securities from an issuer at a specified price.

Fixture Personal property that has been affixed to reality in such a manner as to become part of the realty. Foreign corporation A corporation doing business in any state other than the one in which it is incorporated.

Foreign Corrupt Practices Act A federal statute which prohibits bribing a foreign official, and establishes accounting procedures designed to discover, such briberies.

Form 10-K A form that must be filed with the SEC within 90 days after the end of the fiscal period and which contains current audited financial statements and information regarding the operations of the business and the status of its securities.

Forum non conveniens, doctrine of The power of a court to decline jurisdiction when the convenience of the parties and the ends of justice would be better served by bringing the action in another court.

Franchise A special privilege conferred on someone.

Franchisee A holder of a franchise.

Franchisor A party granting a franchise.

Fungible goods Goods of any type which are by nature considered to be the equivalent of any other good of that type.

Garnishee The person on whom a garnishment is served; one who has in his or her possession the property of someone who owes a debt to another person.

Garnishment A proceeding in which money, property, or credits of a debtor in possession of a third person, the garnishee, are applied to the payment of debts. The process is available only where it is authorized by statute.

GATT The abbreviation for General Agreement on Tariffs and Trade. Treaty covering the treatment of exports and imports for adopting nations.

General intent An intention, purpose, or design, either without a specific plan or without a particular object.

Golden parachutes Lucrative compensation benefits granted to corporate executives in the event they are terminated after a takeover.

Good Under the Uniform Commercial Code, any tangible item capable of being moved other than money, securities, and real estate.

Good faith An intangible quality encompassing honesty, sincerity, and the lack of intent to defraud or take advantage of another.

Goodwill The propensity of customers to return to a business. The patronage of a particular business. As such, it is an intangible asset of a business.

Gratuity A gift.

Gross negligence A conscious or intentional act or omission likely to result in harm to a person or property; a higher level of culpability than simple negligence.

Group boycott A per se violation of the Sherman Antitrust Act which amounts to a refusal to economically deal by two or more.

Handicap A physical or mental impairment that substantially limits one or more of life's major activities.

Hazard communication standard An OSHA standard requiring chemical manufacturers and importers to evaluate the hazards of all chemicals they produce or import, to develop material safety data sheets for each chemical, to label containers holding chemicals with information concerning the chemicals and their hazards, and to so advise their employees about the hazards.

Horizontal merger Acquisition of one company by another company producing the same product or similar product and selling it in the same geographic market.

Horizontal restraint An agreement between two or more competitors to avoid competing with each other.

Hot cargo agreement A form of a secondary boycott involving an illegal agreement that the employer will not deal with nonunion employers or that the employees need not handle nonunion goods.

Imminent hazard An immediate danger resulting from a product defect.

Impeach To challenge the credibility of a witness.

Impleader A procedure whereby a defendant brings a new party into an action on the basis that the new party may be liable to that party.

Implied contract A contract not explicitly created by the parties, but inferred, as a matter of reason and justice, from the circumstances.

Implied warranty A warranty which arises by operation of law although the seller does not express it; for example, that a product is fit for the purpose for which it is intended.

In camera In chambers; in private. A cause is said to be heard in camera either when the hearing is held before a judge or agency official in his or her private office or when all spectators are excluded from the courtroom or agency hearing room.

Incidental damages Damages resulting from a buyer's breach of contract, such as the costs of stopping delivery and reselling the goods; damages resulting from a seller's breach, including the expenses incurred in returning rightfully rejected goods and procuring a replacement.

Incorporation doctrine A doctrine developed by the Supreme Court whereby it has interpreted the Due Process Clause of the 14th Amendment of the Constitution of the United States as incorporating, or absorbing, selected provisions of the Bill of Rights (the first 10 amendments) and thus applying them to the states. Prior to the incorporation doctrine, the Bill of Rights applied only to the federal government.

Independent contractor One who contracts to do work for a principal and maintains the means, method, and manner of accomplishing the result.

Independent regulatory agency A federal agency to which appointments require Senate approval.

Indict *See Indictment.*

Indictment A formal accusation made by a grand jury which charges that a person has committed a crime.

Information *See Bill of information.*

Injunction An order of the court directing someone to do or not to do something.

In personam jurisdiction The power which a court has over the defendant's personas opposed to the power of a court over property.

Insider With respect to federal regulation of securities, an insider is anyone who has knowledge of facts not available to the general public. With regard to Section 16 of the Exchange Act of 1934, an insider is specifically defined as an officer, director, or any security holder owning at least 10 percent of the stock of a corporation.

Inside trading Gains derived by trading on inside information.

Intent A conscious and purposeful state of mind with which a person acts.

Intentional infliction of emotional distress An intentional tort action providing redress to the victims of outrageous conduct that causes severe psychological injury.

Intentional torts A category of civil wrongs giving redress to the victims of willful wrongdoing.

Interpretive rules Rules of a federal agency rendering interpretations of the agency's enabling legislation. Such rules are not binding on the courts. Such rules do not need to be issued according to the procedures of the federal Administrative Procedure Act.

Interpretivism A theory of constitutional law maintaining that the Constitution should be interpreted by resort to its literal language or the intent of the framers, as found in historical accounts of the drafting of the Constitution.

Interrogatories A discovery device consisting of a series of written questions directed by one party to another party.

Interstate commerce Commercial trading, traffic, or the transportation of persons or property from a point in one state to points in other states.

Intervention The act of a nonparty becoming a party to a lawsuit on his/her own initiative.

Intrastate commerce Commerce that is carried out wholly within the limits of a single state.

Invasion of privacy An intentional tort providing redress to the victims whose privacy has been unreasonably intruded on.

Investigative consumer report Information gathered through personal interviews with neighbors, friends, associates, or others.

Involuntary corporate dissolution The dissolution of a corporation by the state for noncompliance of administrative requirements.

Irrevocable letter of credit A letter of credit that cannot be cancelled without the agreement of both buyer and seller.

Judgment non obstante verdicto (judgment n.o.v.) *See Judgment notwithstanding the verdict.*

Judgment notwithstanding the verdict A judge's judgment that is contrary to the verdict of the jury.

Judicial review The process by which the Supreme Court of the United States reviews legislation and refuses to enforce those laws that it declares to be unconstitutional.

Jurisdiction The power of a court or a judicial officer to decide a case; the geographic area of a court's authority.

Jurisdictional standards Standards issued by the National Labor Relations Board for particular industries for purposes of determining whether the board will assert jurisdiction.

Jurisprudence The philosophy of law; the science which studies the principles of law and legal relations.

Labeling defect In the law of product liability, a defect in a product resulting from inadequate labeling.

Labeling standard A standard issued by the Consumer Product Safety Commission requiring that a warning label be attached to a product.

Laboratory conditions Conditions regulated by the National Labor Relations Board to ensure a fair determination of the uninhibited wishes of the employees, during an election campaign.

Labor organization An organization of employees organized for the purpose of dealing with their employer.

Laissez-faire economics A policy whereby government takes a hands-off posture toward economic planning.

Lanham Act A federal act that prohibits the use of any false description or representation in connection with any goods or services introduced into commerce.

Legal relief Money damages. Contrast *Equitable relief.*

Legislation The act of enacting laws; the making of laws by express decree; sometimes means a statute or statutes.

Legislative history The background and events leading up to the enactment of a statute; for example, committee reports and floor debates. Courts use the legislative history of a statute in determining the legislature's intent in enacting it.

Legislative rules Regulations issued by federal agencies pursuant to the federal Administrative Procedure Act. Such rules are binding on courts.

Legislator One who makes laws; a member of a legislative body.

Legislature The department, assembly, or body of government that makes laws for a state or nation.

Letter of credit A letter authorizing one person to pay money or extend credit to another on the credit of the writer.

Libel To defame or injure a person's reputation by a published writing.

License A permit granted by a government authority, person, or business to pursue some occupation or to carry on some business.

Lien A security interest in another's property, usually exercisable on the nonpayment of a debt.

Like grade and quality An element in a price discrimination offense under the Robinson-Patman Act requiring two products that are the subject of price discrimination to be of like grade and quality

Limited partnership A special form of partnership whereby the business is managed by general partners and financed by limited partners who do not participate in the management and who enjoy limited liability.

Liquidation The act or process by which a party settles his or her debt by converting all assets into cash and making distribution to creditors. The term is also used in connection with a Chapter 7 straight bankruptcy proceeding.

Lobbying   Attempts, including personal solicitation, to induce legislators to vote in a certain way or to introduce legislation.

Long-arm statute   A state statute subjecting a nonresident or a foreign corporation to the state's jurisdiction if the person or corporation has committed a tortious wrong or conducted business within the state, or has otherwise had minimal contacts within the state.

Magistrate   A term for a public officer. Commonly, however, the term is applied to judicial officers with limited authority, such as justices of the peace.

Magnuson-Moss Warranty Act   A federal statute that requires certain disclosures in connection with written warranties, imposes restrictions on disclaimers of implied warranties, and establishes a procedure through which consumers may more effectively enforce their warranty rights.

Mandatory subjects of bargaining   Under the National Labor Relations Act, bargaining on wages, hours, and other terms and conditions of employment, including retirement benefits, vacations, rest periods, and work assignments.

Marxist model of justice   A model based on the theory of economic justice: "from each according to his ability, to each according to his needs."

Mediation   The act of a third person who attempts to persuade disputing parties to adjust their positions so as to resolve their dispute.

Meeting competition defense   A defense to price discrimination under the Robinson-Patman Act when the seller's lower price was made in good faith to meet the equally low price of a competitor.

Merchantable   Of good quality; of the quality fit for the purpose for which the good is intended.

Merger   The fusion or absorption of one thing or right into another. For example, a merger occurs when one corporation becomes a part of another corporation.

Merit model of justice   A model based on a concept of justice holding that if any distribution of things of value is based on merit, the distribution is just.

Misrepresentation   An untrue statement that justifies the rescission of a contract.

Modification   A change.

Monopoly   The ownership or control of so large a part of the market supply of a given commodity as to stifle competition and ensure control over prices and competition.

Moot   A question which is no longer a controversy because the issue involved is no longer in dispute.

Morals   Judgments regarding what is right or wrong, good or evil.

Mortgage   A pledge or security of particular property for the payment of a debt.

Most-favored-nation clause   A clause found in most treaties providing that the citizens or subjects of contracting nations may enjoy the privileges accorded by either nation to those of the most favored nation.

Motion   A request to a court or judge for a rule or order favorable to the requesting party, generally made within the course of an existing lawsuit.

Motion for directed verdict   A request that the judge order the entry of a verdict for one party on the grounds that the opposing party has failed to present sufficient evidence for any other verdict.

Nationalization   The act whereby a host country takes the property of an alien for a public purpose.

Natural law   Conception of law as a system of rules and principles for the guidance of human conduct which, independently of enacted law or of the systems peculiar to any one people, might be discovered by the rational intelligence of man, and would be found to grow out of and conform to man's nature.

Necessary and Proper Clause   Clause in U.S. Constitution which authorizes Congress to make all laws necessary and proper to carry out the enumerated powers of Congress and all other powers vested in the federal government.

Negligence   The omission to do something that a reasonable and prudent person, guided by those considerations which ordinarily regulate human affairs, would do, or the doing of something that a reasonable and prudent person would not do.

Negligence per se   Imputation of negligence when the defendant's violation of a statute results in injury to a person who is within the class of persons the statute is designed to protect and which injury is the type the statute is designed to protect against.

Nolo contendere Latin, "I will not contest it." A plea in a criminal action often having the same effect as a guilty plea, except that it may not be used against the defendant in a subsequent civil action. Also known as a no-contest plea.

Nonattainment area An area that has not met the national standards for air quality established under the federal Clean Air Act.

Noninterpretivism A theory of constitutional interpretation maintaining that the Supreme Court may make the determination of constitutionality by referring to values other than those constitutionalized by the framers.

Non-obviousness One of the characteristics of an invention that makes it patentable; if the state of the art at the time of the development was such that the "invention" was obvious, it will not be patentable.

Nonpoint source Nondiscernible and unconfined conveyance, such as overflows from irrigated agriculture.

Nuisance A class of torts that arise from the unreasonable, unwarrantable, or unlawful use by a person of his or her property, or from unlawful personal conduct, which obstructs or injures the rights of another.

Obiter dictum See Dictum.

Offer A proposal or act on the part of one person whereby he or she gives to another the legal power to create a contract.

Offeror Someone who makes an offer.

Oligopolistic A market in which a few large producers dominate.

Open-end credit Revolving charges and credit cards which permit the consumer to pay a part of what is owed.

Opinion of the court The statement by a judge or court of the decision reached in regard to a cause tried or argued before them, expounding the law as applied to the case, and detailing the reasons on which the judgment is based.

Order A command or direction authoritatively given.

Order for relief An order of a court or an administrative agency providing a remedy to someone.

OSHRC Occupational Safety and Health Review Commission; a federal administrative agency established under the Occupational Safety and Health Act; it hears appeals from OSH Act violations.

Over-the-counter market The market for securities traded off the floor of a stock exchange and usually sold through brokerage houses.

Palming off To impose by fraud; to pass off a product as another product by unfair means.

Parent corporation A company which owns over 50 percent of the voting stock of another company, known as its subsidiary.

Parliament The supreme legislative assembly of Great Britain.

Parole evidence Evidence of terms of a written contract other than the written document. When the written document is intended as the parties' final expression of their contract, parole evidence of prior agreements or representations cannot be used to vary the terms of the document.

Partnership An association of two or more persons to carry on as co-owners of a business for profit.

Partnership by estoppel A partnership arising when third parties are erroneously led to rely on the existence of a partnership.

Patent A limited monopoly granted by the federal government to make, use, and sell an invention.

Pattern or practice of discrimination A general policy of treating members of a protected class less favorably than other employees, proved by circumstantial evidence.

Per curiam Latin, "By the court." Used to indicate an opinion by the entire court rather than a single judge. Sometimes refers to a brief statement of the court's decision unaccompanied by any written opinion.

Per se Latin, "By itself." Inherently.

Performance standard A standard issued by the Consumer Product Safety Commission specifying minimum performance criteria for a product.

Personal property That property which has no fixed site and is moveable.

Petitioner A party that files a petition with a court, applying in writing for a court order; a party that takes an appeal from a judgment; a party that initiates an equity action.

Plain meaning rule A rule of statutory construction which requires that the meaning of words in a statute be assigned their plain import unless to do so would result in an absurdity.

Plaintiff A person who brings an action or complaint against a defendant; the party who initiates a suit.

Plea An answer to a complaint or to a material allegation of fact therein. In criminal procedure, the answer of the accused in response to the criminal charge.

Pleadings The formal allegations by the parties of their respective claims and defenses; the complaint, answer, and reply.

Plenary Full; entire; complete; absolute; perfect.

Point source Any discernible and confirmed conveyance of water, such as a pipe, ditch, well, or canal.

Police power The inherent power of a state over persons and property which enables the state to regulate the health, safety, and welfare of society.

Positive Law Law actually or specifically enacted or adopted by proper authority for the government of a society.

Possession The control or custody of property, for one's use and enjoyment, to the exclusion of all others.

Post hoc Hereafter; after this time.

Power of Attorney A written instrument investing an agent with authority to act for a principal.

Precedent A previously decided court case which serves as authority for a subsequent similar case.

Predatory intent An attempt to drive competitors out of business by sacrificing present revenues in the hope of recouping losses through future high prices.

Preemption doctrine The doctrine adopted by the U.S. Supreme Court holding that certain matters are of such a national, as opposed to local, character that federal laws take precedence over state laws. As such, a state may not pass a law inconsistent with the federal law.

Preferential transfer A transfer made during the 90-day period before an insolvent debtor's bankruptcy petition is filed, in which the debtor transfers to the creditor a greater percentage of the debt than would have been received under the distribution provision of the act.

Prejudicial error An error made during a trial which materially affects the rights of a party and thus may be grounds for a reversal of judgment or a new trial.

Premises rule A rule of worker's compensation law that holds that an employee who is injured while on the employer's premises may recover even though the employee was going to or coming from the work site.

Price discrimination Selling to one customer at a price and refusing to sell to another at the same price by someone engaged in interstate commerce.

Price fix The act of establishing a price; a per se violation of the Sherman Antitrust Act, as an unreasonable restraint of trade.

Prima facie Latin, "At first sight." A fact presumed to be true unless disproved by evidence to the contrary.

Prima facie case A case which has proceeded on sufficient proof to that stage at which it supports a judicial finding if evidence to the contrary is disregarded. A litigating party is said to have a prima facie case when the evidence in its favor is sufficiently strong for its opponent to be called on to answer it. A prima facie case, then, is one which is established by sufficient evidence and which can be overthrown only be rebutting evidence adduced on the other side.

Primary-fine injury Injury that occurs when a seller suffers damages as a result of price discrimination by a competitor.

Principal In agency law, the party for whom an agent acts.

Private law As used in contrast to public law, the term means that part of the law which is administered between citizen and citizen or which is concerned with the definition and enforcement of rights in cases where both the person in whom the right inheres and the person on whom the obligation is incident are private individuals.

Private placement An exemption under the Securities Act for transactions by an issuer not involving any public offering.

Privilege A right or advantage particular to an individual or a class.

Privity A mutual or successive relationship,, for example, the relationship between the parties to a contract.

Pro rata Proportionately.

Probable cause Reasonable grounds for belief in the existence of facts. In criminal procedure, reasonable grounds for the belief that a person should be arrested or a warrant issued.

Procedural justice A form of justice that deals with the process used in deciding outcomes.

Procedural law The part of law which concerns the method or process of enforcing rights.

Procedural rules Rules adopted by an administrative agency to govern its internal procedures, such as the handling of charges, the holding of hearings, and the timing of investigations and hearings.

Promissory estoppel A legal theory that allows a promise to be enforced without consideration. The theory applies where the promisee reasonably relies on a promise to his or her detriment and when that reliance is foreseeable to the promisor.

Prosecution A criminal action. The term is also frequently used with respect to civil litigation and includes every step from commencement to final determination.

Prospectus A pamphlet that capsulizes the information contained in the registration statement.

Proximate cause Event(s) or action which, in natural and unbroken sequence, produce an injury that would not have occurred absent the event(s) or action.

Proxy Written authorization given by a shareholder to vote his or her shares at a shareholders' meeting.

Proxy statement A statement containing prescribed information that must be supplied to shareholders before proxies are solicited.

Public law The branch of law concerned with administrative and constitutional law.

Publicly held corporation A corporation whose stock is in the hands of many.

Punitive damages Damages awarded to a plaintiff greater than the amount necessary to compensate his or her loss. They are generally granted where the wrong involves intent, violence, fraud, malice, or other aggravated circumstances.

Quid pro quo The giving of one valuable thing for another.

Real property Land and anything that is permanently attached to land.

Realist conception A conception of law that holds that law is not embodied in abstract principles but in the process of deciding disputes.

Recognition picketing The picketing of an employer by a noncertified union to force the employer to recognize it or the employees to choose it as their representative.

Reconstruction period Period following the Civil War during which the states of the former Confederacy were reintegrated into the Union.

Red herring prospectus In securities law, an advance copy of the statement (prospectus) to be filed with the Securities and Exchange Commission preceding an issue of securities. The copy is marked in red ink, "not a solicitation, for information only."

Redlining The practice of denying mortgage loans to finance property located in specific neighborhoods.

Redress The receiving of satisfaction for an injury sustained.

Relevant market The geographic market composed of products that have reasonable interchangeability for purposes for which they are produced, considering their price, use, and quality. The term, in relation to a case involving an alleged violation of the Sherman Act or the Clayton Act, consists of both a product market and a geographic market.

Reliance damages A measure of money damages for breach of contract that places the victim of the breach in the economic position he or she would have been in had the contract not been made.

Remand To send back. The sending of a case back to the same court out of which it came, for the purpose of having some action taken on it.

Reorganization A type of bankruptcy that permits a financially disturbed business to continue while arrangements for the adjustment of debts are made with creditors.

Res ipsa loquitur Latin, "The thing speaks for itself." Rule of evidence whereby negligence of the defendant is inferred from the circumstances as the result of a reasonable belief that the injury could not have happened without such negligence.

Res judicata Latin, "A matter adjudged." A thing judicially acted on or decided; a rule that a final judgment or decree on the merits by a court of competent jurisdiction is conclusive of the rights of the parties or their privies in all later suits on points and matters determined in the former suit.

Respondeat superior Latin, "Let the master answer." Doctrine which provides that an employer or master is responsible for the acts of an employee or servant committed within the scope of the employment.

Respondent The party that contends against an appeal.

Response costs The costs of federal or state environmental cleanups for which the violator may be ordered to pay.

Restatement A book published by the American Law Institute consisting of that body's restatement of the law in one of several areas, such as torts, contracts, and agency.

Restitution The avoidance of unjust enrichment, accomplished by requiring the recipient of a benefit to pay the reasonable value of the benefit to the party that conferred the benefit.

Restraining order An injunction; a court order prohibiting a party from doing something.

Restraint of trade Contracts or combinations which tend, or are designed, to eliminate or stifle competition, effect a monopoly, artificially maintain prices, or otherwise obstruct commerce as it would be carried on if left to the control of natural or economic forces.

Reverse To overthrow, vacate, set aside, make void, annul, repeal, or revoke, as to reverse a judgment.

Reviewability A term addressing whether a court has the power to review an administrative agency's action.

Revocation The recall of some power, authority, or thing granted.

RICO Racketeer Influenced and Corrupt Organizations Act; a federal statute that makes it a crime to acquire or operate an enterprise by a pattern of racketeering.

Rights model Ethical justification holding that decisions least disruptive of human rights are to be preferred.

Right to know provision A provision within the superfund law requiring owners and occupiers of facilities which produce, use, and store hazardous chemicals to file with local and state officials a material safety data sheet for each hazardous chemical.

Right to sue letter A letter issued by the Equal Employment Opportunity Commission to a complainant after finding probable cause of discrimination and when attempts to conciliate the dispute have failed.

Rulemaking A function of most federal agencies that allows interested parties to comment on proposed rules of an agency before their promulgation.

Rule of reason A restraint against trade that has a procompetitive business purpose and a competitive restraint not beyond that business purpose.

Rule 10b-5 An SEC rule that prohibits fraud in connection with any sale or purchase of securities.

Sale of business doctrine A doctrine rejected by the United States Supreme Court; it holds that the sale of 100 percent of the stock of a business is not a sale of a security for purposes of federal securities law.

Scalping The practice of a securities broker whereby the broker recommends the purchase of a stock for the purpose of inflating its value so that the broker, who had purchased the same stock previously, capitalizes on its sale.

Scienter Knowledge; intent to deceive or defraud.

Secondary boycott In labor law, the term refers to a refusal by union employees to work for, purchase from, or handle products of a secondary employer with whom the union has no dispute, with the object of forcing such employer to stop doing business with the primary employer with whom the union has a dispute.

Secondary meaning A trademark that has developed a new meaning in which it serves to identify specific goods. For example, Nantuckett has a primary meaning of a geographical location; however, it has a secondary meaning—a specific manufacturer's shirts.

Secondary-line injury Injury that occurs when a seller discriminates in price between two competing buyers.

Security A stock, bond, note, investment contract, or other interest involving an investment in a common enterprise with the expectation of a profit to be derived from the efforts of someone other than the investor; an obligation given by a debtor to assure payment of a debt by providing the creditor with a resource that the creditor can use if the debtor defaults on the debt.

Security interest A type of interest held by a creditor in a debtor's property such that the property could be sold on the debtor's default to satisfy the debt.

Seniority By seniority, the oldest worker in point of service, ability, and fitness for the job is the first to be given a choice of jobs, is the first to be promoted within a range of jobs subject to seniority, and is the last to be laid off. This proceeding is followed down the line to the youngest worker in point of service.

Separation of powers A phrase referring to the division of the federal government into three departments or branches: the legislative, which is empowered to make laws; the executive, which is required to carry out the laws; and the judiciary, which is charged with interpreting the laws and adjudicating disputes under the laws. One branch is not permitted to intrude on the domain of another.

Shareholder A person who owns stock in a corporation.

Shipping terms Terms in a contract which govern the shipment of goods. Shipping terms determine such matters as when risk of loss passes and when performance is complete.

Short-swing profits Profits made by an insider through the sale or other disposition of the corporate stock within six months after purchase.

Single trespass A trespass of a single instance.

Situs Situation or location.

Slander The tort of oral defamation.

Social audit A report of a company's social behavior.

Social balance sheet A report in which a company shares information on its social behavior.

Sole proprietorship A business owned by one person.

Sovereign An independent body or state; a chief ruler with supreme power, such as a king.

Sovereign immunity Doctrine preventing a litigant from asserting an otherwise meritorious claim against a sovereign (government).

Specific intent Exercise of intelligent will to commit a crime.

Specific performance A remedy for breach of contract that requires the breaching party to actually perform what he or she had promised to perform in the contract.

Squeeze out The elimination of minority shareholders by the majority shareholders.

Standard deviation A statistical method of measuring the probability that a given result occurred by chance.

Standing A stake in a controversy sufficient to entitle a person to sue and obtain judicial resolution of the controversy.

Stare decisis Latin, "Let the decision stand." Doctrine under which courts stand by precedent and do not disturb a settled point. Under this doctrine, once a court has laid down a principle of law as applied to a certain state of facts, the court adheres to that principle and applies to it all future cases in which the facts are substantially the same.

State action In constitutional law, the term is used to designate governmental action that is necessary for purposes of bringing a constitutional challenge to such action.

State right-to-work statute A state statute authorized by the Taft-Hartley Act whereby an employee may lawfully refuse to join a union certified as the bargaining representative of the employer's employees.

Status quo ante Latin, "The state of things before."

Statute An act of a legislature declaring, commanding, or prohibiting something; a particular law enacted by the legislative department of government. Sometimes the word is used to designate codified law as opposed to case law.

Statute of frauds A statute requiring that certain contracts be supported by written memoranda.

Statute of limitations A statute prescribing the length of time after an event in which a suit must be brought or a criminal charge filed.

Statutory law Law consisting of statutes as opposed to common law, which is judge-made law.

Stay To stop, arrest, or forbear. To stay an order or decree means to hold it in abeyance or to refrain from enforcing it.

Stop order The name of a Securities and Exchange Commission order directing that the effectiveness of a registration statement be suspended. The order also suspends a security issuer's license to use the mails and warns the investing public that the SEC has found the registration statement to be unreliable.

Strict liability Liability without fault. A case is one of strict liability when neither care nor negligence, neither good nor bad faith, neither knowledge nor ignorance exonerate the defendant.

Subject matter jurisdiction A court's authority to hear a particular type of case.

Subpoena A writ ordering a person to appear and give testimony or to bring documents in his or her control.

Subsidiary corporation A corporation of whose shares at least a majority are owned by another corporation, which thus has control over it.

Substantial evidence standard of review The standard of judicial review of agency action whereby a court examines the administrative record to determine if substantial evidence exists to support the agency determination.

Substantiation   A requirement imposed on advertisers by the Federal Trade Commission that they be able to substantiate the truth of their advertising claims.

Substantive law   That part of law which creates, defines, and regulates rights, as opposed to procedural law, which prescribes the methods for enforcing the rights.

Summary judgment   A pretrial decision reached by a trial court, after considering the pleadings, affidavits, depositions, and other documents, on the ground that no genuine issue of fact has been raised.

Summary plan description   Under the Employee Retirement Income Security Act, a statement of any material modifications to a pension plan, annual reports including certified financial statements, and terminal and supplementary reports, if the plan is to be terminated.

Summons   An instrument served on a defendant in a civil proceeding to give the defendant notice that he or she has been sued.

Sunset legislation   A statute which provides that an agency's authority shall expire on a given date unless the legislative body acts to extend it.

Supremacy Clause   A clause in the U.S. Constitution providing that all laws made by the federal government pursuant to the Constitution are the supreme law of the land and are superior to and conflicting state law.

Takeover bid   A bid to assume control or management of a corporation; a tender offer.

Target company   The company intended to be taken over in a takover bid.

Tender offer   An offer to purchase shares of stock, usually made in an attempt to obtain a controlling interest in a corporation.

Terminable at will   The normal employment relationship, absent a contract, whereby an employer may discharge an employee for any nondiscriminatory reason.

Tie-in   When a party offers to provide one good or service only to those who agree to accept another good or service.

Tombstone ad   An advertisement of a stock offering containing language to the effect that the announcement is neither an offer to sell nor a solicitation of an offer to buy any of the securities listed. The actual offer is made only by the prospectus.

Tort   A civil wrong or injury, other than a breach of contract, committed against the person or property of another.

Tortfeasor   A person who has committed a tort.

Trade association   Organizations of competitors with common interests and business pursuits.

Trademark   A word, name, symbol or device used by a manufacturer or merchant to identify goods and distinguish them from those manufactured by others.

Treatise   A book that expounds on a broad area of a subject.

Treaty   An agreement between nations.

Treble damages   Three times actual damages. The remedy provided to a successful plaintiff in certain actions, including antitrust suits.

Trespass   A tort action affording redress for injury committed to the plaintiff by the unauthorized entry on another's land or the interference with another's personal property.

Trust   A legal arrangement whereby property or other assets are secured for beneficiaries by placing legal title and usually management responsibility in a trustee.

Trustee   The person appointed to execute a trust.

Truth in Lending Act   A federal statute that regulates consumer credit by requiring lenders to disclose certain credit terms in a standard way and regulates the cancellation of credit agreements, consumer leasing, and credit card extension and use.

Unconscionable   So unfair or one-sided as to oppress or unfairly surprise a party.

Unfair labor practices   Those practices contained in sections 8(a) and (b) of the NLRA that prohibit specified employer and employee practices, for example, refusing to bargain in good faith.

Uniform Commercial Code   A comprehensive code, drafted by the National Conference of Commissioners on Uniform State Laws, which has been enacted in all of the states.

Union certification   The process by which the National Labor Relations Board certifies a union as the exclusive bargaining representative of a unit of employees in the employer's work force.

Utility model   Ethical justification holding that acts or rules that provide the greatest benefit to the greatest number of people are right or good.

Validation   A statistical corroboration of a selection procedure that has an adverse impact on a protected group.

Variance   Permission to depart from the literal requirements of an administrative regulation

Venue   The particular county or geographic location in which a court with jurisdiction may hear a case.

Vertical merger   A merger between two firms that have a buyer-seller relationship.

Vertical restraint   An agreement between two or more parties at different levels of the distribution process to restrain trade by, for example, inhibiting intrabrand competition.

Vested   Fixed, settled, absolute. Having the character of absolute ownership. With regard to pension plan benefits, vested benefits are not contingent on the employee continuing to work for the employer.

Veto   Latin, "I forbid." The refusal of assent by the executive officer whose assent is necessary to perfect a law which a legislative body has passed.

Vicarious liability   See *Respondeat superior.*

Vis-à-vis   Face to face. One of two things or persons opposite or corresponding to each other. In relation to each other.

Void   Null; ineffectual; having no legal force.

Warrant   A writ from a competent authority in pursuance of law which directs the doing of an act, is addressed to an officer or person competent to do the act, and affords that officer or person protection from damage if he or she does it. In particular, writs are issued by a magistrate or justice, and addressed to a sheriff, constable, or other officer, requiring the latter to arrest someone or to search someone's person or property and seize items of evidence.

Warranty   A promise that a statement is true. In contracts, a written or verbal undertaking or stipulation that a certain statement in relation to the subject matter of the contract is or shall be as it is stated or promised to be.

White collar exemptions   Those executive, administrative, and professional personnel, who are salaried and meet other specified requirements and who are exempt from coverage of the Fair Labor Standards Act.

Work-product doctrine   The doctrine by which certain material prepared by an attorney in anticipation of litigation is protected from discovery.

Work councils   Plant-level committees consisting of supervisory personnel and workers, which decide plant-level matters.

Writ   A court order directing a person to do something.

Wrongful discharge   See *Abusive discharge.*

CHAPTER
EXTENSION FILES

Chapter One   Law and Ethics

With regard to the chapter's discussion of the fundamental legal principle under the heading *Exercise Due Care and Diligence*, consider the following:

While the expectation of due care in the performance of one's job is prevalent in business, from a technical, legal perspective, the requirement that someone exercise due care requires what the law refers to as a duty of due care. The general rule of law in the United States is that one does not have a duty to go to the aid of another who is exposed to peril. For example, the American rule is that even an expert swimmer need not risk his or her life to save a drowning victim. This is not the rule of law in some other countries. In the United States, there are "good Samaritan" statutes that protect from liability people who help someone who is in need of medical help. The case that follows involves the issue of when a person should be held to a duty to render assistance to another. The court recognizes the long-standing rule of "no duty to aid." However, note that fairness prevails when the court distinguishes the facts of the case from the ordinary "good Samaritan" case.

With regard to the chapter's discussion under the heading *Maintain Fiduciary Standards*, the following is the classic case for expressing the fiduciary rule.

MEINHARD V. SALMON
164 N.E. 545 (N.Y. 1928)

Gerry leased to Salmon the Hotel Bristol at the corner of 42nd Street and Fifth Avenue in New York City. The lease was for 20 years. Salmon undertook to change the hotel building for use as shops and offices.

Salmon entered into a venture with Meinhard to obtain the funds to finance the improvements. Under the terms of the venture, Meinhard was to pay to Salmon half of the cost to reconstruct, manage, and operate the property. (This relationship is referred to as a *joint venture* in the law. The court uses the term *joint adventure*. A joint venture is formed for a single purpose and terminates automatically on completion of the purpose. In most respects, a joint venture is like a partnership, and some view joint ventures as a type of partnership.)

Salmon was to pay Meinhard 40 percent of the profits from the first five years of the lease and 50 percent for the remaining years. Each was to bear the losses equally. Salmon was to have sole power to manage the building.

When the lease was coming to a conclusion, Gerry sold the property to a relative also bearing the name Gerry, who became the lessor-owner. With fewer than four months remaining on the lease, this new owner approached Salmon with a new lease, including the Bristol property. Salmon entered into the lease through

Midpoint Realty Company, which he owned and controlled. Salmon did not tell Meinhard about the lease. When Meinhard found out about it, he demanded that the new lease be held in trust as an asset of the venture. Salmon refused that demand.

Meinhard sued. The trial court and an intermediate appellate court found in favor of Meinhard. Salmon appealed to New York's highest appeals court, which affirmed the decision.

Chief Judge Cardozo

The two were coadventurers, subject to fiduciary duties. . . . As to this we are all agreed. The heavier weight of duty rested, however, upon Salmon. He was a coadventurer with Meinhard, but he was manager as well. During the early years of the enterprise, the building, as reconstructed, operated at a loss. If the relation had then ended, Meinhard as well as Salmon would have carried a heavy burden. Later the profits became large with the result that for each of the investors there came a rich return. For each the venture had its phases of fair weather and of foul. The two were in it jointly, for better or for worse.

Joint adventurers . . . owe to one another, while the enterprise continues the duty of the finest loyalty. Many forms of conduct permissible in a workaday world for those acting at arm's length are forbidden to those bound by fiduciary ties. A trustee is held to something stricter than the morals of the marketplace. Not honesty alone, but the punctilio of an honor the most sensitive, is then the standard of behavior. As to this there has developed a tradition that is unbending and inveterate. Uncompromising rigidity has been the attitude of courts of equity when petitioned to undermine the rule of undivided loyalty by the "disintegrating erosion" of particular exceptions. Only thus has the level of the conduct for fiduciaries been kept at a level higher than that trodden by the crowd. It will not consciously be lowered by any judgment of this court.

The owner . . . Mr. Gerry . . . had vainly striven to find a tenant who would favor his ambitious scheme of demolition and construction. Baffled in the search, he turned to the defendant Salmon in possession of the Bristol, the keystone of the project. He figured to himself beyond a doubt that the man in possession would prove a likely customer. To the eye of an observer, Salmon held the lease as owner in his own right, for himself, and no one else. In fact he held it as a fiduciary, for himself and another, sharers in a common venture. . . . The . . . opportunity that was thus an incident of the enterprise, Salmon appropriated to himself in secrecy and silence.

The trouble about his conduct is that he excluded his coadventurer from any chance to compete, from any chance to enjoy the opportunity for benefit that had come to him alone by virtue of his agency.

We have no thought to hold that Salmon was guilty of a conscious purpose to fraud. Very likely he assumed in all good faith that with the approaching end of the venture he might ignore his coadventurer and take the extension for himself. He had given to the enterprise time and labor as well as money. He had made it a success. Meinhard, who had given money, but neither time nor labor, had already been richly paid. . . . [But] [f]or [Salmon] and those like him the rule of undivided loyalty is relentless and supreme. A different question would be here if there were lacking any nexus of relation between the business conducted by the manager and the opportunity brought to him as an incident of management. For this problem, as for most, there are distinctions of degree.

A question remains as to the form and extent of the equitable interest to be allotted to the plaintiff. . . . [A]n equal division of the shares might . . . take away from Salmon the power of control and management which under the plan of the joint venture he was to have from first to last. . . . To that end an extra share should be added to his half.

[Judgment affirmed.]

Case Questions

1. What duty did Salmon breach?
2. Under the circumstances of this case, what does the law require Salmon to do?
3. Suppose you and another student rent an apartment together for the school year. Toward the end of the year, the two of you are not getting along as well as before. The landlord approaches you with an offer to renew the lease. You want to renew the lease, but you have another friend that you would like to live with in the apartment. Can you renew the lease with the landlord, bringing in your other friend as a new tenant, and excluding your current roommate from the opportunity to participate in renewing the lease? Explain.

SOLDANO V. O'DANIELS
190 Cal. Rptr. 310 (Calif. App. 1983)

Darrell Soldano was shot and killed by Rudolph Villanueva at Happy Jack's Saloon. An eating establishment, the Circle Inn, was across the street from Happy Jack's. On the date of the shooting, a patron of Happy Jack's came into the Circle Inn and informed the bartender that a man had been threatened at Happy Jack's. The patron requested the bartender to either call the police or allow him to use the Circle Inn phone to call the police. The telephone was not in a private office but positioned where it could be used by patrons without inconvenience to the Circle Inn's owner or guests. The bartender refused this request. Soldano's son (the plaintiff) sued the owner of the Circle Inn, Howard O'Daniels (the defendant), for the wrongful death of his father. He alleged that the actions of the Circle Inn bartender were a breach of the legal duty that the Circle Inn owed to the decedent. The trial court dismissed the suit and awarded judgment for O'Daniels. The California Court of Appeals reversed the trial court decision and returned the case to that court for trial. What follows is the appellate court decision.

Associate Justice Andreen

Does a business establishment incur liability for wrongful death if it denies use of its telephone to a good samaritan who explains an emergency situation occurring . . . and wishes to call the police?

■   ■   ■

There is a distinction, well rooted in the common law, between action and nonaction.

The fact that the actor realizes or should realize that action on his part is necessary for another's aid or protection does not of itself impose upon him a duty to take such action. . . .

The distinction between malfeasance and nonfeasance, between active misconduct working positive injury and failure to act to prevent mischief not brought on by the defendant, is founded on "that attitude of extreme individualism so typical of Anglo-Saxon legal thought."

Defendant argues that the request that its employee call the police is a request that it do something. . . .

The refusal of the law to recognize the moral obligation of one to aid another when he is in peril and when such aid may be given without danger and at little cost in effort has been roundly criticized. . . .

[S]pecial relationships which create a duty to render aid [include] that of a common carrier to its passengers, an innkeeper to his guest, possessors of land who hold it open to the public, or one who has a custodial relationship to another. A duty may be created by an undertaking to give assistance.

Here there was no special relationship between the defendant and the deceased. It would be stretching the concept beyond recognition to assert there was a relationship between the defendant and the patron from Happy Jack's Saloon who wished to summon aid. But this does not end the matter.

It is time to re-examine the common law rule of nonliability for nonfeasance in the special circumstances of the instant case.

■   ■   ■

Crime is a blight on our society and a matter of great citizen concern.

■   ■   ■

"[T]hat attitude of extreme individualism so typical of Anglo-Saxon legal thought" may need limited re-examination in the light of current societal conditions and the facts of this case to determine whether the defendant owed a duty to the deceased to permit the use of the telephone.

■   ■   ■

[T]he reluctance of the law to impose liability for nonfeasance . . . is in part due to the difficulties in setting standards and making rules workable.

Many citizens simply "don't want to get involved." No rule should be adopted which would require a citizen to open up his or her house to a stranger so that the latter may use the telephone to call for emergency assistance. As Mrs. Alexander in Anthony Burgess's *A Clockwork Orange* learned to her horror, such an action may be fraught with danger. It does not follow, however, that the use of a telephone in a public por-

tion of a business should be refused for a legitimate emergency call. . . .

A business establishment such as the Circle Inn is open for profit. The owner encourages the public to enter, for his earnings depend on it. A telephone is a necessary adjunct to such a place. It is not unusual in such circumstances for patrons to use the telephone to call a taxicab or family member.

■   ■   ■

We conclude that the bartender owed a duty to the plaintiff's decedent to permit the patron from Happy Jack's to place a call to the police or to place the call himself.

It bears emphasizing that the duty in this case does not require that one must go to the aid of another. That is not the issue here. The employee was not the Good Samaritan intent on aiding another. The patron was.

■   ■   ■

The possible imposition of liability on the defendant in this case is not a global change in the law. It is but a slight departure from the "morally questionable" rule of nonliability for inaction absent in a special relationship.

Case Questions

1. Which ethical approach or approaches do you see reflected in the court's opinion? Explain.
2. Analyze the issue of whether one should be under a duty to render assistance to another using the cost/benefit approach. What conclusion do you reach? Explain.
3. Analyze the issue of whether one should be under a duty to render assistance to another using the rights approach. What conclusion do you reach? Explain.
4. Would the result in Soldano v. O'Daniels be different today when cell phones are widespread? Explain.

With regard to the fundamental legal principle under the heading *Act in Good Faith and Deal Fairly with Others*, good faith, honesty and fair dealing are involved in the following case.

IZADI V. MACHADO FORD, INC.
550 So. 2d 1135 (Fla. App. 1989)

Machado Ford (defendant) ran an advertisement in the *Miami Herald*. The ad prominently invited customers to shop at the dealership and receive a trade-in of at least $3,000.00. Very small print at the bottom of the ad said that it applied only to the purchase of an Eddie Bauer Aerostar or Turbo T-Bird.

Izadi (plaintiff) sought to purchase a Ford Ranger pickup, priced at $7,095.00, with $3,595.00 cash, a $500.00 factory rebate, and a trade-in. Machado refused and Izadi sued. The trial court dismissed the complaint. The Florida Court of Appeal reversed.

Chief Judge Schwartz

It is . . . well settled that an allegedly binding offer must be viewed as a whole. . . . We . . . believe that the complaint appropriately alleges that, objectively considered, the advertisement . . . contained just the unqualified $3,000 offer which was accepted by the plaintiff. . . . [T]he case thus is like many previous ones in which it has been held, contrary to what is perhaps the usual rule, that an enforceable contract arises from an offer contained in an advertisement. . . .

■   ■   ■

Machado—although it did not intend to adhere to the $3,000 trade-in representation—affirmatively, but wrongly sought to make the public believe that it would be honored; that, in other words, the offer was to be used as the "bait" to be

followed by a "switch" to another deal when the acceptance of that offer was refused. Indeed, it is difficult to offer any other explanation for the blanket representation of a $3,000 trade-in for any vehicle—which is then hedged in sub-microscopic print to apply only to two models which were not otherwise referred to in the ad. . . . This situation invokes the applicability of a line of persuasive authority that a binding offer may be implied from the very fact that deliberately misleading advertising intentionally leads the reader to the conclusion that one exists.

■   ■   ■

There is entirely too much disregard of law and truth in the business, social, and political world of today. . . . It is time to hold men to their primary engagements to tell the truth and observe common honesty and fair dealing.

Case Questions

1. What was the promise made by Machado Ford? What were its specific terms?
2. How did Machado's apparent bait and switch motive affect the court's analysis and conclusion?
3. Red Owl Pharmacy offers franchises to purchasers for $200,000.00. Scarzano desired to purchase a franchise in Bakersfield, California district. Red Owl executive Randall

Masse told Scarzano that he would first have to sell his house and move to Bakersfield. Scarzano sold his house in West Hartford, Connecticut, packed up and moved. Masse told him that he would have to sell his bakery that he owned in Connecticut. He did. Then he told Scarzano that he would have to put down $2500.00 to have his credit checked. He did. Then Red Owl refused to sign a franchise agreement with Scarzano. How might a court apply fairness to arrive at a just result?

Chapter Two   Nature of Law and Legal Reasoning

An Example of Legal Reasoning

To fully appreciate what is involved in legal reasoning, consider the following three cases, which deal with a single issue: whether the husband or wife of an injured person is entitled to compensation from the wrongdoer for the loss of the victim's spousal services—what the law labels *loss of consortium.*

Deciding a Case of First Impression

Sometimes a court must decide an issue with no statute or prior judicial decision to guide its determination. When this occurs, the court is faced with a case of first impression. A court confronted with this novel situation must determine what the law should be. That situation confronted the Supreme Court of California in the following case involving loss of consortium.

DESHOTEL V. ATCHISON, TOPEKA & SANTA FE RAILWAY CO.
328 P.2d 449 (Calif. 1958)

Eloyce Deshotel's husband was severely injured when a taxicab in which he was a passenger collided with a train. He sued the railway company, the taxicab company, the train engineer, and the cab driver, obtaining a judgment of $290,000. While his case was pending, Eloyce Deshotel (plaintiff) brought a lawsuit against the same defendants. She alleged that as a result of their negligence her husband was injured in such a manner that she had "been denied his care, protection, consideration, companionship, and society" and that "by reason of the loss of consortium of her husband" she had been damaged in the sum of $100,000. The trial court dismissed her claim and awarded judgment for the defendants. Eloyce Deshotel appealed to the Supreme Court of California, which affirmed the trial court decision.

Chief Justice Gibson

The sole question presented is whether a wife whose husband has been injured as the result of the negligence of a third person may maintain an action for loss of "consortium," a term which is used in the opinion to refer to the noneconomic aspects of the marriage relation, including conjugal society, comfort, affection, and companionship. The question is one of first impression in this state, but it has been answered by the courts in many other jurisdictions. In England and in the vast majority of American jurisdictions the wife has been denied the right to recover for loss of consortium.

■   ■   ■

In a number of jurisdictions where the wife has not been allowed recovery, the husband is given such a right if his wife is negligently injured. Plaintiff argues, in effect, that the courts which withhold relief from the wife have relied upon medieval concepts of the marriage relation, that in modern time the marital status of the wife has changed, placing her in a position equal to that of her husband, and that there is no longer any reason to refuse her the kind of redress which he may obtain. Some jurisdictions, however, have denied recovery to the husband as well as to the wife. The law in California with respect to the right of the husband is not settled. In *Meek v. Pacific Electric Ry. Co.*, it was said that damages "could not be obtained by a husband for the loss of his wife's society, or what is termed the *consortium.*" This statement was rejected as "inadvertent dictum" in *Gist v. French* [a decision of a lower-level California court of appeals], which

held that a husband whose wife had been negligently injured could recover not only for the loss of services but also for the loss of cohabitation and society. We agree that the quoted statement in the *Meek* case is dictum, but a statement in the *Gist* case which indicates that the wife may recover for loss of consortium resulting from a negligent injury to her husband is also dictum, and for the reasons hereafter given, the language in the Gist case relating to the wife's rights is disapproved.

It is clear that the granting of relief to the wife for loss of consortium caused by negligent injury to her husband would constitute an extension of common law liability, and the courts are justifiably reluctant to depart from established limitations on recovery. Obviously, such an extension would also involve problems of policy or procedure. A judgment obtained by a husband after he is injured by a third person might include compensation for any impairment of his ability to participate in a normal married life, and, if his wife is allowed redress for loss of consortium in a separate action, there would be danger of double recovery. Any harm she sustains occurs only indirectly as a consequence of the defendant's wrong to the husband, and the measurement of damage for the loss of such things as companionship and society would involve conjecture since their value would be hard to fix in terms of money. Moreover, if a cause of action in the wife were recognized on the basis of the intimate relationship existing between her and her husband, other persons having a close relationship to the one injured, such as a child or parent, would likely seek to enforce similar claims, and the courts would be faced with the perplexing task of determining where to draw the line with respect to which claims should be upheld. . . .

In our view the Legislature rather than the courts can best deal with these problems. For example, the Legislature, if it found this type of suit to be desirable, could define the extent of the liability, designate who may maintain the action, and provide safeguards against the danger of double recovery. . . .

■   ■   ■

The Legislature has not seen fit to alter the common law rule that the wife cannot recover for the loss of consortium resulting from a negligent injury to her husband, and we are of the opinion that any departure from the overwhelming weight of authority in support of that rule should be left to legislative action.

Justice Carter (Dissenting)

I dissent.

It was held in *Gist v. French* [a lower California court of appeals decision] that a husband may recover for loss of consortium resulting from a negligent injury to his wife. This court unanimously denied a hearing on December 14, 1955. The statement in the majority opinion that "The law in California with respect to the right of the husband is not settled" would appear to ignore the very definite holding in the *Gist* case that the husband may recover for the loss of his wife's consortium since only the statement therein concerning the *wife's* cause of action for loss of her

husband's consortium is disapproved.

There is no sound reason for denying either husband or wife a right of recovery for the loss of consortium of the spouse. "The parties to a marriage are each entitled to the comfort, companionship and affection of the other. Any interference with the right of either spouse to the enjoyment of the other is a violation of a natural right as well as a legal right arising from the marriage relation" [Gist v. French]. . . . The statement in the majority opinion that the "granting of relief to the wife for loss of consortium caused by negligent injury to her husband would constitute an extension of common law liability" ignores the present-day status of the wife and her emancipation from old-world concepts that the wife was but a chattel of the husband without either feelings to be injured or rights to be considered.

Case Questions

1. What did the majority opinion mean when it described the issue in the case as "one of first impression in this state?"

2. What did the majority opinion mean when it described as dictum certain statements contained in two earlier cases?

3. Did the majority opinion rely on any precedent-based rationales for its decision? Why or why not?

4. How do the majority and dissenting opinions differ in their discussion of *Gist v. French*?

5. Which policy-based rationales did the majority opinion rely on for its decision? How did the dissenting opinion differ from the majority with respect to the policy questions?

Applying Precedent

Two years after deciding in *Deshotel* that a wife could not sue for loss of consortium, the Supreme Court of California revisited the issue-only this time it was a husband's claim for loss of consortium that was under consideration. An interesting question at that point was should *Deshotel* have applied so that a husband, too, would not be able to recover for loss of consortium, or would the California court join the majority of states in allowing the husband this recovery? Consider the following case:

WEST V. CITY OF SAN DIEGO
353 P.2d 929 (Calif. 1960)

Dorothy West was seriously injured and rendered incompetent as the result of a collision between an automobile she was driving and one operated by a police officer killed in the accident. Her husband brought suit on her behalf against the City of San Diego (defendant) to recover damages she sustained, and, in addition, he sought redress for himself, alleging permanent loss of his wife's services. As a result of the collision, Mrs. West sustained massive brain damage, which reduced her mentality to that of a child four or five years of age. She had been married to Mr. West for 10 years and was 57 years old when she was injured. The jury returned a verdict in favor of the Wests (plaintiffs), awarding $57,828.89 to the wife and $5,000 to the husband. The City appealed to the Supreme Court of California, contending that Mr. West should not have been awarded damages for loss of consortium. The Supreme Court of California reversed that part of the jury's verdict awarding Mr. West compensation for loss of consortium.

Chief Justice Gibson

At common law in England, based on the now outmoded theory that the wife was the husband's inferior and occupied a position in relation to him akin to that of a servant to a master, the husband, but not the wife, was allowed to recover for loss of consortium caused by negligence, and a number of American jurisdictions have followed the common law rule. A few courts grant relief to the wife as well as the husband. Some jurisdictions deny recovery of both spouses.

■　■　■

In 1958 this court was called upon to consider the question of recovery for loss of consortium in *Deshotel v. Atchison, T. & S. F. Ry. Co.,* where a husband had been negligently injured. We held that a wife was not entitled to recover, disap-

proving the dictum to the contrary in the *Gist* case. In so holding, we discussed the various problems of policy and procedure involved. For example, there is a danger of double recovery, and the loss of such things as companionship and society is indirect only and is difficult to measure in terms of money. In the absence of a statute . . . courts would be faced with the perplexing task of determining where to draw the line with respect to similar claims by others having a close relationship to the one injured. We concluded that the Legislature rather than the courts could best deal with these problems and determine whether the wife should be allowed relief. It was pointed out that some of the objections to an action by the wife apply with equal force to one by the husband and that legislation in this field with respect to the husband as well as the wife would be preferable to piecemeal determination of the problems of judicial decision.

There is no sound reason to depart here from the principle that the Legislature is the proper body to decide whether recovery for loss of consortium should be permitted and, if so, under what terms and conditions. Drawing a distinction between spouses on the ground that the husband, unlike the wife, had a right of recovery at common law would be extremely inequitable and, further, would ignore the fact that recognition of his right was based upon the wife's subservient position in the marriage relationship, whereas, under present-day law, spouses are generally regarded as equals.

Justice Peters
(Dissenting)

I dissent. . . .

The majority, in concluding that the judgment as to Mert West should be reversed, hold that, in this state, a husband has no cause of action for the negligent interference with those noneconomic aspects of marriage usually included within the term "consortium." Stated another way, the majority hold that a husband, in this state, is not entitled to recover on his own behalf for a negligent injury to his wife that results in depriving him of his privilege of sexual intercourse with his wife; of the possibility of becoming a father; and of the right of society, care, and comfort of his wife. This holding is unrealistic and unsound.

A large portion of our family law is devoted to protecting the spouses against intentional interference with these conjugal rights. If a wife were to deprive her husband of these rights it would, of course, be a ground for divorce. But, according to the majority, negligent interference resulting in the deprivation of these rights is not compensable. This holding is contrary to the common law, is contrary to the overwhelming weight of authority elsewhere, and is contrary to the public policy of this state.

■ ■ ■

There can be no doubt, and the majority concede, that the common law rule was and is that a husband has such a cause of action. Such right was recognized as early as 1619 in the [English] case of Gay against Lively.

■ ■ ■

The majority opinion is predicated on the false premise that such a right should not exist in the husband because the Legislature has not expressly provided for such a right. . . .

Apparently the majority have overlooked section 22.2 of the Civil Code, which provides: "The common law of England, so far as it is not repugnant to or inconsistent with the Constitution of the United States, or the Constitution or laws of this State, is the rule of decision in all the courts of this State. " If the Legislature has not seen fit to change a common-law rule, at least a common-law rule existing at the time this state was admitted into the Union in 1850, the courts should not repudiate such rule but should follow.

Apparently, in the realization that they are repudiating a common-law rule, and that this should not be done without some good reason, the majority state that because the wife had no such right at common law it "would be extremely inequitable" to grant the right to the husband. This solicitude for symmetry in the law may be laudable but it carries little weight against a settled rule of common law. The common law itself created this lack of symmetry. The point does not have to be labored that the law is not necessarily logical nor symmetrical. Lack of symmetry alone is no sound reason for this court, by judicial fiat, to enter into the legislative field by repudiating a common-law rule that the Legislature itself has not seen fit to repudiate. . . . Moreover, it can be argued with what I submit is sounder logic, that, if symmetry is to be secured, it should be secured by holding that the wife as well as the husband is entitled to maintain such an action. Such a result . . . could be justified on the reasoning that the Legislature, by its many laws freeing women from their common-law disabilities, had evidenced an intent to place the wife in the same position as the husband so far as the right of consortium is concerned.

■ ■ ■

That a husband should recover under the facts of this case for loss of consortium is justified by reason, logic, authority, the common law, and by the public policy of this state. For these reasons I would affirm the judgment in favor of Mert West.

Case Questions

1. What effect did the *Deshotel* decision have on the court majority in *West*?
2. Did the majority opinion rely on a precedent-based rationale for its decision? Explain.
3. Did the majority opinion rely on any policy-based rationales for its decision? Explain.
4. How could the *Deshotel* case have been distinguished from the situation confronting the court in *West*? How did the majority respond to this point? If the court had distinguished *Deshotel,* how would that have affected the precedential weight of the *Deshotel* decision on the court? How did the refusal to distinguish *Deshotel* affect the court's decision?
5. How does the dissenting opinion rely on a precedent-based rationale? Does the dissenting opinion rely on any policy-based rationales? Explain.

Overruling Precedent

The doctrine of stare decisis expresses the policy preference of the courts to stand by precedents and to preserve settled points of law. However, where a court concludes it has made a mistake or that the rule needs to be changed, the court may correct or change the rule. Thus, a court may overrule an earlier case where there is good reason to do so. For example, technological change or changes in social conditions may dictate that the law be altered; or events occurring after an earlier decision may prove that the decision was wrong. It would be ironic if appellate courts, which are empowered to correct the errors of lower courts, lacked the power to correct their own errors. If appellate courts could not correct erroneous or outdated precedents, the law would stagnate.

When a court overrules its earlier case law, it usually goes to great length to explain its action. This usually involves explaining why the earlier decision is wrong, outdated, or otherwise exists as a fishbone in the throat of the law. Having wiped the slate clean, the court then considers the issue anew and explains why it is adopting a new rule in place of its earlier decision. The following case involving a reexamination of the consortium issue shows a court undertaking this rare task.

RODRIGUEZ V. BETHLEHEM STEEL CORP.
525 P.2d 669 (Calif. 1974)

While at work, Richard Rodriguez was struck on the head by a falling pipe weighing over 600 pounds. The blow caused severe spinal cord damage, which left him totally paralyzed in both legs, totally paralyzed in his body below the midpoint of the chest, and partially paralyzed in one of his arms. The injuries were permanent. Because he needed assistance in virtually every activity of daily living, his wife, Mary Anne (plaintiff), gave up her job and undertook his care on a 24-hour basis. At the time of the accident Richard was 22 years old and Mary Anne was 20. The accident occurred only 16 months after their marriage. Mary Anne sued Richard's employer, Bethlehem Steel Corp. (defendant), for loss of consortium. The trial court dismissed her claim, and a California appellate court affirmed the dismissal. She appealed to the Supreme Court of California, which reversed the lower court decisions.

Justice Mosk

In this case we are called upon to decide whether California should continue to adhere to the rule that a married person whose spouse has been injured by the negligence of a third party has no cause of action for loss of "consortium."

■   ■   ■

In affirming the judgment the Court of Appeal . . . indicated its dissatisfaction with the *Deshotel* rule, but correctly deferred to this court for any reconsideration of the doctrine: Presiding Justice Kaus, writing for a unanimous court, stated that "In spite of counsel's eloquent exhortations to the contrary, we must hold that it is up to the Supreme Court to qualify or overrule its decisions. We say this in full recognition of Mary Anne's argument that several Supreme Court cases since *Deshotel* and *West* can be read as undermining the rationale of those holdings." This is a perceptive and accurate reading of our decisions, as we shall explain.

To begin with, we delineate the rationale of *Deshotel* and *West*. . . .

In *Deshotel* . . . the court devised . . . reasons of "policy and procedure" to justify . . . the rule. . . .

We shall show that each of these reasons has been rendered untenable by developments subsequent to *Deshotel*.

Stare Decisis and the Role of the Legislature

■   ■   ■

First and foremost, the *Deshotel* court emphasized that the "overwhelming weight of authority" supports the common law rule, and "the courts are justifiably reluctant to depart from established limitations on recovery." In the 16 years since *Deshotel* was decided, however, there has been a dramatic reversal in the weight of authority on this question. At the time of *Deshotel* the majority of the states denied the wife the right to recover for loss of consortium, while the right was recognized in only five jurisdictions. Today those 5 have grown in number to at least 31. . . .

In these circumstances we may fairly conclude that the precedential foundation of *Deshotel* has been not only undermined but destroyed. In its place a new common law rule has arisen, granting either spouse the right to recover for loss of consortium caused by negligent injury to the other spouse. Accordingly, to adopt that rule in California at this time would not constitute, as the court feared in *Deshotel,* an "extension" of common law liability, but rather a recognition of that liability as it is currently understood by the large preponderance of our sister states and a consensus of distinguished legal scholars.

The second principal rationale of the *Deshotel* opinion was that any departure from the then settled rule denying the wife recovery for loss of consortium "should be left to legislative action." But in the years since *Deshotel* the argument has fared badly in our decisions. As we summarized in *People v. Pierce,* "In effect the contention is a request that courts of law abdicate their responsibility for the upkeep of the common law."

The judicial responsibility to which we referred in *Pierce* arises from the role of the courts in a common law system. In California as in other jurisdictions of Anglo-American heritage, the common law is not a codification of exact or inflexible rules for human conduct, for the redress of injuries, or for protection against wrongs, but is rather the embodiment of broad and comprehensive unwritten principles, inspired by natural reason and an innate sense of justice, and adopted by common consent for the regulation and government of the affairs of men.

"The inherent capacity of the common law for growth and change is its most significant feature. Its development has been determined by the social needs of the community which it serves. It is constantly expanding and developing in keeping with advancing civilization and the new conditions and progress of society, and adapting itself to the gradual change of trade, commerce, arts, inventions, and the needs of the country. . . ."

Whenever an old rule is found unsuited to present conditions or unsound, it should be set aside and a rule declared which is in harmony with those conditions and meets the demands of justice. Although the Legislature may of course speak to the subject, in the common law system the primary instruments of this evolution are the courts, adjudicating on a regular basis the right variety of individual cases brought before them.

■   ■   ■

If upon further analysis it appears the remaining reasons given in *Deshotel* no longer support that rule . . . we shall have no hesitation in abrogating it. Such a step would not be an usurpation of legislative authority, but a reaffirmation of our high responsibility to renew the common law of California when it is necessary and proper to do so.

The Injury Is Indirect, the Damages Speculative, and the Cause of Action Would Extend to Other Classes of Plaintiffs

[T]he *Deshotel* court asserted that "Any harm [the wife] sustains occurs *only indirectly* as a consequence of the defendant's wrong to the husband." The argument was negated 10 years after *Deshotel* in *Dillon v. Legg.* There the issue was whether a driver who negligently runs over a

small child in the street is also liable to the child's mother for emotional shock and resulting physical disorders suffered by the latter when she personally witnessed the occurrence of the accident. Finding such liability, we in effect rejected the argument that the injury to the mother was too "indirect." The critical question, we explained, was foreseeability. . . ." Such reasonable foreseeability does not turn on whether the particular [defendant] as an individual would have in actuality foreseen the exact accident and loss, it contemplates that courts, on a case-to-case basis, analyzing all the circumstances, will decide what the ordinary man under such circumstances should reasonably have foreseen. The courts thus mark out the areas of liability, excluding the remote and unexpected."

Applying these rules to the facts alleged, we were of the opinion in *Dillon* that "Surely the negligent driver who causes the death of a young child may reasonably expect that the mother will not be far distant and will upon witnessing the accident suffer emotional trauma." By parity of reasoning, we conclude in the case at bar that one who negligently causes a severely disabling injury to an adult may reasonably expect that the injured person is married and that his or her spouse will be adversely affected by that injury.

■   ■   ■

The next rationale of the *Deshotel* court was that "the measurement of damage for the loss of such things as companionship and society would involve conjecture since their value would be hard to fix in terms of money." This argument, too, has fared badly in our subsequent decisions. Although loss of consortium may have physical consequences, it is principally a form of mental suffering. We have fully recognized that "One of the most difficult tasks imposed upon a jury in deciding a case involving personal injuries is to determine the amount of money the plaintiff is to be awarded as compensation for pain and suffering. . . . In a very real sense, the jury is asked to evaluate in terms of money a detriment for which monetary compensation cannot be ascertained with any demonstrable accuracy." (*Beagle v. Vasold*) "Yet," we emphasized in *Beagle,* "the inescapable fact is that this is precisely what the jury is called upon to do."

■ ■ ■

The third argument of this group set forth in *Deshotel* is that if the wife's cause of action were recognized "on the basis of the intimate relationship existing between her and her husband, other persons having a close relationship to the one injured, such as a child or parent, would likely seek to enforce similar claims, and the courts would be faced with the perplexing task of determining where to draw the line with respect to which claims should be upheld." Here again the answer was subsequently given in *Dillon v. Legg.* In that case it was likewise urged that any cause of action granted to a mother who witnesses her child's injury could also be asserted by other close relatives present at the scene such as siblings or grandparents, thus involving the courts "in the hopeless task of defining the extent of . . . liability."

We rejected this argument in *Dillon* on the ground that . . . "proper guidelines can indicate the extent of liability for such future cases." Those guidelines . . . are the general principles of negligence law limiting liability to persons and injuries within the scope of the reasonably foreseeable risk.

The Fear of Double Recovery

[T]he *Deshotel* court expressed the concern that "A judgment obtained by a husband after he is injured by a third person might include compensation for any impairment of his ability to participate in a normal married life, and, if his wife is allowed redress for loss of consortium in a separate action, there would be danger of double recovery. . . ."

It is true the rule against double recovery forecloses the wife from recovering for the loss of her husband's financial support if he is compensated for his loss of earnings and earning power, "because the *source* of the wife's right to support is the husband's earning capacity, for impairment of which *he* is entitled to recover." But there is more to the marriage relationship than financial support. "The concept of consortium includes not only loss of support or services, it also embraces such elements as love, companionship, affection, society, sexual relations, solace and more." As to each, "the interest sought to be protected is personal to the wife," so that to compensate her for damage to that interest cannot result in double recovery.

■ ■ ■

All that is necessary to avoid double recovery "is to insure that each element of the damages is separate and distinct from all the others," and in particular that the wife's recovery does not include any damages for loss of her husband's financial support or other items for which he is primarily entitled to be compensated. . . .

We therefore overrule *Deshotel v. Atchison, T. & S.F. Ry. Co.* and *West v. City of San Diego* and declare that in California each spouse has a cause of action for loss of consortium, as defined herein, caused by a negligent or intentional injury to the other spouse by a third party.

Justice McComb *(Dissenting)*

I dissent. I adhere to the view that any change in the law denying the wife recovery for loss of consortium should be left to legislative action. (*Deshotel v. Atchison, T. & S.F. Ry. Co.*)

Case Questions

1. Why did the lower-level court of appeal not simply decline to follow the *Deshotel* and *West* decisions?
2. How did the *Rodriguez* court use precedent-based rationales in overruling its earlier precedents of *Deshotel* and *West*?

3. How did the *Rodriguez* court confront the policy-based rationales used earlier by the court in *Deshotel*?

4. *Deshotel* was decided in 1958. *Rodriguez* was decided in 1974. Which changes in the social conditions in California occurred during this period? Could these changes have influenced the court's decision making? Explain. Do you see any evidence of this in the various majority and dissenting opinions? Explain.

Legislative Interpretation

The following case involves the interpretation of Title VII of the Civil Rights Act, which forbids discrimination in employment on the basis of race, color, sex, religion, and national origin. Three years earlier, in the case of *McDonald v. Santa Fe Trail Trans. Co.*, the Supreme Court had interpreted Title VII to apply to racial discrimination in employment directed against whites.[1] In *McDonald*, several white employees were discharged for misappropriating their employer's property, but their black accomplice was not dismissed. The Court stated that "Title VII . . . prohibits the discharge of `any individual' because of such `individual's race. . . .' Its terms are not limited to discrimination against members of any particular race."[2] *McDonald* left open the issue of the legality of voluntary affirmative action programs. That issue was addressed in the following case.

UNITED STEELWORKERS V. WEBER
443 U.S. 193 (1979)

Kaiser and the United Steelworkers of America (petitioners) entered into a collective bargaining agreement that established training programs to teach unskilled production workers the skills necessary to become craft workers. The program reserved 50 percent of the openings for black employees. This aspect of the program was to continue until the percentage of blacks in the craft work force approximated the percentage of blacks in the local labor force. Before the program began, Kaiser hired only experienced craft workers, almost all of whom were white.

Weber (respondent) brought a class action alleging that junior black employees were accepted into the program ahead of more senior whites. The trial court held that this violated Title VII, and the Fifth Circuit Court of Appeals affirmed. The Supreme Court reversed the circuit court decision.

---

[1] 427 U.S. 273 (1976).
[2] Id. at 278–79.

Justice Brennan

The only question before us is the narrow statutory issue of whether Title VII *forbids* private employers and unions from voluntarily agreeing upon bona fide affirmative action plans that accord racial preference in the manner and for the purpose provided in the Kaiser-USWA plan. That question was expressly left open in *McDonald v. Santa Fe Trail Trans. Co.*

Respondent argues that Congress intended in Title VII to prohibit all race-conscious affirmative action plans. Respondent's argument rests upon a literal interpretation of 703(a) and (d) of the Act. Those sections make it unlawful to "discriminate . . . because of . . . race" in hiring and in the selection of apprentices for training programs. Since, the argument runs, *McDonald v. Santa Fe Trail Trans. Co.* settled that Title VII forbids discrimination against whites as well as blacks, and since the Kaiser-USWA affirmative action plan operated to discriminate against white employees solely because they are white, it follows that the Kaiser-USWA plan violates Title VII.

Respondent's argument is not without force. But it overlooks the significance of the fact that the Kaiser-USWA plan is an affirmative action plan voluntarily adopted by private parties to eliminate traditional patterns of racial segregation. In this context respondent's reliance upon a literal construction of 703(a) and (d) and upon *McDonald* is misplaced. It is a "familiar rule, that a thing may be within the letter of the statute and yet not within the statute, because [the thing is] not within its spirit, nor within the intention of its makers." The prohibition against racial discrimination in 703(a) and (d) of Title VII must therefore be read against the background of the legislative history of Title VII and the historical context from which the Act arose. Examination of those sources makes clear that an interpretation of the sections that forbade all race-conscious affirmative action would "bring about an end completely at variance with the purpose of the statute" and must be rejected.

Congress' primary concern in enacting the prohibition against racial discrimination in Title VII of the Civil Rights Act of 1964 was with "the plight of the Negro in our economy." Before 1964, blacks were largely relegated to "unskilled and semi-skilled jobs."

It plainly appears from the House Report accompanying the Civil Rights Act that Congress did not intend wholly to prohibit private and voluntary affirmative action efforts as one method of solving this problem. The report provides:

> No bill can or should lay claim to eliminating all of the causes and consequences of racial and other types of discrimination against minorities. There is reason to believe, however, that national leadership provided by the enactment of Federal legislation dealing with the most troublesome problems will create an atmosphere conductive to voluntary or local resolution of other forms of discrimination.

Given this legislative history, we cannot agree with respondent that Congress intended to prohibit the private sector from taking effective steps to accomplish the goal that Congress designed Title VII to achieve. The very statutory words intended as a spur or catalyst to cause "employers and unions to self-examine and to self-evaluate their employment practices and to endeavor to eliminate, so far as possible, the last vestiges of an unfortunate and ignominious page in this country's history," cannot be interpreted as an absolute prohibition against all private, voluntary, race-conscious affirmative action efforts to hasten the elimination of such vestiges. It would be ironic indeed if a law triggered by a Nation's concern over centuries of racial injustice and intended to improve the lot of those who had "been excluded from the American dream for so long," constituted the first legislative prohibition of all voluntary, private, race-conscious efforts to abolish traditional patterns of racial segregation and hierarchy.

Our conclusion is further reinforced by examination of the language and legislative history of 703(j) of Title VII. . . . The section provides that nothing contained in Title VII "shall be interpreted to require any employer . . . to grant preferential treatment . . . to any group because of the race . . . of such . . . group on account of" a *de facto* racial imbalance in the employer's work force. The section does not state that "nothing in Title VII shall be interpreted to *permit*" voluntary affirmative efforts to correct racial imbalances. The natural inference is that Congress chose not to forbid all voluntary race-conscious affirmative action.

The reasons for this choice are evident from the legislative record. Title VII could not have been enacted into law without substantial support from legislators in both Houses who traditionally resisted federal regulations of private business. Those legislators demanded as a price for their support that "management prerogatives and union freedoms . . . be left undisturbed to the greatest extent possible." Section 703(j) was proposed by Senator Dirksen to allay any fears that the Act might be interpreted in such a way as to upset this compromise. The section was designed to prevent 703 of Title VII from being interpreted in such a way as to lead to undue "Federal Government interference with private businesses because of some Federal employee's ideas about racial balance or imbalance." Clearly, a prohibition against all voluntary, race-conscious, affirmative action efforts would disserve these ends. Such a prohibition would augment the powers of the Federal Government and diminish traditional management prerogatives while at the same time impeding attainment of the ultimate statutory goals. In view of this legislative history and in view of Congress' desire to avoid undue federal regulation of private businesses, use of the word "require" rather than the phrase "require or permit" in 703(j) fortifies the conclusion that Congress did not intend to limit traditional business freedom to such a degree as to prohibit all voluntary, race-conscious affirmative action.

We therefore hold that Title VIIs prohibition in 703(a) and (d) against racial discrimination does not condemn all private, voluntary, race-conscious affirmative action plans.

Justice Rehnquist
(With whom the Chief Justice joins, dissenting)

The operative sections of Title VII prohibit racial discrimination in employment *simpliciter*. Taken in its normal meaning, and as understood by all members of Congress who spoke to the issue during the legislative debates, this language prohibits a covered employer from considering race when making an employment decision, whether the race be black or white. Several years ago, however, a United States District Court held that "the dismissal of white employees charged with misappropriating company property while not dismissing a similarly charged Negro employee does not raise a claim upon which Title VII relief may be granted." *McDonald v. Santa Fe Trail Trans. Co.* This Court unanimously reversed, concluding from the "uncontradicted legislative history" that "Title VII prohibits racial discrimination against the white petitioners in this case upon the same standards as would be applicable were they Negroes. . . .

We have never wavered in our understanding that Title VII "prohibits *all* racial discrimination in employment, without exceptions for any particular employees. . . ."

Today, however, the Court behaves much like the Orwellian speaker earlier described, as if it had been handed a note indicating that Title VII would lead to a result unacceptable to the Court if interpreted here as it was in our prior decisions. Accordingly, without even a break in syntax, the Court rejects "a literal construction of Section 703(a)" in favor of newly discovered "legislative history," which leads to a conclusion directly contrary to that compelled by the "uncontradicted legislative history" unearthed in *McDonald* and our other prior decisions. Now we are told that the legislative history of Title VII shows that employers are free to discriminate on the basis of race; an employer may, in the Court's words, "trammel the interests of white employees" in favor of black employees in order to eliminate "racial imbalance."

As if this were not enough to make a reasonable observer question this Court's adherence to the oft-stated principle that our duty is to construe rather than rewrite legislation, the Court also seizes upon Section 703(j) of Title VII as an independent, or at least partially independent basis for its holding. Totally ignoring the wording of that section . . . and totally ignoring the months of legislative debates . . . which demonstrate clearly that it was enacted to prevent precisely what occurred in this case, the Court infers from Section 703(j) that "Congress chose not to forbid all voluntary race-conscious affirmative action."

Thus, by a *tour de force* reminiscent not of jurists such as Hale, Holmes, and Hughes, but of escape artists such as Houdini, the Court eludes clear statutory language, "uncontradicted" leg-islative history, and uniform precedent in concluding that employers are, after all, permitted to consider race in making employment decisions.

Case Questions

1. What is the basis for the Court's conclusion that the Kaiser affirmative action plan did not violate Title VII?
2. Which kind of legal reasoning (formalist or purposive) did the Court use? Explain. Which kind of legal reasoning (formalist or purposive) did the dissent use? Explain.
3. Suppose you had been plant manager of the Kaiser plant involved in this case. Would you have agreed to the proposal to adopt the affirmative action plan that actually was adopted by Kaiser and the United Steelworkers? Explain.
4. How would you have decided the issue of the legality of the Kaiser affirmative action program? Explain.

Chapter Three   Business and the Legal System

The Attorney-Client Privilege

There are some limited exceptions to the privilege, but as the next case makes clear, the privilege is strong enough to survive the death of the client.

SWINDLER & BERLIN AND
JAMES HAMILTON V. UNITED STATES
524 U.S. 399 (1998)

White House Counsel, Vincent Foster, met with James Hamilton (Petitioner), an attorney with Swindler & Berlin (Petitioner), to seek legal representation in connection with investigations of the dismissal of White House Travel employees. Hamilton took three pages of handwritten notes during the meeting. Nine days later Foster committed suicide. Thereafter, a federal grand jury issued subpoenas for the handwritten notes as part an investigation by the Office of Independent Counsel into whether various individuals made false statements, obstructed justice or committed other crimes during the investigation into White House Travel firings. Swindler & Berlin and James Hamilton, Petitioners, moved to dismiss the subpoenas on the basis that the notes were protected by the attorney-client privilege. The District Court agreed. The Court of Appeals for the DC Circuit reversed, reasoning "that there is a posthumous exception to the privilege for communications whose relative importance to particular criminal litigation is substantial." The United States Supreme Court granted certiorari.

Chief Justice Rehnquist

The attorney-client privilege is one of the oldest recognized privileges for confidential communications. The privilege is intended to encourage "full and frank communication between attorneys and their clients and thereby promote broader public interests in the observance of law and the administration of justice." The issue presented here is the scope of that privilege; more particularly, the extent to which the privilege survives the death of the client. . . .

The Independent Counsel argues that the attorney-client privilege should not prevent disclosure of confidential communications where the client has died and the information is relevant to a criminal proceeding. There is some authority for this position. One state appellate court, and the Court of Appeals below have held the privilege may be subject to posthumous exceptions in certain circumstances. In *Cohen*, a civil case, the court recognized that the privilege generally survives death, but concluded that it could make an exception where the interest of justice was compelling and the interest of the client in preserving the confidence was insignificant.

But other than these two decisions cases addressing the existence of the privilege after death—most involving the testamentary exception—uniformly presume the privilege survives. . . .

Such testamentary exception cases consistently presume the privilege survives. They view testamentary disclosure of communications as an exception to the privilege: "The general rule with respect to confidential communication . . . is that such communications are privileged during the testator's lifetime and also, after the testator's

death unless sought to be disclosed in litigation between the testator's heirs."

■   ■   ■

Indeed, this Court, in recognizing the testamentary exception, expressly assumed that the privilege continues after the individual's death. The Court explained that testamentary disclosure was permissible because the privilege, which normally protects the client's interests, could be impliedly waived in order to fulfill the client's testamentary intent.

The Independent Counsel contends that the testamentary exception supports the posthumous termination of the privilege because in practice most cases have refused to apply the privilege posthumously. He further argues that the exception reflects a policy judgment that the interest in settling estates outweighs any posthumous interest in confidentiality. He then reasons by analogy that in criminal proceedings, the interest in determining whether a crime has been committed should trump client confidentiality, particularly since the financial interests of the estate are not at stake.

But the Independent Counsel's interpretation simply does not square with caselaw's acceptance of the privilege's survival and with the treatment of testamentary disclosure as an "exception" or an implied "waiver." And the premise of his analogy is incorrect, since cases consistently recognize that the rationale for the testamentary exception is that it furthers the client's intent. . . .

■   ■   ■

Despite the scholarly criticism, we think there are weighty reasons that counsel in favor of posthumous application. Knowing that communications will remain confidential even after death encourages the client to communicate fully and frankly with counsel. While the fear of disclosure, and the consequent withholding of information from counsel, may be reduced if disclosure is limited to posthumous disclosure in a criminal context, it seems unreasonable to assume that it vanishes altogether. Clients may be concerned about reputation, civil liability, or possible harm to friends or family. Posthumous disclosure of such communications may be as feared as disclosure during the client's lifetime.

■   ■   ■

The contention that the attorney is being required to disclose only when the client could have been required to disclose is at odds with the basis for the privilege even during the client's lifetime. In related cases, we have said that the loss of evidence admittedly caused by the privilege is justified in part by the fact that without the privilege, the client may not have made such communications in the first place. This is true of disclosure before and after the client's death. Without assurance of the privilege's posthumous application, the client may very well not have made disclosures to his attorney at all, so the loss of evidence is more apparent than real. In the case at hand, it seems quite plausible that Foster, perhaps already contemplating suicide, may not have sought legal advice from Hamilton if he had not been assured the conversation was privileged.

The Independent Counsel additionally suggests that his proposed exception would have minimal impact if confined to criminal cases, or, as the Court of Appeals suggests, if it is limited to information of substantial importance to a particular criminal case. However, there is no case authority for the proposition that the privilege applies differently in criminal and civil cases. . . . In any event, a client may not know at the time he disclosed information to his attorney whether it would later be relevant to a civil or criminal matter let alone whether it will be of substantial importance.

■   ■   ■

It has been generally, if not universally, accepted, for well over a century, that the attorney-client privilege survives the death of the client in a case such as this. While the arguments against the survival of the privilege are by no means frivolous, they are based on large part on speculation . . . as to whether posthumous termination of the privilege would diminish a client's willingness to confide in a attorney. In an area where empirical information would be useful, it is scant and inconclusive.

. . . [D]irection to look to "principles of the common law as they may be interpreted by the courts of the United States in the light of reason and experience" does not mandate that a rule, once established, should endure for all time. But here the Independent Counsel has simply not made a sufficient showing to overturn the common law rule embodied in the prevailing caselaw. Interpreted in the light of reason and experience, the body of law requires that the attorney-client privilege prevent disclosure of the notes at issue in this case. The judgment of the Court of Appeals is Reversed.

Justice O'Connor, with whom Justice Scalia and Justice Thomas join dissenting.

I agree that a deceased client may retain a personal, reputational and economic interest in confidentiality. But after death, the potential that disclosure will harm the client's interests has been greatly diminished, and the risk that the client will be held criminally liable has abated altogether. . . .

As the Court of Appeals observed, the costs of recognizing an absolute posthumous privilege can be inordinately high. Extreme injustice may occur, for example, where a criminal defendant seeks disclosure of a deceased client's confession to the offense. In my view, the paramount value that our criminal system places on protecting an innocent defendant should outweigh a deceased client's interest in preserving confidences. . . .

A number of exceptions to the privilege already qualify its protections, and an attorney "who tells his client that the expected communications are absolutely and forever privileged is oversimplifying a bit." In the situation where the posthumous privilege most frequently arises—a dispute between heirs over the decedent's will—the privilege is widely recognized to give way to the interest in settling the estate. . . .

Accordingly, I would affirm the judgment of the Court of Appeals. . . .

Case Questions:

1. Are there good reasons for the court to extend the posthumous exception to the privilege to certain criminal cases? What would the dissent say and why?
2. What does the Court mean when it says that principles of law as interpreted by the courts in the light of reason and experience "does not mandate that the rule . . . endure for all time?" What could change to change the rule?

3. How would empirical evidence have helped the Court? What might it show to alter the Court's decision?
4. The U.S. Patriot Act authorizes the eavesdropping on conversations between attorneys and their clients, who are in federal custody. In conjunction with the Patriot Act, the Bureau of Prisons allowed federal agents to tape conversations between a convicted terrorist held in a federal penitentiary and his attorney. Some of the conversations were used to convict the attorney of smuggling communications from his client to his client's followers in violation of the prison rules and law. How do you think the U.S. Supreme Court would rule in this matter? Should this portion of the Patriot Act be upheld? Explain.

Jurisdiction

The following case involving the use of a long-arm statute grapples with what satisfies minimum contacts.

WORLD-WIDE VOLKSWAGEN CORP. v. WOODSON
444 U.S. 286 (1980)

Harry and Kay Robinson (Respondents) purchased a new Audi automobile from Seaway Volkswagen (Seaway), in Massena, New York. The following year the Robinsons left their residence in New York and relocated in Arizona. While passing through the state of Oklahoma, another car struck their Audi in the rear causing a fire which severely burned Kay Robinson and her two children.

The Robinsons sued a number of parties, including the manufacturer of the Audi, its importer, its regional distributor, World-Wide Volkswagen Corp. (World-Wide) (Petitioner), and its retail dealer, Seaway (Petitioner), alleging that the accident was due to the misplacement of the gas tank. World-Wide is incorporated and has its business office in New York, and it distributes vehicles, parts and accessories to retail dealers in New York, New Jersey, and Connecticut. Seaway also is incorporated in New York, and has its place of business in that state. Neither

World-Wide nor Seaway does any business in Oklahoma. They do not do any advertising calculated to reach Oklahoma.

Seaway and World-Wide claimed that Oklahoma's exercise of jurisdiction over them would offend the limitations of Due Process Clause of the Fourteenth Amendment. The Oklahoma trial judge rejected that constitutional claim and the Supreme Court of Oklahoma in effect upheld that ruling. It based its holding on Oklahoma's long arm statute which conferred jurisdiction to the limits permitted by the United States Constitution. Petitioners sought a writ of certiorari which the United States Supreme Court granted.

Justice White delivered the opinion of the Court.

The issue before us is whether, consistently with the Due Process Clause of the Fourteenth Amendment, an Oklahoma court may exercise *in personam* jurisdiction over a nonresident automobile retailer and its wholesale distributor in a products-liability action, when the defendants' only connection with Oklahoma is the fact that an automobile sold in New York to New York residents became involved in an accident in Oklahoma.

■ ■ ■

As has long been settled, and as we reaffirm today, a state court may exercise personal jurisdiction over a nonresident defendant only so long as there exist "minimum contacts" between the defendant and the forum State. The concept of minimum contacts, in turn, can be seen to perform two related, but distinguishable, functions. It protects the defendant against the burdens of litigating in a distant or inconvenient forum. And it acts to insure that the States, through their courts, do not reach beyond the limits imposed on them by their status as coequal sovereigns in a federal system.

. . . We have said that the defendant's contacts with the forum State must be such that maintenance of the suit "does not offend 'traditional notions of fair play and substantial justice.' ". . .

The limits imposed on state jurisdiction by the Due Process Clause, in its role as guarantor against inconvenient litigation, have been substantially relaxed over the years. . . . [T]his trend is largely attributable to a fundamental transformation in the American economy:

> Today many commercial transactions touch two or more States and many involve parties separated by the full continent. With this increasing nationalization of commerce has come a great increase in the amount of business conducted by mail across state lines. At the same time modern transportation and communication have made it much less burdensome for a party sued to defend himself in a State where he engages in economic activity."

■ ■ ■

. . . [T]he Due Process Clause "does not contemplate that a state may make binding a judgment *in personam* against an individual or corporate defendant with which the state has no contacts, ties or relations.". . .

. . . Petitioners carry on no activity whatsoever in Oklahoma. They close no sales and perform no services there. They avail themselves of none of the privileges and benefits of Oklahoma law. They solicit no business . . . [n]or does the record show that they regularly sell cars at wholesale or retail to Oklahoma customers or residents or that they indirectly, through others, serve or seek to serve the Oklahoma market. In short, respondents seek to base jurisdiction on one, isolated occurrence and whatever inferences can be drawn therefrom: the fortuitous circumstance that a single Audi automobile, sold in New York to New York residents, happened to suffer an accident while passing through Oklahoma.

It is argued however, that because an automobile is mobile by its very design and purpose it was "foreseeable" that the Robinsons' Audi would cause injury in Oklahoma. . . .

If foreseeability were the criterion, a local California tire retailer could be forced to defend in Pennsylvania when a blowout occurs there . . . ; a Wisconsin seller of a defective automobile jack could be haled before a distant court for damage caused in New Jersey . . . ; or a Florida soft-drink concessionaire could be summoned to Alaska to account for injuries happening there. . . .

This is not to say, of course, that foreseeability is wholly irrelevant. But the foreseeability that is critical to due process analysis is not the mere likelihood that a product will find its way into the forum State. Rather, it is that the defendant's conduct and connection with the forum State are such that he should reasonably anticipate being haled into court there. The Due Process Clause, by insuring the "orderly administration of the laws," gives a degree of predictability to the legal system that allows potential defendants to structure their primary conduct with some minimum assurance as to where that conduct will and will not render them liable to suit.

When a corporation "purposefully avails itself of the privilege of conducting activities within the forum State," it has clear notice that it is subject to suit there, and can act to alleviate the risk of burdensome litigation by procuring insurance, passing the expected costs on to customers, or, if the risks are too great, severing its connection with the State. Hence if the sale of a product to a manufacturer or distributor such as Audi or Volkswagen is not simply an isolated occurrence, but arises from the efforts of the manufacturer or distributor to serve, directly or indirectly, the market for its product in other States, it is not unreasonable to subject it to suit in one of those States if its allegedly defective merchandise has there been the source of injury to its owners or to others. The

forum State does not exceed its powers under the Due Process Clause if it asserts personal jurisdiction over a corporation that delivers its products into the stream of commerce with the expectation that they will be purchased by consumers in the forum State.

But there is no such or similar basis for Oklahoma jurisdiction over World-Wide or Seaway in this case. . . . It is foreseeable that the purchasers of automobiles sold by World-Wide and Seaway may take them to Oklahoma. But the mere "unilateral activity of those who claim some relationship with a nonresident defendant cannot satisfy the requirement of contact with the forum State."

. . . [I]t is contended that jurisdiction can be supported by the fact that petitioners earn substantial revenue from goods used in Oklahoma. The Oklahoma Supreme Court so found, drawing the inference that because one automobile sold by petitioners had been used in Oklahoma, others might have been used there also. . . .

This argument seems to make the point that the purchase of automobiles in New York, from which the petitioners earn substantial revenue, would not occur *but for* the fact that the automobiles are capable of use in distant States like Oklahoma. Respondents observe that the very purpose of an automobile is to travel, and that travel of automobiles sold by petitioners is facilitated by an extensive chain of Volkswagen service centers throughout the country, including some in Oklahoma. However, financial benefits accruing to the defendant from a collateral relation to the forum State will not support jurisdiction if they do not stem from a constitutionally cognizable contact with that State. In our view, whatever marginal revenues petitioners may receive by virtue of the fact that their products are capable of use in Oklahoma is far too attenuated a contact to justify that State's exercise of *in personam* jurisdiction over them.

Because we find that the petitioners have no "contacts, ties, or relations" with the State of Oklahoma, the judgment of the Supreme Court of Oklahoma is *Reversed*.

Justices Brennan, Marshall, and Blackmun dissent.

Case Questions

1. What is the issue that this case presents?
2. What is the policy behind the Constitution's Due Process Clause in relation to jurisdiction?
3. Would not the respondents know that the automobiles they placed in the stream of commerce would wind up in another state? Why then, is "mere awareness" insufficient to constitutionally confer jurisdiction upon the Petitioners?
4. Change the facts of the case so that there would be jurisdiction in Oklahoma based upon the "purposefully avail" test.
5. CEA is a French research agency that patented a technology for the design and manufacture of liquid crystal displays (LCDs), a type of flat panel display used in computer monitors and television screens. CMO is a Taiwanese manufacturer of LCD products that CEA contends infringes on its patents. CMO's LCD products are sold to original equipment manufacturers (OEMs) that incorporate the LCDs into computer monitors. Although CMO does not have any direct contact with Delaware, it does derive substantial revenue from sales of its products to Delaware. Does this present a case of "sufficient minimum contacts" to justify jurisdictional power by a Delaware court? Is it distinguishable from World-Wide Volkswagen? Explain.

Diversity Jurisdiction

In the following case, the Supreme Court determines what is a corporation's "principal place of business" for purposes of diversity jurisdiction.

THE HERTZ CORPORATION V. FRIEND ET AL.
130 S. Ct. 1181 (U.S. 2010)

Melinda Friend and John Nhieu (respondents) two California citizens, sued the Hertz Corporation (petitioner) in a California state court. They sought damages for what they claimed were violations of California's wage and hour laws. Hertz sought removal to the federal district court, claiming that because it and the respondents were citizens of different states, the federal court possessed diversity-of-citizenship jurisdiction. Respondents, however, claimed that Hertz was a California citizen, like themselves, and therefore diversity jurisdiction was lacking under the federal jurisdiction statute, which provides that "a corporation shall be deemed to be a citizen of any State by which it has been incorporated and of the State where it has its principal place of business." To support its position, Hertz submitted a declaration by an employee relations manager that sought to show that Hertz's "principal place of business" was in New Jersey, not in California. The declaration stated, among other things, that Hertz operated facilities in 44 States; and that California—which had about 12% of the Nation's population – accounted for 273 of Hertz's 1,606 car rental locations; about 2,300 of its 11,230 full-time employees; about $ 811 million of its $ 4.371 billion in annual revenue; and about

3.8 million of its approximately 21 million annual transactions, i.e., rentals. The declaration also stated that the "leadership of Hertz and its domestic subsidiaries" is located at Hertz's "corporate headquarters" in Park Ridge, New Jersey; that its "core executive and administrative functions . . . are carried out" there and "to a lesser extent" in Oklahoma City, Oklahoma; and that its "major administrative operations . . . are found" at those two locations. The District Court concluded that it lacked diversity jurisdiction because Hertz was a California citizen under Ninth Circuit precedent, which asks whether the amount of the corporation's business activity is "significantly larger" or "substantially predominates" in one State. The District Court found that California was Hertz's "principal place of business" under that test because the plurality of each of the relevant business activities was in California, and that the differential between the amount of those activities in California and the amount in the next closest state was significant. The Ninth Circuit Court of Appeals affirmed the District Court, and Hertz appealed to the Supreme Court of the United States. What follows is the Supreme Court's opinion.

Justice Breyer

. . . We conclude that "principal place of business" is best read as referring to the place where a corporation's officers direct, control, and coordinate the corporation's activities. It is the place that Courts of Appeals have called the corporation's "nerve center." And in practice it should normally be the place where the corporation maintains its headquarters—provided that the headquarters is the actual center of direction, control, and coordination, i.e., the "nerve center," and not simply an office where the corporation holds its board meetings (for example, attended by directors and officers who have traveled there for the occasion).

The statute's text deems a corporation a citizen of the "State where it has its principal place of business. The word "place" is in the singular, not the plural. The word "principal" requires us to pick out the "main, prominent" or "leading" place. And the fact that the word "place" follows the words "State where" means that the "place" is a place within a State. It is not the State itself.

A corporation's "nerve center," usually its main headquarters, is a single place. The public often (though not always) considers it the corporation's main place of business. And it is a place within a State. . . .

[A]dministrative simplicity is a major virtue in a jurisdictional statute. Complex jurisdictional tests complicate a case, eating up time and money as the parties litigate, not the merits of their claims, but which court is the right court to decide those claims. Complex tests produce appeals and reversals, encourage gamesmanship, and, again, diminish the likelihood that results and settlements will reflect a claim's legal and factual merits. Judicial resources too are at stake. . . .

Simple jurisdictional rules also promote greater predictability. Predictability is valuable to corporations making business and investment decisions.

A "nerve center" approach, which ordinarily equates that "center" with a corporation's headquarters, is simple to apply comparatively speaking. The metaphor of a corporate "brain," while not precise, suggests a single location. By contrast, a corporation's general business activities more often lack a single principal place where they take place. That is to say, the corporation may have several plants, many sales locations, and employees located in many different places. If so, it will not be as easy to determine which of these different business locales is the "principal" or most important "place."

■   ■   ■

We recognize that there may be no perfect test that satisfies all administrative and purposive criteria. We recognize as well that, under the "nerve center" test we adopt today, there will be hard cases. For example, in this era of telecommuting, some corporations may divide their command and coordinating functions among officers who work at several different locations, perhaps communicating over the Internet. That said, our test nonetheless points courts in a single direction, towards the center of overall direction, control, and coordination. Courts do not have to try to weigh corporate functions, assets, or revenues different in kind, one from the other. Our approach provides a sensible test that is relatively easier to apply, not a test that will, in all instances, automatically generate a result.

■　　■　　■

We understand that such seeming anomalies will arise. However, in view of the necessity of having a clearer rule, we must accept them. Accepting occasionally counterintuitive results is the price the legal system must pay to avoid overly complex jurisdictional administration while producing the benefits that accompany a more uniform legal system.

The burden of persuasion for establishing diversity jurisdiction, of course, remains on the party asserting it. . . .

Petitioner's unchallenged declaration suggests that Hertz's center of direction, control, and coordination, its "nerve center," and its corporate headquarters are one and the same, and they are located in New Jersey, not in California. Because respondents should have a fair opportunity to litigate their case in light of our holding, however, we vacate the Ninth Circuit's judgment and remand the case for further proceedings consistent with this opinion.

Case Questions

1. What is diversity jurisdiction?
2. Where is a corporation a citizen for purposes of diversity jurisdiction?
3. What does the Court decide that "principal place of business" means?
4. Where does the Court say that the nerve center of a corporation will typically be found?

Arbitration

The next case concerning baseball arbitration illustrates the extent to which state courts are required to defer to arbitrator decisions.

MAJOR LEAGUE BASEBALL PLAYERS ASSOCIATION V. STEVE GARVEY
532 U.S. 504 (2001)

In the late 1980s, Major League Baseball Players Association (Association) filed grievances against the Major League Baseball Clubs (Clubs) claiming that the clubs had colluded in the market for free-agent services in violation of the industry's agreement. A free agent is a player who may contract with any Club, rather than one whose right is restricted to a particular Club. In a series of decisions, arbitrators found collusion by the Clubs and damage to the players. Thereafter, the Association and the Clubs entered into an agreement, whereby the Clubs established a $280 million fund to be distributed to injured players. The Association also designed a "Framework" to evaluate the individual player's claims.

The Framework provided that the players could seek an arbitrator's review of the distribution plan. The arbitrator would determine "only whether the approved Framework and the criteria set forth therein have been properly applied. . . . " Under the Framework claims were only legitimate "where evidence exists that a specific offer of an extension was made by a club prior to collusion only to thereafter be withdrawn when the collusion scheme was initiated."

Steve Garvey, a retired highly regarded first baseman, submitted a claim for damages of approximately $3 million. The matter was submitted to arbitration under the Framework. To provide his claim that the San Diego Padres offered him a contract, which was later withdrawn because of collusion, he submitted a copy of a letter from Ballard Smith, the Padres' president and chief executive officer, which stated that Smith offered to extend Garvey's contract, but thereafter the Padres refused to negotiate with Garvey due to collusion of the Clubs.

The arbitrator denied Garvey's claim, stating that there was substantial doubt as to the credibility of the statements in the Smith letter. Garvey appealed to the Federal District Court, who upheld the arbitrator's decision. The Court of Appeals for the Ninth Circuit reversed and remanded the case back to the arbitration panel for further hearings. The case arose to the U.S. Supreme Court when the Major League Player's Association petitioned the court for a writ of certiorari and it was granted.

Per Curiam*

The parties do not dispute that this case arises under . . . an agreement between an employer and a labor organization. Although Garvey's specific allegation is that the arbitrator violated the Framework for resolving players' claims for damages, that Framework was designed to facilitate payments to remedy the Club's breach of the . . . agreement. Garvey's right to be made whole is founded on that agreement.

Judicial review of a labor-arbitration decision pursuant to such an agreement is very limited. Courts are not authorized to review the arbitrator's decision on the merits despite allegations that the decision rests on factual errors or misinterprets the parties' agreement. We recently reiterated that if an " 'arbitrator is even arguably construing or applying the contract and acting within the scope of his authority,' the fact that 'a court is convinced he committed serious error does not suffice to overturn his decision.' " It is only when the arbitrator strays from interpretation and application of the agreement and effectively "dispense[s] his own brand of industrial justice" that his decision may be unenforceable. When an arbitrator resolves disputes regarding the application of a contract, and no dishonesty is alleged, the arbitrator's "improvident, even silly, factfinding" does

---

*Literally, "by the Court." In this case it is a decision that is not authored by one justice but by the majority of justices.

not provide a basis for a reviewing court to refuse to enforce the award.

In discussing the courts' limited role in reviewing the merits of arbitration awards, we have stated that "'courts . . . have no business weighing the merits of the grievance [or] considering whether there is equity in a particular claim.'" When the judiciary does so, "it usurps a function which . . . is entrusted to the arbitration tribunal." Consistent with this limited role, we said . . . that "[e]ven in the very rare instances when an arbitrator's procedural aberrations rise to the level of affirmative misconduct, as a rule the court must not foreclose further proceedings by settling the merits according to its own judgment of the appropriate result."

That step, we explained, "would improperly substitute a judicial determination for the arbitrator's decision that the parties bargained for" in their agreement. Instead, the court should "simply vacate the award, thus leaving open the possibility of further proceedings if they are permitted under the terms of the agreement."

To be sure, the Court of Appeals here recited these principles, but its application of them is nothing short of baffling. The substance of the Court's discussion reveals that it overturned the arbitrator's decision because it disagreed with the arbitrator's factual findings, particularly those with respect to credibility. The Court of Appeals, it appears, would have credited Smith's . . . letter, and found the arbitrator's refusal to do so at worst "irrational" and at best "bizarre." But even "serious error" on the arbitrator's part does not justify overturning his decision, where, as here, he is construing a contract and acting within the scope of his authority.

. . . [E]stablished law ordinarily precludes a court from resolving the merits of the parties' dispute on the basis of its own factual determinations, no matter how erroneous the arbitrator's decision. Even when the arbitrator's award may properly be vacated, the appropriate remedy is to remand the case for further arbitration proceedings. The dissent [in this case] suggests that the remedy . . . is limited to cases where the arbitrator's errors are procedural . . . If a remand is appropriate *even*

when the arbitrator's award has been set aside for "procedural aberrations" that constitute "affirmative misconduct," it follows that a remand ordinarily will be appropriate when the arbitrator simply made factual findings that the reviewing court perceives as "irrational." The Court of Appeals usurped the arbitrator's role by resolving the dispute and barring further proceedings, a result at odds with this governing law.

For the foregoing reasons, the Court of Appeals erred in reversing the order of the District Court denying the motion to vacate the arbitrator's award, and it erred further in directing that judgment be entered in Garvey's favor. The judgment of the Court of Appeals is reversed, and the case is remanded for further proceedings consistent with this opinion.

It is so ordered.

Case Questions:

1. What is the scope of review of a labor arbitration dispute?

2. Under what circumstances in this case would the decision of the arbitrator be overturned by a court? What is the arbitrator's "own brand of industrial justice?"

3. Assume that a contract for an automobile contained sub-microscopic print on the backside that said: "In the event of a dispute the parties shall submit to binding arbitration and not have the right to institute an action in court." The arbitration clause was never brought to the attention of the consumer. How do you think a court should rule in this instance when the consumer seeks to sue in court because of false misrepresentations made by the car dealer concerning the odometer reading? Must it defer to an arbitrator? Why, or why not?

4. Assume that an agreement between a bank and a customer reads:

   All disputes, or claims, or controversies arising from this contract shall be resolved by binding arbitration by one arbitrator selected by the Bank with the consent of the Customer.

A customer maintains that she did not receive certain notifications by the Bank required by law. In order to resolve the dispute the company selects an arbitrator, and the customer agrees to the selection. The customer seeks to certify the case as a class action so that other consumers may take advantage of the arbitration. Is it within the realm of the courts or the arbitrator to determine whether the class action is permissible? Explain. How do you interpret the language of the agreement? To permit this or not?

Chapter Four   The Law of Property

Mislaid Property

The distinctions among abandonment, lost and mislaid property are examined in the next case in order to determine who was entitled to possession of old currency found in a motel room.

TERRY V. A.D. LOCK
343 Ark. 452, 37 S.W. 3d 202 (2001)

Joe Terry and Davis Stocks were stripping motel rooms at the Best Western Motel, in preparation for the renovation of the rooms. While removing some ceiling tiles in room 118 they found a cardboard box that was concealed on the top of the heating and air vent. The box contained $38,310.00 in old dusty currency.

Terry and Stocks, motel renovators, brought an action against the motel owners, seeking a determination that they were the rightful owners of the lost property. An Arkansas trial court held in favor of the motel owners. Terry and Stocks, the finders, appealed the case to the Supreme Court of Arkansas.

Justice Ray Thornton

Property is said to be "abandoned" when it is thrown away, or its possession is voluntarily forsaken by the owner, in which case it will become the property of the first occupant; or when it is involuntarily lost or left without the hope and expectation of again acquiring it, and then it becomes property of the finder, subject to the superior claim of the owner.

Lost Property

"Lost property" is property, which the owner has involuntarily parted with through neglect, carelessness, or inadvertence, that is, property which the owner had unwittingly suffered to pass out of his possession, and of whose whereabouts he has no knowledge. Property is deemed lost when it is unintentionally separated from the dominion of its owner. Popularly, property is lost when the owner does not know, and cannot ascertain, where it is[.] [T]he essential test of lost property is whether the owner parted with the possession of the property intentionally, casually or involuntarily; only in the latter contingency may it be lost property. Property is not "lost" unless the owner parts with it involuntarily and unintentionally, and does not, at any time thereafter, know where to find it. A loss is always involuntary; there can be no intent to part with the ownership of the property.

The finder of lost property does not acquire absolute ownership, but acquires such property interest or right as will enable him to keep it against the entire world but the rightful owner. This rule is not affected by the place of finding, as the finder of lost property has a right to possession of the article superior to that of the owner or occupant of the premises where it is found.

Mislaid Property

"Mislaid Property" is that which is intentionally put into a certain place and later forgotten. The place where money or property claimed as lost is found is an important factor in the determination of the question of whether it was lost or only mislaid. But where articles are accidentally dropped in any public place, public thoroughfare, or street, they are lost in the legal sense. In short, property will not be considered to have been lost unless the circumstances are such that, considering the place where, and the conditions under which, it is found there is an inference that it was left there unintentionally.

A finder of mislaid property acquires no ownership rights in it, and, where such property is found upon another's premises, he has no right to its possession, but is required to turn it over to the owner of the premises. This is true whether the finder is an employee or occupier of the premises on which the mislaid article is found or a customer of the owner or occupant. The right of possession, as against all except the true owner, is in the owner or occupant of the premises where the property is discovered, for the mislaid property is presumed

to have been left in the custody of the owner or occupier of the premises upon which it is found. The result is that the proprietor of the premises is entitled to retain possession of the thing, pending a search by him to discover the owner, or during such time the owner may be considered to be engaged in trying to recover his property. . . .

The finder of the mislaid property must turn it . . . over to the owner or occupier of the premises where it was found; it is the latter's duty to keep mislaid property for the owner. . . . As against everyone but the true owner, the owner of such premises has the duty to defend his custody and possession of the mislaid property, and he is absolutely liable for a misdelivery.

■   ■   ■

. . . Appellant Stocks stated in his affidavit that "the box and its contents appeared to have been located at the site for very long time." Mr. Lock testifies that in 1988 a beam was replaced in room 118 and the box was not discovered at that time. Upon opening the box, a large amount of old, dusty currency was discovered. Neither appellants nor appellees claim to have concealed the property in the ceiling. It is apparent that the box was not lost. The circumstances suggest that it was either abandoned property . . . [or] mislaid property. . . . We hold that the trial court's findings that "the money in controversy was intentionally placed where it was found for its security, in order to shield it from unwelcome eyes . . ." and that the "money was mislaid [property]" were not clearly erroneous.

■   ■   ■

The natural assumption is that the person who concealed the bills in the case at bar was a guest of the hotel. Their considerable value, and the manner of their concealment, indicates that the person who concealed them did so for the purpose of security, and with the intention of reclaiming them. They were, therefore, to be classified not as lost, but as misplaced or forgotten property, and the defendant, as the occupier of the premises where they were found, had the right and duty to take them into his possession and to hold them . . . for the true owner.

■ ■ ■

Affirmed.

Case Questions

1. Would there be a different result if the money had not been old and dusty? Explain.
2. Construct a scenario to explain how the money got where it was found. Is that important when characterizing it? Explain.
3. Should the money revert to the state rather than to the owner of the hotel? Why or why not?

Bailee's Liability

The following case considers the issue of a bailee's liability for the contents of bailed property.

HADFIELD V. GILCHRIST
343 S.C. 88, 538 S.E. 2d 268 (2000)

Mark Hadfield, a medical student, sought to retrieve his Lincoln Continental from a parking lot where his wife had left the car. Since the vehicle was parked in a private parking spot without the permission of the owner, it was towed to a storage facility. The facility, owned by Sam Gilchrist, maintained a chain link fence around the facility and there was an office employee on the lot 24 hours. Periodically, the employee would check on the storage facility. Hadfield went to the facility and paid fees. However, when he went to retrieve the car he found that vandals who had cut a hole in the fence had extensively damaged it. His radio/compact disc players were stolen, the car windows smashed, and the vehicle's computer mechanisms were permanently damaged.

Hadfield sued Gilchrist and a magistrate found Gilchrist liable for $4,035.00 in damages. Gilchrist appealed to the Circuit Court, which affirmed the magistrate's decision. Gilchrist prosecuted a further appeal to the Court of Appeals of South Carolina.

Judge Anderson

A bailment is created by the delivery of personal property by one person to another in trust for a specific purpose, pursuant to an express or implied contract to fulfill that trust.

Bailments are generally classified as being for (1) the sole benefit of the bailor, (2) the sole benefit of the bailee; or (3) the mutual benefit of both.

Bailments, which benefit only one of the parties, the first and second classifications, are often described as gratuitous.

■ ■ ■

"A gratuitous bailment is, by definition, one in which the transfer of possession or use of the bailed property is without compensation." For instance, a gratuitous bailment arises if the bailment is undertaken as a personal favor or is involuntary.

A "gratuitous bailee" acts without expectation of reward or compensation. To show the bailment was for the sole benefit of the bailor, the bailee must establish that it was not expecting compensation. . . .

By contrast, a bailment for the mutual benefit of the parties arises when one party takes the personal property of another into his care or custody in exchange for payment or other benefit.

Although a bailment is ordinarily created by the agreement of the parties, the agreement of the parties may be implied or constructive, and the bailment may arise by operation of law. Such a constructive bailment arises when one person has lawfully acquired possession of another's personal property, other than by virtue of a bailment contract, and holds it under circumstances that the law imposes on the recipient of the property the obligation to keep it safely and redeliver it to the owner. A constructive bailment may occur even in absence of the voluntary delivery and acceptance of the property, which is usually necessary to create a bailment relationship.

Gilchrist argues he towed the vehicle pursuant to the Charleston Municipal Ordinances, and the ordinances are for the sole benefit of the vehicle owners. Accordingly, he contends, the relationship created a gratuitous bailment. We disagree. . . .

■　　■　　■

The vehicle owned by Hadfield was plucked by Gilchrist from . . . private property. . . . Gilchrist acted pursuant to and by virtue of the licensing authority under the city ordinance. Quintessentially, the factual scenario encapsulated in this case is a paradigm of a "constructive bailment." We conclude a constructive bailment, for the mutual benefit of Hadfield and Gilchrist, was created.

Although contractual in nature, and involving the conveyance of personal property, an action for breach of the duty of care by a bailor sounds in tort. . . . Concomitantly, after finding a bailment for mutual benefit exists in this case, we must determine whether Hadfield is entitled to damages. . . .

The degree of care required of a bailee for mutual benefit is defined as ordinary care, or due care, or the degree of care which would be exercised by a person of ordinary care in the protection of his own property. . . .

Under the decided cases in this state, liability of a bailee under a bailment for mutual benefit arises upon a showing that (1) the goods were delivered to the bailee in good condition, (2) they were lost or returned in a damaged condition, and (3) the loss or damage to the goods was due to the failure of the bailee to exercise ordinary care in the safekeeping of the property. The burden of proof in such cases, in the first instance, rests upon the bailor to make out a prima [facie] case. This has been done when the bailor proves that he delivered the goods to the bailee in good condition and their loss or return in a damaged condition. When the bailor has so proven, the burden is then shifted to the bailee to show that he has used ordinary care in the storage and safekeeping of the property.

The burden of proof in this case rests first upon the bailor, Hadfield, to prove the *prima facie case*. He must show: 1) the goods were delivered to the bailee in good condition, and 2) they were lost or returned in damaged condition. When the bailor, Hadfield, has so proven, the burden is then shifted to the bailee, Gilchrist, to show that he has used ordinary care in the good's storage and safekeeping.

Hadfield testified before the magistrate regarding the "nice" condition of the vehicle prior to being towed, and the damage to his vehicle, and the other vehicles on the lot. In addition, he introduced photographs depicting the damage. Thus, Hadfield made out his prima facie case. . . . The burden then shifted to Gilchrist to show that he used ordinary care in protecting the vehicle while in his care.

Gilchrist impounded the cars in a storage lot surrounded by a chain link fence. . . . The fact the guard was not on duty at the impound lot and, considering the only other security for the vehicles was the chain link fence, the lower court judge could have concluded that Gilchrist failed to exercise ordinary care. . . .

We rule that where a city ordinance is utilized as the legal justification for taking possession of a vehicle on private property the person or entity lawfully acquiring possession of the property under the ordinance becomes a constructive bailee as a matter of law. We find a constructive bailment, for the mutual benefit of Hadfield and Gilchrist, was created. Further, we hold an action for breach of duty of care by a bailor, although contractual in nature, sounds in tort. We conclude the burden of proof in a constructive bailment case rests first upon a bailor to prove a *prima facie* case and, once so proven, the burden shifts to the bailee to show use of ordinary care in the storage and safekeeping of the property. Accordingly, the order of the Circuit Court is
AFFIRMED.

Case Questions

1. Would the result have been different had the court found this to be a gratuitous bailment? Explain.
2. What specifically is the alleged negligent act or omission committed by Gilchrist that led to liability? Do you agree that this is sufficient?
3. Why is this a constructive bailment? What type of bailment does the court construct?
4. Assume that the owner of the vehicle left it to be fixed at a garage. Employees repaired it and left it parked outside with the keys in the car. The car was stolen and damaged. Would the garage owner be liable? Do you need additional facts? Explain.

Fixtures—Adaptation

Consider the following case involving a posh estate and items in dispute that were consistent with its décor.

PAUL V. FIRST NATIONAL BANK
369 N.E.2d 488 (Ohio Common Pleas 1976)

The Longs died in an airplane crash. Among other things, they left a posh estate. Plaintiff, Paul, entered into a contract for $575,000 for the purchase of the estate—a 17-room, elegant stone house situated on a 97-acre picturesque estate of landscaped, rolling terraces, referred to as "Long Acres."

The purchase contract included all "fixtures." Before Paul took possession, heirs living in the house removed certain items. They included lighting fixtures, metal cranes and garden statues, an ornamental well housing, a statue of Mercury, and a walnut organ bench. Paul sued the estate representative, First National Bank, and the heirs of the estate for wrongful taking. The trial court found for the plaintiff.

Judge Black

In *Masheter v. Boehm . . . the* Supreme Court [of Ohio] designated . . . six "facts" to be considered in determining whether an item is a fixture:

1. The nature of the property;
2. The manner in which the property is annexed to the realty;
3. The purpose for which the annexation is made;

4. The intention of the annexing party to make the property a part of the realty;

5. The degree of difficulty and extent of any loss involved in removing the property from the realty; and

6. The damage to the severed property which such removal would cause.

. . . [T]he expression of "a comprehensive and generally applicable rule of law" about fixtures has bedeviled the courts for years and is complicated by the need for different definitions in those situations where the relationship between the parties is different. Nevertheless, the six considerations listed in *Masheter v. Boehm* are pertinent and applicable in the interpretation of "all fixtures relating to said real estate. . . ."

■   ■   ■

Using the Supreme Court's considerations, the light "fixtures" (there is no other available word) from the swimming pool, the stable apartment and the chapel are clearly fixtures in contemplation of law. . . . They are of a type universally recognized as fixtures. This is true even though the pool "fixtures" were hung on brackets and could be unplugged and simply lifted off the brackets. But they were designed and produced solely and only for the swimming pool, from the same design as was used for the light fixture in the porte cochere (which was not removed). Further, the poles from which they were taken are barren and incomplete without them.

The three metal cranes and the four garden statues also meet five of the six criteria, in the judgment of the court. The "nature" of these items is that they were a part of the total elegance of Long Acres. They are not the type of fixture which would be commonly found on other lawns or in other gardens, but they are an integral part of this sumptuous country estate. The cranes were "annexed" by being bolted or screwed into concrete foundations in a manner similar to the annexation of the marble table in the Great Hall, an item clearly admitted by all defendants to be a fixture passing with the real estate. The 4 garden statues . . . were not simply placed on top of their col-

umns, but were held in place by 6-inch pipe protruding from the columns into the bases of the statues. The purpose of fixing these into position was to ensure their presence and preservation as part and parcel of the landscape and approach to Long Acres. These cranes and statues were not items moved about at the whim of the owner or according to the seasons: they were permanent emplacements, intended to be part of the continuing visual effect of the estate. While no great difficulty was encountered in removing any of them, their absence is a source of loss. The cranes were prominent in the approach to the front door, and that approach is damaged without them. . . . The removal of the statues leaves the columns on which they stood barren and incomplete; the columns appear to have been vandalized.

. . . [T]he ornamental well housing, the Mercury statue and the organ bench, were not attached in a permanent way. However, interpreting the contract from its four corners, in the light of all the facts and circumstances in evidence, the Court concludes that these items were "appurtenances" to the real estate, both in contemplation of law and in interpretation of this word as used in the purchase contract.

■   ■   ■

All three items . . . form a part of the character of Long Acres and enhance the style of its elegance. They are appurtenant to Long Acres in the sense that they are necessarily connected with the use and enjoyment of this country estate. They are incidental to the total value of this estate. The source of that value is not only the grand design but also all of the details whereby that design is executed: the location of the house on the property, the sweep of the driveway as it approaches the porte cochere, the spread-out location of the barns and other outbuildings, the majesty of the formal gardens, the spaciousness of the lawns on every side, and all the details of the exterior and interior of the mansion itself.

To allow the heirs to walk off with an organ bench, leaving the built-in organ behind would be plainly ridiculous. You cannot play an organ while standing up, and no ordinary bench will do.

The Mercury statue is pictured in two photographs included in the appraisal of Long Acres which was considered by plaintiff before purchase. It may have been moved from the pedestal from time to time by the Long family. . . . But interpreting the contract in the light of all facts and circumstances in evidence, the Court concludes that these items pass[ed] with the real estate.

■　　■　　■

[The court ordered damages due to the wrongful taking of the fixtures.]

Case Questions

1. What issue does this case present?
2. What do you think the intention of the Longs were regarding each item? Why?
3. Change the facts such that the items would not be considered fixtures?
4. How could the parties to the contract have clarified the sale and reduced the possibility of a lawsuit?

Patentable Subject Matter

The following case, involving genetically engineered bacteria, discusses and illustrates the breadth of the interpretation of the statutory subject matter.

DIAMOND V. CHAKRABARTY
447 US 303 (1980)

Chakrabarty, a microbiologist (respondent), filed an application for a patent relating to his invention of a human-made, genetically engineered bacteria capable of breaking down multiple components of crude oil. Because of this property, which is possessed by no naturally occurring bacteria, Chakrabarty's invention is believed to have significant value for the treatment of oil spills.

The United States Patent Office held that live, human-made micro-organisms were not patentable subject matter under the statute. The Court of Customs and Patent Appeals (now the Court of Appeals for the Federal Circuit) reversed, holding that the fact that the micro-organisms are alive is without significance for application of the law. The Supreme Court affirmed the Court of Customs and Patent Appeals.

Chief Justice Burger

The question before us in this case is a narrow one of statutory interpretation requiring us to construe 35 U.S.C. § 101, which provides: "Whoever invents or discovers any new and useful . . . manufacture, or composition of matter . . . may obtain a patent therefore. . . ."

■　　■　　■

. . . [T]his Court has read the term "manufacture" . . . in accordance with its dictionary definition to mean "the production of articles for use from raw or prepared materials by giving to these materials new forms, qualities, properties, or combinations, whether by hand-labor or by machinery. . . ." Similarly, "composition of matter" has been construed consistent with its common usage to include "all compositions of two or more substances and . . .

all composite articles, whether they be the results of gases, fluids, powders or solids. . . ." In choosing such expansive terms as "manufacture" and "composition of matter," modified by the comprehensive "any," Congress plainly contemplated that the patent laws would be given wide scope.

■ ■ ■

. . . The Committee Reports accompanying the 1952 Act inform us that Congress intended statutory subject matter to "include any thing under the sun that is made by man. . . ."

This is not to suggest that § 101 has no limits or that it embraces every discovery. The laws of nature, physical phenomena, and abstract ideas have been held not patentable. . . . Thus, a new mineral discovered in the earth or a new plant found in the wild is not patentable subject matter. Likewise, Einstein could not patent his celebrated law that $E = mc^2$; nor could Newton have patented the law of gravity. Such discoveries are "manifestations of . . . nature, free to all men and reserved exclusively to none."

Judged in this light, respondent's micro-organism plainly qualifies as patentable subject matter. His claim is not to a hitherto unknown natural phenomenon, but to a nonnaturally occurring manufacture or composition of matter . . . a new bacterium with markedly different characteristics from any found in nature and one having the potential for significant utility. His discovery is not nature's handiwork, but his own; accordingly it is patentable subject matter under § 101.

■ ■ ■

The petitioner's second argument is that micro-organisms cannot qualify as patentable subject matter until Congress expressly authorizes such protection. . . . The briefs present a gruesome parade of horribles. Scientists, among them Nobel laureates, are quoted suggesting that genetic research may pose a serious threat to the human race. . . .

It is argued that this Court should weigh these potential hazards in considering whether respon-

dent's invention is patentable subject matter under § 101. We disagree. The grant or denial of patents on micro-organisms is not likely to put an end to genetic research or to its attendant risks. . . .

What is more important is that we are without competence to entertain these arguments—either to brush them aside as fantasies generated by fear of the unknown, or to act on them. . . . Congress is free to amend § 101 so as to exclude from patent protection organisms produced by genetic engineering. . . . Or it may choose to craft a statute specifically designed for such living things. But, until Congress takes such action, this Court must construe the language of § 101 as it is. The language of that section fairly embraces respondent's invention.

Case Questions

1. The language of the patent statute quoted by the Court (". . . any new and useful . . . manufacture or composition of matter . . .") was actually written in the first patent statute by Thomas Jefferson in 1793. Do you feel that Jefferson intended the language to cover a living micro-organism? Analyze.

2. Do you think the Court was unduly swayed by the obvious utility of the invention? Explain.

3. The Court dismisses the argument of scientists that genetic engineering could pose a serious threat to the human race. In authorizing patent ability of genetically engineered micro-organisms, is the Court acting in the best interests of society? Discuss.

4. A researcher at a large pharmaceutical firm successfully isolated a biologically pure micro-organism believed to be extremely useful in producing a well-known antibiotic at significantly lower costs. Evidence was presented that while the micro-organism was known to exist in nature, it never existed in the biologically pure form. Can the researcher obtain a patent on this micro-organism? Analyze.

Copyright Owner's Rights

The fair use doctrine has been incorporated into the copyright statute, and is discussed in the following case involving the electronic duplication and transfer of copyrighted musical recordings.

A & M RECORDS V. NAPSTER, INC.
239 F. 3d 1004 (9th Cir. 2001)

A & M Records, plaintiffs, are engaged in the commercial recording, distribution and sale of copyrighted musical compositions and sound recordings. Defendant, Napster, Inc., facilitates the transmission of audio musical recordings in an MP3 file format from one user to another, by electronic transfer and duplication. Through Napster's Musicshare software, available free from Napster's Internet site, network servers and server-side software users were able to engage in "peer-to-peer" file sharing. Napster also provides technical support for indexing, searching and chatting, all to assist the downloading and uploading of MP3 files.

Circuit Judge Beezer

The district court . . . determined that the plaintiff's exclusive rights under §106 were violated: "here the evidence establishes that a majority of Napster users use the services to download and upload copyrighted music. . . . And by doing that . . . the uses constitute direct infringement of the plaintiffs' musical composition, recordings." The district court also noted that "it is pretty much acknowledged . . . by Napster that this is infringement." We agree that plaintiffs have shown that Napster users infringe at least two of the copyright holders' exclusive rights: the rights of reproduction and distribution. Napster users who upload names to the search index for others to copy violate plaintiffs' distribution rights. Napster users who download files containing copyrighted music violate plaintiffs' reproduction rights.

■ ■ ■

Napster contends that its users do not directly infringe plaintiff's copyrights because the users are engaged in fair use of the material. Napster identifies three specific alleged fair uses: sampling, where users make temporary copies of a work before purchasing; space-shifting, where users access a sound recording through the Napster system that they already own in audio CD format; and permissive distribution of recordings by both the new and established artists.

The district court considered factors listed in 17 U.S.C. § 107, which guide a court's fair use determination. These factors are: (1) the purpose and character of the use; (2) the nature of the copyrighted work, (3) the "amount and substantiality of the portion used" in relation to the work as a whole; and (4) the effect of the use upon the potential market for the work or the value of the work. The district court first conducted a general analysis of Napster system uses under §107, and then applied its reasoning to the alleged fair uses identified by Napster. The district court concluded that Napster users are not fair users. We agree. We first address the court's overall fair use analysis.

1. Purpose and Character of the Use

The factor focuses on whether the new work merely replaces the object of the original creation or instead adds a further purpose or different character. In other words, this factor asks "whether and to what extent the new work is 'transformative.' "

The district court first concluded that downloading MP3 files does not transform the copyrighted work. This conclusion is supportable. Courts have been reluctant to find fair use when an original work is merely retransmitted in a different medium.

This "purpose and character" element also requires the district court to determine whether the allegedly infringing use is commercial or noncommercial. A commercial use weighs against finding a fair use but is not conclusive on the issue. The district court determined that Napster users engage in commercial use of the copyrighted materials largely because (1) "a host user sending a file cannot be said to engage in a personal use when distributing that file to an anonymous requester" and (2) "Napster users get for free something they would ordinarily have to buy." The district court's findings are not clearly erroneous.

Direct economic benefit is not required to demonstrate a commercial use. Rather, repeated and exploitative copying of copyrighted works, even if the copies are not offered for sale, may constitute a commercial use. In the record before us, commercial use is demonstrated by a showing that repeated and exploitative unauthorized copies of copyrighted works were made to save the expense of purchasing authorized copies. . . .

2. The Nature of the Use

Works that are creative in nature are "closer to the core of intended copyright protection" than are more fact-based works. The district court deter-

mined that plaintiffs' "copyrighted musical compositions and sound recordings are creative in nature . . . which cuts against a finding of fair use under the second factor." We find no error in the district court's conclusion.

3. The Portion Used

"While 'wholesale copying does not preclude fair use per se,' copying an entire work 'militates against a finding of fair use.' " The district court determined that Napster users engage in "wholesale copying" of copyrighted work because file transfer necessarily "involves copying the entirety of the copyrighted work." We agree. We note, however, that under certain circumstances, a court will conclude that a use is fair even when the projected work is copied in its entirety.

4. Effect and Use on Market

"Fair use, when properly applied' is limited to copying by others which does not materially impair the marketability of the work which is copied." "[T]he importance of this [fourth] factor will vary, not only with the amount of harm, but also with the relative strength of the showing on the other factors." The proof required to demonstrate the present or future market harm varies with the purpose and character of the use. . . .

Addressing this factor, the district court concluded that Napster harms the market in "at least" two ways: it reduces audio CD sales among college students and it "raises barriers to the plaintiffs' entry into the market for the digital downloading of music." The district court relied on evidence plaintiffs submitted to show that Napster use harms the market for their copyrighted musical compositions and sound recordings. In a separate memorandum the order regarding the parties' objections to the expert reports, the district court examined each report, finding some more appropriate and probative than others. . . .

■ ■ ■

The district court cited both the Jay and Fine Reports in support of its finding that Napster use harms the market for plaintiffs' copyrighted musical compositions and sound recordings by reducing CD sales among college students. The district court cited the Teece Report to show the harm Napster use caused in raising barriers to plaintiffs' entry into the market for digital downloading of music. The district court's careful consideration of defendant's objections to these reports and decision to rely on the reports for specific issues demonstrates proper exercise of discretion in addition to a correct application of the fair use doctrine. Defendant has failed to show any basis for disturbing the district court's findings.

We, therefore, conclude that the district court made sound findings related to Napster's deleterious effect on the present and future digital download market. Moreover, lack of harm to an established market cannot deprive the copyright holder of the right to develop alternative markets for the works. Here . . . the record supports the district court's finding that the "record company plaintiffs have already expended considerable funds and effort to commence Internet sales and licensing for digital downloads." Having digital downloads available for free on the Napster sys-tem necessarily harms the copyright holders' attempts to charge for the same downloads.

[The Court] did not abuse [its] discretion in reaching the above fair use conclusions, nor were the findings of fact with respect to fair use considerations clearly erroneous. . . .

■　　■　　■

Affirmed in part.

Case Questions

1. In what ways has Napster infringed on A & M Records copyrighted material? Explain.
2. What are the four factors to be considered when determining fair use?
3. MP3 format is a lesser quality than CDs. Would not the MP3s actually motivate users to purchase recordings that they would not otherwise purchase after listening to the MP3 recordings, and thus increase the demand for the recordings? Explain.
4. What can Napster now do to avoid infringement while distributing music recordings electronically? Explain.

Federal Registration and Remedies

The following case involves the trademark of a color.

QUALITEX COMPANY V. JACOBSON PRODUCTS CO.
514 U.S. 159 (1995)

Plaintiff, Qualitex, used a special shade of green-gold color on pads that it manufactured and sold to dry cleaning firms for use on dry cleaning presses. Jacobson Products, defendant, a competitor, sold presses with similar colored pads. Qualitex registered the special green-gold color as a trademark.

Qualitex sued Jacobson for trademark infringement and unfair competition. The district court found in favor of Qualitex. The Ninth Circuit Court of Appeals set aside the trademark infringement claim on the basis that one cannot register a "color alone" as a trademark. The Circuit Courts of Appeals were split on this issue and the United States Supreme Court granted certiorari.

Justice Breyer

The question in this case is whether the Trademark Act . . . (Lanham Act) permits the registration of a trademark that consists, purely and simply, of a color. We conclude that, sometimes, a color will meet ordinary legal trademark requirements. And, when it does so, no special legal rule prevents color alone from serving as a trademark.

■   ■   ■

The Lanham Act gives a seller or producer the exclusive right to "register" a trademark, and to prevent his or her competitors from using that trademark. Both the language of the Act and the basic underlying principles of the trademark law would seem to include color within the universe of things that can qualify as a trademark. The language of the Lanham Act describes that universe in the broadest of terms. It says that trademarks "include any word, name, symbol, or device, or any combination thereof." Since human beings might use as a "symbol" or "device" almost anything at all that is capable of carrying meaning, this language, read literally, is not restrictive. The courts and the Patent and Trademark Office have authorized for use as a mark a particular shape (of a Coca-Cola bottle), a particular sound (NBC's three chimes), and even a particular scent (of plumeria blossoms on sewing thread). If a shape, a sound, and a fragrance can act as symbols why one might ask, can a color not do the same?

A color is also capable of satisfying the more important part of the statutory definition of a trademark, which requires that a person "use" or "intend to use" the mark "to identify and distinguish his or her goods, including a unique prod-

uct, from those manufactured or sold by others and to indicate the source of the goods, even if that source is unknown." True, a product's color is unlike "fanciful," "arbitrary," or "suggestive" words or designs, which almost *automatically* tell the customer that they refer to a brand. The imaginary word "Suntost," or the words "Suntost Marmalade," on the jar or orange jam immediately would signal a brand or a product "source"; the jam's color does not do so. But, over time, customers may come to treat a particular color on a product or its packaging (say, a color that in context seems unusual, such as pink on a firm's insulating material or red on the head of a large industrial bolt) as signifying a brand. And, if so, that color would have come to identify and distinguish the goods—*i.e.*, "to indicate" their "source"—much in the way that descriptive word on a product (say, "Trim" on nail clippers or "Car-Freshener" on deodorizer) can come to indicate a product's origin. In this circumstance, trademark law says that the word (*e.g.*, "Trim"), although not inherently distinctive has developed "secondary meaning." . . . Secondary meaning" is acquired when " in the minds of the public, the primary significance of a product feature . . . is to identify the source of the product rather than the product itself". . . .

We cannot find in the basic objectives of trademark law any obvious theoretical objection to the use of color alone as a trademark, where that color has attained "secondary meaning" and therefore identifies and distinguishes a particular brand (and thus indicates its "source"). In principle, trademark law, by preventing others from copying the source-identifying mark, "reduce[s] the customer's costs of shopping and making purchasing decisions," for it quickly and easily assures a potential customer that *this* item—the item with the mark—is made by the same producer as other similarly marked items that he or she liked (or disliked) in the past. At the same time, the law helps assure a producer that it (and not an intimidating competitor) will reap the financial, reputation-related awards associated with a desirable product. The law thereby "encourage[s] the production of quality products," and simultaneously discourages those who hope to sell inferior products by capitalizing on a consumer's inability quickly to evaluate the quality of an item offered for sale. . . .

. . . Neither can we find a principled objection to use of color as a mark in the important "functionality" doctrine of trademark law.

. . . This court consequently has explained that, "in general terms, a product feature is functional," and cannot serve as a trademark, "if it is essential to the use or purpose of the article or if it affects the cost or quality of the article," that is, if exclusive use of the feature would put competitors at a significant non-reputation-related disadvantage. Although sometimes color plays an important role (unrelated to source identification) in making a product more desirable, sometimes it does not. And, this latter fact—the fact that sometimes color is not essential to a product's use or purpose and does not affect the cost or quality—indicates that the doctrine of "functionality" does not create an absolute bar to the use of color alone as a mark.

It would seem, then, that color alone, at least sometimes, can meet the basic legal requirements for use as a trademark. It can act as a symbol that distinguishes a firm's goods and identifies their source, without serving any other significant function. . . . Accordingly, unless there is some special reason that convincingly militates against the use of color alone as a trademark, trademark law would protect Qualitex's use of green-gold color on its press pads.

Respondent Jacobson Products says that there are four special reasons why the law should forbid the use of a color alone as a trademark. We shall explain, in turn, why we, ultimately, find them unpersuasive.

First, Jacobson says that, if the law permits the use of color as a trademark, it will produce uncertainty and irresolvable court disputes about the shades of a color a competitor may lawfully use. . . .

We do not believe, however, that color, in this respect, is special. Courts traditionally decide quite difficult questions about whether two words or phrases or symbols are sufficiently similar, in context, to confuse buyers. . . .

Second, Jacobson argues, as have others, that colors are in limited supply. Jacobson claims that, if one of many competitors can appropriate a particular color for use as a trademark, and each competitor then tries to do the same, the supply of competitors will soon be depleted. Put in its strongest form, this argument would concede that "hundreds of color pigments are manufactured and thousands of colors can be obtained by mixing." But, it would add that, in the context of a particular product, only some colors are usable. By the time one discards colors that, say, for reasons of customer appeal, are unstable, and adds the shades that competitors cannot use lest they risk infringement of a similar registered shade, then one is only left with a handful of possible colors. And, under these circumstances, to permit one, or a few, producers to use colors as trademarks will "deplete" the supply of usable colors to the point where a competitor's inability to find a suitable color will put that competitor at a significant disadvantage.

This argument is unpersuasive, however, largely because it relies on an occasional problem to justify a blanket prohibition. When a color serves as a mark, normally alternative colors will likely be available for similar use by others. . . .

■   ■   ■

. . . *Third*, Jacobson points to many older cases—including Supreme Court cases—in support of its position. In 1878, this Court described the common-law definition of trademark rather broadly to "consist of any symbol, figure, letter, form, or device, if adopted and used by a manufacturer or merchant in order to designate the goods he manufactures or sells to distinguish the same from those manufactured or sold by another." Even though these statements amounted to dicta, lower courts interpreted them as forbidding protection for color alone.

These Supreme Court cases, however, interpreted trademark law as it existed *before* 1946, when Congress enacted the Lanham Act. The Lanham Act significantly changed and liberalized the common law to "dispense with mere technical prohibitions" most notably, by permitting trademark registration of descriptive words where they had acquired "secondary meaning." The Lanham Act extended protection to descriptive marks by making clear that (with certain explicit exceptions not relevant here) "nothing . . . shall prevent the registration of a mark used by the applicant which has become distinctive of the applicant's goods in commerce." . . .

■   ■   ■

Fourth, Jacobson argues that there is no need to permit color alone to function as a trademark because a firm already may use color as part of a trademark, say as a colored circle or colored letter or word. . . . The first part of this argument begs the question. One can understand why a firm might find it difficult to place a usable symbol or word on a product (say, a large industrial bolt that cus-

tomers normally see from a distance); and, in such instances, a firm might want to use color, pure and simple, instead of color as part of the design. . . .

Having determined that a color may sometimes meet the basic legal requirements for use as a trademark and that respondent Jacobson's arguments do not justify a special legal rule preventing color alone from serving as a trademark we conclude that the Ninth Circuit erred in barring Qualitex's use of color as a trademark. For these reasons, the judgment of the Ninth Circuit is *Reversed.*

Case Questions

1. The Lanham Act defines a trademark to include any "word, name, symbol, or design." Into which category did the court place "color"?
2. What is the secondary meaning? How does it relate to color in this case? Explain.
3. What if a firm wanted to use a rainbow consisting of all the colors in the spectrum as a trademark? Would the Court have a problem with this?
4. The Yellow Transit Company having painted its taxicabs "yellow" for more than forty years filed an application to register the trademark "yellow" for taxicabs. What action should be taken on the application by the patent office? Explain.

Chapter Five   The Law of Contractual Transactions

Advertisements Constituting an Offer

One exception to the general rule that advertisements do not constitute offers, involves a limited offer directed to a limited number of people, and is illustrated in the following classical case.

LEFKOWITZ V. GREAT MINNEAPOLIS SURPLUS STORE
86 N.W. 2d 689 (Minn. 1957)

Great Minneapolis (Defendant) ran an advertisement in the Minneapolis newspaper that read:

> "Saturday 9 A.M. sharp
> 3 Brand New Fur Coats
> Worth to $100.00
> First Come, First Served
> $1 Each"

The following Saturday essentially the same ad was run again, but it also expressed "First Come, First Served" for a Black Lapin Stole for $1.00. Lefkowitz (Plaintiff) was the first one in the store at the appropriate counter and demanded the coat and the stole, tendering $1.00 for each as advertised. Great Minneapolis refused to sell to Mr. Lefkowitz on the grounds that a house rule disqualified men from taking advantage of the offer.

Lefkowitz sued the Store and received a money damage award. Defendant appealed the case.

Justice Murphy

1. The defendant contends that a newspaper advertisement offering items of merchandise for sale at a named price is a "unilateral offer" which may be withdrawn without notice. He relies upon authorities which hold that, where an advertiser publishes in a newspaper that he has a certain quantity or quality of goods which he wants to dispose of at certain prices and on certain terms, such advertisements are not offers which become contracts as soon as any person to whose notice they may come signifies his acceptance by notifying the other that he will take a certain quantity of them. Such advertisements have been construed as an invitation for an offer of sale on the terms stated, which offer, when received, may be accepted or rejected and which therefore does not become a contract of sale until accepted by the seller; and until a contract has been so made, the seller may modify or revoke such prices or terms. . . .

■   ■   ■

There are numerous authorities which hold that a particular advertisement in a newspaper or circular letter relating to a sale of articles may be construed by the court as constituting an offer, acceptance of which would complete a contract. . . .

The test of whether a binding obligation may originate in advertisements addressed to the general public is "whether the facts show that some performance was promised in positive terms in return for something requested."

The authorities above cited emphasize that, where the offer is clear, definite, and explicit, and leaves nothing open for negotiation, it constitutes an offer, acceptance of which will complete the contract. The most recent case on the subject is Johnson v. Capital City Ford Co. in which the court pointed out that a newspaper advertisement relating to the purchase and sale of automobiles may constitute an offer, acceptance of which will consummate a contract and create an obligation in the offeror to perform according to the terms of the published offer.

Whether in any individual instance a newspaper advertisement is an offer rather than an invitation to make an offer depends on the legal intention of the parties and the surrounding circumstances. We are of the view on the facts before us that the offer by the defendant of the sale of the Lapin fur was clear, definite, and explicit, and left nothing open for negotiation. The plaintiff having successfully managed to be the first one to appear at the seller's place of business to be served, as requested by the advertisement, and having offered the stated purchase price of the article, he was entitled to performance on the part of the defendant. . . .

2. The defendant contends that the offer was modified by a "house rule" to the effect that only women were qualified to receive the bargains advertised. The advertisement contained no such restriction. This objection may be disposed of briefly by stating that, while an advertiser has the right at any time before acceptance to modify his offer, he does not have the right, after acceptance,

to impose new or arbitrary conditions not contained in the published offer. . . .

Affirmed.

Case Questions

1. Is this an ethical result? Why?
2. What if the store would have inserted in the advertisement, "Women Only"? Would that have changed the result? Explain.
3. How is this case distinguished from a "house for sale" advertisement?
4. What does this case have in common with the reward cases?
5. Do you think that the general rule that an advertisement is not an offer is ethical? Explain.

Statute of Frauds

In the following case the court discussed issues relating to the requirement of consideration and the Statute of Frauds' requirement of a writing.

DAVIES V. MARTEL LABORATORY SERVICES, INC.
545 N.E.2d 475 (Ill. App. 1989)

Janet Davies (Plaintiff) sued Martel Laboratory Services, Inc. (Defendant) for breach of an oral contract for permanent employment. The trial court dismissed Davies' complaint. Davies appealed, and the Appellate Court of Illinois reversed the trial court's dismissal and remanded the case for further proceedings. What follows is the appellate court's decision.

Presiding Justice Murray

Plaintiff Janet Davies appeals from an order of the circuit court of Cook County dismissing her . . . complaint for breach of an oral contract for permanent employment against defendant Martel Laboratory Services, Inc. She argues that the trial court erred in granting Martel's motion to dismiss her complaint based on its determination that she

failed to establish consideration for an enforceable contract of permanent employment and that the court erred in granting Martel's motion based on its finding that her cause of action was barred by the Statute of Frauds. For the reasons set forth below, we reverse and remand the cause for further proceedings.

■   ■   ■

Davies . . . filed [a] . . . complaint in the trial court, the subject of this appeal, alleging that Martel hired her in April 1980 to perform oil analyses and mapping work until approximately March 1, 1983. During that time she was an employee at will. In the latter part of February 1983, however, she attended a dinner conference with Harold Flynn, Martel's president. At that time Flynn "made an offer [to her] to alter, change and modify the terms and conditions of [her] contract of employment." The terms and conditions were that she "would be made a Vice-President of MARTEL earning $40,000.00 per year" if she "would obtain an MBA Degree" and, if she accepted the offer then and there, "she would immediately be designated a permanent employee of MARTEL and also appointed a member of the President's Council for which she would assume and become responsible for a policy making role for MARTEL." Flynn also promised that Martel would contribute one-half of her expenses incurred in obtaining her MBA, while she would be responsible for the other one-half. She immediately accepted the offer, thereby becoming a permanent employee. On March 1, one week later, she attended her first meeting as a member of the President's Council. In the fall of 1983, she enrolled at Northwestern University to begin an MBA program. Davies' complaint further alleged that she continued working, assuming additional duties and responsibilities as a "policy maker for MARTEL." On October 12, 1984, Martel terminated her employment without cause.

In response to Davies' complaint, Martel filed a motion to dismiss. On April 20, 1988, the trial court granted Martel's motions, finding that Davies failed to demonstrate consideration for Martel's oral promise of permanent employment and that her claim was also barred by the Statute of Frauds. A subsequent motion by Davies to amend her complaint was denied by the court, and this appeal followed.

To be enforceable, an oral contract for permanent employment, like any other contract, must be supported by sufficient consideration. It is also well settled that any act or promise which is of benefit to one party or a disadvantage to the other is a sufficient consideration to support a contract.

In the instant case, Martel contends that Davies suffered no disadvantage or detriment and therefore the trial court correctly ruled that her complaint was insufficient in law because it failed to allege sufficient consideration. Specifically, Martel contends that Davies' pursuit of an MBA degree was in fact a benefit to her, making her more marketable, and not a disadvantage or detriment. While this fact may be true, it is not necessarily legally so. The words "benefit" and "detriment" in contract cases involving consideration have technical meanings. "Detriment" as used in determining the sufficiency of consideration to support a contract means " 'legal detriment as distinguished from detriment in fact. It means giving up something which immediately prior thereto the promisee was privileged to retain, or doing or refraining from something which he was then privileged not to do, or not to refrain from doing.' " (*Hamilton Bancshares, Inc. v. Leroy* (1985), 131 Ill. App. 3d 907, 913, quoting 1 Williston, Contracts § 102A, at 380-82 (3d ed. 1957).) For example, a promise to give up smoking may be a benefit to the promisee's health, but a promise to give up smoking is also a legal detriment and sufficient consideration to support a contract.

In the present case, Davies did not have to obtain an MBA degree and expend her own time and money in doing so in order to continue as an at-will employee of Martel's; she could have continued to perform oil analyses and mapping work rather than enter the ivied walls of Northwestern. Nor does it appear that Davies was obligated to serve as a member on Martel's President's Council and to assume additional duties and responsibilities. In other words, Davies was privileged to refrain from serving on Martel's council and from pursuing an MBA degree. By giving up her privilege to refrain from so acting, Davies clearly could be said to have suffered a legal detriment, which would constitute sufficient consideration to support the alleged oral contract between the parties. Based on the foregoing, and in light of the fact that a motion to dismiss admits all facts well pleaded together with all reasonable inferences which can be drawn from those facts, we find that Davies' amended complaint sufficiently alleged consideration in support of the contract at issue.

We also find, contrary to Martel's argument, that the trial court erroneously applied the Statute of Frauds to bar Davies' claim of breach of contract. The Statute of Frauds requires that any contract that cannot be performed within one year must be in writing. Martel contends that the alleged oral contract of permanent employment was incapable of being performed within one year, based on the fact that it was "contingent on plaintiff obtaining an MBA degree, that an MBA program at Northwestern University involves two years of study for full-time students and five years for part-time students, and that Davies did not even enroll in the program until the fall of 1983," more than six months after the oral contract.

Based on the foregoing, the oral contract would be unenforceable under the Statute of Frauds if in fact it was pleaded by Davies in her amended complaint that her permanent employment was contingent upon her obtaining an MBA degree. However, that is not the oral agreement pleaded by Davies. Rather, Davies pleaded that she would be immediately designated a permanent employee of Martel and also appointed a member of Martel's President's Council if she accepted the terms and conditions of the offer "then and there" (made a *commitment* to pursue an MBA degree and serve as a member of the President's Council), which she did do. On the other hand, the obvious inferences of the complaint unrebutted by anything in the record are that Davies' appointment as a vice-president of the company was predicated on her attaining the MBA, not the permanent employment promise. The fact that she could not complete the MBA program within one year might be a Statute of Frauds defense to that portion of the oral contract whereby Martel promised to make her a vice-president and pay her $40,000 annually. It is not a defense, however, to the promise to make her a permanent Martel employee, which she accepted immediately.

Moreover, we further observe that the Statute of Frauds has no application where there has been part performance by one of the contracting parties in reliance upon the agreement. Here, whether in fact Davies relied on Flynn's alleged oral promise and enrolled in the MBA program based on that promise, as she alleges in her amended complaint, is a question of fact that could not be decided on a motion to dismiss her amended complaint.

In light of the foregoing, the judgment of the circuit court of Cook County is reversed and the cause remanded for further proceedings.

Reversed and remanded.

Case Questions

1. Why did the appellate court find that Davies' complaint alleged sufficient consideration in support of the contract at issue in the case?

2. The appellate court stated that [*t*]*he words "benefit" and "detriment" in contract cases involving consideration use technical meanings.* What is the technical meaning of "detriment" for purposes of the doctrine of consideration?

3. Martel argued at the oral argument between Martel and Davies was unenforceable according to the provision of the Statute of Frauds that requires a contract that cannot be performed within one year to be in writing. Why was the appellate court not convinced by that argument?

4. If the oral argument had been that Davies' permanent employment was contingent upon her obtaining an MBA degree, would the agreement have been enforceable? Explain. If not, what should Davies do under such circumstances? If you were in Davies position how difficult would it be for you to ask the president of the company to put his promise in writing? When you want someone to put their oral promises in writing can you think of a way to express the request so that they might accede in the request? How would you politely respond if the other person were to say, "What's the matter, don't you trust me?"

5. What would be the effect of proof by Davies that she relied on Flynn's oral promise and enrolled in the MBA program based on that promise? Explain.

Promissory Estoppel

In the following case, the Illinois Supreme Court adopt promissory estoppel as an affirmative cause of action that can be used to enforce a promise that otherwise is not recognized as enforceable as a contract under traditional contract law.

NEWTON TRACTOR SALES, INC., V. KUBOTA TRACTOR CORPORATION ET AL
233 Ill. 2d 46 (Ill. 2009)

Plaintiff-Appellant, Newton Tractor Sales, Inc (Newton) sued defendants Kubota Tractor Corporation and Michael Jacobson, a local Kubota representative (collectively, Kubota) claiming promissory estoppel. The trial court granted summary judgment in favor of Kubota. Newton appealed, and the appellate court affirmed. Newton then appealed to the Supreme Court of Illinois, which reversed the trial and appellate courts' judgments, and returned the case to the trial court for further proceedings.

Justice Garman

BACKGROUND

In 2002, Newton owned and operated a dealership that sold farm equipment. In November 2002, Newton began negotiations to purchase another nearby dealership, Vandalia Tractor & Equipment, Inc. (VTE). VTE at that time was being operated by two brothers, Tim and Ron Emerick.

Newton was at first reluctant to purchase VTE. Newton decided it could not buy VTE without having a local partner with which to run the dealership. Eventually, one of VTE's salesmen, Mike Cripe, agreed to partner with Newton. Newton then proceeded in its attempt to purchase VTE. The negotiations between Newton and VTE culminated in an asset purchase agreement signed by both parties on July 10, 2003. Among the provisions of that agreement was section 8.11, which allowed Newton to cancel the asset purchase agreement if it was unable to obtain authority to sell New Holland, Agco or Kubota products. If any one of those man-

ufacturers denied Newton a license to sell its products, Newton could rescind the agreement.

At the time Newton and VTE entered into the asset purchase agreement, VTE was an authorized dealer for Kubota, a manufacturer of a line of farm equipment. VTE was also authorized to sell other lines of equipment. As part of purchasing VTE, Newton became the authorized dealer for several lines of equipment previously sold at VTE's dealership.

The authority to sell Kubota products, however, was not included within the asset purchase agreement. Instead, Kubota required Newton to submit an application to Kubota's local representative, defendant Michael Jacobson. On June 19, 2003, Newton submitted its application to Jacobson along with financial statements. That application had not been approved at the time Newton and VTE entered into the asset purchase agreement.

In its complaint, Newton alleges that its officers met with Tim Emerick and Jacobson on July 25, 2003. At that meeting, Jacobson explained that Newton could not have their application processed until Kubota had approved termination of Kubota's existing relationship with VTE. Jacobson presented a voluntary termination agreement to VTE. Newton alleges that Tim Emerick told Jacobson he would not sign the termination agreement if Newton were not going to become the authorized Kubota dealer. Newton alleges Jacobson responded by saying, "They [Newton] will be the dealer."

Newton claims that in reliance on this statement by Jacobson, it allowed Tim Emerick to sign the termination agreement. Tim Emerick in his affidavit confirmed that he would not have signed the termination agreement if Newton was not going to be the authorized Kubota dealer. Newton claims to have further relied on Jacobson's statements by selling Kubota products under VTE's dealership number and performing $ 28,500 in warranty work on Kubota equipment.

On July 28, 2003, Jacobson submitted an internal memo recommending that Newton become the authorized Kubota dealer. In an analysis dated July 29, 2003, Jacobson indicated that "Vandalia Tractor & Equip. was purchased by Newton Tractor Sales, Inc. dba Vandalia Tractor Sales, Inc. Dealer Buy-out w/out interruption of Kubota sales & service." On August 12, the application was approved at Kubota's division level. However, Newton's application was subsequently denied by Kubota's corporate office. According to Jacobson, Newton was informed of the decision on August 25, 2003, and was invited to submit further information to Kubota. Newton did so, but Kubota did not change its position on Newton's application. In late September, Kubota had its products removed from the former VTE dealership in Vandalia.

ANALYSIS

The doctrine of promissory estoppel is a common law doctrine. . . .

To establish a claim, the plaintiff must prove that (1) defendant made an unambiguous promise to plaintiff, (2) plaintiff relied on such promise, (3) plaintiff's reliance was expected and foreseeable by defendants, and (4) plaintiff relied on the promise to its detriment.

■   ■   ■

Having concluded that promissory estoppel has previously been recognized as a cause of action, we now address Kubota's policy arguments. . . .

Even if Illinois case law were not conclusive as to whether promissory estoppel is available as an affirmative cause of action, we would be unwilling to accept Kubota's argument that promissory estoppel should be limited solely to defensive actions. Kubota asserts that promissory estoppel is limited only to "enforcing a plaintiff's promise (to the defendant's benefit) as to an intended abandonment of the legal right the plaintiff is intending to enforce." Under this theory, promissory estoppel is available to a defendant debtor who seeks to prevent the plaintiff creditor from charging interest where the plaintiff had previously promised not to charge any. Similarly, Kubota contends the doctrine may also be used to allow a defendant tenant to avoid summary ejectment when the plaintiff landlord had promised not to require written notice for renewing the lease.

Kubota is correct that "it is often said that promissory estoppel is most extensively recognized and most frequently applied where there is a promise as to an intended abandonment of existing rights." . . .

Although promissory estoppel is most extensively recognized with respect to the abandonment of existing legal rights, . . . "[m]any courts and other legal authorities have taken a much broader view of promissory estoppel, which permits the doctrine to be used as a 'sword' in any situation where a promise has been made which was relied upon by the promisee to his detriment in such a manner as to make it a fraud or injustice not to enforce the promise." ... *People's National Bank of Little Rock v. Kinebarger Construction Co.,* (noting promissory estoppel "is an attempt by the courts to keep remedies abreast of increased moral consciousness of honesty and fair representations in all business dealings")... We, therefore, reject Kubota's argument that this court should recognize promissory estoppel only so far as is consistent with what Kubota calls its "traditional limitations."

... Kubota suggests that allowing an affirmative cause of action in promissory estoppel would undermine public policies underlying contract law in two ways. First, Kubota contends that promissory estoppel could result in otherwise unenforceable unilateral contracts. Second, Kubota contends that parties will be hesitant to enter preliminary negotiations for fear of being held to statements made in those negotiations.

With respect to the first issue, Kubota points in particular to relationships in the field of development and construction. In construction, before a general contractor is awarded a bid, it must approach one or more subcontractors for their respective bids on specific parts of the overall project. Kubota expresses concern that promissory estoppel, as an affirmative action, would "erode the incentives for parties to carefully consider and detail the contractual terms and obligations in their relationships, and it would unfairly and unnecessarily expose one of the parties to unilateral obligations." Citing a North Carolina case, Kubota argues that promissory estoppel would "force the subcontractor to be bound if the general contractor uses his bid, even though the general contractor is not obligated to award the job to that subcontractor."

... [W]e remain convinced that allowing promissory estoppel as a cause of action will not affect the existing relationship between general contractors and their subcontractors and suppliers. Therefore, we reject Kubota's first public policy argument.

We next address Kubota's second public policy argument. Kubota has argued that recognizing an affirmative action under promissory estoppel will result in reluctance to enter into commercial negotiations for fear of being obligated to perform contracts that have not been fully negotiated.

... Here, we believe that Kubota misunderstands the equitable nature of promissory estoppel. ... Thus, courts may appropriately limit relief to only those damages suffered as a result of justifiably relying on the other party's promise. ...

... Where there has not been mutual assent, and the terms are not sufficient to constitute a contract, damages may appropriately be limited to restoring plaintiff to the position he was in prior to relying, to his detriment, on the promise. Thus, we reject Kubota's concerns that promissory estoppel would somehow undermine preliminary negotiations.

For the foregoing reasons, we reiterate that Illinois law provides for an affirmative cause of action under the doctrine of promissory estoppel.

CONCLUSION

For the foregoing reasons, we conclude that promissory estoppel is an affirmative cause of action in Illinois, reverse the judgments of the appellate and [trial] courts, and remand to the [trial] court for further proceedings consistent with this opinion.

Case Questions

1. What is required to enforce a promise under the doctrine of promissory estoppel?
2. What policy arguments did Kubota raise for why promissory estoppels should not be recognized as an affirmative claim?
3. Why did the court reject Kubota's policy arguments?
4. Do you think the court is correct with regard to the policy implications of recognizing promissory estoppels as an affirmative claim?
5. Does this case essentially mean that your kindergarten teacher was right after all when you were taught: "Don't make any promises that you don't intend to keep!"?

Unconscionability

As the following case illustrates, the concept of unconscionability may be applied in commercial transactions.

ART'S FLOWER SHOP, INC. V. C & P TELEPHONE CO.
413 S.E.2d 670 (W.Va. 1992)

Art's Flower Shop (plaintiff) contracted with C & P (defendant) to place an ad in C & P's Yellow Pages. C & P failed to run the ad and Art's sued. A clause in the contract limited C & P's liability to twice the price of the ad. The trial court held that Art's damages were so limited. The West Virginia Supreme Court reversed.

Justice Brotherton

[I]n many commercial transactions, some inequality of bargaining power exists. Since many of these situations may not revolve around an unconscionable contract despite that inequality, something more is required.

■   ■   ■

The end result of this analysis is that the liability clause in the 1978 contract between C & P and Art's Flower shop is void for unconscionability. The positions of C & P and Art's Flower Shop were grossly unequal: C & P had the only Yellow Pages directory in the area. As a monopoly, C & P had the right to make the Yellow Pages an integral part of their regular white pages directory and the name recognition to make it successful. No evidence was presented of a comparable, meaningful alternative to a Yellow Page advertisement. . . . Art's Flower Shop . . . obviously was in no position to bargain for the contract.

The final element in the analysis is the determination of whether unfair contract terms exist. While the contract terms are valid in and of themselves, the limitation of out-of-pocket damages experienced as a result of C & P's omission of a contracted-for advertisement to twice the cost of the ad is unreasonably favorable to C & P. Under the terms of the liability clause in the contract, C & P's negligent omission could cost a client its livelihood, yet C & P would be liable for only minimal costs, no matter how damaging its omission. Such a result cannot stand. Contrary to C & P's assertions, radio and TV advertisements, flyers and other methods of advertising Art's services are inadequate and costly compared to the Yellow Pages advertisements.

Case Questions

1. Was it significant that this was a commercial contract rather than a consumer contract? Explain.
2. What factors led the court to find that Art's had no meaningful choice but to agree to the damage limitation? Could Art's have advertised elsewhere? Should that matter?
3. What factors led the court to find the limitation oppressive? Could there be any commercially legitimate reason for the damage limitation? Explain.
4. Jones, a welfare recipient, agreed to purchase on credit a freezer for $900.00 plus finance charges, property insurance, and credit life insurance. The total cost amounted to $1,439.69. The retail value of the freezer was

$300.00. Was this contract unconscionable? Why or why not?

5. Williams purchased a chair from Walker-Thomas Furniture Co. for $54.67, on credit. In fine print on the reverse side of the credit agreement a clause provided that if Williams made additional credit purchases, all payments would be allocated pro rata to each purchase. In the event of default Walker-Thomas retained the right to repossess the goods.

Over the course of several years, Williams made numerous additional credit purchases from Walker-Thomas. She then defaulted on one payment. At the time of default Williams had paid $1,400.00 on a total debt of $1,800.00. However, because of the pro rata allocation of her payment she was not credited with fully paying for any items. Her outstanding balance on the first chair she had bought was 25 cents. If Walker-Thomas seeks to repossess all of the items will it succeed? Explain.

Illegality—Covenant Not to Compete

The following case examines what factors are significant when determining whether a covenant not to solicit is enforceable.

WILEY V. ROYAL CUP, INC.
370 S.E.2d 744 (Ga. 1988)

Wiley (defendant) was district sales manager for Royal Cup (plaintiff). Wiley's employment contract provided that for one year after termination of employment, he would not disclose any of Royal Cup's business methods; sales, service, or distribution techniques; prices; or customer names and addresses. It also provided that for two years after termination, Wiley would not solicit business in 18 Georgia counties from anyone who had been a Royal Cup customer or who had been solicited by Royal Cup during the two years before termination. The trial court enjoined Wiley from breaching both provisions. The Georgia Supreme Court affirmed in part and reversed in part.

Justice Gregory

In a case involving a covenant not to compete, we held that territorial restrictions which relate to the territory in which the employee worked are generally enforceable. Those restrictions which relate to the territory in which the employer does business but the employee did not work will not be enforced absent a showing by the employer of the legitimate business interest sought to be protected.

It appears that the justification for this difference in treatment is that a court will accept as prima facie valid a covenant related to the territory where the employee was employed as a legitimate protection of the employer's investment in customer relations and good will. Thus a court will enforce an agreement prohibiting an employee from pirating his former employer's customers served by the employee during the employment, at the employer's direct or indirect expense. Conversely, a court will not accept as prima facie valid a covenant related to the territory where the employer does business where the only justification is that the employer wants to avoid competition by the employee in that area.

We apply this same requirement to a territorial restriction in a covenant not to solicit. In the case before us, the territorial restriction goes beyond the area in which Wiley served the customers of Royal Cup: Wiley is prohibited from soliciting customers in Bartow and Hall counties, counties in which Royal Cup does business, but where, it is undisputed, Wiley has never worked on behalf of Royal Cup. We conclude that the effect of this territorial restriction is not to protect the legitimate business interests of Royal Cup, but to prevent Wiley from competing against Royal Cup in these counties. As such, the territorial restriction is unreasonable and must fall.

■   ■   ■

[T]he entire covenant not to solicit is void. The trial court erred in holding it is enforceable against Wiley.

Wiley complains that the trial court erred in holding the covenant not to disclose is valid.

■   ■   ■

[I]n determining the reasonableness of a covenant not to disclose, the courts must consider "(1) whether the employer is attempting to protect confidential information relating to the business, such as . . . methods of operation, names of customers, personnel data . . . and (2) whether the restraint is reasonably related to the protection of the information." In this case the covenant specifically prohibits the disclosure of methods of operation and prices used by Royal

Cup, as well as the names of Royal Cup's customers. Wiley has acknowledged in his employment contract that these items constitute confidential information. We hold that this restraint, imposed on Wiley for a period of one year may be enforced independently of a covenant not to compete whether it is in the same or distinct provisions of the employment agreement.

Justice Weltner
(Dissenting)

I respectfully dissent.

■   ■   ■

[A] covenant prohibiting solicitation of the employer's customers is less restrictive than a covenant prohibiting competition. . . ."

■   ■   ■

[W]e do not apply to such covenants all of the limitations that pertain to covenants not to compete.

Rather, the inquiry should be whether *in this case* it is unreasonable to require a district sales manager to covenant not to solicit his employer's customers in an 18 county area when, in twelve of those counties, Royal Cup had customers. Where Royal Cup had no customers, the restraint upon Wiley is almost illusory, as it prohibits the solicitation of "customers" that do not exist.

I suggest that this limitation is entirely reasonable. Wiley should be held to his covenants.

Case Questions

1. What is the difference between a covenant not to compete and a covenant not to solicit?
2. Why did the majority hold that the covenant not to solicit was void in this case? Why did Justice Weltner disagree?
3. The court voided the entire covenant not to solicit. Should it have enforced the covenant in the counties where Wiley had worked? Why or why not?

4. If the court refused to enforce any part of the covenant not to solicit, why did it enforce the covenant not to disclose confidential information?

5. Jackson was employed as a hairdresser for Hair Salon, Inc. Jackson's employment contract prohibited Jackson from competing within a five-mile radius of the Hair Salon store for two years after leaving Hair Salon's employ. Is the covenant not to compete enforceable? Why or why not?

Parol Evidence Rule

In the following case, the court must determine whether the parol evidence rule applies to limit the terms of a contract to the writing signed by the parties.

HINKEL VS. SATARIA DISTRIBUTION & PACKAGING, INC.
20 N.E.2d 766 (Ind. App. 2010)

Mark Hinkel (Appellant) was hired to work for the Sataria Distribution and Packaging, Inc. (Appellee). Hinkel was allegedly promised a year's worth of salary and insurance coverage if he were ever terminated involuntarily, but his written employment contract did not provide for severance pay or post-employment benefits. Hinkel was soon terminated, and he did not receive the severance package he says he was promised. Hinkel sued for breach of contract. The trial court entered summary judgment in favor of Sataria. Hinkel appealed, and the Indiana appellate court affirmed the decision of the trial court. What follows is the opinion of the appellate court.

Vaidik, Judge

Hinkel was employed by Refractory Engineers, Inc. and Ceramic Technology, Inc. John Jacobs was the owner of Sataria. In late August or September 2005, Hinkel and Jacobs met to discuss working together. Jacobs offered Hinkel a job at Sataria. Hinkel had reservations. Jacobs told him, "Mark, are you worried that I'll f*** you? If so, and things don't work, I'll pay you one (1) year's salary and cover your insurance for the one (1) year as well. But let me make it clear, should you decide this is not for you, and you terminate your own employment, then the agreement is off." Jacobs later sent Hinkel the following written job offer:

Hinkel signed the offer and resigned from his other employers. He began working at Sataria in September 2005. According to Hinkel, Jacobs reiterated the severance promise again in November 2005 and December 2005.

Sataria terminated Hinkel's employment involuntarily on January 23, 2006. Sataria paid Hinkel six weeks of severance thereafter. Hinkel brought this action for breach of contract ... against Sataria. He claimed that Sataria owed him the severance package that Jacobs promised. Sataria moved for summary judgment. The trial court granted Sataria's motion. Hinkel now appeals.

According to Hinkel, Jacobs orally promised him a year's salary and insurance coverage if he were ever involuntarily terminated. Sataria argues that any alleged oral promises are barred from consideration by the parol evidence rule.

The parol evidence rule provides that "[w]hen two parties have made a contract and have expressed it in a writing to which they have both assented as the complete and accurate integration of that contract, evidence . . . of antecedent understandings and negotiations will not be admitted for the purpose of varying or contradicting the writing." *Dicen v. New Sesco, Inc.* (quoting 6 Arthur Linton Corbin, *Corbin on Contracts* § 573 (2002 reprint)) This rule "effectuates a presumption that a subsequent written contract is of a higher nature than earlier statements, negotiations, or oral agreements by deeming those earlier expressions to be merged in to or superseded by the written document." 11 Richard A. Lord, *Williston on Contracts* § 33:1 (4th ed. 1999).

The first step when applying the parol evidence rule is determining whether the parties' written contract represents a complete or partial integration of their agreement. If the contract is completely integrated, constituting a final and complete expression of all the parties' agreements, then evidence of prior or contemporaneous written or oral statements and negotiations cannot operate to either add to or contradict the written contract

In addition,

> The test of [parol evidence] admissibility is much affected by the inherent likelihood that parties who contract under the circumstances in question would simultaneously make both the agreement in writing which is before the court, and also the alleged parol agreement. The point is not merely whether the court is convinced that the parties before it did in fact do this, but whether reasonable parties so situated naturally would or might obviously or normally do so. . . . The vast majority of courts assessing the admissibility of parol evidence at common law apply this test. This test is commonly known by the adverbs used by the courts which apply it, and might be variously called the "naturally" test, the "naturally and normally" test, the "ordinarily" test, or any of a host of words used by the courts to indicate that parties similarly situated might reasonably have believed it appropriate to keep the two agreements separate. Moreover the test can be stated in the affirmative or the negative; either way the key question is the same. Thus, one way to ask the question is whether the nature of the collateral agreement was such that,

Dear Mark,
    This is written as an offer of employment. The terms are as described below:

1. Annual Compensation:	$ 120,000
2. Work Location:	Belmont Facility
3. Initial Position:	Supervisor Receiving Team
4. Start Date:	08/19/2005
5. Paid Vacation:	To be determined
6. Health Insurance:	Coverage begins 09/01/2005 pending proper
	Enrollment submission

Please sign and return.

if the parties had agreed to it, they would naturally have included it in their writing. Asked in this way, if the answer is that they would have, and they did not, they engaged in "unnatural" behavior, and evidence of the alleged agreement is inadmissible.

11 *Williston on Contracts* § 33:25.

Here, Jacobs and Hinkel negotiated the terms of Hinkel's employment before completing their written contract. Jacobs allegedly promised Hinkel that he would receive one year of salary and benefits if he were ever terminated involuntarily. The parties then executed their written agreement. The written employment offer specified Hinkel's compensation, work location, title, start date, and the date on which his insurance coverage would begin. It did not provide that Hinkel would receive severance pay or benefits following termination. Hinkel signed the letter and began working at Sataria. In light of all the relevant evidence, we find as a matter of law that Hinkel's contract represented a complete integration of the parties' employment agreement. Jacobs allegedly promised Hinkel a severance package, but the written contract enumerates both compensation and insurance coverage while saying nothing of post-employment salary and/or benefits. The offer leaves one term to be decided—paid vacation—but the contract imports on its face to be a complete expression with respect to salary and insurance. And since a lucrative severance provision would "naturally and normally" be included in an employment contract, its glaring omission here further supports the conclusion that Hinkel's written contract superseded any alleged prior oral promises. We hold that the written contract constituted a final representation of the parties' agreement, and any contemporaneous oral agreements that the parties made as to severance are not subject to interpretation.

Crone, Judge, dissenting

I respectfully dissent because I disagree with the majority's conclusion that Jacobs's oral promise to Hinkel regarding a severance package is "bar-red from consideration by the parol evidence rule." I do so for two reasons.

First, I believe that a genuine issue of material fact exists regarding whether the parties intended for Jacobs's written job offer to Hinkel to be completely integrated, i.e., a "final and complete expression of all the parties' agreements[.]" Although not conclusive, the offer—a one-page document with six bullet points for a position paying $120,000 per year—does not contain an integration clause. More persuasive is its statement that Hinkel's vacation terms were yet to be determined, which indicates to me that the parties had not yet reached agreement on that issue. Based on the foregoing, a factfinder reasonably could conclude that the offer is more akin to a memorandum of understanding and represents only a partial integration of the parties' agreements, and that therefore the parol evidence rule would not apply to bar consideration of Jacobs's oral promise regarding the severance package.

Second, the terms of the severance package do not vary from or contradict the terms of the written offer, but merely cover that which was not covered in the offer. As such, even assuming that the offer is completely integrated, the terms of the severance package would not be barred by the parol evidence rule. See *Malo v. Gilmaan* ("[P]arol evidence may be admitted to supply an omission in the terms of the contract. . . . Using parol evidence to supply an omission will not modify the written agreement, but merely adds to it."). Therefore, I would reverse the trial court's grant of summary judgment in favor of Sataria and remand for further proceedings.

Case Questions

1. What is the parol evidence rule? How does this rule of evidence determine what is in fact the substance of a contract?
2. According to the court, what is the purpose of the parol evidence rule?
3. What is required before the parol evidence rule applies and excludes evidence of ancil-

lary agreements? How do the majority and dissenting opinions view the facts of the case with regard to whether this requirement has been met? With which opinion do you agree? Explain.

4. If you were in Hinkel's position, what should you do to make sure that the employment contract includes the severance pay and post-employment benefits?

5. Do you see how the parol evidence rule would be important to companies that employ agents to sell their products and services to consumers, especially when the agents are paid on commissions and have an incentive to make promises to consumers that are not included in the written sales contracts? Explain.

Chapter Six   The Law of Injuries (Tort Law)

Punitive Damages

The following U.S. Supreme Court case defines the constitutional limits on the award of punitive damages.

STATE FARM MUTUAL AUTOMOBILE INSURANCE CO. VS. CAMPBELL
538 U.S. 408 (2003)

Curtis Campbell, while driving with his wife passed six vans travelling ahead of them on a two-way highway. Ospital, who was coming in the opposite direction swerved onto the shoulder, lost control of his car, and collided with another vehicle. Ospital was killed and the person in the other vehicle was rendered permanently disabled. The Campbells were not injured. Although investigators fixed the blame on Mr. Campbell, State Farm Insurance, the Campbell's insurance carrier refused offers to settle for the $50,000.00 policy limit. State Farm assured the Campbells that "their assets were safe, that they had no liability for the accident, that [State Farm] would represent their interests, and that they did not need to procure separate counsel." The jury determined that Mr. Campbell was at fault, and a judgment was rendered in the amount of $185,849.00.

At first State Farm refused to cover the excess liability in the amount of $135,849.00. The Campbells were told by State Farm's lawyer: "You may want to put for sale signs on your property to get things moving." State Farm refused to appeal the case.

The Campbells sued State Farm for bad faith refusal to settle, fraud and intentional infliction of emotional distress. (While that suit was pending State Farm paid the entire judgment.) The trial court granted State Farm's motion for summary judgment on the grounds that State Farm eventually paid the judgment. The trial court's decision was overturned by the Utah Court of Appeals. On remand the jury found that the refusal to settle was unreasonable because there was a substantial likelihood of an excess verdict. Evidence was admitted concerning State Farm's business practices for over 20 years in numerous states. The jury awarded the Campbells $2.6 million in compensatory damages and $145 million in punitive damages, which was reduced by the trial court to $1 million and $25 million respectively. Both parties appealed and the Utah Supreme Court reinstated the $145 million punitive damages award.

Justice Kennedy

. . . Compensatory damages "are intended to redress the concrete loss that the plaintiff has suffered by reason of the defendant's wrongful conduct." By contrast, punitive damages serve a broader function; they are aimed at deterrence and retribution. . . .

While States possess discretion over the imposition of punitive damages, it is well established that there are procedural and substantive constitutional limitations on these awards. The Due Process Clause of the Fourteenth Amendment prohibits the imposition of grossly excessive or arbitrary punishments on a tortfeasor. . . . The reason is that "[e]lementary notions of fairness enshrined in our constitutional jurisprudence dictate that a person receive fair notice not only of the conduct that will subject him to punishment, but also of the severity of the penalty that a State may impose." . . . To the extent an award is grossly excessive, it furthers no legitimate purpose and constitutes an arbitrary deprivation of property. . . .

■   ■   ■

In light of these concerns, in [*BMW of North America Inc. v. Gore*] we instructed courts reviewing punitive damages to consider three guideposts: (1) the degree of reprehensibility of the defendant's misconduct; (2) the disparity between the actual or potential harm suffered by the plaintiff and the punitive damages award; and (3) the dif-

ference between the punitive damages awarded by the jury and the civil penalties authorized or imposed in comparable cases. . . .

■   ■   ■

Under the principles outlined in *BMW of North America, Inc. v. Gore,* this case is neither close nor difficult. It was error to reinstate the jury's $145 million punitive damages award. We address each guidepost of *Gore* in some detail.

■   ■   ■

"[T]he most important indicium of the reasonableness of a punitive damages award is the degree of reprehensibility of the defendant's conduct." We have instructed courts to determine the reprehensibility of a defendant by considering whether: the harm caused was physical as opposed to economic; the tortious conduct evinced as indifference to or a reckless disregard of the health or safety of others; the target of the conduct had financial vulnerability; the conduct involved repeated actions or was an isolated incident; and the harm was the result of intentional malice, trickery, or deceit, or mere accident. . . . It should be presumed a plaintiff has been made whole for his injuries by compensatory damages, so punitive damages should only be awarded if the defendant's culpability, after having paid compensatory damages, is so reprehensible as to warrant the imposition of further sanctions to achieve punishment or deterrence.

Applying these factors in the instant case, we must acknowledge that State Farm's handling of the claims against the Campbells merits no praise. The trial court found that State Farm's employees altered the company's records to make Campbell appear less culpable. State Farm disregarded the overwhelming likelihood of liability and the near-certain probability that, by taking the case to trial, a judgment in excess of the policy limits would be awarded. State Farm amplified the harm by at first assuring the Campbells their assets would be safe from any verdict and by later telling them, postjudgment, to put a for-sale sign on their house. While we do not suggest there was error in awarding punitive damages based upon State Farm's conduct toward the Campbells, a more modest punishment for this reprehensible conduct could have satisfied the State's legitimate objectives, and the Utah courts should have gone no further.

The Campbells have identified scant evidence of repeated misconduct of the sort that injured them. Nor does our review of the Utah courts' decision convince us that State Farm was only punished for its actions toward the Campbells. Although evidence of other acts need not be identical to have relevance in the calculation of punitive damages, the Utah court erred here because evidence concerning reprehensibility was even more tangential. For example, the Utah Supreme Court criticized State Farm's investigation into the personal life of one of its employees and, in a broader approach, the manner in which State Farm's policies corrupted its employees.

■   ■   ■

Turning to the second *Gore* guidepost, we have been reluctant to identify concrete constitutional limits on the ratio between harm, or potential harm, to the plaintiff and the punitive damages award. . . . We decline to impose a bright-line ratio which a punitive damages award cannot exceed. Our jurisprudence and the principles it has now established demonstrate, however, that, in practice, few awards exceeding a single-digit ratio between punitive and compensatory damages, to a significant degree, will satisfy due process.

■   ■   ■

Nonetheless, because there are no rigid benchmarks that a punitive damages award may not surpass, ratios greater than those we have previously upheld may comport with due process where "a particularly egregious act has resulted in only a small amount of economic damages." . . . The converse is also true, however. When compensatory damages are substantial, then a lesser ratio, perhaps only equal to compensatory damages, can reach the outermost limit of the due process guarantee. The precise award in any case, of course, must be based upon the facts and circumstances of the defendant's conduct and the harm to the plaintiff.

In sum, courts must ensure that the measure of punishment is both reasonable and proportionate to the amount of harm to the plaintiff and to the general damages recovered. In the context of this case, we have no doubt that there is a presumption against an award that has a 145-to-1 ratio. The compensatory award in this case was substantial; the Campbells were awarded $1 million for a year and a half of emotional distress. This was complete compensation. The harm arose from a transaction in the economic realm, not from some physical assault or trauma; there were no physical injuries; and State Farm paid the excess verdict before the complaint was filed, so the Campbells suffered only minor economic injuries for the 18-month period in which State Farm refused to resolve the claim against them.

■   ■   ■

The third guidepost in *Gore* is the disparity between the punitive damages award and the "civil penalties authorized or imposed in comparable cases." We note that, in the past, we have also looked to criminal penalties that could be imposed. . . . Punitive damages are not a substitute for the criminal process, and the remote possibility of a criminal sanction does not automatically sustain a punitive damages award.

. . . The most relevant civil sanction under Utah state law for the wrong done to the Campbells appears to be a $10,000 fine for an act of fraud, an amount dwarfed by the $145 million punitive damages award. The Supreme Court of Utah speculated about the loss of State Farm's business license, the disgorgement of profits, and possible imprisonment, but here again its references were to the broad fraudulent scheme drawn form evidence of out-of-state and dissimilar conduct. This analysis was insufficient to justify the award.

■   ■   ■

An application of the *Gore* guideposts to the facts of this case, especially in light of the substantial compensatory damages . . . likely would justify a punitive damages award at or near the amount of compensatory damages. The punitive award of $145 million, therefore, was neither reasonable nor proportionate to the wrong committed, and it was an irrational and arbitrary deprivation of the property of the defendant. The proper calculation of punitive damages under the principles we have discussed should be resolved, in the first instance, by the Utah courts.

The judgment of the Utah Supreme Court is reversed, and the case is remanded for proceedings not inconsistent with this opinion.

Case Questions

1. How should the Utah courts respond? What should be the award in order to be consistent with this opinion? Why?
2. What are the facts in this case that tend to mitigate the punitive? What are the facts that tend to aggravate the punitive?
3. Construct a scenario in which more than a single-digit multiple for punitive would pass constitutional muster.
4. How do you think that this case will impact future settlements involving punitive damages?

Intentional Infliction of Emotional Distress

In the following case, the court considers whether an employer's termination of an employee amounts to intentional infliction of emotional distress.

DEBRA AGIS V. HOWARD JOHNSON COMPANY
355 N.E.2d 315 (Mass. 1976)

Debra Agis (plaintiff) sued the Howard Johnson Company and Roger Dionne, manager of the restaurant in which she was employed (defendants), to recover damages for mental anguish and emotional distress allegedly caused by her summary dismissal from such employment. The trial court dismissed Agis's claim. Agis appealed to the Supreme Judicial Court of Massachusetts, which reversed the trial court's dismissal and remanded the case for a trial.

Justice Quirico

Briefly, the allegations in the plaintiffs' complaint . . . are the following. Debra Agis was employed by the Howard Johnson Company as a waitress in a restaurant known as the Ground Round. On or about May 23, 1975, the defendant Dionne notified all waitresses that a meeting would be held at 3 P.M. that day. At the meeting, he informed the waitresses that "there was some stealing going on," but that the identity of the person or persons responsible was not known, and that, until the person or persons responsible were discovered, he would begin firing all the present waitresses in alphabetical order, starting with the letter "A." Dionne then fired Debra Agis.

The complaint alleges that, as a result of this incident, Mrs. Agis became greatly upset, began to cry, sustained emotional distress, mental anguish, and loss of wages and earnings. It further alleges that the actions of the defendants were reckless, extreme, outrageous and intended to cause emotional distress and anguish. In addition, the complaint states that the defendants knew or should have known that their actions would cause such distress.

■   ■   ■

[O]ne who, by extreme and outrageous conduct and without privilege, causes severe emotional distress to another is subject to liability for such emotional distress even though no bodily harm may result. However, in order for a plaintiff to prevail in a case for liability under this tort, four elements must be established. It must be shown (1) that the actor intended to inflict emotional distress or that he knew or should have known that emotional distress was the likely result of his conduct, (2) that the conduct was "extreme and outrageous," was "beyond all possible bounds of decency" and was "utterly intolerable in a civilized community," (3) that the actions of the defendant were the cause of the

plaintiff's distress, and (4) that the emotional distress sustained by the plaintiff was "severe" and of a nature "that no reasonable man could be expected to endure it." These requirements are "aimed at limiting frivolous suits and avoiding litigation in situations where only bad manners and mere hurt feelings are involved," and we believe they are a "realistic safeguard against false claims. . . ."

Testing the plaintiff Debra Agis's complaint by the rules stated above, we hold that she makes out a cause of action and that her complaint is therefore legally sufficient. [W]e believe that the "[plaintiff] has alleged facts and circumstances which reasonably could lead the trier of fact to conclude that defendant's conduct was extreme and outrageous, having a severe and traumatic effect upon plaintiff's emotional tranquility." Because reasonable men could differ on these issues, we believe that "it is for the jury, subject to the control of the court," to determine whether there should be liability in this case. [T]he judgment must be reversed and the plaintiff Debra Agis must be given an opportunity to prove the allegations which she has made.

Case Questions

1. What are the requirements for the tort of intentional infliction of emotional distress?

2. Do you agree with the court that the defendants' alleged conduct was sufficiently extreme and outrageous to constitute the tort of intentional infliction of emotional distress?

3. What should a company do when conducting investigations into possible employee theft in order to avoid exposure to liability for the tort of intentional infliction of emotional distress?

4. ABC Company suspected that a manager of one of its stores was stealing from the company. As part of its investigation, ABC executives interviewed the manager, required the manager to take a polygraph (lie detector) test,

and refused the manager's request that he be allowed to take his medication, which was Valium, a mood relaxant. As a result of its investigation, ABC concluded that the manager was guilty of theft and terminated the manager's employment. The manager went to see his psychiatrist, who admitted him to the mental institution. The manager sued ABC for intentional infliction of emotional distress. Should the manager win? Explain.

Intrusion into Seclusion

Questions arise as to whether drug testing in the work place constitutes an invasion of privacy. The following case illustrates the position of one court.

JANICE RUSHING V. HERSHEY CHOCOLATE—MEMPHIS
U.S. App. LEXIS 27392 (2000)

Janice Rushing, the plaintiff, was employed by Hershey, the defendant, for 17 years, in a non-sensitive safety job position. During her employment she consented to and took a urinalysis drug test as part of the mandatory company policy. Her test was inconclusive. Rushing refused to submit to additional urinalysis. She was terminated.

Rushing was never cited for deficiencies in her work and she never tested positive for drugs. She filed an action in wrongful discharge based upon a right to privacy, which she alleged was violated. Hershey moved for a dismissal, which the U.S. District Court granted. Rushing appealed to the United States Court of Appeals for the Sixth Circuit.

Circuit Judge Clay

Tennessee law recognizes the common law tort of invasion of privacy. Under Tennessee law, "'a person who unreasonably and seriously interferes with another's interest in not having his affairs known to others or his likeness exhibited to the public is liable to the other.'" Liability for invasion of privacy attaches only if (1) the defendant should have realized that his conduct would be offensive to persons of ordinary sensibilities; and, (2) the intrusion goes beyond the limits of decency.

An action for invasion of privacy may be asserted as one of four common law privacy torts: (1) intrusion into a person's seclusion, solitude or person affairs; (2) public disclosure; (3) false light; or (4) appropriation of one's likeness. Here Rushing has only asserted a claim for intrusion. One is liable for intrusion if he "'intentionally intrudes, physically or otherwise, upon the solitude or seclusion of another or his private affairs or concerns, . . . and the intrusion would be highly offensive to a reasonable person.'"

With these legal principles in mind, we conclude that Rushing's claim fails for two reasons: (1) there was no intrusion—physical or otherwise; and (2) Rushing's urinalysis test results were not a matter which she had a right to keep private in an employment setting.

In order for Rushing to state a claim for invasion of privacy based on intrusion upon her seclusion or solitude, she must allege that an intrusion took place. In *Baggs,* several of the plaintiffs asserted actions against their employer for invasion of privacy after they were terminated for refusing to submit to drug testing. The court held that those plaintiffs had no cause of action for invasion of privacy because "there was no intrusion" since the plaintiffs didn't actually take the test.

Baggs bears a striking resemblance to the case at bar. Here, as in *Baggs,* Rushing refused to submit to drug testing. Because Rushing refused to submit to the drug test, she cannot now complain that her privacy was invaded by that same test.

■　■　■

Because a claim for intrusion requires that an actual intrusion take place, and Rushing neither alleges that an intrusion took place nor provides a sufficient factual basis for this Court to infer that an intrusion took place, we conclude that Rushing's claim for invasion of privacy based upon intrusion must fail.

■　■　■

Furthermore, we conclude that Rushing's claim must fail because she did not allege facts that show that the drug tests implicated interests for which she had a right of privacy. Although there is no Tennessee case law specifically addressing the subject, Tennessee and other courts have indicated that employers may require an employee to take drug tests related to employment without committing an invasion of privacy.

■　■　■

Rushing attempts to argue she should not have been required to submit to a drug test because Her-

shey did not have particularized suspicion or probable cause to suspect that Rushing was under the influence of drugs while on the job. Rushing further argues that she should not have been required to submit to drug testing because she did not occupy a safety-sensitive position. This Court finds that these arguments are unpersuasive and unsupported by authority.

. . . Rushing attempts to attach to private employers standards [that] which have traditionally been applied to government action.

■　■　■

We therefore conclude that Rushing has failed to point to a privacy interest in the results of her urinalysis test, which presumably would reveal nothing more than whether she was under the influence of drugs while on the job. Moreover, we conclude that Hershey has a right to require its employees to submit to drug tests as long as they are not intrusive, i.e., the manner in which the program is conducted is not intrusive and the testing methods would not reveal private medical facts other than drug use.

Case Questions

1. What interest does Hershey have in keeping a drug free work place? Should it matter that Rushing was in a non-sensitive safety position and that her work was good? Explain.

2. Do you think the result would be different if the drug test required the extraction of blood? The taking of a swatch of hair? A saliva swab? Explain.

3. Draft a policy on drug testing in the work place that includes notice, procedure and consequence of non-compliance and test failure.

Proximate Cause

The following case, involving the placement of a telephone booth, illustrates the application of the negligence elements of duty and proximate cause.

BIGBEE V. PACIFIC TELEPHONE AND TELEGRAPH CO.
665 P. 2d 94 (Calif. 1983)

At approximately 12:20 A.M., Charles Bigbee was standing in a public telephone booth outside the Fortune Liquor Store on Century Boulevard in Inglewood, California. The phone booth in which Bigbee was standing was one of two booths in the parking lot of the store. They were close to the store's front wall, between the front door and the sidewalk bordering the boulevard, near an entrance to the parking lot. Bigbee occupied the booth nearer the street, 15 feet from the curb. Century Boulevard is a six-lane thoroughfare with a posted speed limit of 40 miles per hour.

At the same time Charles Bigbee was placing his phone call, an intoxicated Leona Roberts lost control of her car, veered off Century Boulevard into Fortune's parking lot, and crashed into the booth where Bigbee was standing. As Bigbee later told his story, he saw Roberts's car coming and attempted to get out of the booth but the door "jammed and stuck, trapping" him inside. Bigbee was severely injured as a result of the crash.

Bigbee sued Roberts and the companies allegedly responsible for serving her alcoholic beverages. A settlement was reached as to these defendants. In addition, Bigbee sued the companies he claimed were negligent in the design, location, installation, and maintenance of the telephone booth, which included Pacific Telephone and Telegraph Co. (defendant), the owner of the booth.

The companies filed a motion for summary judgment. In their motion, they argued that the facts demonstrated a lack of two elements essential to Bigbee's negligence claim: (1) the existence of a duty to protect Bigbee from the injuries he suffered, and (2) that their conduct could be found to be the proximate cause of Bigbee's injuries. The trial judge granted the companies' motion and entered judgment against Bigbee. Bigbee appealed to the Supreme Court of California, which reversed the summary judgment and ordered the trial judge to proceed with a trial.

Chief Justice Bird

Defendants contend that their duty to use due care in the location, installation, and maintenance of telephone booths does not extend to the risk encountered by plaintiff and that neither their alleged negligence in carrying out these activities nor any defect in the booth was a proximate cause of plaintiff's injuries. These contentions present the same issue in different guises. Each involves this question—was the risk that a car might crash into the phone booth and injure plaintiff reasonably foreseeable in this case?

Turning to the merits of this case, the question presented is a relatively simple one. Is there room for a reasonable difference of opinion as to whether the risk that a car might crash into the phone booth and injure an individual inside was reasonably foreseeable under the circumstances set forth above?

In pursuing this inquiry, it is well to remember that foreseeability is not to be measured by what is more probable than not, but, includes whatever is likely enough in the setting of modern life that a reasonabl[y] thoughtful [person] would take account of it in guiding practical conduct. One may be held accountable for creating even "the risk of a slight possibility of injury if a reasonabl[y] prudent [person] would not do so." Moreover, it is settled that what is required to be foreseeable is the general character of the event or harm—e.g., being struck by a car while standing in a phone booth—not its precise nature or manner of occurrence.

Here, defendants placed a telephone booth, which was difficult to exit, in a parking lot 15 feet from the side of a major thoroughfare and near a driveway. Under these circumstances, this court cannot conclude as a matter of law that it was unforeseeable that the booth might be struck by a car and cause serious injury to a person trapped within. A jury could reasonably conclude that this risk was foreseeable. This is particularly true where, as here, there is evidence that a booth at this same location had previously been struck.

Indeed, in light of the circumstances of modern life, it seems evident that a jury could reasonably find that defendants should have foreseen the possibility of the very accident which actually occurred here. Swift traffic on a major thoroughfare late at night is to be expected. Regrettably, so too are intoxicated drivers who lose control of their cars and crash into poles, buildings or whatever else may be standing alongside the road they travel—no matter how straight and level that road may be.

Where a telephone booth, which is difficult to exit, is placed 15 feet from such a thoroughfare, the risk that it might be struck by a car veering off the street, thereby causing injury to a person trapped within, cannot be said to be unforeseeable as a matter of law.

It is no consequence that the harm to plaintiff came about through the negligent or reckless acts of Roberts. If the likelihood that a third person may act in a particular manner is the hazard or one of the hazards which makes the actor negligent, such an act whether innocent, negligent, intentionally tortious, or criminal does not prevent the actor from being liable for harm caused thereby. Here, the risk that a car might hit the telephone booth could be found to constitute one of the hazards to which plaintiff was exposed.

Considering the case law and the circumstances of this case, this court cannot conclude as a matter of law that injury to plaintiff, inflicted by negligent or reckless third party drivers, was unforeseeable. Just as we may not rely upon our private judgment on this issue, so the trial court may not impose its private judgment upon a situation, such as this, in which reasonable minds may differ.

Justice Kroniger
(Dissenting)

I respectfully disagree with this court's holding that the negligent siting theory of plaintiff's case should be submitted to the trier of fact.

To hold that defendants could be found liable for locating the booth where they did is tantamount to holding that one may be found negligent whenever he conducts everyday activities on or adjacent to the public sidewalk. It will go far toward making all roadside businesses insurers of safety for wayward travelers.

There is no suggestion of anything defendants might reasonably have done differently with respect to siting except simply not to maintain a telephone in the vicinity at all. Public telephones have, in fact, long been maintained adjacent to streets and highways for the convenience of the public, despite the obvious but remote risks.

Case Questions

1. Compare and contrast the majority and dissenting opinions.
2. Which fact does the court draw on to support its conclusion that the question of breach of duty and proximate cause are proper jury

questions? Over the last century the role of the American jury in negligence cases has enlarged. How do you think this trend affects business?

3. Assume that a vegetable stand operating on the side of a country road results in a patron being injured by a reckless operator of an

automobile. Under *Bigbee*, would the vegetable stand owner be liable? Explain. What about a particularly flashy billboard that results in auto accidents when drivers are distracted? Explain.

4. Are there any strategies that businesses might take to counter the results in *Bigbee*?

Injury

The following is a negligence case involving a popular fast food chain.

SUTTON V. ROTH, L.L.C. AND MCDONALD'S CORPORATION
2010 U.S. App. LEXIS 1310 (Fourth Circuit Court of Appeals, 2010)

Frank Sutton, (Plaintiff-Appellant), a customer who suffered burns from eating a fried chicken sandwich, sued Roth, L.L.C. and McDonald's Corporation (Defendants-Appellees), a franchise owner and a fast food corporation, for negligence under Virginia law. The U.S. District Court granted summary judgment in favor of McDonald's and, after trial, granted judgment as a matter of law in favor of Roth, L.L.C., the franchise owner. Sutton appealed. The court of appeals vacated the district court's judgment and returned the case to the district court for further proceedings.

Shedd, Circuit Judge

Around 1:30 a.m. on August 8, 2005, Sutton, along with his wife, adult son, and a work associate (Bill Giffon), stopped to refuel at the Daniel Boone Truck Stop in Duffield, Virginia. While refueling, the group noticed a McDonald's restaurant attached to the truck stop's convenience store. Roth owns this restaurant as a franchisee of McDonald's Corporation.

Because their vehicles were too big to fit through the restaurant's drive-thru, Sutton and his entourage went inside the restaurant/convenience store to order. When they entered, Sutton noticed that the partition between the McDonald's restaurant and the convenience store was closed. Sutton asked the convenience store clerks whether the McDonald's restaurant was still open, and they replied that it was. Sutton returned to the partition and called for a McDonald's employee, but no one answered. The convenience store operators then informed Sutton that the McDonald's employees were outside, behind the restaurant.

Sutton went outside and found two young women in McDonald's uniforms talking with two young men. Sutton asked them if the restaurant was still open, and they replied affirmatively. Sutton walked back inside, and the two women met him at the partition. Sutton placed and paid for his order. He then watched the two women go into the restaurant. Shortly thereafter, the women returned with Sutton's change and his order. Sutton's group then went to a small table in the convenience store to eat.

When Sutton bit into his fried chicken sandwich, "grease flew all over his mouth." (Testimony of Bill Giffon). As Sutton described it, "the grease from the inside of the chicken sandwich spread out all over my bottom lip, my top lip, down onto my chin." Sutton immediately dropped his sandwich, and his wife took ice out of her drink, put it into a napkin, and began to dab his face. Almost instantly, blisters appeared on Sutton's lips.

After tending to his face, Sutton sought out the two McDonald's employees to report the incident. Unable to find them inside, Sutton went back outside, where he found them again talking with two young men. He told them what had happened and showed them the blisters on his lips and chin. One of the women responded, "This is what happens to the sandwiches when they aren't drained completely." After they finished eating, Sutton and his entourage left the truck stop.

The next morning Sutton discovered that some of the blisters on his lips had bled onto his pillow. At this point, he realized that his burns were worse than he initially thought. Two days after the accident, he returned to the restaurant to file an incident report with the manager on duty. Four days after the accident, Sutton went to an urgent care facility for medical attention; there he was told that the burns would heal naturally over the next month.

Sutton's lips continued to bother him over the next few months. Because sunlight and heat irritated his burns, Sutton's lips consistently bothered him during his work of refurbishing and assembling outdoor amusement rides. Sutton declined specific jobs if he knew the necessary work would aggravate his lips.

Seven months after the accident Sutton sought additional treatment for his injuries. Dr. Donnelly, an ear, nose, and throat specialist, treated Sutton

with lip balm, and he instructed Sutton to avoid excessive exposure to sunlight. Sutton visited Dr. Donnelly on a regular basis for ongoing observation and treatment.

Sutton sued Roth and McDonald's Corporation for negligence . . . under Virginia law, seeking $ 2,000,000 for lost wages, medical bills, and pain and suffering.

■   ■   ■

The district court then found that because Sutton had failed to demonstrate any evidence of a standard of care, his claim failed as a matter of law.

■   ■   ■

[W]e now must determine whether, under the law of Virginia, Sutton presented evidence of a standard of care at trial.

Under Virginia law, government standards, industry standards, or the reasonable expectations of consumers can constitute evidence of a standard of care in a products liability case. Describing these different types of evidence, we have said that:

> *While government and industry standards are readily identifiable for a given product at a given time, the reasonable expectation of purchasers requires a factual examination of what society demanded or expected from a product. This may be proved from evidence of actual industry practices, knowledge at the time of other injuries, knowledge of dangers, the existence of published literature, and from direct evidence of what reasonable purchasers considered defective at the time.*

■   ■   ■

After reviewing all of Sutton's admissible evidence, we find that Sutton presented sufficient evidence of a standard of care in the form of reasonable consumer expectation. First, Roth's employee's statement constitutes evidence of "actual industry practice." Second, Sutton's companions' reactions to his injury are evidence of "what reasonable purchasers considered defective." Sutton's wife removed ice from her soda, put it in a napkin, and tried to put it on Sutton's chin. Giffon described the incident by saying "grease flew all over his mouth." Sutton threw the sandwich down. The consumers did not expect Sutton's fried chicken sandwich to contain a hot pocket of grease, and Roth's employee's statement serves as strong corroboration for the reasonableness of this expectation. These facts reveal "what society demand[s] or expect[s] from" a fast-food, fried chicken sandwich. Under Virginia law, this constitutes evidence of a standard of care. The district court, therefore, erroneously granted judgment as a matter of law in favor of Roth. For these reasons, the district court's decision must be reversed . . . .

Based on these findings, we vacate the district court's orders . . . and we remand this case to the district court for further proceedings consistent with this opinion.

Davis, Circuit Judge, dissenting

In order to make out a prima facie case of negligence . . . a plaintiff must establish . . . a relevant standard of care . . . .

. . . Sutton's burden of proof is not remotely satisfied merely by testimony from himself and his son that they (together with their dinner companions) thought the chicken sandwich was "negligently prepared" or "defective." Rather, the test is an objective one, informed by societal standards. Sutton never undertook to offer such evidence . . . .

. . . Sutton presented no expert testimony establishing a standard of care for the preparation of fast foods. This failure was and is fatal to his case because, as a matter of law, however "hot," the sandwich was, . . . expert testimony is ordinarily necessary to establish the appropriate standard of care. The employee's alleged statement that, "This

is what happens to the sandwiches when they aren't drained completely," does not establish the requisite standard of care, or substitute for such evidence.

For the reasons stated above, I respectfully dissent.

Case Questions

1. What element of negligence is at issue in this case?
2. What sort of evidence does the court say is used to establish the standard of care in a negligence case?
3. Why did the dissenting judge maintain that Sutton had failed to establish the relevant standard of care? In the dissenting judge's view, what evidence should Sutton have provided?
4. How can you use what the court and the dissenting opinion have to say about establishing the standard of care in your everyday business experience? For example, if you were employed in a food chain restaurant what would you look to for guidance in determining whether your actions and decisions measure up to the standard of care expected of you?
5. In response to this case the *New York Times*, ran an editorial under the banner *A Nonfrivolous Suit* stating:

   > *If Mr. Sutton prevails, expect his case to become a talking point for critics of civil lawsuits and a late-night punch line. What they should be saying is that companies that sell food to the public have an undeniable responsibility to ensure their products are safe. That's no joke.*

   Do you agree or disagree with *Times* editorial? Explain.

Res Ipsa Loquitur

In the following case the court considers the application of res ipsa loquitur in the context of "exclusive control" of a chair.

TRUJEQUE V. SERVICE MERCHANDISE CO.
872 P.2d 361 (N.M. 1994)

Carmen Trujegue was shopping at Service Merchandise, when she decided to sit down on a chair provided for shoppers' convenience. The chair broke as she sat upon it, and caused injury to her arm.

Trujeque sued Service Merchandise and at trial the court instructed the jury that "Trujegue had the burden of proving that the chair was under the 'exclusive control and management' of Service Merchandise," and further defined exclusive control as follows:

> In order to prove that the defendant had exclusive control and management over the instrumentality causing plaintiff's accident and injuries plaintiff must show from the evidence that others did not have an opportunity of equal access to the instrumentality.

The jury found for the defendant, and the Court of Appeals affirmed. The Supreme Court of New Mexico granted certiorari to review the case.

Justice Ransom

. . . The doctrine of res ipsa loquitur applies only when evidence establishes that in the ordinary course of events an injury would not occur except through negligence of the person in exclusive control and management of the injuring instrumentality. . . . Generally, cases in which the theory of res ipsa loquitur is presented fall into two categories: those in which the defendant directly uses an instrumentality so as to cause injury, and those in which the defendant is in charge of, created, or last controlled an instrumentality that inexplicably becomes dangerous and injures the victim outside of the defendant's presence. . . . The case at [hand] falls into the second category.

. . . In order to make a . . . case from which the jury may infer that the defendant is liable for the damages caused by the instrumentality outside of the defendant's presence, the plaintiff must provide evidence of the character of the occurrence and of the exclusive control of the defendant. The plaintiff's burden may vary according to the facts of the case. . . .

While the two "collapsing chair" cases in New Mexico . . . imply that a showing of ownership, management, and possession of chairs in a business establishment with many invitees is sufficient to establish exclusive control, they do not expressly state what the plaintiff's burden is in those cases. There are, however, many cases from other jurisdictions expressly holding that such a showing is sufficient. . . .

We are aware one jurisdiction holds that because chairs in use are under the control of the user, the exclusive control element cannot be met as a matter of law. This argument has been widely criticized as a ridiculous conclusion. . . . We believe that [this] theory . . . is an "overly rigid interpretation of the requirement of exclusive control," and that it is "artificial and ignores the purpose of the requirement that defendant have exclusive control."

That third parties may have had access to the chair did not preclude Service Merchandise from having exclusive control and management of the chair within the meaning of the doctrine of res ipsa loquitur, and did not preclude a reasonable inference that Service Merchandise was responsible for a danger within its use. Once Trujeque established that an accident occurred that normally does not occur absent negligence and that Service Merchandise owned, maintained, and provided the chair for use by its customers on the store's premises, she satisfied her burden of making a . . . case from which the jury could infer negligence. Service Merchandise could then choose to present no evidence or choose to rebut the inference by offering evidence that a latent manufacturing defect was the cause of the collapse or perhaps that some third party bore responsibility for the collapse of the chair. It has long been held that

> [a]ll that the plaintiff should be required to do in the first instance is to show that the defendant owned, operated, and maintained, or controlled and was responsible for the management and maintenance of, the thing doing the damage. . . . When he has done this, he has cast a burden on the defendant, who may then proceed to show that the accident was occasioned by . . . other causes for which he was not responsible.

"[R]es ipsa loquitur means that the facts of the occurrence warrant the inference of negligence, not that they compel such an inference; . . . that they call for explanation or rebuttal, not necessarily that they require it; that they make a case to be decided by the jury. . . ." Trujeque met her burden, and instructing the jury that she also had to prove that no other party had an opportunity of equal access to the chair was reversible error. We reverse and remand for a new trial.

Case Questions

1. Define res ispsa loquitur.
2. When is res ipsa loquitur applicable? Why was it applicable in this case?
3. What was the problem with the jury instructions?
4. What is a stack of chairs overhead "within the business establishment" fell, struck a patron and injured her? Would res ipsa loquitur be applicable?
5. Simpson was a paying guest at the Econo Lodge Motel in Durham, North Carolina. Simpson was given room number 27. After checking into the room, he went into the bathroom to take a shower in the combination bathtub-shower. He adjusted the hot and cold water control knob to a comfortable temperature. He then pulled out the shower-bath control knob so that the water came out of the shower head. After Simpson finished his shower, he pushed in the shower-bath control knob. The water from the shower head stopped, but moments later, a sudden burst of scalding hot water gushed out from the shower head hitting him. He jumped to get away from the hot water, slipped, lost his balance and fell on the tile floor, sustaining injuries to his left leg and knee. Simpson sued Econo Lodge, claiming that it was liable to him for negligence under the doctrine of res ipsa loquitur. Is Simpson correct? Explain.

Abnormally Dangerous Activities

In the following case, the court considers whether a fireworks display qualifies as an abnormally dangerous activity for purposes of imposing strict liability.

KLEIN V. PYRODYNE CORPORATION
810 P.2d 917 (Wash. 1991)

Danny and Marion Klein (plaintiffs) were injured when an aerial shell at a Fourth of July fireworks exhibition went astray and exploded near them. Pyrodyne Corporation (defendant) is a pyrotechnic company hired to set up and discharge the fireworks. The Kleins sued Pyrodyne in tort under the theory of strict liability. The trial court granted summary judgment in favor of the Kleins. Pyrodyne appealed to the Supreme Court of the State of Washington the trial court's holding that strict liability was the appropriate standard of liability. The Supreme Court of Washington affirmed the trial court decision favoring the Kleins.

Justice Guy

The Kleins contend that strict liability is the appropriate standard to determine the culpability of Pyrodyne because Pyrodyne was participating in an abnormally dangerous activity. . . .

The modern doctrine of strict liability for abnormally dangerous activities derives from *Rylands v. Fletcher* in which the defendant's reservoir flooded mine shafts on the plaintiff's adjoining land. *Rylands v. Fletcher* has come to stand for the rule that "the defendant will be liable when he damages another by a thing or activity unduly dangerous and inappropriate to the place where it is maintained, in the light of the character of that place and its surroundings."

The basic principle of *Rylands v. Fletcher* has been accepted by the Restatement (Second) of Torts (1977). Section 519 of the Restatement provides that any party carrying on an "abnormally dangerous activity" is strictly liable for ensuing damages. . . . The essential question is whether the risk created is so unusual, either because of its magnitude or because of the circumstances surrounding it, as to justify the imposition of strict liability for the harm that results from it, even though it is carried on with all reasonable care.

. . . Anytime a person ignites aerial shells or rockets with the intention of sending them aloft to explode in the presence of large crowds of people, a high risk of serious personal injury or property damage is created. That risk arises because of the possibility that a shell or rocket will malfunction or be misdirected. Furthermore, no matter how much care pyrotechnicians exercise, they cannot entirely eliminate the high risk inherent in setting off powerful explosives such as fireworks near crowds.

The dangerousness of fireworks displays is evidenced by the elaborate scheme of administrative regulations with which pyrotechnicians must comply. . . .

[R]elatively few persons conduct public fireworks displays. Therefore, presenting public fireworks displays is not a matter of common usage.

Pyrodyne argues that . . . fireworks are a common way to celebrate the Fourth of July. . . . Although fireworks are frequently and regularly enjoyed by the public, few persons set off special fireworks displays. Indeed, the general public is prohibited by statute from making public fireworks displays insofar as anyone wishing to do so must first obtain a license.

. . . In this case, the fireworks display was conducted at the Puyallup Fairgrounds. Although some locations—such as over water—may be safer, the Puyallup Fairgrounds is an appropriate place for a fireworks show because the audience can be seated at a reasonable distance from the display.

. . . This country has a long-standing tradition of fireworks on the Fourth of July. That tradition suggests that we as a society have decided that the value of fireworks on the day celebrating our national independence and unity outweighs the risks of injuries and damage.

In sum, we find that setting off public fireworks displays . . . is an activity that is not "of common usage" and that presents an ineliminably high risk of serious bodily injury or property damage. We therefore hold that conducting public fireworks displays is an abnormally dangerous activity justifying the imposition of strict liability.

■   ■   ■

Policy considerations also support imposing strict liability on pyrotechnicians for damages caused by their public fireworks displays, although such considerations are not alone sufficient to justify that conclusion. Most basic is the question as to who should bear the loss when an innocent person suffers injury through the nonculpable but abnormally dangerous activities of another. In the case of public fireworks displays, fairness weighs in favor of requiring the pyrotechnicians who present the displays to bear the loss rather than the unfortunate spectators who suffer the injuries.

In addition, the rule of strict liability rests not only upon the ultimate idea of rectifying a wrong and putting the burden where it should belong as a matter of abstract justice, that is, upon the one of the two innocent parties whose acts instigated or made the harm possible, but it also rests on problems of proof: One of these common features is that the person harmed would encounter a difficult problem of proof if some other standard of liability were applied. For example, the disasters caused by those who engage in abnormally dangerous or extra-hazardous activities frequently destroy all evidence of what in fact occurred, other than that the activity was being carried on. Certainly this is true with explosions of dynamite, large quantities of gasoline, or other explosives. In the present case, all evidence was destroyed as to what caused the misfire of the shell that injured the Kleins. Therefore, the problem of proof this case presents for the plaintiffs also supports imposing strict liability on Pyrodyne.

Case Questions

1. What is the principle of *Rylands v. Fletcher*?
2. What essentially determines whether strict liability for abnormally dangerous activities will be imposed?
3. What factors does the court weigh in determining whether an activity is one that qualifies for strict liability?
4. What are the policy reasons for imposing strict liability for abnormally dangerous activities?
5. The Tittles purchase land in the country and built a house there. Two years later, IMAC Corporation began blasting operations in connection with strip mining on adjacent property approximately 300 feet from the Tittles' home. The Tittles claim that the blasting has caused cracks in the foundation and the plasterboard of their house. If the Tittles sued IMAC Corp., under the tort theory of strict liability, should they win? Explain.

Chapter Seven   The Law of Business Organizations

Apparent Authority

The following case details the principles involving apparent authority.

HAMILTON HAULING INC. V. GAF CORPORATION
719 S.W. 2d 841 (Mo. App. 1986)

Bajt was a purchasing agent for GAF. His duties included the purchase of raw materials necessary for day-to-day plant production, including wood chips. Bajt entered into a 10-year contract with Hamilton Hauling for the purchase of $6 million worth of wood chips. This was the only long-term contract Bajt had ever entered into on behalf of the company, although he had purchased wood chips before by purchase order. Company policy required approval at corporate headquarters for long-term contracts. Bajt never sought approval, nor did he inform anyone at corporate headquarters of the contract.

When GAF found out about the contract, the company refused to honor it, maintaining that Bajt lacked agency authority. Hamilton Hauling maintained that Bajt possessed apparent authority. Hamilton Hauling sued GAF. At the trial, a jury found in favor of GAF. The Missouri Court of Appeals affirmed the trial court decision.

Judge Dixon

It is generally held that when a principal "holds out" another as possessing certain authority, thereby inducing others reasonable to believe that authority exists, the agent has apparent authority to act even though as between himself and the principal, such authority has not been granted. Apparent authority differs from actual authority in that the principal communicates directly with a third person to create apparent authority; to create actual authority, the principal communicates directly with the agent.

When a principal has by his voluntary act placed an agent in such a situation that a person of ordinary prudence, conversant with business usages and the nature of the particular business, is justified in persuming that such an agent has authority to perform a particular act on behalf of his principal, the principal is estopped . . . from denying the agent's authority to perform the act.

It must be emphasized that the third party must reasonably rely on the authority held out by the principal. . . . Apparent authority is that which a reasonably prudent man, using diligence and discretion, in view of the principal's conduct would suppose the agent to possess.

Establishment of apparent authority by direct, express statements is obvious. The other methods of creating apparent authority by "position" and by "prior acts" have both been recognized. . . .

Wynn v. McMahon Ford Co. exemplifies the apparent authority that may be generated by an agent's position. In *Wynn,* defendant's agent [was] designated as used car sales manager, [and] was placed by defendant in a managerial position. The court found that persons dealing with the agent could reasonably believe that he had authority to conclude transactions. . . .

Apparent authority may result from a prior relation of agent and principal. The principal by allowing an agent to carry out prior similar transactions may create an appearance of authority of the agent to carry out such acts.

There was no evidence to show that GAF knowingly permitted Bajt to enter into the contract in question. Bajt had never entered into a long-term contract before. Bajt admitted he did not send a copy of the contract to corporate headquarters and no one at GAF seemed to know about the contract. Clearly, the contract was made in violation of internal corporate policy and nothing was presented to show that GAF generally "ignored" its policy in making long-term multi-million dollar contracts. . . .

Hamilton Hauling claims Bajt's authority came from his position[.] [H]owever, there was no evidence of any sort in this case as to the usual authority of purchasing agents generally. There was nothing to support an inference that a vendor dealing with a purchasing agent expects that agent to have the power to make a contract like the long-term agreement in evidence. . . . There was no evidence that Bajt had ever entered into a long-term contract on behalf of GAF; in fact, Bajt admitted that in all his years at GAF, he had not made any other such contract. Bajt was not clothed with apparent authority by virtue of his position. Moreover, there was no evidence to support Hamilton's claim that he reasonably relied on Bajt's authority. Hamilton admitted that the contracts he had entered into with other corporations were signed at corporate headquarters, not locally. . . .

The judgment favoring GAF is affirmed.

Case Questions

1. What is the issue this case presents?
2. Why did the court hold that apparent authority was absent?
3. What could Hamilton Hauling have done to avoid the problem? Explain. What should Bajt insist on in order to avoid the problem in the future?
4. Assume that Bajt entered into a similar contract for five years. Would the result be different? What about one year?

Piercing the Corporate Veil

The next case, involving a bar, an uninsured motorist, and injured plaintiff, discusses the parameters of piercing the corporate veil.

BAATZ V. ARROW BAR
452 N.W. 2d 138 (S.D. 1990)

Kenny and Peggy Baatz (appellants) were injured while riding a motorcycle; they were struck by Roland McBride, who crossed the center line of the street with his automobile. McBride was uninsured.

The Baatzes allege that Arrow Bar (appellee) served alcoholic beverages to McBride while he was already intoxicated, before the accident. Arrow Bar was incorporated and Edmond and LaVella Neuroth were shareholders of the corporation. Arrow Bar did not have insurance. The Baatzes sought to pierce the corporate veil and to hold the Neuroths liable. The trial court entered summary judgment in favor of the Arrow Bar and the Neuroths. The Supreme Court of South Dakota affirmed.

Justice Sabers

Baatz claims that . . . the corporate veil should be pierced, leaving the Neuroths, as the shareholders of the corporation, individually liable. A corporation shall be considered a separate legal entity until there is sufficient reason to the contrary. When continued recognition of a corporation as a separate legal entity would "produce injustices and inequitable consequences," then a court has sufficient reason to pierce the corporate veil. Factors that indicate injustices and inequitable consequences and allow a court to pierce the corporate veil are:

1. fraudulent representation by corporation directors;
2. undercapitalization;
3. failure to observe corporate formalities;
4. absence of corporate records;
5. payment by the corporation of individual obligations; or
6. use of the corporation to promote fraud, injustice or illegalities.

When the court deems it appropriate to pierce the corporate veil, the corporation and its stockholders will be treated identically.

Baatz advances several arguments to support his claim that the corporate veil of Arrow Bar, Inc. should be pierced, but fails to support them with facts, or misconstrues the facts.

First, Baatz claims that since Edmond and LaVella personally guaranteed corporate oblig-ations, they should also be personally liable to Baatz. However, the personal guarantee of a loan is a contractual agreement and cannot be enlarged to impose tort liability. . . . Baatz also argues that the corporation is simply the alter ego of the Neuroths, and . . . the corporate veil should be pierced. Baatz' discussion of the law is adequate, but he fails to present evidence that would support a decision in his favor in accordance with that law. When an individual treats a corporation "as an instrumentality, through which he [is] conducting his personal business," a court may disregard the corporate entity. Baatz fails to demonstrate how the Neuroths were transacting personal business through the corporation. In fact, the evidence indicated the Neuroths treated the corporation separately from their individual affairs.

Baatz next argues that the corporation is undercapitalized. Shareholders must equip a corporation with a reasonable amount of capital for the nature of the business involved. Baatz claims the corporation was started with only $5,000 in borrowed capital, but does not explain how that amount failed to equip the corporation with a reasonable amount of capital. . . .

Finally, Baatz argues that Arrow Bar, Inc. failed to observe corporate formalities because none of the business signs or advertising indicated that the business was a corporation. Baatz cites [a South Dakota statute] as requiring the name of any corporation to contain the word corporation, company, incorporated, or limited or an abbreviation for such a word.

. . . [T]he "mere failure upon occasion to follow all the forms prescribed by law for the conduct of corporate activities will not justify" disregarding the corporate entity. . . .

Therefore, we affirm summary judgment dismissing the Neuroths as individual defendants.

Justice Henderson
(Dissenting)

This corporation has no separate existence. It is the instrumentality of shareholders, officers, and employees. Here, the corporate fiction should be disregarded. . . .

Peggy Baatz, a young mother, lost her left leg; she wears an artificial limb. Kenny Baatz, a young father, has had most of his left foot amputated; he has been unable to work since this tragic accident. Peggy uses a cane. Kenny uses crutches. Years have gone by since they were injured and their lives have been torn asunder.

Are the Neuroths subject to personal liability? It is undisputed by the record that the dismissed defendants (Neuroths) are immediate family and stockholders of Arrow Bar. By pleadings . . . it is expressed that the dismissed defendants are employees of Arrow Bar. Seller of the Arrow Bar would not accept Arrow Bar, Inc., as buyer. Seller insisted that the individual incorporators, in their individual capacity[,] be equally respon-

sible for the selling price. Thus, the individuals are the real party in interest and the corporate entity, Arrow Bar, Inc., is being used to justify any wrongs perpetrated by the incorporators in their individual capacity. Conclusion: Fraud is perpetrated upon the public. At a deposition of Edmond Neuroth (filed in this record), this "President" of "the corporation" was asked why the Neuroth family incorporated. His answer: "Upon the advice of counsel, as a shield against individual liability." . . .

Therefore, I respectfully dissent.

Case Questions

1. What are the circumstances under which a corporate veil may be pierced?
2. Why do the majority and dissent arrive at different conclusions on the issue of whether the corporate veil should be pierced? Should the difference make it clear that reasonable minds can differ and, hence, summary judgment is inappropriate? Explain.
3. What is undercapitalization? Is there an objective way to measure it? Do you favor a statute that would establish minimum levels of capitalization? Explain.
4. Do you favor a law requiring bars to be fully insured in order to be licensed to sell alcoholic beverages? Explain.

Business Judgment Rule

Consider the business judgment rule in connection with the next case involving a board's decision to the sell the company.

SMITH V. VAN GORKOM
488 A.2d 858 (Del. 1985)

Trans Union was a publicly traded corporation in the railcar leasing business. Van Gorkom was the chief executive officer and chairman of the board of directors.

He owned 75,000 shares of company stock out of 20 million outstanding shares.

Van Gorkom located a social acquaintance, Pritzker, who offered to purchase the company at a price of $55 a share. The stock was selling for about $38 a share on the open market. Van Gorkom called a meeting of the board and made a 20 minute presentation to the board concerning the proposal. After two hours, the board approved the Pritzker proposal.

Shareholders sued Van Gorkom and the company directors. The Delaware Court of Chancery held that the defendants were protected under the business judgment rule. The plaintiffs appealed the judgment, and the Supreme Court of Delaware reversed.

Judge Horsey

Under Delaware law, the business judgment rule is the offspring of the fundamental principle that the business and affairs of a . . . corporation are managed by or under its board of directors. . . . The business judgement rule exists to protect and promote the full and free exercise of the managerial power granted to Delaware directors. The rule itself "is a presumption that in making a business decision, the directors of a corporation acted on an informed basis, in good faith and in the honest belief that the action taken was in the best interest of the company."

The determination of whether a business judgment is an informed one turns on whether the directors have informed themselves "prior to making a business decision, of all material information reasonably available to them."

■   ■   ■

Under the business judgment rule there is no protection for directors who have made "an unintelligent or unadvised judgment." A director's duty to inform himself in preparation for a decision derives from the fiduciary capacity in which he serves the corporation and its stockholders. Since a director is vested with the responsibility for the management of the affairs of the corporation, he must execute that duty with the recognition that he acts on behalf of others. Such obligation does not tolerate faithlessness or self-dealing. But fulfillment of the fiduciary function requires more than the mere absence of bad faith or fraud. Representation of the financial interests of others imposes on a director an affirmative duty to protect those interests and to proceed with a critical eye in assessing information of the type and under the circumstances present here.

■   ■   ■

On the record before us, we must conclude that the Board of Directors did not reach an informed business judgment . . . in voting to "sell" the Company for $55 per share pursuant to the Pritzker cash-out . . . proposal. Our reasons, in summary, are as follows:

The directors (1) did not adequately inform themselves as to Van Gorkom's role in forcing the "sale" of the Company and in establishing the per share purchase price; (2) were uninformed as to the intrinsic value of the Company; and (3) given these circumstances, at a minimum, were grossly negligent in approving the "sale" of the Company upon two hours' consideration, without prior notice, and without the exigency of a crisis or emergency.

Without any documents before them concerning the proposed transaction, the members of the Board were required to rely entirely upon Van Gorkom's 20-minute oral presentation of the proposal. No written summary of the terms . . . was presented; the directors were given no documentation to support the adequacy of [a] $55 price per share for sale of the Company; and the Board had before it nothing more than Van Gorkom's statement of his understanding of the substance of an agreement which he admittedly had never read, nor which any member of the Board had ever seen.

■   ■   ■

A substantial premium (difference between stock price and sales price) may provide one reason to recommend [the proposal], but in the absence of other sound valuation information, the fact of a premium alone does not provide an adequate basis upon which to assess the fairness of an offering price. . . .

The record is clear that Van Gorkom and other members of Trans Union's Board knew that the market had consistently undervalued the worth of Trans Union's stock, despite steady increase in the Company's operating income in the seven years preceding. . . .

■   ■   ■

. . . [T]here was no call by the Board . . . for any valuation study or documentation of the $55 price per share as a measure of the fair value of the Company in a cash-out context. It is undisputed that the major asset of Trans Union was its cash flow. Yet, at no time did the Board call for a valuation study taking into account that highly significant element of the Company's assets.

■   ■   ■

The record also establishes that the Board accepted without scrutiny Van Gorkom's representation as to the fairness of the $55 price per share for sale of the Company—a subject that the Board had never previously considered. The Board thereby failed to discover that Van Gorkom had suggested the $55 price to Pritzker. . . .

■   ■   ■

None of the directors . . . were investment brokers or financial analysts. Yet the Board did not consider recessing the meeting until a later hour that day (or requesting an extension . . .) to give it time to elicit more information as to the sufficiency of the offer, either from inside Management or from Trans Union's own investment banker, Salomon Brothers, whose Chicago specialist in merger and acquisitions was known to the Board and familiar with Trans Union's affairs.

■   ■   ■

We conclude that Trans Union's Board was grossly negligent in that it failed to act with informed reasonable deliberation in agreeing to the Pritzker . . . proposal. . . .

■   ■   ■

We hold, therefore, that the Trial Court committed reversible error in applying the business judgment rule in favor of the director defendants in this case.

REVERSED and REMANDED for proceedings consistent herewith.

Case Questions

1. What issue does this case present?
2. For what reasons did the court find that Board was not protected by the business judgment rule?
3. Why is the market price not necessarily a fair price?
4. What questions would you as a board member want to ask before making a decision?
5. Assume that the board entered into an agreement with Pritzker, another "suitor" came along and offered $75/share for the buyout. What should the board do and why?

Chapter Eight   Equal Employment Opportunity

Disparate Impact

In the following case, the Supreme Court applies the disparate impact approach to a case brought under the Age Discrimination in Employment Act (the ADEA). Note that the application of the disparate impact approach is narrower in cases involving the ADEA than in cases brought under Title VII. This is because of differences in the text of the two federal laws. The ADEA contains a separate provision not found in Title VII. The ADEA includes a defense for "reasonable factors other than age" (the RFOA).

SMITH v. CITY OF JACKSON, MISSISSIPPI
125 S. Ct. 1536 (2005)

In revising its employee pay plan, the City of Jackson, Mississippi (Respondent) granted raises to all police officers and police dispatchers in an attempt to bring their starting salaries up to the regional average. Officers with less than five years' service received proportionately greater raises than those with more seniority, and most officers over 40 had more than five years of service. A group of older officers (Petitioners) filed suit under the Age Discrimination in Employment Act (ADEA), claiming that they were adversely affected by the plan because of their age. The District Court granted the City summary judgment. The Court of Appeals affirmed, ruling that disparate-impact claims are unavailable under the ADEA. The Supreme Court of the United States affirmed. The following is the Supreme Court's decision.

Justice Stevens

We . . . hold that the ADEA does authorize recovery in "disparate-impact" cases. . . . Because, however, we conclude that petitioners have not set forth a valid disparate-impact claim, we affirm.

■   ■   ■

In determining whether the ADEA authorizes disparate-impact claims, we begin with the premise that when Congress uses the same language in two statutes having similar purposes, . . . it is appropriate to presume that Congress intended that text to have the same meaning in both statutes. . . .

In *Grigges [vs. Duke Power Co.]*, a case decided four years after the enactment of the ADEA, we considered whether §703 of Title VII prohibited an employer "from requiring a high school education or passing of a standardized general intelligence test as a condition of employment in or transfer to jobs when (a) neither standard is shown to be significantly related to successful job performance, (b) both requirements operate to disqualify Negroes at a substantially higher rate than white applicants, and (c) the jobs in question formerly had been filled only by white employees as part of longstanding practice of giving preference to whites." Accepting the Court of Appeals' conclusion that the employer had adopted the diploma and test requirements without any intent to discriminate, we held that good faith "does not redeem employment procedures or testing mechanisms that operate as 'built-in headwinds' for minority groups and are unrelated to measuring job capability."

We explained that Congress had "directed the thrust of the Act to the *consequences* of employment practices, not simply the motivation." We relied on the fact that history is "filled with examples of men and women who rendered highly effective performance without the conventional badges of accomplishment in terms of certificates, diplomas or degrees. Diplomas and tests are useful servants, but Congress has mandated the commonsense proposition that they are not to become masters of reality." And we noted that the Equal Employment Opportunity Commission (EEOC), which had enforcement responsibility, had issued guidelines that accorded with our view. We thus squarely held that §703(a)(2) of Title VII did not require a showing of discriminatory intent.

■　　■　　■

Griggs, which interpreted the identical text at issue here, thus strongly suggests that a disparate-impact theory should be cognizable under the ADEA. . . .

[T]extual differences between the ADEA and Title VII make it clear that even though both statutes authorize recovery on a disparate-impact theory, the scope of disparate-impact liability under ADEA is narrower than under Title VII. The first is the RFOA provision . . . *[The RFOA provision provides that it shall not be unlawful for an employer "to take any action otherwise prohibited . . . where the differentiation is based on reasonable factors other than age."]*

Turning to the case before us, . . . the disparate impact is attributable to the City's decision to give raises based on seniority and position. Reliance on seniority and rank is unquestionably reasonable given the City's goal of raising employees' salaries to match those in surrounding communities. In sum, we hold that the City's decision to grant a larger raise to lower echelon employees for the purpose of bringing salaries in line with that of surrounding police forces was a decision based on a "reasonable factor other than age" that responded to the City's legitimate goal of retaining police officers. While there may have been other reasonable ways for the City to achieve its goals, the one selected was not unreasonable. Unlike the business necessity test, which asks whether there are other ways for the employer to achieve its goals that do not result in a disparate impact on a protected class, the reasonableness inquiry includes no such requirement.

Accordingly, while we do not agree with the Court of Appeals' holding that that the disparate-impact theory of recovery is never available under the ADEA, we affirm its judgment.

Case Questions

1. Describe the disparate impact approach to determining the existence of illegal job discrimination and how that approach differs from the disparate treatment approach.

2. In which types of cases will the disparate impact approach and the disparate treatment approach be applied?

3. How is the disparate impact approach different in cases brought under ADEA and cases brought under Title VII of the Civil Rights Act? Is the protection against disparate impact discrimination as strong under the ADEA as it

is under Title VII? Why or why not? Which is easier to prove: that an employer's policy or practice is necessary or that it is reasonable? Under Title VII an employer charged with disparate impact discrimination must justify the practice as a business necessity to avoid liability, but under the ADEA, when an employer is charged with disparate impact discrimination, it must only show that the practice was reasonable.

4. Is it enough to avoid liability under either Title VII or the ADEA that the employer can prove that its policy or decision is not motivated by discrimination?

5. What are the practical implications of *Smith vs. City of Jackson, Mississippi?* Suppose an employer's hiring criteria can be shown to statistically have a negative impact on employees over age forty. What must the employer be able to prove to avoid liability?

The Bona Fide Occupational Qualification

The following case illustrates how courts evaluate the BFOQ.

UNITED AUTO WORKERS v. JOHNSON CONTROLS, INC.
499 U.S. 187 (1991)

Johnson Controls (respondent) manufactured automobile batteries. It prohibited fertile women from working in jobs where they would be exposed to lead. It imposed the ban after eight employees became pregnant and had blood lead levels that could endanger their fetuses.

The United Auto Workers (petitioners) sued respondent for violating Title VII. The trial court granted summary judgment for respondent. The Seventh Circuit Court of Appeals affirmed. The Supreme Court reversed.

Justice Blackmun

The bias in Johnson Controls' policy is obvious. Fertile men, but not fertile women, are given a choice as to whether they wish to risk their reproductive health for a particular job. . . . The policy excludes women with childbearing capacity from lead-exposed jobs and so creates a facial classification based on gender. . . .

■　■　■

We therefore turn to the question whether Johnson Controls' fetal-protection policy is one of those "certain instances" that come within the BFOQ exception.

The BFOQ defense is written narrowly, and this Court has read it narrowly. . . . Johnson Controls argues that its fetal-protection policy falls within the so-called safety exceptions to the BFOQ. . . .

■　■　■

Our case law . . . makes clear that the safety exception is limited to instances in which sex or pregnancy actually interferes with the employee's ability to perform the job. This approach is consistent with the language of the BFOQ provision itself, for it suggests that permissible distinctions based on sex must relate to ability to perform the duties of the job. Johnson Controls suggests, however, that we expand the exception to allow fetal-protection policies that mandate particular standards for pregnant or fertile women. We decline to do so. Such an expansion contradicts not only the language of the BFOQ and the narrowness of its exception but the plain language and history of the Pregnancy Discrimination Act.

■　　■　　■

We have no difficulty concluding that Johnson Controls cannot establish a BFOQ. Fertile women, as far as appears in the record, participate in the manufacture of batteries as efficiently as anyone else. Johnson Controls' professed moral and ethical concerns about the welfare of the next generation do not suffice to establish a BFOQ of female sterility. Decisions about the welfare of future children must be left to the parents who conceive, bear, support, and raise them rather than to the employers who hire those parents. Congress has mandated this choice through Title VII, as amended by the Pregnancy Dis-

crimination Act. Johnson Controls has attempted to exclude women because of their reproductive capacity. Title VII and the PDA simply do not allow a woman's dismissal because of her failure to submit to sterilization.

Case Questions

1. What was Johnson Controls' motivation for excluding fertile women from jobs involving exposure to lead?

2. What must an employer prove to establish a BFOQ?

3. Do you think that removing the ban on fertile women will result in large numbers of women taking jobs involving exposure to lead? Why or why not?

4. An employer requires that its director of Latin American marketing be male. The position involves extensive travel to Latin America to deal with present and potential customers. Business meetings are often held in hotel rooms. Many Latin American customers would find conducting business with a woman in a hotel room offensive to their cultural customs and mores. They generally prefer to do business with men and would probably switch to a competitor if the employer's Latin American marketing director were female. Does the employer's refusal to consider females for the position violate Title VII? Why or why not?

Harassment

In the following case, the Supreme Court sets the standard for determining when there is hostile environment sexual harassment.

HARRIS V. FORKLIFT SYSTEMS, INC.
510 U.S. 117 (1993)

Teresa Harris worked as a manager at Forklift Systems. Charles Hardy was Forklift's president. Throughout Harris' time at Forklift, Hardy often insulted her because of her gender and often made her the target of unwanted sexual innuendos. Hardy told Harris on several occasions, in the presence of other employees, "You're a woman, what do you know" and "We need a man as the rental manager." Hardy occasionally asked Harris and other female employees to get coins from his front pants pocket. He threw objects on the ground in front of Harris and other women, and asked them to pick the objects up. He made sexual innuendos about Harris' and other women's clothing.

When Harris complained to Hardy about his conduct, Hardy said he was surprised that Harris was offended, claimed he was only joking, and apologized. He also promised he would stop, and based on this assurance Harris stayed on the job. But a month later, Hardy began anew: While Harris was arranging a deal with one of Forkift's customers, he asked her, again in front of other employees, "What did you do, promise the guy . . . some [sex] Saturday night?" Harris collected her next paycheck and quit.

Harris then sued Forklift, claiming that Hardy's conduct had created an abusive work environment for her because of her gender. The district court held that Hardy's conduct did not create an abusive environment. The court found that Hardy's comments "were not" so severe as to be expected to seriously affect [Harris's] psychological well being. The court of appeals affirmed, and Harris appealed to the Supreme Court of the United States, which reversed. The following is the Supreme Court's opinion.

Justice O'Connor

Title VII of the Civil Rights Act of 1964 makes it "an unlawful employment practice for an employer . . . to discriminate against any individual with respect to his compensation, terms, conditions , or privileges of employment, because of such individual's race, color, religion, sex, or national origin." As we made clear in *Meritor Savings Bank* v. *Vinson,* this language "is not limited to 'economic' or 'tangible' discrimination. The phrase 'terms, conditions, or privileges of employment' evinces a congressional intent 'to strike at the entire spectrum of disparate treatment of men and women in employment,'" which includes requiring people to work in a discriminatorily hostile or abusive environment. When the workplace is permeated with "discriminatory intimidation, ridicule, and insult," that is "sufficiently severe or pervasive to alter the conditions of the victim's employment and create an abusive working environment," Title VII is violated.

This standard, which we reaffirm today, takes a middle path between making actionable any conduct that is merely offensive and requiring the conduct to cause a tangible psychological injury. As we pointed out in *Meritor,* "mere utterance of an . . . epithet which engenders offensive feelings in an employee," does not sufficiently affect the conditions of employment to implicate Title VII. Conduct that is not severe or pervasive enough to create an objectively hostile or abusive work environment—an environment that a reasonable person would find hostile or abusive—is beyond Title VII's purview. Likewise, if the victim does not subjectively perceive the environment to be abusive, the conduct has not actually altered the conditions of the victim's employment, and there is no Title VII violation.

But Title VII comes into play before the harassing conduct leads to a nervous breakdown. A discriminatorily abusive work environment, even one that does not seriously affect employees' psychological well being, can and often will detract from employees' job performance, discourage employees from remaining on the job or keep them from advancing in their careers. Moreover, even without regard to these tangible effects, the very fact that the discriminatory conduct was so severe or pervasive that it created a work environment abusive to employees because of their race, gender, religion, or national origin offends Title VII's broad rule of workplace equality. . . .

We therefore believe the District Court erred in relying on whether the conduct "seriously affect[ed] plaintiff's psychological well being" or led her to "suffe[r] injury." Such an inquiry may needlessly focus the factfinder's attention on concrete psychological harm, an element Title VII does not require. Certainly Title VII bars conduct that would seriously affect a reasonable person's psychological well being, but the statute is not limited to such conduct. So long as the environment would reasonably be perceived, and is perceived, as hostile or abusive, there is no need for it also to be psychologically injurious.

This is not, and by its nature cannot be, a mathematically precise test. We need not answer today all the potential questions it raises, nor specifically address the EEOC's new regulations on this subject. But we can say that whether an environment is "hostile" or "abusive" can be determined only by looking at all the circumstances. These may include the frequency of the discriminatory conduct; its severity; whether it is physically threatening or humiliating, or a mere offensive utterance; and whether it unreasonably interferes with an employee's work performance. The effect on the employee's psychological well being is, of course, relevant to determining whether the plaintiff actually found the environment abusive. But while psychological harm, like any other relevant factor, may be taken into account, no single factor is required.

■　　■　　■

We therefore reverse the judgment of the Court of Appeals, and remand the case for further proceedings consistent with this opinion.

Case Questions

1. What kind of harassment was involved in this case: quid pro quo or hostile environment? Explain. What is the difference between the two types of sexual harassment?

2. What standard does the Court apply in determining whether there is illegal sexual harassment?

3. What factors does the Court say should be considered in determining whether an environment is hostile or abusive? Suppose an employee complained to you about sexual harassment. What questions should you ask the employee?

4. Does the Court's opinion provide greater clarity or confusion as to when there will be illegal sexual harassment? Explain. Will the opinion likely lead to more or less litigation? Explain. What should an employer do to reduce the likelihood of charges of sexual harassment?

5. Suppose an employee complains of harassment based on race, religion, national origin, age, or disability. Does the approach taken by the Court reach those forms of harassment? Explain.

Age

In the following case, the Supreme Court considers whether younger employees can bring reverse age discrimination cases against their employer.

GENERAL DYNAMICS LAND SYSTEMS, INC., V. CLINE
540 U.S. 581 (2004)

General Dynamics (petitioner) and the United Auto Workers negotiated a new collective bargaining agreement that provided retiree health benefits only to those employees who were at least fifty years old at the time of the new agreement. A group of employees who were in their forties (collectively, Cline) sued, claiming that the terms of the new agreement violated the ADEA. The district court dismissed their complaint. The court of appeals reversed the district court's decision. General Dynamics appealed to the Supreme Court of the United States, which reversed the court of appeals and reinstated the district court's dismissal of the complaint. What follows is the Supreme Court's opinion.

Justice Souter

The Age Discrimination in Employment Act of 1967 (ADEA) or Act forbids discriminatory preference for the young over the old. The question in this case is whether it also prohibits favoring the old over the young. We hold it does not.

■ ■ ■

Congress chose not to include age within discrimination forbidden by Title VII of the Civil Rights Acts of 1964, being aware that there were legitimate reasons as well as invidious ones for making employment decisions on age. Instead it called for a study of the issue by the Secretary of Labor, who concluded that age discrimination was a serious problem, but one different in kind from discrimination on account of race. . . .

Congress then asked for a specific proposal, which the Secretary provided in January 1967. . . .

The testimony at both hearings dwelled on unjustified assumptions about the effect of age on ability to work. . . . The record . . . reflects the common facts that an individual's chances to find and keep a job get worse over time; as between any two people, the younger is in the stronger position, the older more apt to be tagged with demeaning stereotype. Not surprisingly, from the voluminous records of the hearings, we have found . . . nothing suggesting that any workers were registering complaints about discrimination in favor of their seniors.

Nor is there any such suggestion in the introductory provisions of the ADEA, which begins with statements of purpose and findings . . . (The findings stress the impediments suffered by "older workers . . . in their efforts to retain . . . and especially to regain employment,"); "the [burdens] of arbitrary age limits regardless of potential for job performance,"; the costs of "otherwise desirable practices [that] may work to the disadvantage of older persons,"; and "the incidence of unemployment, especially long-term unemployment [which] is, relative to the younger ages, high among older workers." The statutory objects were "to promote employment of older persons based on their ability rather than age; to prohibit arbitrary age discrimination in employment; [and] to help employers and workers find ways of meeting problems arising from the impact of age on employment.

■ ■ ■

Such is the setting of the ADEA's core substantive provision prohibiting employers and certain others from "discriminat[ion] . . . because of [an] individual's age" whenever . . . the individual is "at least forty years of age . . . The prefatory provisions and their legislative history make a case that we think is beyond reasonable doubt, that the ADEA was concerned to protect a relatively old worker from discrimination that works to the advantage of the relatively young.

Nor is it remarkable that the record is devoid of any evidence that younger workers were suffering at the expense of their elders, let alone that a social problem required a federal statute to place a younger worker in parity with an older one. Common experience is to the contrary, and the testimony, reports, and congressional findings simply confirm that Congress used the phrase "discriminat[ion] . . . because of [an] individual's age" the same way that ordinary people in common usage might speak of age discrimination any day of the week. One commoplace conception of American society in recent decades is its character as a "youth culture," and in a world where younger is better, talk about discrimination because of age is naturally understood to refer to discrimination against the older.

This same, idiomatic sense of the statutory phrase is confirmed by the statute's restriction of the protected class to those 40 and above. If Congress had been worrying about protecting the younger against the older, it would not likely have ignored everyone under 40. The youthful deficiencies of inexperience and unsteadiness invite stereotypical and discriminatory thinking about those a lot younger than 40, and prejudice suffered by a 40-year-old is not typically owing to youth, as 40-year-olds sadly tend to find out. The enemy of 40 is 30, not 50. ("[T]estimony indicated [40] to be the age at which age discrimination in employment becomes evident"). Even so, the 40-year threshold was adopted over the objection that some discrimination against older people begins at an even younger age; female flight attendants were not fired at 32 because they were too young. Thus, the 40-year threshold makes sense as identifying a class requiring protection against preference for their juniors, not as defining a class that might be threatened by favoritism toward seniors.

■   ■   ■

We see the text, structure, purpose, and history of the ADEA . . . as showing that the statute does not mean to stop an employer from favoring an older employee over a younger one. The judgment of the Court of Appeals is reversed.

Case Questions

1. Does the Court's decision allow employers to grant preferential treatment to older workers? Explain. Why or why not? Explain.

2. Have you observed employment discrimination against younger workers? If so, what is your reaction to it? Do you think that the law should prohibit discrimination against younger as well as older workers? (Some state statutes prohibit age discrimination directed against both younger as well as older workers.)

3. What are the practical implications of the Court's decision with regard to employee benefits? If you were in senior management at General Dynamics, what might you have done regarding the company's health care benefits if the Court had decided in favor of the younger workers?

4. Suppose an employer wishes to reduce its workforce. Can it offer an early retirement incentive program that offers a lump-sum payment of a year of pay for anyone over a certain age who wishes to retire? Explain.

5. Do you agree with the Court's decision to allow employment practices and policies that benefit older workers even if the policies adversely impact younger workers? Explain.